Emotional Safety

Emotional Safety

Viewing Couples Through the Lens of Affect

DON R. CATHERALL

Routledge
Taylor & Francis Group
New York   London

Routledge is an imprint of the
Taylor & Francis Group, an informa business

Routledge
Taylor & Francis Group
270 Madison Avenue
New York, NY 10016

Routledge
Taylor & Francis Group
2 Park Square
Milton Park, Abingdon
Oxon OX14 4RN

© 2007 by Taylor & Francis Group, LLC
Routledge is an imprint of Taylor & Francis Group, an Informa business

Printed in the United States of America on acid-free paper
10 9 8 7 6 5 4 3 2 1

International Standard Book Number-10: 0-415-95451-7 (Perfect)
International Standard Book Number-13: 978-0-415-95451-8 (Perfect)

Library of Congress Cataloging-in-Publication Data

Catherall, Donald Roy, 1946-
    Emotional safety : viewing couples through the lens of affect / Don R. Catherall.
        p. cm.
     ISBN 0-415-95451-7 (hc : alk. paper)
     1. Marital psychotherapy. 2. Family psychotherapy. I. Title.
     [DNLM: 1. Couples Therapy--methods. 2. Affect. WM 430.5.M3 C363e 2006]

    RC488.5.C38 2006
    616.89'1562--dc22   2006011585

Visit the Taylor & Francis Web site at
http://www.taylorandfrancis.com

and the Routledge Web site at
http://www.routledgementalhealth.com

For Kim,
who knows all my buttons,
and generally refrains from pushing them.

Contents

Foreword

Every once in a while you meet a psychotherapist who works equally well and equally comfortably with both individuals and couples. Professional therapists differ greatly in their willingness and ability to tolerate the intense emotion generated by couples whose discomfort had been so great that they agreed to accept the interpersonal exposure inherent to therapy. Most therapists set up strict rules to protect themselves as well as those who seek their aid: "Fighting not allowed." "Bring the conflicts, not the rage." "You guys are going to have to respect the therapy process enough to handle yourselves differently in here." Even those few couples who are able to accept such tepid commands see them as paradoxical and of little personal benefit. Supervisors, trainers, and mentors of couple therapists are often heard to say that success in their field is due far less to training than individual talent or quirks of personality.

Not so, says Don Catherall in this credible and eminently sensible book. Most beginning couple therapists are told that therapy will be approachable and simple if you can get the participants to leave their affect at home. But Dr. Catherall echoes the spirit of Diane Keaton's character in the film *Sleeper* when Woody Allen, displaced two centuries into the future, showed terror as she handed her lunch guests tiny pellets of cholesterol. She laughed at his fear: "You guys were throwing out the best part." To a more recent generation, "It's the affect, stupid!"

Let Catherall teach you how to recognize the full range of affect—the ancient, intrinsically pleasant and unpleasant subcortical mechanisms that have evolved into spotlights that focus attention on whatever requires our best neocortical equipment. Listen as he explains interpersonal attachment and the affective experiences that foster or interfere with it. Focus on what he means by emotional safety, learn how to provide it for your clients, and teach them how to make it work at home. Study transcripts of sessions in which he demonstrates exactly what he means by every theory described. Imagine yourself working with each of *his* patients. Remember clients of your own who get derisive every time a spouse asks for help or looks like he or she is going to cry. Even better, test-drive some of his ideas about emotional safety next time your own spouse/partner complains that you are "really mean," that you are "impossible," or that you "don't care" about his or her needs. Name calling is about shame, and the more you know about your own experience of shame, the better will you be able to make therapy both understandable and a process so positive that your patients will look forward to their sessions. After all, we are just people too, and one of the reasons we know a lot about those who visit us is that wonderful line from the old Pogo cartoon: "We have met the enemy and he is us."

There is another aspect of this book that you will really like. Each chapter contains both clinical wisdom and references to professional literature where you can learn even more about this material. Some of the citations are strictly for the professional education of the reader, other references contain analogues you will find useful when doing psychotherapy, and many will make you walk around for days trying to figure out why they stick in your mind.

Dr. Catherall does not draw the line between psychotherapy and teaching—if they are supposed to learn, then we have got to teach! Vehicles of change include anecdotes from our practice, stories about our own lives, movies and books that helped us understand something otherwise obscure. Never once does this author even come near the intrinsically shaming suggestion that the therapist is well and the client is sick. It is the study of shame that forces all of us to give up the pretensions and disguises we use when trying to cover some perceived personal defect. Affect is universal and in constant play—every session reveals us even as it does them. Psychotherapy that takes for granted the psychology of affect encourages us to grow during every session we hold and makes us exemplars of an examined life.

As a scholar of affect in general and shame in particular, and a writer whose work Dr. Don Catherall has incorporated into his system of therapy, it is a pleasure to express my own pride that ideas so long in their development continue to find their way into the clinical literature. Whether you pick up this fascinating book as a psychotherapist looking for new ways out of old traps, or as a partner in a troubled relationship wishing only a more enjoyable life, you will savor the process of learning that now approaches you.

Donald L. Nathanson, M.D.
Executive Director
The Silvan S. Tomkins Institute
Clinical Professor of Psychiatry and
Human Behavior
Jefferson Medical College

Preface

Understanding the client in individual therapy is a challenge, but working with two individuals and their relationship to each other can seem to be more than twice as challenging. Some partners are so reactive to everything the other partner says that their therapists get overwhelmed by the speed at which emotions appear and interactive events occur in the session. Indeed, some therapists choose not to work with couples because they find it so difficult to keep up with everything that is going on in the room.

Do the Partners Even Know What They Are Fighting About?

One of the most persistent problems encountered by couple therapists is the couple that is caught in a cycle of repetitive, unresolved conflict—the fight that seems to recur without end. The slightest issue can somehow flare up into the repetitive conflict, and the partners have the déjà vu experience that they've had this fight many times before. It is never resolved, though the immediate fight may stop when the partners are just too exhausted to continue or one partner gives in. Therapists too can get exhausted by sessions of endless conflict, especially if they are struggling to make sense of what the fight is really about.

The Difficulty With Couple Therapy Is in Not Understanding What Is Going On

The thing that makes couple therapy overwhelming is simply not understanding what is going on. Consider how confusing it is to watch a sports event if you don't know the rules. But your entire view of the experience changes when you understand what is going on. Instead of watching seemingly aimless activity, you are able to track specific events and appreciate the whole of the experience. The partners who fight over anything do not know what they are fighting about. If the therapist doesn't know, chaos reigns.

The Right Model Makes All the Difference

The therapist's theoretical model determines whether she will be able to make sense of what is occurring in the session—and intervene effectively—or whether she will be confused and overwhelmed by the onslaught of data. A sound theoretical model is like a pair of eyeglasses, or a microscope, or a telescope—it provides a means of seeing what is missed by the unaided eye. The proper lens can transform and organize seemingly senseless data into a clear, meaningful picture.

What Makes a Strong, Useful Model?

The more a model requires the user to rely upon unproven assumptions, the more the model must introduce idiosyncratic devices to explain special circumstances and the weaker the model becomes. In my opinion, the strength of a model is determined by: (a) the extent to which it requires the acceptance of hypothesized constructs, (b) the breadth of human behavior it explains, (c) the overall coherence it derives from its core constructions, (d) its simplicity, and (e) its appeal on the level of common sense.

The best models: (a) require that few assumptions be taken on faith, (b) account for a large range of behavior, (c) consistently explain that diverse range of behavior on the basis of the same set of core principles, (d) are clear and simple enough to actually be useful during the course of a psychotherapy session, and (e) make sense to the clients as well as the therapist.

In Couple Therapy, You Need to Understand What Is Happening *As It Occurs*

When I first trained in couple therapy, it was popular to categorize couples according to the character structure of the individuals involved. This didn't work for me because my diagnostic assumptions too often proved to be wrong. I was seeing the partners at their worst moments—when they were extremely upset because of problems in their most important relationship—and they became very different people when their relationships improved. So I moved away from models that emphasized pathology and deficits and sought to understand the core concerns that drove the partners' behavior.

What Do All Effective Couple Therapies Have in Common?

At this stage of the research in the field of couple therapy, several approaches have been shown to be effective. These include: *behavioral couple therapy, emotionally focused couple therapy, insight-oriented couple therapy*, and *integrative couple therapy*. These various approaches emphasize different aspects of the treatment and propose different mechanisms of change. Although some have been shown to work better than others, all have demonstrated effectiveness.[1] It seems clear that a significant element leading to therapeutic change must be among the nonspecific factors in the treatment situation, some aspect of couple therapy that all effective approaches have in common. The nature of that common factor is not yet established; several major reviews have reached the same conclusion: The research on couple therapy has not yet been able to demonstrate what mechanisms of change are operating in those therapies that result in improvement (Gottman, 1998; Lebow, 2000; Snyder, Castellani, & Whisman, 2006).

I Think It Is About Safety

Often, the only place where the partners feel safe enough to even explore their concerns is in the consulting room of the couple therapist, where each partner is protected from attack, treated with respect, and remains free from judgment. The safety provided by the couple therapist makes it possible for many couples to finally make some progress in addressing their concerns. I believe the mechanism that is shared by all effective forms of couple therapy is that safety, and it is specifically *emotional safety.*[2]

What Makes a Person Feel Emotionally Unsafe?

Many different areas of difficulty appear in intimate relationships, but the emotional problems that underlie them boil down to two realms of human need— esteem and attachment. *Problems in intimate relationships occur because at least one partner perceives a threat, either to his self-esteem or to the relationship.* The issues that populate the realms of esteem and attachment are the driving forces—what the partners are fighting about—and affect (the biological core of emotion) supplies the lens to enable us to see those issues with clarity. The emotional safety model enables couple therapists to see the essential emotional interaction that underlies all activity in an intimate relationship.

The Emotional Safety Model

The emotional safety model views intimate partners through the lens of affect, focused on the two realms of attachment and esteem, to determine whether each partner feels safe. If either partner feels that the attachment of his or her esteem is threatened, then the couple does not have emotional safety.

The emotional safety model is not so much a method of treatment as it is a way of thinking about treatment, a model to help the clinician see what is happening as two partners struggle with their emotional relationship. It is, as the book's title suggests, a lens through which couple therapists can view their clients and make sense of what is going on. As a theoretical model for thinking about couple treatment, it is not restricted to a single treatment approach. It can potentially enhance any approach to couple therapy, although it is more compatible with some approaches than others. It is probably the most compatible with Susan Johnson's *Emotionally Focused Couples Therapy* (1996/2005 EFCT),[3] which focuses on two of the central elements in this model—emotion and the attachment relationship—and with Harville Hendrix's Imago Relationship Therapy (Hendrix, 1988, 1993) which pays particular attention to another central element in this model—the partners' views of each other. But it also shares components and works well with several other approaches, including insight-oriented and object-relations approaches, cognitive-behavioral approaches, systemic approaches, and integrative approaches.[4]

What You Will Learn in This Book

In the first half of this book you will learn how to view your clients through the lens of affect. Affect theory is a relatively recent player on the stage of metapsychological theories, but it is an extremely powerful player. Donald Nathanson (Nathanson, 1992) opened my eyes to the implications of affect theory with his groundbreaking work on shame. This book focuses on the interactive implications of shame, as well as other affects, and advances modern affect theory into the realm of interpersonal relationships. As you develop a theoretical foundation in this model, you will be able to:

- identify the emotional concerns underlying your clients' problems;
- identify one partner's specific concerns about the other partner's attachment;
- identify one partner's specific concerns about how he or she is viewed by the other partner;
- identify the underlying scripts that shape the partners' affect life;
- identify exactly what it is that each partner is reacting to;
- express clients' concerns with greater clarity than they themselves can;
- help each client to feel truly understood and supported, even as you show a similar level of understanding and support for the partner.

In the second half of this book you will learn how to apply the model. The goal of the therapy is the establishment and maintenance of emotional safety, and every intervention derives from that fundamental orientation. You will learn to:

- establish a consensually accepted view of the nature of the problem;
- identify the specific issues and realms in which each partner feels threatened;
- identify each partner's maladaptive reactions and help the partners see how their reactions create threat for each other;
- help the partners understand each other and learn to be sensitive to each other's sensitivities;
- help the partners see the systemic pattern their reactions create, so that neither partner is to blame for the recurring problem;
- help the couple to repair a partner's damaged esteem;
- help the couple to heal a partner's attachment injuries;
- guide the partners in establishing emotional safety through maintaining positive esteem and attachment security;
- identify exactly what each partner must do to achieve and maintain emotional safety;
- prepare the partners to reachieve emotional safety on their own when they encounter the inevitable fluctuations in safety that occur in all relationships.

A Caveat About Books on Intimate Relationships

This book contains examples of individuals and couples who exemplify various points. In all cases, details have been altered in order to protect the identities of the actual people upon whom these examples are based. Additionally, a book on relationships inevitably must contend with the problem of personal pronoun gender. Every person is subject to the issues discussed in this book; the dynamics of an emotional relationship are not confined to males or to females or to heterosexual, married couples. Thus, my use of personal pronouns is arbitrary. I have chosen to use the feminine form when referring to the therapist and the masculine form when referring to an individual partner. I tried to vary my use of the sexes when discussing the dynamics between two partners.

The exceptions are when I specifically address one sex or the other and when I describe the dynamics among couples. I found that it was easier to identify partners as "he" and "she" when I wished to describe each partner's role in complex interactions (it was better than Partner A and Partner B). In no way is this meant to imply that these patterns are specific to the sexes. Some patterns are more common (for example, it is more often the case that the man withdraws and the woman wants to talk about the relationship), but virtually every pattern appears in the opposite form as well.[5]

Put on These Lenses and Take It for a Test Drive

The real test of a model like this one is its utility, and that will be determined by you, the couple therapists who read this book. The model should enhance your understanding and help you to see what your clients cannot. Once you understand the model, you should be able to address the core emotional issues that underlie your clients' recurring problems. Then your role will be to help them understand and address those issues so they can achieve and maintain emotional safety in their relationship.

Once intimate partners achieve emotional safety, they can increase their intimacy and create a more meaningful connection—if they so choose. But these latter events are not the goals of the emotional safety model; though they are frequently the results. Every couple must determine the levels of intimacy, dependence, and autonomy that they choose to have in their relationship, and every couple starts from their own unique starting place.

Our job is to help them remove the impediments and achieve emotional safety with each other. Where they go from there is up to them.

Acknowledgments

The model presented in this book is built on the pioneering work of two original theorists and the elaborations of that work by two contemporary clinicians who applied the theories to clinical contexts. The original theorists are Silvan S. Tomkins, who developed modern affect theory, and John Bowlby, who developed attachment theory. Donald Nathanson took one aspect of affect theory—regarding the importance of shame and the feelings one has about the self—and developed it beyond Tomkins's original ideas. Nathanson's book, *Shame and Pride* (1992), opened my eyes to the dimension of couples' relationships which I call esteem. Susan Johnson took Bowlby's attachment theory and developed an approach to couples treatment that brings the issue of attachment to life in a way that no one else has matched. Her work, and her book, *Creating Connection: The Practice of Emotionally Focused Couple Therapy* (1996/2005), helped me to appreciate the centrality of attachment in couples' relationships. In addition to the conceptual clarity provided by these visionary theorists, my thinking about couples' relationships has been aided by the findings of many excellent researchers, most notably that of John Gottman.

The measure of any metapsychological theory is its value in creating models to guide clinical work. To borrow William Blake's metaphor, a clinician's reach is largely confined by his grasp of what drives human behavior. It is because of the work of Tomkins, Nathanson, Bowlby, Johnson and Gottman that my grasp of the behavior of couples has grown so much larger, and I believe this has extended my reach.

This book pays considerable attention to the emotion of shame. My understanding of the power of shame is based largely in my own capacity and tendency to experience this life-shaping emotion. That "felt knowledge" has been elaborated by: (a) my reading of the marvelous works of Silvan Tomkins and Donald Nathanson; (b) my clients (who educate every enlightened therapist); and (c) a special group of colleagues with whom I worked at the Phoenix Institute in Chicago: Skip Shelton, who first introduced me to affect theory and the power of shame, and who continues to teach me and be a positive model for me; Eleanore Feldman, whose warmth and incisive mind have helped me see many things; Joe McDonald, whose integrity rubs off on everyone around him; Ruth Engel, who makes you feel you're the only person in the world when you talk to her; and Chris Johnson, who has known most everything in this book much longer than me.

I am also indebted to the mental health professionals who thoughtfully reviewed the manuscript, helped me to clarify my thinking, and offered encouragement and support throughout. These were my wife, Kim Cather-all; and my colleagues Skip Shelton, Joe McDonald, Blair Barbour, and Don Nathanson (who invested a lot of time to help a colleague he'd never met). Since I work extensively with couples, I have been able to apply my understanding of affect theory and attachment to the world of intimate relationships. But I stand on the shoulders of giants. When I get it right, it is because my education has succeeded and I have been able to see clearly. I owe that to the giants—Drs. Tomkins, Nathanson, Bowlby, and Johnson, and all my colleagues and clients. When I get it wrong, it is because I still gaze at the world from my own myopic point of view.

Part I
Theory and Foundation

1
The Problem

Kurt and Sally walked into my office looking subdued and uncomfortable. Kurt smiled briefly; Sally rolled her eyes. They both seemed a bit embarrassed to be back to see me. We had completed a course of therapy 2 years earlier and they had left feeling pretty good about their relationship. Now here they were again, looking as glum as they did at the beginning of the previous therapy. I inquired about what had brought them back to see me. They both hesitated, then Sally started talking.

"Well, I guess we're here because of the same problems as before. Kurt doesn't really want to be married. He's too busy for a wife and family. He's always got something more important to do."

Kurt closed his eyes and sighed. "She's right about one thing, not much has changed. Everything I do is still wrong." He paused, then added sarcastically, "and nothing Sally does is ever wrong."

Sally looked at him and said, "That's not what you told your sister. You said that I couldn't do anything right at home so that's why I do my volunteer work." Sally turned to me and said, "Kurt doesn't think I'm any good as a mother."

Kurt responds in an exasperated tone, "I never said you were not a good mother. I've always said you were a good mother." He takes a deep breath and says, "I just told her that you missed working and being a mother wasn't enough—that you needed to be doing something where you get positive feedback from adults." He gestured at me, "We learned that here the last time."

Sally says, "Well, I certainly never get positive feedback from you, do I? Not that you're ever around to give it."

I felt a sinking feeling inside. Here we go again. It looked like Kurt and Sally had lost all the gains they had achieved in their previous course of therapy.

In the field of couple therapy, couples like Kurt and Sally are typically characterized as *conflictual*—two people who cannot agree on practically anything. Sometimes their disagreement is heated; sometimes it is a calmer description of their never-ending differences. In either case, there is an underlying, painful conflict that they have never been able to resolve. That conflict is always lurking in the vicinity, ready to spring into life over the most trivial interaction. However, for many other couples, the problem is not so overt.

Gil and Marian had a relationship that appeared positive in many respects. They led a very active life and enjoyed a variety of sports and other outdoor activities together. They were very social and spent a great deal of time with friends, both individually and as a couple. They were both intelligent, accomplished people, yet the level of their conversation with each other was superficial. They seldom expressed intense feelings or made emotional demands on each other. They each claimed to want greater physical intimacy in their relationship, but neither of them ever took the risk of actively trying to initiate it.

Periodically, they would have conflict. One fight was precipitated by Gil's confession that he was bored at a gathering with Marian's family. Marian wanted to know what he meant by "bored" and, within a few minutes, was accosting him about his passivity and failure to engage anyone in meaningful interaction. He reacted by attacking her for never saying what she really wanted of him. The conflict quickly escalated to a level at which neither of them was listening to the other; each was only making critical comments about the other. After such a fight, they would steer clear of each other for several days. Then they would begin to interact in a more formal tone. Eventually they would start to relax around each other and resume their usual pattern. At some future point, however, another burst of conflict would flare up, and they would go through the avoidance cycle once more.

Gil and Marian do not disagree on everything; they are more able to enjoy themselves as a couple than Kurt and Sally. Yet they often end up in an atmosphere of tension and excessive caution. Each partner holds back out of a fear of "things going bad" and somehow causing the relationship to lapse into a conflict that they won't be able to resolve. When such conflict is triggered, it is likely to dominate the relationship for the rest of the day or even longer. Couples like Gil and Marian might be characterized as *avoidant*. Each partner learns to tiptoe around the other's feelings, trying not to say anything that will set the other partner off.

An Underlying Lack of Safety

Both of these couples had a similar problem, though its outward manifestations were very different. In both cases, the partners did not feel emotionally safe with each other. Their relationships were burdened by a feeling that the partners had to tread carefully or some nebulous underlying conflict would flare into life. This feeling of not being emotionally safe showed itself in the two common forms that plague couples who have this problem: either (a) a heightened state of reactivity that results in repetitive, unresolved conflict, or (b) an ongoing state of disconnection that results in a superficial, unsatisfying relationship. Most couples with this problem fall into one of these two categories or a mixture of both.

Neither of these couples had been able to identify the exact nature of this problem, but each of the four partners was aware of it. They each lived with an underlying dread of triggering the conflict into life. Nor is this to say that these couples had failed to make progress in couple therapy. They had each resolved a variety of issues and even found some level of tolerance for those perpetual issues that are based on personality differences. But the recurring nature of their conflicts was not driven by the array of issues that they resolved in therapy. Those issues simply provided the content for their fights.

The reason that they fought—or avoided each other for fear of fighting—is the subject of this book. I use the term "fighting" to reflect the tone that characterizes their conflicts. Basically, *a conflict qualifies as a fight when the partners start to feel they are in danger of suffering a significant personal loss.* Of course, what will be lost is usually unclear, and the individuals are really not sure why they are so riled up. Many couples sense this and will acknowledge that they don't really know what they're fighting about or they will say that the fight is surely about something other than the issue that comprises the content of the fight.

Couple therapy can either help couples like these to resolve the series of surface issues, or it can help them to resolve the underlying problem, the thing that leads them to fight rather than discuss and negotiate their issues. Sometimes resolving the surface issues is enough. Some couples use therapy for that purpose and are satisfied to return to their normal relationship. But for most couples, resolving the content issues is never enough because there is an endless stream of such issues. Those couples can only find peace by finally confronting and resolving the underlying problem.

Two Realms of Potential Threat

Beneath the surface with these couples, each partner has an underlying feeling that he (or she) is not emotionally safe, that the couple is never far from something happening that will result in harm—either to the individuals or to the relationship. Consequently, the partners operate like they are in hostile territory. They don't completely let down their guard with each other, and each partner remains on the lookout for the perception of threat. Some partners deal with this feeling of unsafety by withdrawing and revealing only part of themselves. Some deal with it by leaping to their defense at the least appearance of what they perceive to be a threat. Some become emotionally numb and stifle the passion out of their lives.

The underlying problem of not feeling safe with each other is largely confined to two discreet spheres of functioning, two realms in which the perception of threat occurs. Each partner is concerned about: (a) him- or herself, which is contained in the realm of esteem, and (b) the relationship, which is contained in the realm of attachment. The majority of conflict in relationships occurs in the realm of esteem, but that conflict is driven by the perception of threat, and threat can be perceived in either realm. When the therapist understands the nature of the partners' perceptions of threat in these realms, she has a distinct advantage in being able to help them.

What They're Fighting Over

I spent many years helping couples resolve the issue-oriented conflicts that they brought to therapy. Sometimes I was successful, but many times I knew that we had not really resolved the underlying problem that made them so terribly sensitive to each other. I could see unresolved concerns hanging over every interaction. Our sessions were filled with arguments about who is right, who hurt whom, whose version of reality is the correct one, and, most of all, who is to blame. Sometimes I could help those couples by teaching them to communicate better, especially to listen better. Yet I myself couldn't hear what the argument was really about. It was when I finally got what the endless argument is really about that the seed for this book began to grow in my mind.

When the conflict is overt, the recurring argument is always the same: Each partner tries to correct the way that he or she is being portrayed by the other. They respond defensively. "I didn't say it like that." "That's not what I meant." "You're the one that got us into this." "So you're saying it's really my fault." *The argument stems from the clash between his efforts to change her view of him and her efforts to change his view of her. The underlying problem that fuels this recurring conflict is in the realm of esteem—how partners value themselves and each other.* The realm of esteem is communicated in the views of self and other expressed by each partner. Such expressions may be direct or they may be very subtle and indirect. He may communicate that he views her as unable to handle something by simply saying so, "You aren't able to do that," by indirect implication, "So who are you going to get to help you with that?", or most of all, by tone of voice, "You mean you're going to do it by *yourself*?"

The conflict erupts when a partner reacts to how he feels he is being portrayed or viewed by the other partner. Of course, if a partner's self-esteem is strong enough or his sense of self is sufficiently developed, he may be able to ignore the negative way he perceives he is seen or being portrayed by her. But when he does react, his goal is invariably to refute the way he perceives he is being portrayed by her (even when it is unspoken or what he thinks is only in her mind). *It is as though he cannot see himself the way he wishes to be seen if she sees him otherwise.* Partners thus fight to defend themselves against a perceived loss of esteem.[1] What they have to lose is their own good standing in each other's eyes, and the underlying fear is that they will be humiliated if they lose that good standing. Losing the fight can mean suffering profound humiliation, and that is why some partners become so terribly invested in winning arguments that seem trivial on the surface.

As I came to see this more clearly, I found myself paying less attention to what was said and more attention to how it was said. Communication in an intimate relationship is not restricted to the words that are spoken; what is even more important is the tone in which the words are said. The tone of our communications conveys another whole language of meaning. That other language is called affect (pronounced a-fekt), and it is present in most of the communications between intimate partners. Affect is the biological component of emotion, and we often convey it without even noticing. An upset partner may be able to hide his feelings behind the words he uses, but it is much harder to hide the affective tone with which those words are said.

We convey affect in our tone of voice, our posture, our behavior, and especially in our facial expressions. When she accosts him about his tone, or his body language, or something he has done (or not done), or the look on his face, she is not being goofy and finding problems where none exist; she is addressing her perception of something that was conveyed in the language of affect. When he denies his behavior meant anything, or argues that his tone or his look was not as she perceived it, he may be unaware of what he has conveyed. Or she may have misperceived what she thought she saw or what she feared his behavior meant. Or he may be playing dumb and relying on the fact that the language of affect can be difficult to identify. In my experience, when partners perceive some kind of negative affective message, they're almost always responding to something real—though they may overestimate its intensity.

Why They're Fighting Over It

When two people enter into an intimate relationship, they bond and open themselves up to each other. Among other things, this means that he allows her feelings about him to influence his feelings about himself, and she allows his feelings about her to influence her feelings about herself. Literally, her view of him affects his view of himself, and vice versa. This is one of the primary elements of being vulnerable—being open enough to your partner's view of you to allow it to influence your own view of yourself. One of the core premises of this book is that *it is primarily through affective tone that intimate partners convey their views of each other*!

An intimate connection is wonderful when the feelings are positive; her positive view of him helps him to feel even better about himself. Thus, people in love are lovely to be around. But the same connection can be devastating when the feelings are not positive; her negative view of him can make him feel terrible. When he perceives her view of him to be negative, he reacts. This is the basis of most recurring conflict; partners react by trying to argue with the other partner's view of them to get the partner to see that he or she is wrong.

In the course of arguing for how he should be seen, he often conveys a negative view of her—leading her to react similarly and creating a repetitive argument that never ends.

The Relationship

So are there sources of legitimate conflict outside the repetitive argument that will influence how each partner will be portrayed? In fact, there are all kinds of sources of legitimate conflict and couples argue about them plenty. The difference is in the tone of the argument and the impact it has on the relationship. It is like the difference between a debate over issues and a personal attack. Couples usually come for therapy when one or both partners feel that the arguing (or the distancing) is destroying the relationship.

Although any source of conflict can lead to the destructive kind of arguing (or distancing), there is one area that ranks above all the others. That area is the relationship itself. This conflict usually takes the form of one partner developing concern about the other partner's investment in the relationship and expressing his concern by attacking, criticizing, or otherwise portraying the other partner negatively. She responds by defending herself, and the repetitive cycle commences. Once a couple becomes locked into a repetitive cycle, whether of conflict or distance, neither partner feels safe enough to be completely open and vulnerable in the relationship. They have lost the key element that makes intimate relationships work—emotional safety.

Emotional Safety

The emotions of greatest relevance in our intimate relationships are those that we have about ourselves and our partners. Those emotions cluster in two distinct areas of human need—the esteem emotions, which reflect how we value ourself and our partner, and the attachment emotions, which reflect our caring for and dependence on our partner. It is much safer and easier for her to talk with him about how upset she is when the source of her upset feelings is someone or something other than him. But if he thinks she is attributing her upset feelings to something he has done, it now impinges on his feelings about himself. The repetitive argument is likely to appear if he tries to argue her out of her feelings about him, or it may go underground if he withdraws and tries to avoid the impact of her view of him. In either case, his sensitivity about how she views him interferes with the quality of their connection.

Conflict in an intimate relationship can stem from a variety of sources; it is only the recurring variety that tends to settle into the realm of esteem. And the perception of threat to the emotional safety of the relationship occurs in both realms, *attachment* and *esteem*. If her love and commitment begin to decline, then he will experience his attachment as being threatened. If her valuing of him declines (she may still love him but is not so sure she likes him), then he will experience his esteem as being threatened. When a threat appears in either realm, the result is a loss of emotional safety in the relationship.

Depending on how partners manage these kinds of events, conflict is likely to emerge. If the threat appears in the attachment realm, partners often react by attacking in the esteem realm. Now the conflict is in the realm of esteem, which is where most people have their open conflicts. Regardless where the conflict originates, if it is not resolved, most people eventually pull back from the emotional connection in order to protect themselves—which then constitutes a threat in the realm of attachment for the other partner.

This is the great irony: Two people get together because they feel so comfortable and open with each other, and then, over time, they come to hide themselves from each other. They end up distant and distrustful, and the intimate space between them becomes a zone of danger, a place where the potential for feeling worse outweighs the prospects of feeling better.

How They Fight Over It

The primary avenue through which he interprets her view of him and she interprets his view of her is not the language of words, it is the language of affect. It is in the invisible realm of affect that the unresolved conflict is fought. Couples in the danger zone are defensive with each other, quick to interpret each other's feelings and intentions as hostile, critical, or insensitive. The central issue is usually each partner's concern about the relationship itself, the attachment. But when the conflict has shifted into the realm of esteem, as it so often does, each partner's concern for how he or she will be viewed in the relationship becomes primary. When they fight, they fight to defend themselves from the humiliation of being found unfit, not good enough, inferior, incompetent, a loser. The conflict may or may not take place in the language of words, but it always takes place in the language of affect.

Some people speak of affect as though it is synonymous with emotion, but the two are different. Indeed, the difference between affect and emotion accounts for much of the misunderstanding that occurs in intimate relationships. Silvan Tomkins (1962) established that affects are our innate biological capacities, the prewired part of emotion. We are all born with the same basic set of affects, but our emotions develop on the basis of our unique experiences. Thus, the emotions of anger and shame experienced by someone who was brutalized in childhood will be very different from the anger and shame emotions of someone who grew up in a secure, loving environment. Yet the affects broadcast by these different people may be fundamentally the same; it is the internal meaning that differs. This creates fertile ground for misunderstanding: We transmit our feelings through the common language of affect, but we tend to interpret others' affective messages through our idiosyncratic language of emotion.

The conflict can take many forms. He may deny that he did what she seems to be accusing him of doing; he may argue that it is something wrong with her that causes her to feel this way; he may discount her feelings and suggest she is overreacting; or he may put up a wall and do his best to be unaffected by her feelings. Any of these (and many other) ways of reacting is likely to make her feel he doesn't care about her or, worse yet, to feel he is conveying a negative view of her. If she now responds by trying to argue him out of his feelings about her (that she perceives him to be having), then the repetitive conflict moves into a full-fledged fight.

The Role of Shame

The reactivity that keeps these recurring conflicts alive is most often based on one particular affect—shame. Shame plays a preeminent role with those couples who keep having the same argument over and over. A number of books have been written about shame in relationships, but just as with my inability to hear what the endless argument is really about, those authors didn't get it either. Their focus is always on the behavior of shaming, which is certainly a central part of the problem, but helping couples to heal and create emotional safety requires much more than just putting a halt to shaming.

Intimate relationships are subject to the endless argument because of a series of "mosts": *Our most shameful views of ourselves are most easily activated by those people who matter most to us.* The prospect of shame makes intimate relationships dangerous. It is not possible to have intimacy without shame, and the greater the intimacy, the greater the potential for shame to emerge. This is one of the built-in dilemmas of life; the only way to avoid it is to avoid intimacy. Unfortunately, the avoidance of intimacy is a common solution to the problem of shame, not only among single people but among couples who have been together for years.

However, the amazing thing about shame is that it can either drive partners apart or it can bring them closer together. When intimate partners can safely go into their shame with each other, they decrease their mutual hurtfulness and increase their intimate connection. *The secret is for partners to act on their shame rather than react to it.* The unhealthy shame people avoid separates them from those they love; but healthy shame can help them to connect despite their limitations.

Recurring Conflict

Recurring conflict almost always occurs in the realm of esteem. This is not to say that the issues being fought over are not important. Often, they are very important. But absent a concern about esteem, most partners can discuss their differences in a reasonable tone. If a partner sees or hears himself portrayed negatively by the other partner, then he is likely to feel he has been maligned, and this can lead to a loss of self-esteem. His responses then become oriented toward protecting himself or establishing his rightness, and the resolution of the content issue is skewed by these factors. This may make more sense with an example.

Say my wife and I are discussing how we will pay for our children to go to college (an actual issue in our lives and certainly an important one). We get into how we will reduce our spending and she suggests that I could drive a less expensive car (or do without golf or a fishing trip or whatever). Depending upon how she says this (or more accurately, how I perceive her tone when she says it), I may hear a note of criticism in her comment and take offense at it. Is she saying that I am driving a more expensive car than we can afford, that I put myself ahead of my children and don't care about their education? Of course, she very well may not be saying these things, but my sensitivity about how I am being viewed by her makes me highly attuned to the slightest suggestion of negativity.

If I experience her comment as a slur, then my entire mood shifts. Even if I try to suppress it and act like it didn't happen, my response is likely to have an edgy tone. This is when she is likely to ask, "Is something wrong?" She has picked up on that tonal change and wants to get things back on track. Of course, my usual answer is, "No, everything's fine." After all, I don't want her to know that I am so sensitive—that could influence her to see me less positively and my esteem would suffer for a different reason. But now I'm in a bad mood, and our continued interaction has a greater likelihood of deteriorating into conflict.

Or I might not try to hide my reaction by suppressing my mood shift. Instead, I may just counterattack by pointing out the ways in which she has spent too much money. She then may feel compelled to defend herself, and the entire discussion turns into a fight over money. When this happens, most couples focus on the content issue. Since the entire fight ended up being about money, they are likely to view their differences over money as the problem. The underlying problem that turned a difficult discussion into a fight is missed entirely. That underlying problem was my sensitivity to how I am viewed in the relationship, the profound shift in my mood that resulted when I felt I was being portrayed negatively, and how I dealt with that.

The Roots of Sensitivity

We are all sensitive to how we are viewed in our intimate relationships. But some people are so sensitive that there seems to be nothing so minor that they don't react to it. They take everything personally. For people this sensitive, an intimate relationship is a field of landmines and every step has the potential to blow up in their faces. Other people are not so sensitive that they react to everything. They may have only occasional encounters that pierce their ability to peacefully coexist with their partners. Yet they too may be dismayed at how devastated they can feel when they do have the occasional conflict with their partners. Such people often learn to dilute the power of their relationship by sacrificing intimacy.

But some people are able to maintain their closeness and intimacy even when they disagree with (their perception of) how they are viewed by their partners. They don't fight because they don't have a need to change their partners' view or fend it off by discounting their partners' credibility. They can agree to disagree and still trust their partners. These people usually have a strong sense of self and good self-esteem. Their feelings about themselves are not easily disrupted by how their partners view them.

Of course, some couples come to therapy without repetitive, unresolved conflicts. Sometimes these couples come to therapists for help in resolving specific issues, such as differences over religion, extended family, or the choice to have children. We therapists tend to work differently with these couples because we implicitly recognize that they do not have a significant underlying problem, though perhaps they can still be helped to have a stronger relationship.

Our ability to determine that one couple does not have an underlying problem while another has a deeper problem (disguised by surface issues) is an example of our own sensitivity to affective tone. Therapists are typically better at sensing affective tone than the average person. After all, we spend our days working in that domain. But even natural talent can be developed. In the coming chapters, you will learn to improve your ability to recognize affect, and you will acquire a vocabulary to describe what it is that you are seeing and hearing, especially in the all-important realms of attachment and esteem that underlie every intimate relationship.

The Language of Affect

Look at the image of a survivor of some carnage and, knowing nothing of her language, culture, beliefs, or circumstances, you can still recognize in the fixed action patterns of her facial muscles the unmistakable lineaments of grief.

Robert Sapolsky, 1997, p. 100

There are over six thousand different languages actively spoken on planet Earth, yet humans from vastly different cultures are still able to communicate. A smile, a gentle touch, averted gaze, an angry look—these things transcend the barriers of spoken language. Two lovers may sit and stare into each other's eyes and never say a word, yet they communicate volumes through the common language of *affect*. It is the unifying factor that underlies the many different languages of words. Every human being is born possessing the language of affect; it is the language through which the newborn infant expresses his feelings and his needs. Though affect may reside in the background when we communicate in casual relationships, it is never far away when we communicate with the people in our intimate relationships.

The views of self and other that determine the tone of our relationships are heavily laden with affect. Indeed, these views develop almost completely in response to the language of affect. The most fundamental view is of the self; it determines how we present ourselves to the world, how we feel about ourselves, and how we will behave throughout our lives. Many of our life choices derive from our view of self and are based on experiences in which we succeeded or failed, felt competent or incompetent, or were seen positively or negatively by others. These kinds of experiences shaped us into the people we are today.

The Physiology of Emotion

Emotions do not exist only in our thoughts; our emotions occur on a physiological level throughout our bodies. This is why we distinguish thoughts from emotions by referring to our heads versus our hearts (or our "gut feelings"). The word affect refers to this biological aspect of emotion, literally the physiological changes that we feel in our bodies. When someone says he is having a *feeling*, he is announcing his awareness of an affect.

The Innate Affects of Infants

Babies are born with the capacity to experience and express affects, as we all know from the baby's first cry when he is spanked into life. One can discern these feeling states in babies from birth; they are obviously capable of having feelings, such as pleasure, interest, and displeasure. When the baby experiences these feelings, he is communicating his needs through the language of affect.

When the baby is upset, the mother knows by the baby's affective display. A well-attuned mother soon learns to read her baby's cries and knows what he needs because she is able to *feel what he is feeling.* Her empathic understanding of what the baby is feeling is based on her own affects, which resonate in concert with the baby's affective expressions. This quality of *affective resonance* is one of the fundamental properties of affect (i.e., our own affects will resonate with the affective display of another person). Thus, the mother not only understands her baby's needs and feelings, she is able to communicate her own feelings to the baby! So when the baby is upset, mother is able to convey a calm, gentle feeling that soothes the baby.

It is instructive to examine how the mother soothes the baby. She doesn't soothe the infant simply by cooing and being calm. She begins by tuning into, and resonating with, the baby's affect state. Often, a mother speaks to her infant and exhibits an affective display on her own face that parallels that of the baby. "Oh, we're not happy, are we?" She then proceeds to shift her own affect to a more soothing tone. "It's going to be okay." And the baby responds by following her lead; he resonates with her more positive affect and is soothed. Thus, affective resonance plays a major role in the infant's intimate experience of being soothed by the mother.

This, then, is the language of affect. Before we develop spoken language, our entire repertoire of communication with others is achieved through the display of affect. As we mature and learn to use spoken language, our repertoire broadens. But we never stop communicating on an affective level; we simply supplement it with words and symbols.

The Empathic Wall

Donald Nathanson (1992) states that the inherently contagious nature of affect—especially in a close relationship where there is a high degree of affective resonance—leads to two developmental tasks that all infants have to learn. They must acquire the ability to (a) moderate the display of their own affects and (b) be able to tune out the affects of others. Without these abilities, we all would go through life constantly overstimulated by others and overstimulating to others. This is a large part of what makes infants so fascinating—it is thoroughly enjoyable to watch the unmoderated display of interest and enjoyment on an infant's face. Their interest and pleasure stimulates our own interest and pleasure. But when they are upset, we feel that as well—the contagious effects of the infant's negative affect can be extraordinarily distressing. Most infant abuse stems from situations in which an adult is unable to soothe an infant's unmoderated anguish.

When an individual is able to control the impact of others' affects on him, we say that he has developed an *empathic wall*. Without the ability to employ an empathic wall, he would lose his ability to be an individual; he would constantly be resonating to the affects broadcast by those around him. Of course, if his empathic wall is maintained in a rigid all-or-nothing fashion, he will be insensitive and blind to other people's affects. Fortunately, most people have more control over their empathic walls than that, though their control may not be conscious. They can "walk in another's shoes," resonating to the other person's affects and recognizing what the other is feeling, and then they can employ their wall and protect themselves from a continuing resonance.

Sometimes it is necessary to intensify one's empathic wall. For example, the physician who must inflict pain (e.g., stitching a wound) in the course of a necessary medical procedure may need a stronger empathic wall or he or she might be overwhelmed by the other person's pain and therefore unable to function effectively to help. The example of the mother soothing the infant shows her both tuning in to the infant's affect and then maintaining enough of a wall that she doesn't get too absorbed in the infant's distress and can instead lead the infant to a more pleasant state.

Healthy adults generally are able both to moderate their own affective displays and block out the affective displays of others, dampening the impact of affect in both directions. But these ways of controlling affect are usually accomplished in degrees. Most people still display a certain amount of their affect states, particularly through their facial expressions, and are still likely to be affected by others' affect displays, though they may be able to dampen the impact. Thus, healthy adults are able to increase and decrease their empathic walls. However, the better acquainted we are with someone, the harder it is to erect an empathic wall and block our tendency to resonate with his or her affects. A person may not be upset by a newscast of people suffering in other parts of the world, but it is harder to avoid being upset by the pain of people with whom he is close.

People have the greatest difficulty employing their empathic walls in their closest relationships. Affective resonance is very high between intimate partners; it is difficult to block out a partner's affects. When the feelings occurring in the relationship are positive, it can be very pleasurable for both partners. But when the feelings are negative, it can be extraordinarily discomfiting. Furthermore, the excessive use of an empathic wall between partners can cause the other partner to feel abandoned. This often gets expressed in her questioning whether he really is who she thought he was.

The display of affects is easiest to read in infants, who must rely exclusively on the expression of unmoderated affect for their communication. It becomes more complicated as children develop and begin to assemble their affects with what they are learning in the world. The assemblage of affect with what has been learned creates *emotion*.

Emotion Is Affect Plus Learning

The words affect and emotion are often used interchangeably, but they are not the same, and it is important to understand the distinction between them. Affects are the core ingredients of emotion, but affects alone have no moral meaning such as we attribute to our emotions; they are simply neurological events that are triggered by certain conditions. Silvan Tomkins (1962, 1963, 1991, 1992) identified nine innate affects, but they can be mixed (coassembled) like the primary colors to produce a vast range of affective experience.

As the person experiences and reexperiences various affective states, he acquires a set of memories associated with each distinct state. Tomkins proposed that those memories are encoded as images that include all the elements from the original scene in which the affect state occurred. Over time, the knowledge assembled within an affective state will include all the scenes associated with that affective state, as well as what was learned from those experiences. The word *emotion* refers to that coassembly of (a) an affect (or a combination of affects), (b) the set of scene images from earlier experiences of that affect state, and (c) what the individual has learned in relation to that particular affect state.

Since we each have different life experiences, it follows that we each experience different emotions. Your experience of the emotion of anger will be different from mine, even though the innate affect *anger-rage* is the same for both of us. *The language of affect is universal, while the language of emotion is unique to each person.* This accounts for much of the misunderstanding that occurs between partners!

Affects are short-lived, lasting only seconds at the longest, but a person may stay in emotional states for a very long time if the affect continues to be triggered. For example, the situation causing the affect may not change or the person may continue to recall memories that trigger the affect.

Affects Provide Motivation

Silvan Tomkins studied the display of affect in the infant and identified nine affects that we are born with that provide the foundation for all emotional experience throughout our lives. I have emphasized the role of affect in *inter*personal communication, especially in an intimate relationship, but Tomkins was focused on the *intra*personal role of affect. He concluded that the function of the affects is to provide motivation, and that they do so by amplifying the event that triggers them. Information alone does not lead to action until affect gets involved. You may notice a predator stalking you, but your motivation to run for your life comes from your fear.[1]

Tomkins's theory of the motivational function of affect brings a greater understanding of the complexity of human behavior. When the drives were viewed as the primary source of motivation, every behavior had to be explained by reducing it down to which drive was running the show. But affect theory shows how any drive can recruit an affect.[2] Consider the range of events that precipitate anger. People can get angry because others want something from them or because others don't want something from them. They can be angry because they are hungry or thirsty or because another person won't accept their gifts of food or drink. They can be angry about the state of the world or about their neighbor's good fortune. We could create similar examples substituting fear for anger.

The same flexibility applies to the positive affects—enjoyment and interest. One person may derive pleasure from playing video games, while another may get his pleasure from building things. Some people enjoy others' misfortunes, while others enjoy making personal sacrifices for the good of the group. The positive affects can even be recruited by our need to protect ourselves. Years ago I attended an event produced by model train enthusiasts who spent many long hours creating miniature worlds in their yards and basements. I was intrigued by the depth of their interest and asked several what motivated them to pursue such a painstakingly intense enterprise. I was surprised to receive the same response several times—a shrug and the comment, "it keeps me out of trouble." Indeed, learning to direct our interest into productive activities is an adaptive way to avoid more destructive activities.

Some people work hard out of interest or pleasure, while others are motivated by anger or greed. Affects can be recruited into a variety of different situations, satisfying different needs and drives. But the couple therapist's interest is primarily in the role affect plays in communication.

The Language of Affect

If you smile at me, I will understand, because that is something everybody everywhere does in the same language.

Crosby, Stills and Nash, "Wooden Ships"

Tompkins emphasized the role of affects as the primary motivational system among individuals, but affects serve a second purpose, which is fully as important as their role in motivating the individual. Affects are at the very core of our ability to communicate with one another. As the stanza from the song in the epigraph to this section observes, we are able to communicate on an affective level even when we lack a shared language. Affects are the substance of the initial connection between mother and infant. How could we ever have developed language if we did not have some common understanding to build upon? Affects are the Rosetta stone that ancient man used to develop spoken words. Before there was "Yes, I agree," there was a smile and a nod.

The role of affect in communication does not stop with its capacity to provide an initial shared understanding for spoken language. Because of affective resonance, affects allow us to not only communicate but also to *influence* each other. When his display of affect causes her affects to resonate, then his personal motivation system has directly influenced her personal motivation system. Sometimes that influence is as simple as his smile stimulating her to smile. But, of course, it is not always that simple. Depending upon what is going on with her (what *emotions* she brings to the situation), she may interpret and react to his smile with something very different. She may be influenced but not in the direction he had in mind.

The Affects

Tomkins categorized the affects as follows: two positive affects (*interest-excitement* and *enjoyment-joy*), one neutral affect (*surprise-startle*), three negative affects (*fear-terror, distress-anguish*, and *anger-rage*), and three affects that operate to limit or moderate the other affects (*disgust, dissmell*, and *shame-humiliation*).[3]

Bear in mind that the fundamental function of affects is to motivate, and they do so by amplifying the events that activate them. In Tomkins's words, affect "either makes good things better or bad things worse" (1979, p. 203). Without the amplification, we might not be sufficiently motivated to act or to act quickly enough. The positive affects motivate us to seek, continue, or increase the situation that triggers them; the negative affects motivate us to avoid or diminish the situation producing them; and the moderator affects motivate us to stop doing what another affect was motivating us to do.

Shame Affect

The affect of greatest interest to the couple therapist is the moderator affect of shame-humiliation. Shame affect serves to overrule the positive affects of interest-excitement and enjoyment-joy. Shame affect is triggered when we encounter some impediment to our pursuit of a source of interest or pleasure. Shame affect usually constrains us from continuing to pursue the activity that provoked the positive affect (thus, it is moderating one of the two positive affects). In other words, shame affect causes the person to *disengage* from a pursuit or activity.[4]

An example of shame affect at work is when his interest in a romantic evening gets shut down because she indicates she is too tired. He experiences a letdown—this is an example of shame *affect* but not the emotion we know as shame. He may or may not have an accompanying *emotional* response to the situation. But if his desire was initially strong, which requires the shutting down of that feeling to be correspondingly powerful, then his momentary feeling of frustration/disappointment will be intense.

The other two moderator affects, disgust and dissmell, are generally associated with appetitive drives—for example, helping the thirsty person refuse to drink a foul liquid—but they are sometimes coassembled with shame in social situations. When shame affect is assembled with disgust, something that was being taken in (including a love object) is expelled. When it is assembled with dissmell, the person holds back from something that appeared desirable (again, including a love object).

Script Theory and the Unique Nature of Emotion

We are not born with shame about our sexuality or fear/anxiety about algebra tests; innate affects generally are not associated with specific experiences. These things are learned, and the learning depends upon our unique experiences. Some people look forward to algebra tests, while others become very anxious about them. Most of these differences derive from our personal histories (some of us were good at math; others had failure experiences that made us feel stupid in that domain). As we mature, we develop sets of expectations and attitudes associated with all kinds of situations. This is how our emotional life develops.

Tomkins used the word *scenes* to refer to the memories of previous affect experiences and the word *scripts* to refer to the patterned sets of scenes, and what was learned from those scenes, that we come to associate with specific situations. The scripts an individual develops over the course of his life shape his experience of emotional situations; he is likely to interpret an emotional situation according to the script it most closely resembles. Our sets of scenes include how we reacted and what we learned, so our scripts can also dictate our reactions when we have an emotion.

Thus, everyone's emotions are different, and many people's emotional reactions are largely predefined. For one person, encountering a plea for help may elicit a feeling of compassion and a response that produces pleasure when the help is provided, while for another, such an event may provoke feelings of anger and disgust, followed by feelings of resentment if the help is provided. The difference lies in each person's unique experiences and the scripts he developed as a result of those experiences.

A person's scripts play a key role in forming personality, helping determine a person's reactions, attitudes, and values. For example, if an individual's anger was triggered in situations in which he concluded that someone was trying to take advantage of him, he may acquire an orientation that centers on not letting people take advantage of him. Sometimes the conclusions people draw are not rational ("Everyone takes advantage of me"), and these irrational thoughts become part of the scripts composing their emotions. *Since affects amplify the events that produce them, we all can have difficulty recognizing how irrational some of our scripts may be when we are in the grip of the affect.*

However, when we are not caught up in the affect, we are more able to recognize irrational thoughts.

Affective Tone

Just about every action we pursue involves some level of affect, since affects are the largest source of our motivation. Intimate partners have significant levels of affect involved in their relationship. Virtually every interaction in an intimate relationship carries an *affective tone*. Since it is primarily in her eyes that he sees himself (and vice versa), her affective tone exerts a profound influence on how he sees and feels about himself. After people move on from their earliest attachments, they generally resist letting anyone have that much power to determine how they will see and feel about themselves, until they fall in love and form a new attachment. Then, once more, they let someone be important enough to them to influence how they see themselves.

Adults in an intimate relationship go through a process of affective resonance that is similar to that of mother and infant. They look into each other's eyes, tune in to each other's affect state, and influence each other's affect state. During the infatuation stage of falling in love, this mutual experience of affective resonance is absorbing and uplifting. The interest-excitement and enjoyment-joy affects that are resonating between the two lovers are immensely pleasurable. Of course, such highly positive affects create the context for especially powerful experiences of shame affect when impediments are encountered.

I will end this chapter with a short example of the power of affective tone when it occurs between intimate partners. In the following interaction, no one got particularly upset or reacted badly at the time, but feelings about the interaction surfaced several times in subsequent weeks.

Sean (excitedly): Hey, guess what? I got tickets so we can go to a Notre Dame game while we're in Chicago.
Linda: Oh, okay. Sure, I know that's important to you.
Sean: Well, uh, yeah. (pause) Look, we don't have to go if you're not interested.
Linda: No, that's fine. It's your alma mater; I know how much that means to you.
Sean: Well, I don't want you to go just for me.
Linda: Sean, it's fine. Really. I'll put it on my schedule.

What Sean later admitted was that he was looking for Linda to sound excited about the prospect of attending the game with him. What he heard in the tone of her response was that she was willing to go, but she was not enthusiastic about it. For him, that made the experience entirely different, and he then had difficulty being excited about it himself. But notice how the interaction can be interpreted quite differently if the affective tone is heard differently. If Linda's initial response had exclamation points ("Oh, okay. Sure!") or if the word emphasis were different ("I *know* that's important to you" versus "I know that's important to *you*") or if it was accompanied by a different tone of voice, then it can come across very differently. Try reading the above interaction again and making the same words produce very different affective tones. The way affective tone is heard shows how partners can experience the same interaction and yet disagree vehemently about what happened.

In our intimate relationships, we become so sensitized to our partners' affective tone that we can pick up on it in a single word or gesture, especially if it is negative. Sometimes he interprets her negative affective tone to be about her ("Linda doesn't get excited about football"), and sometimes he interprets it to be about him ("She thinks my interests are dumb"). When he interprets her affective tone to be (a) negative and (b) about him, then his negative scripts about himself are most easily triggered ("I'm just not interesting enough for her").

The language of affect plays a major role in most communications that occur within intimate relationships. It is easy to recognize its importance when people are yelling at each other, but its influence is also there during quieter times. Every intimate partner is highly attuned to the other partner's affective tone, and many partners are reactive to any negative tone they pick up from their partners. His capacity to manage his reaction when he picks up distressing affective tone from her is influenced by: (a) his capacity to employ his empathic wall, (b) his capacity to self-soothe his own affective response, and (c) the scripts that he brought to the relationship. Remember, whenever there is a significant amount of affect involved in communication between partners—especially if the affect is not acknowledged openly—then there is great potential for misunderstanding.

Conclusion

This chapter has described the language of affect, but more than that, it has provided the foundation for therapists to be able to view their clients through the lens of affect. The lens of affect is composed of conceptual tools: an understanding of the basic affects, the function of the scenes and scripts that combine with affects to form emotions, the power of affective resonance, the need for affective walls, the motivating power of affects, the relationship between affect and emotion, the influence of the inevitable background of affective tone that hovers over every interaction in an intimate relationship, and the particular power of shame affect to suddenly and completely halt a positive experience by amplifying the impediment so that it looms larger than the positive affects that preceded it. In the next chapter we will see the extraordinary influence affective tone exerts on relationships in the realms of attachment and esteem.

3

Realms of Affect: Attachment and Esteem

Couple therapists can talk to their clients about the problems that occur at home, but real change doesn't tend to happen until they can address the partners' immediate, affective experience as it occurs in the consulting room. Experienced couple therapists track the affective events that occur in each partner throughout the course of the therapy session; they can usually describe the exact sequence of events that preceded a significant moment. Therapists may or may not choose to intervene in response to any particular affective event, but they recognize that those events are occurring and thus have a choice about whether to intervene and how to intervene. Those decisions are based largely on the therapist's understanding of the meaning of the affective events, so the therapist's model for understanding affective events is a crucial component of the therapy.

Though therapists have always paid attention to affective events, emotion has often been viewed as secondary to other aspects of the relationship, such as problem solving or distribution of power. However, over the past decade, more couple therapists and researchers have focused on the affective dimension of the relationship. The model of affective events that has proven most useful in couple therapy is John Bowlby's attachment theory, especially as it has been applied in Susan Johnson's Emotionally Focused Couple Therapy. Bowlby conceived of attachment as a fundamental need that starts in infancy and continues throughout life. When people are securely attached, they are more able to venture out into the world and function well. But when they sense that their attachment relationship is threatened, they become fearful and uncertain, often reacting in ways that might further alienate their partners.

Attachment theory differed from traditional psychoanalytic theories in the extent of its emphasis on the person's actual experiences; it focused on the individual's outer environment rather than the more subjective internal environment emphasized by many elements of traditional psychoanalytic theory.[1] Susan Johnson has noted how attachment theory is essentially a theory of trauma; it "describes and explains the trauma of deprivation, loss, rejection, and abandonment by those we need the most."[2] Her approach to couple therapy is to repair disrupted attachment and restore the "secure base and safe haven" the partners have lost.

The Concept of Attachment

Bowlby used the term *attachment* to refer to a particular kind of relationship in which a person forms an emotional bond to another person. Attachment relationships occur throughout life, but Bowlby's research and primary focus were on the attachments of very young children. He developed his ideas about the nature of attachment by studying what happens when the attachment relationship is disrupted. He observed very young children who were separated from their mothers for medical reasons and found that a consistent pattern occurs when an infant's dependent relationship with his mother is severed. The infant goes through three phases, which Bowlby termed *protest*, *despair*, and *detachment*. During the first phase, protest, the infant is visibly distressed. "He will often cry loudly, shake his cot, throw himself about, and look eagerly towards any sight or sound which might prove to be his missing mother" (Bowlby, 1969, p. 28).

During the second phase, despair, the infant's behavior suggests increasing hopelessness. His activity diminishes or ends and he becomes withdrawn and inactive. During this stage, the infant stops making demands on people in his environment and appears to be in a deep state of mourning. But it is the third stage, detachment, that is the most deceptive. The infant begins to show more interest in his surroundings again. He no longer rejects the nurses and can even smile and be sociable. Bowlby noted that observers often misunderstand this stage, thinking that the infant has recovered. However, the difference shows when the mother visits.

> [T]here is a striking absence of the behavior characteristic of the strong attachment normal at this age. So far from greeting his mother he may seem hardly to know her; so far from clinging to her he may remain remote and apathetic; instead of tears there is a listless turning away.[3] He seems to have lost all interest in her. (Bowlby, 1969, p. 28)

From these observations of what happens when an attachment bond is disrupted, Bowlby theorized about what the attachment bond does when it is working well. He concluded that a sound attachment provides the infant with a fundamental feeling of security that allows him to relax and tolerate the inevitable demands of life without undue distress. Bowlby's discoveries about the disruptions in the bond offered a new way of understanding infants (and adults) who seem to live with near constant distress. He contended that they may lack the fundamental security provided by a strong bond; in the language of attachment theory, they may have an *insecure attachment*. The child who has an insecure attachment no longer feels confident that he can depend upon his mother to be there when he needs her.

The child who reaches the detachment stage has learned to protect himself from the distress of not being able to depend upon his mother by no longer caring whether she is there for him. For an adult, the equivalent might be to participate in a relationship without allowing the other person to become too important or else to avoid intimate relationships altogether.

Bowlby's Working Models

Bowlby contended that the child develops internalized representations of self and other, which he called internal working models, and that these models determine the person's approach to relationships throughout life. He emphasized the value of secure attachment in helping individuals handle the stresses and demands of life. Bowlby theorized that a secure attachment requires that the person have a model of self as deserving of a secure attachment, as well as a model of the other as reliably attached. He felt that these models are formed in childhood, but they can be revised as a result of subsequent experience in adult attachment relationships.

Expanding Attachment Theory

In subsequent years, Bowlby and other theoreticians who followed him developed attachment theory further by delineating various subtypes of insecure attachment. Researchers established the importance of secure attachment among very young children in areas such as *separating* from mother and *exploring* strange situations.[4] A secure attachment allowed children to separate more easily; it was the insecurely attached child who was clingy with mother, fearful that mother might not continue to be there if he separated. When the child was placed in new and strange situations, a secure attachment with mother provided a secure base from which the child could more confidently explore his new environment.

Over the past two decades, attachment theory has increasingly been applied to adults and their love relationships. Researchers have developed instruments designed to measure attachment security among adults.[5] The measures are based on Bowlby's theory that a person's level of attachment security is a reflection of the person's internal working models of self and other. There is an ever-increasing amount of research being done on the relationship between attachment security and adult relationships, and the findings of this research consistently support the value of secure attachment on marital satisfaction.[6]

The essence of attachment theory for adult relationships is the importance of the attachment relationship and the disruptive impact of insecure attachment. Simply understanding this helps us make sense of the extreme emotions that can occur in an intimate relationship when the attachment bond is threatened. However, there is a significant difference in the research on adult attachment from that done with children and infants. All of the child and infant research is observational and is focused on external signs of distress and confidence. Using self-report measures, the adult attachment research is more focused on the internal working models, including the working model of the self.

The adult research has moved into an arena that was never accessible in the attachment research conducted with children.

The Adult's Working Models

There has been criticism of some of this research on adult attachment, based on an aspect of the working models that goes back to Bowlby's original formulations.[7] Bowlby suggested that people with secure attachments feel more competent and function better in life. This certainly appears to be the case, but it should not be taken to mean that all feelings of competence stem from secure attachment. This may be the case with infants, but it is not the case with adults. A secure attachment enhances an adult's feelings of competence, but *a significant portion of an adult's feelings of competence stems from his evaluation of his capacity to deal with the demands of life, independent of his intimate relationship*!

The current approach to researching adult attachment, which categorizes positive versus negative views of the self as aspects of attachment security, tends to conflate attachment security with the individual's view of his competence to meet the demands of life. This other realm, which is also contained in the person's working model of self, is related to, yet independent from, attachment per se. Events in the attachment relationship can certainly affect a person's evaluation of his competence to deal with life, but that evaluation is based on much more than his suitability for attachment.

The existence of a nonattachment realm of the working models has immense relevance for couple therapy because it is primarily in this other realm that the majority of conflict occurs. This is the realm of esteem; clinical work with couples is greatly aided by separating the realm of esteem from the realm of attachment.

The Realms of Attachment and Esteem

The emotional safety model views the working models of self and other as being composed of two principal realms: *attachment* and *esteem*.[8] These two realms contain the affective messages that play the central roles in the emotional dramas of distressed couples. *The realm of attachment is largely composed of feelings about the relationship and the other partner's commitment and reliability. The realm of esteem is largely composed of feelings about the self and the other partner as a person* (rather than as a partner). These two realms occasionally overlap but generally can be clearly distinguished. The better the couple therapist is able to see the affective communications occurring in these two realms, the greater the precision and impact of her interventions.

The Realm of Attachment

The realm of attachment refers to those affects that have to do with the emotional bond that is the foundation of every love relationship. That bond of attachment produces feelings of dependence associated with the partner, and *that inevitable dependency places each partner in a position of vulnerability since either partner can sever the bond*. Problems arise when a partner feels the bond is threatened; this is the source of insecurity in a love relationship. Some individuals cannot tolerate being so vulnerable and consequently position themselves in such a way that it is the other partner who is made to feel insecure about the relationship. Some individuals deal with their feelings of insecurity by aggressively pursuing the other partner, which often has the paradoxical effect of driving the other partner farther away. Some individuals try to avoid any insecure feelings by taking control of the relationship.

Needless to say, there are a variety of ways in which partners get into trouble because of their discomfort with the vulnerability that goes with the territory of a love relationship. The realm of attachment affects primarily refers to: the love that comprises the bond (and the longing for it when it seems to be lacking), the fears associated with the potential loss of the bond, and the distress associated with loss of the bond.

The Realm of Esteem

The realm of esteem refers to those affects that have to do with the self and how the self is judged and valued. This includes the partner's feelings about his own self as well as his feelings about the self of the other partner. Feelings about one's own self (the components of self-esteem) are the most important of these, but feelings about the self of the partner (other-esteem) are also very important because of their ability to activate the partner's positive/negative feelings about himself. The realm of esteem affects is composed of the positive and negative feelings experienced and expressed about the self and the partner.

A secure attachment is a source of positive self-esteem, but it is only one source, and the realm of esteem includes many other sources. Feeling worthy of secure attachment can make a person feel lovable, but it does not make one feel competent or adequate to function in the world. *Feelings of self-worth are derived from secure attachments, but feelings of competence and adequacy are derived primarily from experiences outside the attachment relationship.* The realm of esteem includes a person's evaluations of both his self-worth and his competence, and competence usually plays the greater role. Some partners try hard to obtain their feelings of competence and adequacy strictly from within the relationship, and that generally results in problems.

There is considerable value in separating the realms of attachment and esteem; different affects and emotions populate the two realms and entail significantly different responses in the treatment situation. Let us look more closely now at these different realms and consider some of the implications for couple therapy.

Realms of Emotion

The couple therapist attends to the affect in the room, but the partners seldom experience singular moments of pure affect—what they experience internally is, of course, emotion. Their affective states are almost always composed of an affect or mixture of multiple affects assembled with: (a) memories of earlier scenes of similar affective states and (b) scripts that dictate the nature of those states and how they will be handled.[9] The partners each bring a rich history of affect-laden scenes and scripts derived from previous relationships and experiences of self. This entire emotional package constitutes the working models of self and other.

Attachment emotions involve the relationship, including his love of her and his commitment to the relationship, as well as his perception of her love for him and her commitment to the relationship. Esteem emotions focus on the Self of each partner, thus there are not only the emotions of Self-esteem but also an Other-esteem dimension in which he is attuned to how she views him and through which he conveys his view of her.[10] Attachment and esteem emotions thus occupy distinct territories, but they overlap at times.

For example, if he perceives that she views him as not adequate in some respect (his perception of her Other-esteem emotions), he might conclude that it constitutes a threat to her love for him or her commitment to the relationship (her *attachment*). In that case, her Other-esteem view is activating an attachment concern for him. Most of the time, however, his perception of her Other-esteem view will impact his Self-esteem view (his view of himself as competent/adequate). Similarly, if he perceives her to be questioning her attachment to him (her Other-attachment emotions), it will activate attachment concern for him. But it could also stir concern in the realm of his self-esteem if he already has sufficient doubts about his competence/adequacy. The primary area of overlap between the two realms is that component of self-esteem that reflects one partner's view of whether the other finds him worthy of attachment.[11]

Much of the literature on adult attachment treats all feelings of self-worth as an aspect of attachment security. It is certainly true that secure attachment contributes to feelings of positive self-worth, but there are many more sources of esteem. For example, a common problem is when one partner does not feel adequate in the esteem realm. His concern about his adequacy may have nothing whatsoever to do with his perception of the quality of the other partner's attachment. Perhaps he is struggling in his career or some other realm of functioning outside of their relationship. However, if he seeks to supplement his esteem through increased involvements outside the relationship, then his decreased involvement within the relationship may activate her attachment concerns. Now his esteem issue has become a relationship issue. If she feels too vulnerable to directly express her attachment needs, she may instead increase her focus on him, which often results in increased criticism of him, which increases his concern about his Self-esteem.

Now the couple is likely to get caught in the cycle of critical pursuer and defensive distancer, and the therapist may view his esteem problem as originating in the relationship. But, in fact, it originated elsewhere; it is simply that the way he dealt with it set off a dynamic in the relationship. A different scenario occurs when he attempts to deal with his flagging self-esteem (again from an external source) by seeking more approval from his partner. If she fails to provide him with the needed boost in esteem, he may react as though she has caused his problem.

The Concept of the Object

> Emotions occur in one of two types of circumstances ... when the organism processes certain objects or situations with one of its sensory devices ... [and] when the mind of an organism conjures up from memory certain objects and situations and represents them as images in the thought process.

> **Antonio Damasio, 1999, p. 56**

In object relations theory, the mental representation referred to as an object is often treated as if it were the *source* of certain affects. An internal representation of a critical parent seems to generate the feelings associated with that parent. But in affect theory, the concept of the object is more akin to its use in grammar (i.e., the element of a sentence that receives the action of a verb or is governed by a preposition). In affect theory, *an object is simply whatever is aimed at by drive or affect.*[12] In that sense, the self and the other are images in the mind that serve as the objects of many affects.

Cognitive theory has focused on our capacity to retain and organize our perceptions so that we develop a map of the world that allows us to operate effectively. Cognitive theorists use the word *schema* (plural is schemata) to refer to the mental image that is the fundamental component of such a map. The psychoanalytic view treats objects, such as the self, as schemata that provoke emotions. From that perspective, I can have a negative view of myself (schema), which then makes me feel bad (emotion). But Tomkins's script theory provides a very different perspective. *The negative view of myself does not exist independent of the emotion; it is part of the emotion!*[13] Although my bad feelings about myself can be activated by any part of the emotion (scenes, script, affects), affect is by far the most powerful activator. Thus, my spouse can display a negative view of me, but without the affect, and I may laugh with her. But if I perceive her negative view of me to include negative affect, then my bad feelings about myself is much more likely to be activated.

The Self

The sense of self is fundamentally one's view of oneself. Since that view is (a) laden with affect, (b) contained in a multitude of scenes from throughout life, and (c) endowed with scripts that define it, *the view of self is essentially an emotion*. Emotions we have about certain things, such as ourselves or our deities, take on the stature of *beliefs* when we accept the actuality or validity of those things.[14] We come to believe we are this or that, and that belief becomes our reality. As a belief, it becomes part of our repertoire of concepts with which we build our view of the world. We may be able to talk about the belief without activating the underlying affects, but *when we activate the underlying affects, the belief about ourselves then becomes our immediate reality*.

Most people have at least two very different beliefs about themselves—a positive or good self and a negative or bad self. The good self is a composite of the emotions containing positive affects, and the bad self is a composite of the emotions containing negative affects. There may be more than two views of the self, of course, and this can vary from person to person. But considering the vast number of scenes that involve the self, the self scripts would almost certainly coalesce into relatively cohesive views of self—much as averages become more stable when drawn from larger pools of numbers. Since there are two separate categories of emotion likely to be directed at the self (positive versus negative), most people are likely to develop at least two very different beliefs related to the self. The same reasoning suggests that there will be a minimum of two beliefs about the other. These beliefs about self and other acquire tremendous importance in influencing the individual throughout life.

Growth of the Self

D. W. Winnicott, a pediatrician who became a psychoanalyst, introduced a different way of thinking about the self. He emphasized the infant's utter *dependence* on the adult caretaker, but noted that there is a reciprocal relationship; the infant influences the mother even as the mother influences the infant. Winnicott (1963) theorized that the self grows out of this complex relationship between infant and mother. He also changed the way people viewed infants when he contended that it was insufficient to think about an infant alone; we have to think about the mother-infant unit in order to appreciate the true complexity of an infant's mental life and the phenomenal importance of dependence on another. Thus, the infant's initial view of self is inordinately influenced by the mother's view of the infant. However, *over time, the growing child begins to develop a view of self that stems from more sources than just the mother's view* (as the infant moves from a state of dependence toward a state of relative independence).

Daniel Stern's (1985) studies of the relationship between infants and their caretakers led him to echo Winnicott's suggestion that the self develops as an aspect of relationship. Prior to Stern's research, most theorists conceived of infants as relatively passive recipients of parental attention. Freudian theory suggested that infants did not have a sense of themselves as separate beings, that they experienced themselves as fused with their mothers. That view of development portrayed the child as progressing toward ever greater levels of separateness.[15] Stern's research suggested that the opposite is closer to the truth. He showed that infants are aware of their separateness, and he described development as a progressive growth of the self and a seeking of closeness. Further, he observed how infants are highly active in the process.[16] Stern emphasized how that connection-seeking process occurs primarily on the level of affect. The infant and the mother are able to share their subjective experience with each other through a process of affective communication, which he termed interaffectivity (Stern, 1985).

Stern's research findings challenged the dominant view of development (i.e., that the self grows *away* from mother toward greater levels of independence and separateness). The complexity occurs in the growth of the self from additional sources and the infant's efforts to have that emerging self recognized and validated by mother.

Nathanson's concept of the empathic wall adds an important dimension to these ways of thinking about the development of the self, because the development of self occurs in concert with the development of the ability to block out one's resonance with the affects of others. Without the capacity to erect an empathic wall, the developing child would be constantly resonating to the affects of others. The empathic wall is thus a crucial component in the development of the self system.[17] Winnicott (1963) made essentially the same point when he emphasized the importance of the capacity to be alone. He contended that the child has not truly mastered the capacity to be alone until he is able to be *alone in the presence of the mother.* Clearly, the ability to be alone in the mother's presence hinges on the child's ability to block out the mother's affects.

This focus on the importance of the empathic wall may appear to be similar to the traditional emphasis on separateness as a goal of development, but they actually differ in a very important way. The developmental model of separateness emphasizes a steady growing apart; it implies that the goal for the child is to be increasingly less dependent and less identified with the parent. The affect theory emphasis on the development of the empathic wall does not need to posit a growing apart. Instead, it emphasizes the development of an *essential relational ability*, an ability that facilitates greater closeness and connection in relationships.[18] The individual who lacks an empathic wall is doomed to avoid closeness because he will lose his sense of himself (and his functioning may therefore decline) if he gets too close to another person. But the individual with a healthy empathic wall is able to maintain great closeness and still retain his distinctive individuality.

The Self-to-Self Connection

> Intimacy is an interaffective process through which the inmost parts of the self are communicated to the other by tangible displays of affect.
>
> Vernon C. Kelly, Jr., 1996, p. 73

In the 1980s, feminist theorists at Wellesley College's Stone Center took a strong stand against the traditional emphasis on greater separateness as the healthy product of growth.[19] They contended that development of the self only occurs when the individual experiences herself as being fully *in connection* with another person.[20] Their model of development posits that the self grows *within* our most intimate connections, that it is only in those connections that we can discover ourselves, confront ourselves, and expand ourselves. Rather than portraying intimacy as a potential obstacle to development of an independent self, the Stone Center model views intimacy as the primary arena in which development occurs.[21] The more the self is seen in all its complexity (including its differences), the more it develops.

The realm of esteem includes many aspects of the view of self that are not part of the attachment relationship. But *personal growth* (defined as positive change in one's view of self) *flows from an attachment relationship.* The more an individual wants to grow, the more he makes his view of self accessible to his intimate partner. The partner has access to both realms of the working model of the self, the view of self as worthy of love and the view of self as competent to meet the demands of life. If her view of him is largely assembled out of positive affects, then he experiences a strong, positive view of self (and good self-esteem). But if her view contains negative affects, his self-view/emotion will be affected in that direction. This is why people can be so sensitive to how they are portrayed by their partners.

Vernon Kelly (1996) applied the affect model to the experience of intimacy. He emphasized the importance of the ability and the desire of each person to expose the inmost self to the other through the process of interaffectivity. The theorists of the Stone Center describe this intimacy experience as the fundamental ingredient in personal growth. It is in those moments of greatest intimacy, when the self is fully exposed to the other person, that one's fundamental view of self is most accessible to being altered. This is the case because the self is not simply an experience of affect—it is a view, a set of scripts, and an object of affects. In other words, the sense of self contains all the components of an emotion. The scripts that define us do not live independent of the affects; there is no internal object per se. It is only when we direct affects at our internal view of self that we are ever aware of having a self.[22]

Realms of Affect but Filled With Emotions

The affects that primarily concern the couple therapist can be grouped into the realms of attachment and esteem. But, of course, the experience of the two partners is not one of simple affects—they are experiencing emotions. This means the affects are mixed in with (a) scenes from the past, (b) possibly other affects, and (c) scripts defining the experience and the person's response. Each person in the room potentially can pick up on the affects being transmitted, but each person is also prone to interpret those affective communications through his or her own idiosyncratic emotions. The therapist has the advantage of not being emotionally involved the way the partners are, so she is less likely to distort the affective messages through the filter of her own unique emotions. However, if the therapist's own emotions get activated, she becomes more prone to distorting her perceptions of the partners' affects by interpreting those affective messages through the filter of her own emotions. This is the essence of what is commonly referred to as *countertransference*.

The fact that the therapist can perceive the partners' affective messages without imposing her own emotions on the interpretation of those messages does not mean that she necessarily will understand the exact nature of a partner's emotional experience. She still must determine the emotional meaning for that individual. But she will be more likely to hear his description of his feelings without imposing her own emotional interpretation.

Primary Versus Secondary Emotions

Many individuals develop scripts for certain difficult emotions that immediately shift the person from the difficult emotion to a different emotional state, a secondary emotion.[23] This can occur so rapidly that the individual never has any awareness of the initial emotional response; instead, he views the secondary emotion as the whole of the experience. For example, the person who gets angry when he has a frightening experience may fail to recognize the fear that preceded the shift into anger. Therapists are accustomed to this phenomenon, and they commonly try to help the individual recognize the primary emotion that was so quickly evaded.

This shifting away to secondary emotions is a very common experience in distressed relationships, and couple therapists are often in the position of trying to help a partner identify the underlying or primary emotion. The situation is even more difficult when the partners remain focused on content issues. The therapist must help the partners recognize not only that the content of the conflict may not be the most relevant dimension, but that the emotions that are visible may not be the whole story on the emotional dimension of the conflict. Once the content issues have been cleared aside, the therapy can focus on the underlying emotional issues. The challenge then may be to help the partners (or one partner) to gain access to the underlying primary emotion (such as feelings of hurt that often underlie anger).

However, even when a primary emotion has surfaced, the emotional reaction may not be completely understood because of the relationship between the realms of esteem and attachment. Each realm can produce disturbing emotions that individuals may have learned to shift away from, and secondary emotions in one realm can lead back to primary emotions in the other realm. The most common pattern is secondary emotions in the esteem realm obscuring primary emotions in the attachment realm. The situation is complicated further by the fact that events in each realm often provoke events in the other realm.

For example, if he feels that she is less than fully committed and may leave, he will perceive the attachment to be threatened and will likely experience emotions associated with insecure attachment. But his experience of threatened attachment can also stir up his feeling that he is inadequate and responsible for her reduced commitment—a primary feeling in the realm of esteem. Or, if she feels inadequate as a person (a primary emotion in the esteem realm), it can stir her concern that he would not want to remain with such a person—a primary feeling in the realm of attachment. Thus, layers of emotions are not always primary versus secondary. The significance of both realms—we each have needs to feel (a) securely attached and (b) competent to fare on our own—means that individuals can have primary emotions in each realm.

The validity of primary emotions in both realms is important because of the tendency to view our clients as not "really feeling" the secondary emotion ("You're not really angry so much as hurt"). The secondary emotion is real, of course, but it is serving a defensive purpose to protect the individual from the greater vulnerability associated with the primary emotion. However, the link between two primary emotions in the separate realms (as in the example of the person with low self-esteem who then fears the partner is not likely to remain attached) is not defensive because neither emotion serves the function of avoiding the other one.

Some adult attachment theorists have tended to imply that a secure attachment inevitably results in good self-esteem. Although it is certainly true that a history of secure attachment is a major source of good feelings about the self (usually characterized as feeling worthy of love), individuals in secure attachment relationships can still have fluctuations in esteem because of events outside the relationship or historical difficulties with esteem. And when one partner's esteem goes down, it often has an impact on the attachment relationship. Similarly, it is a greater challenge to maintain self-esteem when one is having difficulties in one's attachment relationship. Often the distress in one realm of the relationship stems from the *solutions* a partner is attempting to use in dealing with difficulties in the other realm. Here is an example of a session in which we dealt first with content, then esteem, and finally attachment issues (a common sequence).

The session began with Ruth complaining of Frank's constant criticism. Even when she is telling him factual events about her life before they got together, he corrects her. She complains that he finds something wrong with everything she does. She begins a discussion of their endless conflict around the rehabbing of their house.

Frank and Ruth are rehabbing the house themselves. Frank was upset earlier in the week because nothing was getting done. Ruth notes several things she has done, and Frank says that is the point—she starts several projects at once but never finishes any of them. I ask for clarification about the process of working together on these projects. Frank explains that they plan their work together, make an agreement on their priorities, but then Ruth does not follow through with the priorities they have developed as a couple.

I note the need to move from generalities to the specific issue that came up earlier in the week.

Ruth was in charge of stripping the wood on the window frames. She had reached the point where she needed to do a window that was high in the stairway. She couldn't work on that window until a proper scaffolding was constructed, and that was Frank's job. They had agreed that this particular window was next on Ruth's agenda, but when the time came to do it, she worked on a door in another part of the house instead. When I asked why, she said it was because the scaffolding was not set up. I inquired about their arrangement for Frank to know when he was supposed to put up the scaffolding. He interjected that all she had to do was ask him and pointed out that he had put it up right away when she eventually did ask several days later.

I pursued Ruth's reasons for not asking Frank to put up the scaffolding. Since her performance of her job was dependent upon his doing his job, I figured that this was where the breach first occurred. Ruth revealed that she is reluctant to ask Frank to do something, even when she has his prior agreement, because he is likely to complain that he cannot do it right then or to suggest alternatives. This response makes her feel that she should have anticipated the situation and thought of alternative solutions. In Ruth's words, "He makes me feel that I should have been able to figure it out on my own." In other words, it stirs her view of herself as not very competent. We were moving into the realm of esteem.

I drew Ruth out on this point. Basically, she inhibits many of her ideas because she fears Frank will shoot them down if she expresses them. Frank entered the discussion, noting his background with a scholarly university where all ideas were subjected to intense, critical scrutiny. He suggests Ruth is simply used to an environment where ideas are accepted uncritically. I continue to draw Ruth out on the many ways in which she withholds her thoughts because she expects Frank to correct her. Eventually, I summarize Ruth's withholding actions; I note the effect of Frank's criticism on her self-esteem; and I mention several examples of the kinds of situations in which *she had withheld. The final example notes how she even fails to ask his help to set up the scaffolding in order to do her part in a project they have agreed to pursue.*

Then I shift to Frank. I note his reaction to the window-stripping incident; and I suggest that I want to know about something a little different. I want to know if he can sense that she is holding back and what that is like for him. I am now trying to move the discussion into the realm of attachment. Frank begins to describe feelings of disconnection (like they are "just roommates," "living parallel lives," and so forth). As I encourage him to expand on these feelings, his desire for greater connection becomes increasingly visible. When I eventually direct Ruth's attention to Frank's obvious desire to be closer to her, she expresses surprise. She felt he didn't want to be closer to her because he is always so critical of her.

This was near the end of the session, so I summarized the cycle that they get caught up in. Frank wants to be closer but mostly expresses his displeasure with the lack of closeness through criticism (he acknowledges he learned to be quite critical in his family of origin). Ruth wants to be responsive to Frank but pulls away from his criticism because it is hard on her esteem (she acknowledges historical difficulty with feeling good about herself). When Frank senses her pulling back, he tends to become more critical. And the more critical he becomes, the more she pulls back. They are caught in a vicious cycle. I emphasize that Frank wants to be closer and that Ruth wants to be responsive and work together as an effective team, but that they must both be watchful for the cycle that they so easily fall into.

This case is an example of how the couple therapy session can move through the realms of content issues to esteem issues to attachment issues. The most significant of these is the attachment realm—where the very existence of the relationship is at stake—and that is where the therapy often ends up. But not always. For some couples, esteem issues are so prominent for one or both partners that the attachment is threatened because of the problems in the realm of esteem. Ruth is such a person. All her life she has struggled with self-esteem (she is actually a highly accomplished professional, which makes little difference to her vulnerability to feeling bad about herself).

Frank also has esteem issues—why else would he need to make his partner feel inferior?—but we did not get into his esteem issues in this session, and it may not even be necessary in future sessions. He has adopted an aggressive stance of superiority, apparently learned in his family of origin, that may serve him in more casual relationships but is clearly problematic in an intimate relationship. If he can learn to treat Ruth with greater sensitivity (to her esteem issues), then perhaps it will not be necessary to delve into Frank's difficulties with self-esteem.

My final intervention is classically systemic. I identified the circular nature of the problematic cycle. Each partner is responding to the other partner's response, consequently neither individual is the problem. The problem is the cycle that they get caught up in together, and they can work together to change that pattern.

In the next chapter, we will look more closely at the realms of attachment and esteem and how they are founded on the affectively toned views of self and other that are expressed by each partner.

4
Realms of Emotion: Views of Self and Other

According to affect theory, there are a variety of drives that motivate human behavior.[1] However, the power of the drives to motivate is relatively weak, so the drives recruit the much more powerful affects. Many of the drives are necessary to the ongoing survival of the individual organism, such as drives to obtain food, water, shelter, and a constant flow of oxygen. Some of the drives are not necessary to immediate survival, but are related to longer-term goals such as reproduction. And at least two drives are oriented specifically toward aspects of human relations. The drive to attach has obvious value to an organism that is helpless and dependent for such an extended period in early life (much longer than any other species). There also appears to be a drive to develop a sense of an independent self that is competent to survive unaided. In a sense, these two are related, but sometimes they also seem to conflict.

If for no other reason, our extended period of dependence in early life makes it crucial for us to be an extremely social animal. No human survives without the extensive assistance of others. The development of a *sense of self* among humans surely exceeds that of other animals not only because of our intelligence and capacity for language, but because it emerges from a matrix of such intense social connections. The emergence and definition of an individual self is a social phenomenon; it originates in our most intimate (and dependent) relationships and continues to be subject to the influence of social relations throughout life. In adult intimate relationships, the sense of self of each person is soothed and held by the secure attachment to the partner, and it is buoyed and strengthened by the positive regard of the partner. But when the sense of self is threatened, the relationship cannot be safe.

Self and Attachment

The attachment relationship is not only the primary source of security for the individual, it is also the primary locus of personal growth. Throughout our lives, we have the greatest opportunity to grow when we are fully engaged in an attachment relationship. *Intra*personal events, such as *how* we feel about ourselves and *who* we choose to be, are heavily influenced by what happens in our attachment relationships.

Adults approach potential attachment relationships with two distinct areas of need in the esteem realm. The first is the need for a secure attachment relationship in which the self can feel worthy of love by a valued human being.[2] This is the area of esteem that flows directly from the attachment realm. The second area is the more general need for esteem (i.e., to feel competent and adequate as a member of society, as a man or a woman, as a student, a worker, an athlete, a citizen, and so forth). This area of esteem has some overlap with the attachment relationship, but it also encompasses the individual's life outside the attachment relationship. A secure attachment can make it easier for an individual to explore the world outside the sphere of the attachment, but as every parent learns when children move out into the world, there are a multitude of events and situations that have an impact on a person's esteem—and these experiences are independent of the person's feelings of being worthy of an attachment (though they can still affect the person's feelings in that realm).

Since the self originally grows within the parent-child relationship, the child's initial definition and valuing of self are products of the attachment relationships with the parents. However, as the child begins to move out into the world, the sources of self-definition and self-esteem expand far beyond the attachment relationship. By the time he enters into an adult attachment relationship, his sense of self is generally well established. Yet a sense of competence, adequacy, and even the nature of a person's self-definition are never established once and for all; they ebb and flow with the exigencies of life. When life brings powerful change into a person's life, his self-definition must change in response; he cannot adapt effectively if he maintains a rigidly defined self.

When a partner forms an adult attachment, he allows the other partner access to his feelings and beliefs about himself. If she sees him differently than he sees himself, then he must deal with that difference in some manner. He might change his own view or his behavior to be more like she sees him or wants him to be; he might resist the way she sees him and try to convince her to change her view of him; or he might disengage from the attachment relationship in order to reduce her influence over how he feels about himself. Of course, he may be able to tolerate her different view without it disrupting either his own view of self or their mutual connection.[3] *To the extent that he needs her to see him as he wishes to be seen (because he would be unable to see himself that way if her view differed), then he gives her the power to make him feel either good or bad about himself.* The more power his partner has to influence his self-esteem, the more the adult relationship resembles the relationship between parent and child.

The Dynamic Emotional Realms

Many practitioners fail to conceptualize their clients' experience in terms of esteem because they think of esteem as a stable variable that does not fluctuate radically in the course of a couple therapy session. This view of esteem probably stems from the fact that research in this area has generally treated esteem as a fixed quantity (i.e., people are categorized as having low self-esteem or high self-esteem). Similarly, research on attachment has convinced many clinicians that individuals fall into discrete categories of attachment security. In actuality, when we characterize someone's level of attachment security or their self-esteem, we are describing their *average* orientation, referred to as *attachment style* or level of self-esteem.[4]

The emotional safety model regards esteem and attachment security as dynamic variables that fluctuate within a relationship in direct response to what occurs within the relationship. Certainly, each partner brings historical vulnerabilities and sensitivities to the relationship, and these influence each partner's perceptions and experiences of esteem and attachment security. However, historical vulnerabilities and sensitivities do not act in a vacuum; they interact with what occurs in the relationship. And the *most important events in any intimate relationship are the affective events.*

The affective events of greatest interest to the couple therapist are each partner's feelings about himself and his partner. When a partner has a good feeling about himself and an attitude that the other partner is trustworthy, then the inevitable little problems that occur in the relationship do not tend to turn into bigger problems. But if he doesn't feel good about himself, or if he's distrustful of his partner, or if he perceives that his partner doesn't trust him, or that she feels bad about herself and blames him for that, then little problems are likely to turn into bigger problems.

Views of Self and Other

The early work on attachment focused on infants and young children, but the modern emphasis is on how adults approach their intimate relationships. The research on attachment focuses on the primary orientation that character-izes an individual's approach to relationships, referred to as attachment style. Attachment theorists regard this style as largely forged in early attachment experiences; however, most agree that it can be amended in adult attachment relationships (such as marriage or psychotherapy). If an individual started out with *secure* attachments, then he is more likely to expect that others can be trusted and relied upon and that he himself is worthy of others' care. But if his early attachment experiences were not secure, then he goes through life with less confidence in relationships, and is more likely to withdraw and give up on a relationship (than someone who has a better history of attachments). In the most severe cases, people with an extensive history of insecure attachments either avoid forming any new attachments and never have adult intimate rela-tionships or are extraordinarily clingy in their attachment relationships.[5]

Theorists in the attachment field came up with a variety of categories of insecure attachment based on their particular observations. Until the late 1980s, most research posited three types of attachments: secure, anxious-resistant, and avoidant.[6] The secure and avoidant categories showed up soundly in the research, but the anxious-resistant category produced less definitive findings (Bartholomew & Horowitz, 1991). Bartholomew and Horowitz developed an attachment schema that "considered all four categories that are logically derived by combining the two levels of self-image (positive vs. negative) with the two levels of image of others (positive vs. negative)" (1991, p. 227). An individual can have a view of self as positive and worthy of others' care (Good Self) or as negative and not worthy of others' care (Bad Self), and a view of the other as reliable and trustworthy (Good Other) or as unreliable and untrustworthy (Bad Other).[7] Bartholomew and Horowitz combined the positive/negative views of self and other into a standard two-by-two factorial design that produced the four basic attachment styles (see Figure 4-1).

Bartholomew's grouping, based on the individual's fundamental views of self and other as being either good or bad, replicated the secure and avoidant categories but eliminated the third category, anxious-resistant, and replaced it with two additional categories. This new grouping revealed information that was obscured when the mixed views of self and other were lumped into one category. One category contained a positive view of self and a negative view of the other. People in this category experienced discomfort when they became

	Positive Self (less dependent)	Negative Self (more dependent)
Positive Other (less avoidant)	*Secure* Good Self Good Other	*Preoccupied* Bad Self Good Other
Negative Other (more avoidant)	*Dismissing* Good Self Bad Other	*Fearful* Bad Self Bad Other

Figure 4-1 Bartholomew's Model of Adult Attachment.
From Kim Bartholomew and Leonard M. Horowitz, "Attachment Styles Among Young Adults: A Test of a Four-Category Model," by K. Bartholomew and L. M. Horowitz, 1991, Journal of Personality and Social Psychology, Vol. 61, No. (2), pp. 226–244, 1991, APA. Adapted with permission.

too close to others. Bartholomew labeled this category as *dismissing*. The other category contained a negative view of self and a positive view of the other. People in this category experienced anxiety when they became too distant from the other person. Bartholomew labeled this category as *preoccupied*. In effect, the previous category of anxious-resistant was capturing two separate groups of people; one group was anxious (the preoccupied style) and the other was resistant (the dismissing style). Now there was one form of secure attachment and three types of insecure attachment (the third type was termed *fearful*; it contained people who had negative views of both self and other).

Separating the preoccupied from the dismissing styles helped to illuminate some underlying issues regarding these people's approach to dependency and autonomy. Individuals with the preoccupied style tended to be very dependent upon their partners and deemphasized autonomy, while individuals with the dismissing style placed greater importance on their autonomy and viewed dependency more negatively. This led Bartholomew and Horowitz to note the psychological issues represented by the two axes of their model. The horizontal axis, which reflects the view of self, also predicts dependency. People with a poor view of self appear to have greater dependency needs and require greater external validation. The vertical axis, which reflects the view of other, also predicts avoidance of intimacy. People with a poor view of other are more invested in avoiding closeness. The components in this model factor independently; dependency versus independence (based on view of self) and intimacy-seeking versus avoidance of intimacy (based on view of other) are not the same thing. The most relevant dimensions underlying these differences appear to be the polarized views of self and other.

Today's prevalent view of the different attachment styles is the four-category model developed by Griffin and Bartholomew (see Figure 4-2).[8] People whose views of self and other are positive fall in the *secure* category and they approach relationships with confidence. People who see themselves negatively but the other positively are labeled *preoccupied/anxious*; their focus is on pleasing their partners. People who see themselves positively but view their partners negatively can readily form relationships but are labeled *dismissing* because of the lengths to which they go to emphasize independence and dismiss dependency. The people who see both themselves and the other negatively are labeled *fearful/avoidant*. They have difficulty even entering into relationships.

If Bob and Carol and Ted and Alice represented the four attachment styles identified by Bartholomew and Horowitz, they might look like this:

Secure Bob enters into a relationship rather easily. He trusts that his partner always means well and forgives her when she lets him down. He trusts that she loves him because, after all, he's a pretty good guy.

Anxious Carol enters into a relationship with concern that she may not please her partner. She makes up for this by focusing on him and his needs. When there are problems, she assumes they are her fault and she is quick to try to be better. She's not certain of her partner's love because, after all, there are so many ways in which she falls short.

Dismissing Ted enters into a relationship with a casual attitude. He remains distant most of the time and expects his partner to come to him. Excessive closeness makes him uncomfortable. He is focused on his need for autonomy and may view his partner as wanting to be "joined at the hip." He conveys the feeling that the relationship is not all that important to him because, after all, he knows he could always find someone else. Dismissing Ted is most likely to partner up with anxious Carol (after all, they both agree that he's great and she ain't).

Avoidant Alice rarely enters into a relationship. When she does, she is wary and expects things to not work out. She is distrustful and prone to look for evidence that her partner cannot be trusted. Worse than that, she believes that her partner will want nothing to do with her if he really gets to know her well enough. She suffers from the Groucho Marx syndrome[9] and assumes that anyone who is interested in her is probably defective in some way himself.

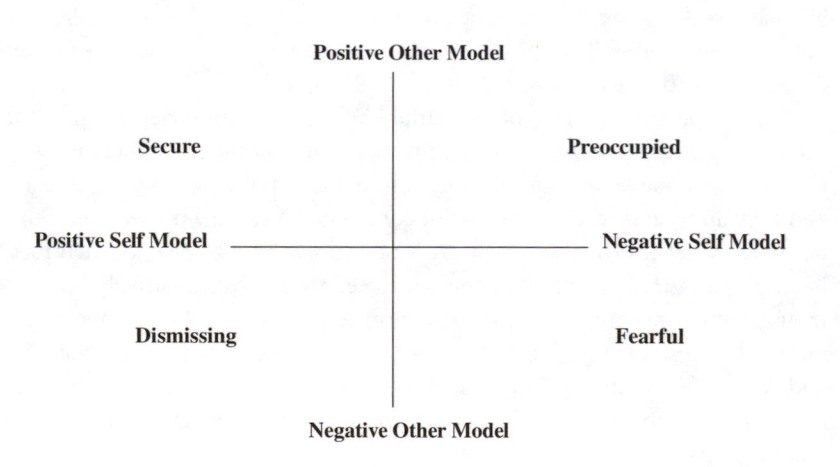

Figure 4-2 Griffin and Bartholomew's Four-Category Model of Adult Attachment.
From Dale Griffin and Kim Bartholomew, "Models of the Self and Other: Fundamental Dimensions Underlying Measures of Adult Attachment," by D. Griffin and K. Bartholomew, 1994, *Journal of Personality and Social Psychology,* Vol. 67, No. (3), pp. 430–445, 1994, APA. Reprinted with permission.

The combination of view of self and view of other helps us to understand the basis of individuals' general approach to relationships. These overarching views actually span the two realms of attachment and esteem. Bad Self may mean the self is not lovable (attachment), or it may mean the self is not adequate (esteem). And Bad Other may mean the other is not reliable (attachment), or it may mean the other is critical and disapproving (esteem). Thus, it is helpful to distinguish between these realms.

Additionally, this view is still at the level of a general orientation; it doesn't address the moment-to-moment experience that produces the dance of conflict and avoidance that comprises the underlying problem for distressed couples. To make greater sense of that dance, we need to be fluent in the language through which it is expressed.

Emotional Views of Self and Other

From the point of view of affect theory, the views of self and other that determine Bartholomew's attachment styles are actually emotions. They contain affects, scenes, and scripts. As emotions, they generally are not activated until the affect within the emotion is triggered. Our emotions about ourselves and others, both positive and negative, do not simply pop out of nowhere; they are activated by discrete events (either an internal event, such as a thought, or an external event, such as the partner's tone of voice). If an individual has an abundance of scenes involving one particular emotion, then he may be more sensitive to stimuli that activate that emotion, but he still requires some triggering event.

When a person has enough positive emotions about himself, he develops a cohesive identity—a core view of self—that is positive. But this does not mean that he is immune to feeling bad about himself or viewing himself negatively. Everyone has some negative emotions about him- or herself, even if he or she grew up with the most secure of attachment relationships. People categorized as having secure attachments are simply less easily triggered to feel negatively about themselves or their partners, and they bounce back more readily when they have been triggered. But even the apparently secure partner in an intimate relationship can feel negative emotion about himself or his partner if he encounters the right trigger.

Through the Lens of Affect

Viewing the events in therapy through the lens of affect allows couple therapists to quickly make sense of the rapid affective changes that often occur in couple therapy. The model focuses on the partners' immediate affective experience in terms of the specific emotions each partner has regarding himself and the other partner—the attachment and esteem emotions. By tracking the sequence of events that precede fluctuations, the therapist is able to develop hypotheses about what is going on between the two partners in the realms of attachment and esteem. In effect, the therapist is attuned to the underlying dimensions of attachment and esteem, no matter what is going on at a content level.

In my opinion, all good therapists do this implicitly. However, the more overt their attunement to these realms, and the more they possess a conceptual language that allows them to readily articulate what is occurring in these realms, the greater the likelihood that their interventions will be direct, immediate, and make sense to the partners. As a rule, delayed interventions in couple therapy tend to miss the fleeting moments of affect that make all the difference in helping partners to understand what is occurring between them. In the next chapter, we will learn to better distinguish the emotions of attachment and esteem.

5
Mapping the Terrain of the Emotional Relationship

Affective messages in the realms of attachment and esteem are influenced by the context, the nature of the relationship, and the content of the communications, as well as the emotional history each partner brings to the relationship. But the most essential aspect of all meaningful messages in the attachment relationship is the affective tone! Much of what is communicated in daily life may say little about the two partners, but every interaction has the potential to convey powerful affective messages in the realms of attachment and esteem. From the perspective of emotional safety, those affective messages in the realms of esteem and attachment are composed of relatively distinct emotional states. Even though there is an enormous range of possible emotions, the particular emotions that most impact emotional safety consistently fall into identifiable categories.

The Esteem Emotions

When a person's positive emotions about himself are enhanced, he has an emotional view of self that Donald Nathanson (1992) has termed *pride*. When his positive emotions about himself are impeded and his negative feelings about himself are activated, he feels *shame*. This shame is the complete emotion, not simply shame affect. In addition to scenes from the past that are laden with shame affect, shame emotion contains scripts in which the self is portrayed negatively. *Shame emotion is activated when a person's positive view of himself is impeded.* This is the emotion we commonly recognize as shame, and it is always about the self. Nathanson has labeled the continuum of feelings about the self as the shame-pride axis, noting that it operates like a seesaw—when one end is up, the other is down. In terms of the model being discussed here, the Self Axis of the esteem realm contains the shame-pride axis.

We can identify a similar axis that refers to an individual's feelings about the other person—the Other Axis of the esteem realm. When a partner has a generally positive feeling state related to the other partner, he has an emotional view of the other that we can call *acceptance*. When his positive emotions about the other are impeded and his negative feelings about the other are activated, he feels *disapproval*. The Self and Other Axes comprise the core emotions contained in the realm of esteem (see Figure 5-1).[1]

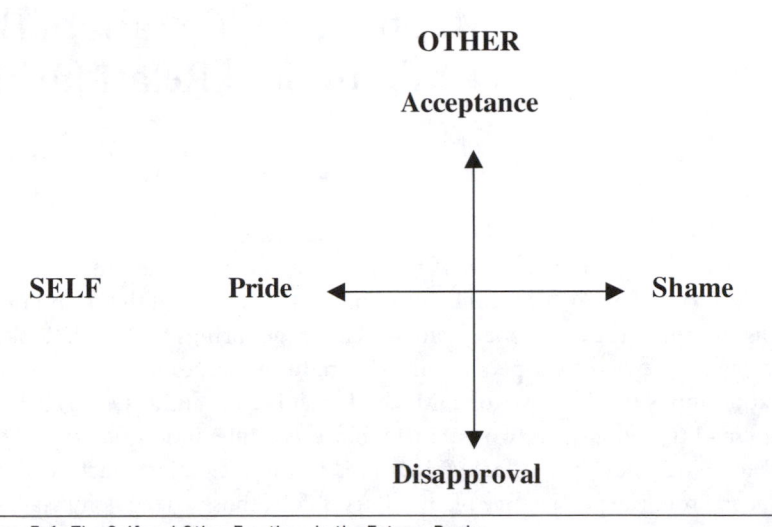

The Esteem Emotions

OTHER

Acceptance

SELF **Pride** ←——————→ **Shame**

Disapproval

Figure 5-1 The Self and Other Emotions in the Esteem Realm.
The horizontal axis contains the central esteem emotions related to the self, and the vertical axis contains the central esteem emotions related to the other.

There is a considerable body of research demonstrating (a) the power of people's perceptions of the extent to which their partners (the other) value them and (b) the relationship between the perception of the other's regard and an individual's own self-esteem.[2] People who have lower self-esteem and doubts about themselves are less inclined to perceive their partners as valuing them highly (Murray, Holmes, Griffin, Bellavia, & Rose, 2001). Thus, having low self-esteem makes a person more likely to react to affective messages that suggest the partner is thinking poorly of him or her.

The Attachment Emotions

From the cradle to the grave, humans desire a certain someone who will look out for them, notice and value them, soothe their wounds, reassure them in life's difficult places, and hold them in the dark.

Susan M. Johnson, 2005, p. 34

The emotions of the attachment realm have to do with the partners' loving of each other and their commitment to the relationship.[3] If he questions his love or commitment, or if he fails to behave in a loving way, then she feels insecure in regard to her personal future in the relationship and she may feel distrustful in regard to his participation in the relationship. Thus, the Self Axis of the attachment realm is marked by pleasure at one pole and distress at the opposite pole. The negative emotions that arise in the realm of attachment have to do with the potential loss of the secure relationship; they include fears and feelings of rejection, abandonment and uncertainty, as well as suspiciousness and distrust of the partner's commitment. The Other Axis of the realm of attachment is marked by feelings of trust at one pole and distrust at the opposite pole (see Figure 5-2).

Just These Emotions?

The four emotions associated with each of the two axes (Self and Other) are intended to capture the continua of people's emotions related to self and other in their intimate relationships. This should not be interpreted to mean that this limited set of emotions comprises the only emotions about self and other that occur within the realms of esteem and attachment. Rather, they represent the central emotional positions that occupy the poles of the two axes in each of the two realms. Emotions closer to the middle of the spectrum may be relatively neutral, but the majority of the esteem and attachment emotions cluster into groups that are distinctly positive or negative.[4] This clustering is a natural consequence of the nature of the innate affects: The positive affects serve to motivate us to increase, maintain, or approach the stimulus/source; the negative affects motivate us to decrease or avoid the source.

The Attachment Emotions

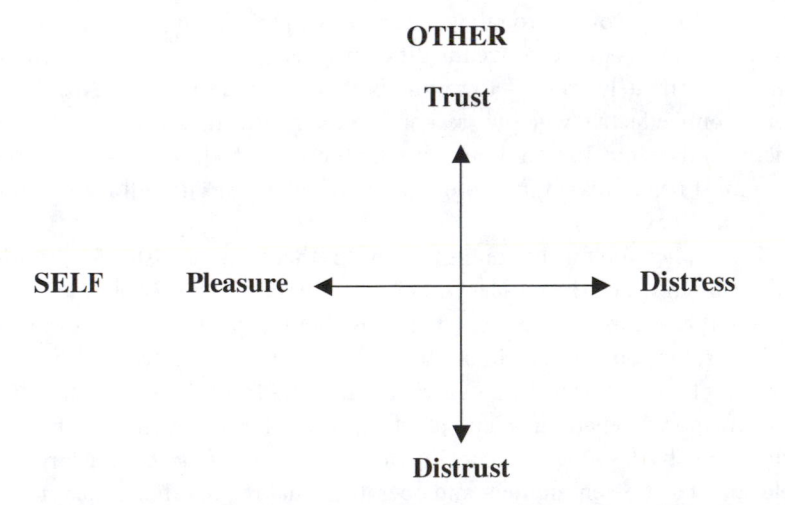

Figure 5-2 The Self and Other Emotions in the Attachment Realm.
The horizontal axis contains the central attachment emotions related to the self, and the vertical axis contains the central attachment emotions related to the other.

The emotional states on these axes are mutually incompatible—when an individual is experiencing the emotion at one end of the axis, he cannot also be experiencing the emotion at the other end of the axis. In this respect, one emotion or the other dominates at any given moment. This helps us to better understand the experience of ambivalence or mixed feelings. Although individuals generally have emotions from both ends of the axes, they don't experience them simultaneously. They may have specific emotions that are assembled out of combinations of seemingly contradictory affects, but that is as close as they will come to a singular emotional state that could be labeled as ambivalence. However, because individuals in a volatile attachment relationship can shift very rapidly from one end of an axis to the other, they can experience and express contradictory emotions sequentially. It is this rapid shifting of emotional states that produces the emotional display that is usually associated with "mixed" emotions or ambivalence.

Self and Other Axes

The two axes of Self and Other occupy both realms, esteem and attachment, but their relative potential to cause problems in the relationship differs. *Perceptions of the other's negative affects usually play the greater role in the realm of esteem, while a perceived lack of positive affects in the other usually plays the greater role in the realm of attachment.* The perception of disapproval by the partner (she is disapproving of me) is the most common activator of shame. The perceived lack of positive affects (she shows no signs of love for me) is the most common activator of distress (in the self) and distrust (of the other), especially in situations in which the distressed partner expected the other partner to come through with something loving. It is very important for couple therapists to recognize the difference between esteem and attachment threats. Ultimately, we seek to restore both acceptance and active loving, but we are only effective when we respond to the realm the individual is experiencing at the time. Esteem issues usually precede attachment concerns. If so, they must be addressed in that order or our interventions will not touch the individual's experience.

The implication for the couple therapist is that she must listen for the affective realm in which the problem is being manifested, and then she must intervene in that realm. If a partner complains about hurtful things the other says and does, his complaints will usually fall in the realm of esteem. If, however, the complaints are mostly about what is missing from the relationship, then they are more likely in the realm of attachment. Most of the time, both realms will be involved, sooner or later. The therapist's goal is to track which realm is relevant at any given moment and operate in that realm. This simple strategy makes a profound difference in the therapist's effectiveness.

Obviously, problems in the attachment realm are the greater threat to the relationship. Perhaps for that reason, it is the realm that is usually harder to reach. Therapists may have to spend considerable time addressing esteem issues before they get to the attachment issues. One clear exception is when there is an overt threat in the attachment realm, such as an affair or a stated intention to leave the relationship. However, even in these cases, it may take considerable time before the couple can talk about the positive, loving behaviors and affects they have found to be missing and are longing for in the relationship. When this subject is brought up in anger, it may lead to pacification efforts, but it usually does not lead to resolution or healing. The prospect for actual healing of attachment issues occurs when partners can access and express the underlying pain and longing for positive attachment.

The Terrain of the Emotional Relationship

An individual's immediate experience in the realms of esteem and attachment can be represented by creating a graph defined by the two axes of Self- and Other-emotions. The resulting graph is an emotional analog to the two-by-two factorial design employed by Bartholomew and her colleagues (Griffin, Horowitz). In this graphic representation, Bartholomew's categories for view of self and view of other have been replaced with the self and other axes from the realms of attachment and esteem (see Figure 5-3).

The vertical axis is the Other Axis, containing acceptance and trust at one end (the Good Other end of Bartholomew's design) and disapproval and

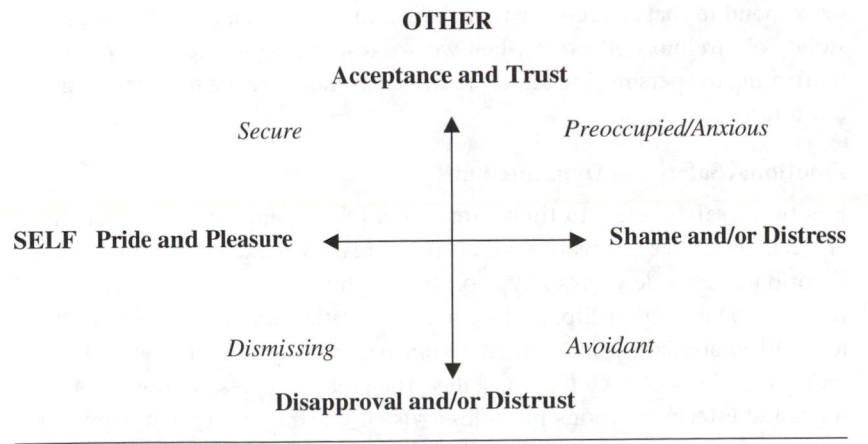

Mapping the Terrain of the Emotional Relationship

OTHER

Acceptance and Trust

Secure   *Preoccupied/Anxious*

SELF   Pride and Pleasure ← → **Shame and/or Distress**

Dismissing   *Avoidant*

Disapproval and/or Distrust

Figure 5-3 The Self and Other Emotions in Both Realms.
The horizontal axis contains the central attachment and esteem emotions related to the self, and the vertical axis contains the central attachment and esteem emotions related to the other. Bartholomew's attachment styles appear in the four quadrants.

distrust at the other end (Bad Other). The horizontal axis is the Self Axis, containing pride and pleasure at one end (Good Self) and shame and distress at the other (Bad Self). The four quadrants of the graph have been labeled with the attachment styles created by Bartholomew's design.

In an adult intimate relationship, complete *emotional safety* only occurs when each partner is experiencing the positive ends of both axes in both realms. To state it differently, *feelings of shame or distress, or the perception of disapproval or distrust in the other partner, eventually tend to lead to a loss of emotional safety.* Partners are largely unable to achieve satisfying levels of intimacy when the relationship does not feel safe. Notice that this graph is basically the same as Bartholomew's model, except that we have identified the emotions that are at the heart of the Good Self, Bad Self, Good Other, and Bad Other representations. Furthermore, there are two emotions at the deepest ends of each axis, representing the emotions of attachment and the emotions of esteem. *Reexamining the graph with an emphasis on the emotions driving those views of self and other allows us to see the relationship through the lens of affect.* It is the affects assembled in those emotions that provide the motivation; this is what is of greatest interest to the couple therapist.

Thus, the person who is fearful and anxious is experiencing some mixture of shame or distress combined with acceptance and trust, while the dismissive partner has pride but is distrustful or disapproving. It is the affects assembled in those various emotions that are operating on the person. If the person shows sadness/distress, he is probably experiencing threat in the realm of the attachment. If he is experiencing shame, often seen in his reactivity, then his threat is in the realm of esteem. The lens of affect helps us to see what is really driving the person, often more clearly than he can see himself. When we respond to that sadness, or that shame, the individual finally feels understood. We are most effective when we are responding to the affects that are motivating the person. The affects in these emotions are the ultimate target of our interventions.

Emotional Safety Is a Dynamic Entity

Emotional safety refers to those times in a relationship when both partners are (relatively) free of negative affects in the realms of esteem and attachment. Emotional safety describes a type of relationship, a location on the terrain of the emotional relationship, and a time in a relationship. I use these multiple terms to emphasize the fluid and dynamic nature of feelings of safety. Partners move in and out of such feeling states. The graphic representation of attachment and esteem emotions provides a visual illustration of what happens as a partner's emotions about himself and his partner shift him in and out of the safe zone. The terrain of the emotional relationship provides a map for tracking the dynamic changes in esteem and attachment that occur between partners as different emotions are activated in the relationship. When positive feelings about self and other are activated, the individual feels safe. Thus, the quadrant defined by the positive ends of both axes is the safe zone. But when negative feelings about himself or his partner are activated, he moves out of the safe zone and into one of the unsafe quadrants where he feels distressed, shameful, distrusting, or disapproving of his partner.

It is instructive to note the difference between the two realms in the Other Axis. In the attachment realm, an individual's attachment security is reflected in his feelings of trust versus distrust *toward* the partner. As I indicated earlier, the activators of distrust tend to be the lack of positive, loving indicators from the partner (except in the case of overt attachment threats). But in the esteem realm, an individual's self-esteem is influenced by his perception of acceptance versus disapproval *from* the partner. *As a rule of thumb, when a partner complains of what the other doesn't do, that individual is expressing attachment concerns. And when a partner complains of what the other does do, that individual is more often expressing esteem concerns.*

Movement Through the Terrain of the Emotional Relationship

The individual's emotional state is represented by his position on the map of the terrain of the emotional relationship. However, his *movement* through that terrain is most heavily influenced by his *partner's* position on the graph, which is the Other Axis on his own graph. It is his perception of her affective tone that has the greatest power to move him along the Self Axis. If he perceives her to be disapproving, that can activate his shame (which might lead him to feel bad about himself, or might lead him to defensively activate his own disapproving feelings about her). And if he perceives her to be distrustful, then he remains cautious and is less likely to move toward greater openness and vulnerability.

It is probably this dimension of couple therapy—the power of the partners' perceptions of each other's affective tone to either facilitate or obstruct movement—that accounts for the increasingly supported finding that couple therapy can often help people resolve individual issues, but individual therapy rarely helps people resolve their couple issues.[5] Individual therapy can help a partner see the issues he contributes to the relationship, but *his movement in the relationship hinges on his perception of the other partner's affective tone.* The perception of a partner's disapproval or distrust is a powerful obstacle; typically each partner waits to see a sign of change in the other partner's affective tone before venturing onto the path of greater openness and vulnerability.

The power of couple therapy is that it creates the possibility for *both* partners to venture onto that path simultaneously, thus creating a change in the affective tone on both sides of the relationship. When couples finally begin to achieve movement, it is common to hear each partner attribute his or her personal change to the changes perceived in the other partner. Such comments can easily cause the couple to slip back into conflict in the esteem realm if a partner feels he is being blamed for the problems that have supposedly now been corrected. The therapist can help prevent this particular form of slipping back by emphasizing the systemic nature of the pattern of interaction that the couple was caught in—basically identifying each partner's part while noting that neither partner was in control of the destructive cycle, as well as by emphasizing the power of each partner's perceptions of the other partner's affective tone.

The couple therapist can use the graphic representation of the terrain of the emotional relationship to track each partner's movement, ultimately seeking to help the partners increase their time in the safe zone. Successful couple therapy not only helps partners spend more time in the safe zone, but also provides them with tools for getting their relationship back into the safe zone when one or both of them has slipped into the unsafe zone. This is something that occurs in all effective couple therapy, but the graph provides the clinician with a map that may help her to visualize the process and perhaps better understand each partner's specific emotional experience. A better grasp of each partner's emotional experience can, in turn, influence the clinician's choice of interventions. We must take a very different tack in therapy when a partner is struggling with distrust than when he is dealing with disapproval.

In addition to understanding the key emotion that each partner is grappling with, the couple therapist also wants to have a clear grasp of the pattern of the couple's movement through the terrain of the emotional relationship. Couples vary in this regard. For example, some couples (or some individuals) slip back into the safe zone slowly as they begin to relax and trust more, while others jump into it by suddenly opening up and revealing deep vulnerabilities. Needless to say, the latter group often finds that such an abrupt experience of safety can prove to be very fragile; it can blow up in their faces and catapult them into deeper levels of unsafety.

The research construct of attachment style describes the quadrant where an individual is most likely to go when feeling unsafe (e.g., the person with shame issues goes to the upper right, the person with distrust goes lower left, and the person with both goes lower right), but this is only their most common response. Especially in therapy sessions in which new experiences are occurring, partners may enter domains of emotion that they less often experience. For example, the shame-bound partner who typically blames herself (upper right) may begin to experience feelings of anger at her partner and move into the disapproval end of the Other-Esteem category (lower left).[6]

The primary trigger for movement in the relationship, or the primary obstacle to movement, is affective tone. In the next chapter, we will look more closely at how affects work their reciprocal influence among intimate partners.

Why Partners Matter: The Power of Affective Resonance

Something happens to a person when he enters into an intimate relationship. Suddenly, another person has a power to influence him that exceeds that of anyone else in his life. That power is not simply about influencing decisions and behavior; it extends to how he feels. His intimate partner can make him feel good just by being with him, but she also has the power to make him feel very bad. Over time, his partner's ability to make him feel bad is refined to the point where she may be able to set off his bad feelings with just a look. What is it about intimate relationships that can give someone such power to make people feel so good or so terrible?

Heightened Attunement

We were in our sixth session together. The previous week was a break-through; Fred finally felt Linda heard and accepted his anger (at his family of origin), and Linda felt Fred finally showed concern for how she was feeling. I never know after such sessions whether the couple will maintain the progress or whether they will have an even bigger falling out precipitated by the increased vulnerability. But Fred and Linda had held on to the gain and had a good week, their first in a very long time. During the session, we talked more about what they had learned in the previous session. Linda explained that her difficulty hearing Fred's anger at his family of origin was based in part on his telling her that she was angry with him for his being angry at his family. She explained that his problems with his family of origin had never made her angry, but his assumption that she was angry did make her angry.

Fred sat quietly while Linda explained all of this. He did not change his body posture, and he seemed to be listening carefully. But I did notice a change in Linda's manner. She was talking more slowly, hesitantly, and I felt she was being cautious. I could still see nothing different going on with Fred, so I asked Linda what was going on with her. She said she thought Fred was angry. I asked Fred if he was, and he confirmed that he was (after a moment or two of avoiding the question). We discussed it and clarified that Fred had thought she was recanting some of the acceptance she had expressed the previous week. Further discussion resolved the issue; Linda was not changing what she had said, only trying to explain further why she had gotten shut down and angry herself.

The interesting thing about this interaction was that I had no clue that Fred had gotten angry. I didn't notice any facial reactions, although I assume Linda saw something in his face. But he didn't cross his arms, shift his body away from her, sigh loudly, or any of the more common ways that I usually recognize a shift in a client's affect state. But Linda spotted it, and when we talked about it, she said that she always knows when Fred is upset with her. Despite the discussion about Fred's mistaken assumptions about Linda's anger, they both agreed that Linda always knows when Fred is angry. She said she can see it in his eyes, or even from his tone of voice over the phone.

Research on the processes that occur within relationships has improved markedly in recent years. Modern researchers monitor the affect dimension of couples' interactions with physiological devices, using computers to merge the synchronized data streams from the two partners (Gottman & Notarius, 2002). The result is an increasingly sophisticated description of the process of nonverbal, affective communication that flows between intimate partners. What is emerging from this research is a picture of two people who are acutely attuned to each other's ongoing affective states. When one partner experiences a slight shift in affect, the other partner responds with her own shift. The mechanism that accounts for this dynamic connection is the same *affective resonance* that allows mothers and infants to communicate.

The Adult Intimate Relationship

[W]hen we share that which is most personal (and authentic) about ourselves, we open ourselves up to the influence of those with whom we have shared.

Karen Prager, 1995, p. 4

An adult intimate relationship is built on the bonds of love. In that respect, it is much the same as the intense bond that the infant experiences toward the mother, except that the emotional structure of the adult is more elaborate. The bonds of adult intimacy are influenced by all the attachment relationships that each person has previously participated in, especially the earliest one between infant and caregiver. However, this does not mean that an adult-adult relationship is the same as an adult-infant relationship. It is not. Adults differ from infants in many important respects, including the level and intensity of their dependency needs, their capacity to restrain their own needs in order to attend to the other person's needs, their ability to erect an empathic wall to the other person's affect, their ability to moderate their own display of affect, and their capacity to function autonomously.

In the relationship between an adult and an infant, the adult is more able to suppress her own needs and attend to the needs of the infant. In adult relationships, both individuals should be willing and able to suppress their personal needs for the benefit of the relationship. When one individual fails to do this, an imbalance develops in the relationship. Similarly, a healthy adult intimate relationship is balanced on the affective level. Each partner is attuned to the other's emotional experience and willing to moderate his own affective display when necessary. However, one of the marks of an intimate relationship is that affect can be displayed more openly. This is a central component of what brings people together. They feel comfortable relating to each other without working so hard at moderating their affect. They inhibit less and connect on a deeper level of emotion.

When two adults first engage in an intimate relationship, they are highly attuned to each other. They usually spend a fair amount of time talking about themselves and getting to know each other on a more intimate level. We might say that they are getting to know each other on an emotional level by learning more about the nature of the scripts that each carries. Their relationship is reminiscent of the caregiver-infant relationship because affective resonance is high and their use of empathic walls is very low (they do not block their affective resonance to each other). The affective tone of the relationship is dominated by interest-excitement and enjoyment-joy, and so the relationship feels great and the bonds of attachment grow.

However, over time, other affects enter the relationship as issues such as autonomy, dependency, and identity are negotiated. This results in a progressive unfolding of issues in an adult intimate relationship. A similar progression occurs in the mother-infant attachment relationship, often involving the same issues. The primary difference is that the adult relationship is more mutual and symmetrical.

Experiencing the Other's Affective Tone

The pattern in this research is clear: Affective tone is more important than the content of dialogue or whether couples can problem solve particular issues.

Susan Johnson, 2003, p. 371

An adult's capacity to love and attach to another adult is heavily influenced by the scripts and scenes he carries from his previous attachment relationships. When an adult falls in love, his positive feelings about the other—including his scripts of trust and acceptance—are activated. But if his previous attachment experiences have not been good, and he has many distress and shame scripts, then he is probably very sensitive to any indications that his partner is feeling distrust or disapproval. Each of these scripts carries an *affective tone*, determined by the affects that are assembled within the specific script.

By lowering their empathic walls and sharing their inner selves with each other, intimate partners achieve a high degree of *affective resonance* in their relationship—they each resonate with subtle nuances of the other's affect. The result is that they are each able to experience themselves and the relationship largely as they perceive their partners to be feeling, just as in their earliest attachment experiences.[1] The positive versus negative nature of these perceived views of self and other is primarily determined by the *affective tone* of the other person's view.[2]

Affective Tone in the Attachment Realm

When he is attuned to her affects in the Other Axis of the attachment realm, he is noticing her feelings about him. Specifically, he is attuned to affects that signify love and caring for him. He perceives these affects in her face when she engages with him, in her behaviors when she comforts him and they do things together, and even in her tone of voice when she talks about him to others. The existence of many positive affects helps him to feel the pleasure of being securely attached. However, there are three situations that can threaten his attachment security and activate distress: (a) one is simply a lack of these positive affects, (b) another is some overt behavior by her that contradicts the positive affects (moving out, having an affair), and (c) the other is his having too many negative scripts from previous attachment relationships that increase his sensitivity to the slightest indication of distrust from her. Any of these can disrupt his feeling of attachment security.

Affective Tone in the Esteem Realm

The perceived affective tone of his partners' feelings in the Other Axis of the esteem realm plays a major role in how he feels about himself; it is both a central component and a major activator of his self scripts.

As infants and young children, we initially define ourselves and develop our repertoire of emotions about ourselves—our pride and shame scripts—in response to the quality of our interactions with our caretakers and the affective tone they convey toward us. Since our capacity for affective resonance preceded our development of language, some of these self scripts are preverbal, memories of feelings about ourselves that we cannot even put into words. As adults, we continue to be sensitive to affective tone cues that can activate feelings about the self, and sometimes we may not even understand where these feelings come from.[3]

Positive affective tone in his partner's view of him (her acceptance scripts) helps him to maintain positive emotions about himself (his pride scripts), but negative affective tone in her view of him (her disapproval scripts) tends to activate negative feelings about himself (his shame scripts).

The Power of the Positive

> We've talked all night about me. Enough about me, let's talk about you.
> So tell me, what did you think of my performance?
>
> Old actors' joke

When a person engages in an intimate relationship, he allows his perception of his partner's feelings about him and the relationship—the affective tone of (a) her view of him and (b) her attachment to him—to influence his overall feeling of security in the relationship, much as he did when he was a dependent child in his earliest attachment relationships. This is how an adult intimate relationship can heal someone with issues of distress, distrust, shame, or emptiness.[4] If the relationship is a positive one, then he can develop his feelings of pride and trust, and many of his scripts of shame and distrust can be disassembled.

The disassembling of negative scripts would translate as a change in his emotional life. The events could still be recalled, but the affects assembled with those memories would be lessened in intensity and perhaps even relinquished. This is the kind of healing that occurs in long-term psychotherapy and in good marriages. It is, quite literally, a change in the person's emotions.

The Power of the Negative

> Why don't you love me like you used to do? . . .
> My hair's still curly and my eyes are still blue.
>
> Hank Williams, Sr.
> "Why Don't You Love Me Like You Used To Do?"

As an intimate relationship develops, the possibility of triggering distrust and disapproval becomes more likely. Part of this is due to the simple fact that spending more time together creates more opportunities for negative things to happen. But it is also true that the intense positive affects associated with a new relationship generally decline as the partners become more familiar with each other. Interest-excitement is highest with novel experiences; it is harder to activate this affect when the experience is common (some couples are able to maintain the intensity of interest-excitement affect through heightened sexual activity).[5]

Most people work the hardest at being thoughtful and other-oriented when they are in the throes of an exciting new relationship. As partners begin to take the relationship, and each other, more for granted, they may not work as hard at pleasing each other. And they begin to reveal more of themselves, the parts that are not as attractive. At some point, distrust or disapproval gets triggered.

Esteem Issues

> We become anxious about others seeing us too accurately, not so much
> because they might condemn us, but because we will be forced to see
> parts of ourselves that others see—parts that, until the public exposure,
> we have concealed from our own scrutiny.

Carl Goldberg, 1991, p. 58

As the relationship evolves to include disapproval scripts, it becomes less safe.
The idea of revealing oneself, initially such an exciting and energizing experience, becomes a more dangerous proposition.[6] Revealing himself to her may
meet with her disapproval, and the affective tone of her disapproval can then
activate his shame, which makes him feel terrible and may cause him to see
an aspect of himself that he normally disavows. If a partner relies extensively
upon disavowal and the relationship causes him to encounter more of his
shame than he can tolerate, then he may inhibit himself and distance from her
in order to preserve his self-esteem. By attempting to reveal only those parts
of himself that elicit approval from his partner, he is actually trying to control
how he feels about himself (though he may still blame it on his partner).

When he experiences his disapproval of her, it is likely to activate her shame
(even though the content of his disapproval scripts probably differs from the
content of her shame scripts), because the affects in her shame emotion can
resonate with the affects in his disapproval. She is vulnerable to being triggered
because: (a) some portion of the affects assembled in her shame script is similar
to (resonate with) the affects assembled in his disapproval script, and (b) she is
identified as the negative object in both his disapproval script and her shame
script. As a result of her affective resonance and identification with the Other
in his disapproval script, she is vulnerable to being triggered into her shame. It
is primarily through the phenomenon of affective resonance that partners can
be easily triggered. Figure 6-1 shows the steps a partner may go through as his
perception of the other partner's disapproval activates his shame.

Feeling Misunderstood

As I noted in Chapter 2, partners' emotions are different because of their different
biographies (i.e., the different historical experiences that produced the idiosyncratic scenes and scripts assembled in each emotion). The thing they have in
common, though, is their experience of their affects. When he resonates with the
affective tone of her view of him, it is activating a similar affect that is assembled
in one of his self scripts. However, the specific nature of their respective scripts—
the cognitive component of emotion, as well as the other affects and the intensity
of those affects assembled in the emotion—is almost always different, sometimes
extremely different. Yet he is likely to interpret her feeling about him as being
much the same as his own self-script that has been activated.

Her Disapproval Triggers His Shame through Affective Resonance

He is in his Safe Zone.

Something happens to activate her Disapproval (it may or may not have to do with him).

He perceives (a) the affects of her Disapproval and (b) the fact that he is the object of her Disapproval.

The affects which he perceives to be in her Disapproval script resonate with the affects in one of his Shame scripts.

His Shame emotion is activated.

He attributes her disapproval to be fundamentally the same as the content of his shame scripts.

Figure 6-1 How Disapproval Triggers Shame.

Communication in an intimate relationship can be difficult because, in effect, *the language of affect is universal but the language of emotion is specific to each individual and his or her unique experience.* We complicate our communication further by naming our emotions as if they were simple affects. But they are not simple, they are idiosyncratic elaborations of the underlying affects. We resonate to those underlying affects, thinking the other person is experiencing the same emotion (or its reciprocal) as that activated in us. The potential for emotional miscommunication is huge!

If her mild annoyance with him triggers his emotion that includes a scripted view of himself as an unwanted pest, then that is how he will feel she views him. His reaction, if negative, can then take the two of them into more negative territory. If he responds with a reciprocal disapproval emotion, they may have conflict. If he responds by pulling away from her to protect his esteem, he may stimulate distress in her and activate her attachment concerns. The problems generated by interpreting affective messages through one's idiosyncratic emotions are most commonly first encountered in the realm of esteem, but they can easily move into the realm of attachment. The power of affective resonance to trigger negative self scripts (shame) is probably the single largest contributing factor to the phenomenon of misunderstanding and feeling misunderstood in intimate relationships.

When Mary was late for their marital therapy session, Jerry was irritated because he had warned her that he would have to leave a few minutes early to make a business appointment. His irritation was visible and he acknowledged that he was "a bit pissed" that she hadn't made a greater effort to be on time. Mary's reaction was to hang her head and talk about how bad she was—clearly suggesting that this was a sign of some deep defect in her personality. As the session wore on, Mary actually became angry at herself and was unable to talk about anything but that. Finally, I asked Mary how she felt Jerry saw her at that moment. The disgust and loathing that she described was shocking to Jerry, who hastened to correct her impression. He had been mildly irritated at first but was beyond that within a few minutes.

Mary grew up with an abusive father. He never actually hit her; his abuse was emotional. When she failed to do almost anything less than perfectly, he would berate her and make her feel that she was beneath contempt. Her shame was thus composed of many of those same attitudes. Jerry rarely expressed negative feelings toward Mary but when he did, it often triggered Mary's self-loathing and disgust with herself. Soon she would move into anger at herself.[7] She had considerable difficulty believing that Jerry really did not see her in these same miserable terms. In Mary's eyes, Jerry's view became her father's view when her shame was triggered. Part of what this misunderstanding led to was that Mary remained distant from Jerry for fear of "enraging" him. In actuality, Mary had had the good sense to marry a very gentle, nonexplosive man.[8]

It is as though they were talking about accelerating in a car and he was picturing a sedate sedan while she was picturing a fire-breathing, thousand horsepower race car. She was upset because she could not tolerate having such a powerful negative affect seemingly directed at her, and he complained that he was not free to express his feelings. They often used the same words to describe the emotions, thus it was difficult for her to recognize that the feelings she was experiencing (and attributing to him) far exceeded what he was experiencing. The affect in Jerry's disapproval script (triggered by her tardiness) resonated with the affect in one of Mary's shame scripts and activated her shame, which was then expanded to encompass the entire assemblage of her shame script, which included disgust affect, among other things. Mary was an abuse survivor and hence had colossal shame scripts. The couple's potential for misunderstanding was just as colossal.

The Nature of Anxiety

Anxiety is an emotion that involves the affect fear-terror. We can be anxious about specific feared events happening or we can have a general anxiety about something bad happening. Like all the emotions, anxiety differs from one person to the next according to the affects and scripts that are assembled out of an individual's unique experiences. Many people have specific fears that predominate because of their histories.[9] Someone who has a history of being abandoned naturally has a fear of being abandoned; someone who has been betrayed has anxiety about being betrayed, and so forth. There is no single source of anxiety—we each have many different scripts that involve anxiety—but the primary thing that distinguishes anxiety from overt fear is that anxiety is generally about things that *may* happen, while fear is a response to something that is perceived to *be* happening.[10]

The most common sources of anxiety within intimate relationships are attachment fears (fear of losing the attachment), esteem fears (fear of being exposed as inadequate or unlovable), and trauma fears (fear of some traumatic event, usually related to the individual's history). Any of these realms can be related to another. For example, the individual who fears he will be exposed as inadequate may also fear that his inadequacy will cause him to be found unfit for the attachment (a case of primary emotions in the realms of attachment and esteem).

Previous negative experiences in any of the three realms (attachment, esteem, trauma) can heighten a partner's sensitivity to potential trouble in that realm. The wife who lost a parent in a transportation accident (attachment and trauma) may become anxious whenever the husband goes on a business trip. The husband who has considerable shame can have his anxiety activated by any indication of disapproval from his partner, however minor. People with a history of unsafe relationships often have a very low threshold of sensitivity to negative affective tone in their partner's voice, posture, or facial display. Any inkling of negative tone can then trigger their anxiety. He may grimace when he bumps his toe and she wants to know if he is upset with her.

Anxiety about the relationship can be activated by something that has nothing to do with the partner—a person's own thoughts. He can begin to think of possible things that might happen and make himself anxious. People who are perpetually anxious have fallen into a pattern of thoughts that constantly envision the possibility of dire outcomes. Still, within an intimate relationship, the most common triggering stimulus is *perceived negative affective tone indicating a distrust or disapproval script* in the partner. Once an individual is anxious, he tends to watch the partner carefully for any indication of negative affect.

Rebuilding the Empathic Wall

Recall now that one of the fundamental differences between attachment and esteem is that attachment concerns are generally about what is missing in the partner's affects, but esteem concerns are generally about what is present in the partner's affects. When he feels assaulted by active disapproval from her, the best defense (against feeling bad every time it occurs) is for him to intensify his empathic wall so that he does not resonate with her negative affects about him.[11] Partners often find this difficult to do. For one thing, putting up a wall interferes with intimacy; the positive affects are blocked out along with the negative affects. This is unsatisfying to both partners; the individual maintaining the wall may look less distressed, but he only does this because it feels so bad to have his shame activated by his partner's negative affect. A better goal is to be able to use the wall in a discriminating fashion, and only employ it when there is a danger of shame being triggered. If this is done sensitively, the partner experiencing disapproval may not feel abandoned and the intimate connection will be preserved. However, if the disapproving partner does feel abandoned, this will likely only add to her feeling of disapproval (more fuel on the fire) and increase the disconnection.

A different kind of solution is also commonly pursued. Rather than maintain the empathic wall at an optimal level, one partner simply controls how much of himself is actually accessible to the other partner. Irene Stiver (1997) referred to this as strategies of disconnection (i.e., revealing only the acceptable parts of the self [and disconnecting the unacceptable parts of the self] in order to maintain a connection). The problem with this strategy is that the quality of the intimate connection is compromised. An individual may not feel fully loved and accepted if he is keeping significant parts of himself out of the connection. Thus, this strategy to protect oneself in the realm of esteem creates new concerns in the realm of attachment and places the individual in a dilemma.

Mature individuals who are able to maintain a high level of intimacy are usually adept at creating an empathic wall. This is not the kind of wall that keeps others out; it is simply a refined ability to control one's own affective resonance and to apply it in a discriminating fashion. We all have to learn to do this during childhood or we would be constantly flooded by others' emotions. Part of developing an intimate relationship is lowering empathic walls. And for many people, part of maintaining an intimate relationship is being able to raise empathic walls when needed—but without disrupting the caring and concern for the other person.[12]

One of the keys to successful intimacy is the ability to simultaneously erect one's empathic wall while remaining close and caring toward the partner. This sounds counterintuitive to people who feel intimacy means complete, unimpeded openness. Certainly it can be overdone, but briefly and judiciously employing empathic walls can help partners control their tendency toward shame and allow them to focus on their own affective experience rather than reacting to the partner's affective experience. This particular area of vulnerability in the realm of esteem is the initial source of most relational difficulties. When it is not addressed adequately, the difficulties rapidly expand into the realm of attachment. In the next chapter, we will see why the emotion of shame has such power to disrupt intimacy.

Why Esteem Matters: The Power of Shame and Pride

The realm of esteem refers to the emotions that are activated about the self and the partner's self. The self emotions lie along the axis between feeling very positive about the self, represented by the emotion of pride, and feeling very negative about the self, represented by the emotion of shame. Every partner's pride or shame can be activated by his perception of the other partner's acceptance or disapproval, so intimate partners all learn the power of their other-esteem emotions to influence their partners, but it is each individual's self-esteem emotions that play the major motivating role in the realm of esteem. And of the two poles of the self-esteem emotional continuum, it is shame that plays the primary role in disrupting emotional safety in intimate relationships. Indeed, shame plays a greater role in shaping personality than most people realize. We will begin this chapter by looking more closely at the power of shame.

Shame Shapes Our Lives

Invariably the smallest person on the team, Bobby could show his worth by fighting harder, by playing even with broken bones, by never giving up. In a sense his whole life was a test—a test to overcome his greatest fear: that he was inadequate.

Ronald Steel[1]

Imagine you are waiting at a red light in a large intersection. In your rear view mirror, you can see the woman in the car behind you has adjusted her mirror so that she can check her makeup. In the car to your right, a muscular young man in a tight T-shirt is stroking his biceps. The car to your left is an expensive luxury car with an older male driver and a beautiful young female passenger. The car in front of you is an old beater with a bumper sticker that reads "My Mercedes is in the shop." Are any of these people currently experiencing shame? Probably not, but past encounters with shame surely are playing a role in their current behavior.

Have you ever run out of gas? It's a disconcerting experience that can produce a variety of affects, including shame affect and often fear. After you've had the distressing experience of running out of gas, you're likely to keep a better eye on the fuel gauge. It becomes second nature for experienced drivers; they automatically scan the gauge when they start the ignition. We can say that their behavior has been *shaped* by the experience of running out of gas. It would be wrong to say that experienced drivers are in constant fear of running out of gas. They are not feeling fearful. But their previous experience has taught them to be more watchful for a certain condition, and they have incorporated that watchfulness into their daily behavior. This is how shame shapes people's behavior—they know how it feels to run out of gas, so they learn to protect themselves against letting it happen again. Once a person has incorporated that learned knowledge, it becomes automatic—part of who he or she is.

Shame operates in a similar fashion; it is an extremely powerful motivator. It not only motivates us at the moment when we experience it, but its residue (the shame scenes and scripts) continues to motivate us as we go forward with our lives. We are all highly motivated to avoid any situation that might activate our shame!

Concern about experiencing shame can stop a person from entering many different kinds of situations. To make matters worse, an individual's vulnerability to having his shame activated is heightened by his anxiety about the prospect of having his shame activated. So people learn to avoid many kinds of situations—perhaps by physically avoiding them ("No thanks, I don't care to play") or perhaps by changing the situation in some fundamental fashion ("How about if we don't keep score?"). Whether a person learns to avoid certain kinds of situations, master them, change them, or pursue something else in their place, the pattern becomes a central part of who that person is. We each shape our lives so as to avoid or minimize our experience of shame.

Since shame exerts such a pervasive influence on our individual lives, it inevitably follows us into our relationships and influences those as well.[2] In fact, it is primarily in interpersonal relationships that shame's potential for destructiveness is unleashed. And it starts with the shame scripts about the self that people bring to their relationships.

Shame Scripts

People seldom think of shame as a pervasive emotion; most people regard the actual experience of shame as a rare event in their lives. This is because they label their difficulties in terms of other emotions,[3] such as frustration, disappointment, feeling hurt or disgusted with themselves, and they reserve the label of shame for only one particular flavor of emotion.[4] Then they go to great lengths to avoid experiencing that emotion.

An additional reason that most people fail to recognize their experience of shame emotion is that their scripted response to the activation of shame is to launch into a secondary emotion, such as anger, with such speed that they never pause to recognize the primary emotion. Instead, they view their reaction as the whole of the emotional experience. Yet when we look carefully, we often can see shame in some of the smallest examples.

Two men arrive late for a meeting because they misunderstood the memo that announced the time. One smiles and shrugs; the other is angry at the person who wrote the ambiguous memo.

These two men have radically different reactions to being caught in an embarrassing posture. One may have a script that says "Embarrassing situations simply reveal my humanity, and the human condition is pretty funny." His typical response—as much a part of the script as the view of himself—may be to laugh at himself in situations like this. Yet for his companion, the same situation might elicit a shame response, with a script that says "Once again I have been revealed to be inferior." His reaction is to get angry at the perceived source of his bad feeling. That reaction can become so automatic that he completely loses his awareness of the moment of shame that preceded the reaction. Instead, he believes that certain events just "make him mad"—rather than that certain events activate his shame and he reacts by getting angry.[5]

Something to Prove

I am the greatest! I am the king!

**Cassius Clay (subsequently known as Muhammad Ali)
upon defeating world heavyweight champion Sonny Liston in
February 1964**

Past shame can pursue a person throughout an otherwise fine life. We see it all around: people overdoing things in their haste to prove something. What are they proving? They are proving that they are okay, acceptable, significant, and not someone with reason to feel filled with shame. And who are they proving it to? They are proving it to themselves. This is the case even when the individual seems to have proven he is the greatest of all. When people insist they are the greatest, they are banishing their shame. They are winning, but the real battle is not with everyone else, it is with their shame. Though they may be fiercely competitive toward everyone, the only opponent that matters is within themselves. The harder they work at proving something, the greater the power of their shame!

An individual's propensity for shame can be diminished by increasing his positive feelings about himself. When he feels he has earned the right to feel good about himself, he's able to relinquish the centrality of the shame scripts that may have dominated his feelings about himself. The result is a movement away from shame and toward pride. But that is different from drawing others' attention to our sources of pride. Trying to manage others' impressions of us so that they see our prideful parts and not our shameful parts is a form of avoidance of shame.[6] It does nothing to build pride, and thus it leaves us vulnerable to having our shame activated.

The Power of Shame and Pride

In the movie *Back to the Future*, Michael J. Fox portrays Marty McFly, a young man who goes back into the past and influences the lives of his parents when they were in high school. Before Marty first leaves the present, his father is a drab, insignificant person who is easily ignored and commands no respect. He lacks self-confidence and cowers before his tyrannical boss, Biff. But after Marty has influenced the past and returns to the present, his father is a suave, confident man and Biff is the cowering subordinate. The difference is attributed to one apocryphal moment in which Marty's influence leads his father to stand up to the school bully (Biff as a teenager) instead of hanging his head in shame and submitting.

These two very different portrayals of Marty's father represent a man whose life is dominated by shame versus a man whose life has been shaped by healthy pride. And the movie captures the idea that a single moment of facing up to one's shame can change the entire direction of a person's life. Of course, this is the kind of simplification created for the movies, yet I believe its appeal is based on our innate grasp of the truth underlying this simplified story. Living a life shaped by pride rather than shame often begins with one courageous step!

Replacing Shame With Pride

When I was a child, my mother used to read a Golden Book story to me about a little train named Tootles. Tootles had a problem with leaving the train track and roaming through the fields because he loved to smell the buttercups. At the end of the day, Tootles would return to the station with grass caught up in his undercarriage, and the engineer would know that Tootles had left the track again. He was concerned about Tootles leaving the tracks and tried to figure out what he could do about it. He knew that Tootles, who was basically a good little train, knew to turn away from red flags and toward green flags. So the engineer arranged for the townspeople to hide in the field of buttercups. When Tootles left the tracks and veered into the field, a townsperson would jump out from behind a bush and wave a red flag. Tootles would turn away, only to encounter another red flag. Tootles kept encountering red flags until he was headed back toward the tracks—that's when the engineer jumped out with a green flag. Tootles was very happy finally to encounter a green flag and, after that, he was content to stay on the tracks.

Shame is a red flag. Every time we encounter it, it turns us away from the direction in which we were heading. When we finally encounter a green flag, we are encouraged to head in that direction. Thus, our course through life is shaped by our avoidance of the red flags of shame and our pursuit of the green flags of pride. Doing something to increase the pride end of the shame-pride axis can help to diminish shame, especially if the pride-inducing behavior is in the same domain as the shame (e.g., the football player who fumbles the ball can recover from his shame by making a touchdown). The development of pride is one of the primary strategies that people employ to overcome their shame.

The Development of Pride

A person's early shame experiences can deter him from pursuing certain activities in life. This is how the avoidance of potential sources of shame can shape a person's life. But pride-inducing experiences can have a similar impact, only in the opposite direction. Just as a person can fall into a chasm of shame and give up on himself, so can a person discover his abilities and build success upon success. Pride always involves action toward a goal (or memories of past actions).[7] The more successes an individual has, the greater his confidence grows, and the more he is willing to attempt that which the shame-prone person assumes to be impossible. The greatest source of pride is successfully facing challenges, especially situations that previously produced shame or have the potential to produce shame.

The pursuit of pride is more adaptive than the avoidance of shame because it can allow the person to remain in those challenging situations that previously produced shame. When an individual has sufficient confidence (and support) to stay with a challenge and apply himself, he often is able to turn failure into achievement and shame into pride. And the more successes he has at converting shameful situations into pride-inducing situations, the more confident he becomes.

The Role of Self Emotions in Defining the Self

We learn from our shame and pride experiences both explicitly and implicitly.[8] Sometimes a person might say to himself, "I will never do that again." Other times, he may not articulate anything yet he learns to shy away from the kind of situations that produced the shame and gravitate toward the kinds of situations that produced pride. This is probably part of the process through which personality develops. Even when a person makes explicit decisions, he often forgets the decision and the circumstances that spawned it and retains only the learned behavior. Thus, shying away from certain kinds of situations and toward others becomes part of who the individual is. He no longer thinks of his daily choices in life as having anything to do with shame or pride; it is simply his style, his personality, his preference.

Shame and pride play a major role in shaping every person's life. An individual may forget about the time he humiliated himself trying to dance or to play baseball, he just becomes someone who is not interested in dancing or playing baseball. And he may also forget the first time he excelled at preparing food or playing Scrabble, he just knows that he enjoys cooking and playing Scrabble.

This is how our self-emotions contribute to the development of who we are and how we see ourselves. Imagine the potential turmoil if another person acquires the power to alter these fundamental views of self. Kelly (1996) defines the revealing of the inmost self as an essential aspect of intimacy. *Engaging in an intimate attachment relationship means giving another person access to our self-emotions.* When that access results in increased positive emotions about the self, it is intoxicating; but when that access results in increased negative emotions about the self, it can be excruciating.

Healthy Shame, Healthy Pride

> In small doses, shame is a prod to self-improvement. ... Healthy responses to feeling shame derive from our willingness to examine openly, and to do something constructive about, those aspects of ourselves that cause us to feel badly and that we can reasonably change.
>
> **Carl Goldberg, 1991, p. 274**

The successful pursuit of pride-inducing experiences not only diminishes shame, it builds self-esteem. We try to help children find pride in their accomplishments because we know of its power to motivate and reward. Many successful people have built their lives around the pursuit of pride-inducing experiences. This is not the kind of unhealthy pride that is viewed negatively; that kind of pride generally refers to an exaggerated, unduly high opinion of oneself that causes the person to be arrogant. Rather, *the pride that counters shame is more of a delight in one's accomplishment.* This kind of pride yields a greater sense of competence, dignity, and self-esteem. In a very real sense, shame yields poor self-esteem, and healthy pride yields good self-esteem.

Healthy pride usually does not make other people feel shame. We're happy for the individual who conquers challenges by overcoming a handicap or excelling at a difficult task. When the runners in the marathon finally cross the finish line, everyone smiles and cheers them on, sharing their well-deserved pride with them. The onlookers are not shamed by the runners' success. Yet shame often still plays a role in the activities that produce healthy pride. Many people who achieve pride-inducing accomplishments were originally motivated by experiencing some degree of shame and vowing to overcome it. Ironically, many prideful accomplishments might not have occurred were it not for the motivational power of shame.

Shame also comes in a healthy form. Remember, the reason we experience shame affect in the first place is to amplify impediments so that we will be motivated to stop when our positive feelings would otherwise motivate us to run right into the obstacle. This is the adaptive nature of shame; it serves to keep us out of trouble, to recognize our limitations. Like Tootles' red flags, our healthy shame helps keep us on track. Shame is the governor on our motivational system; its job is to protect us, and it is the fundamental source of our efforts to improve ourselves.

Unhealthy Shame

> Under police questioning, he whimpered, held his head in his hands and stared morosely at the floor.

The above quote is from an Associated Press article by Brian Carovillano about former Rhode Island police detective Jeffrey Scott Hornoff, who served 6 years of a life sentence for murder until the actual murderer came forward and confessed. Hornoff's only offense was adultery and lying about it to police. "Am I guilty of something? Yes, I am. I broke my sacred wedding vows and for that I will never forgive myself." This man experienced such intense shame and guilt about his adulterous behavior that he apparently failed to adequately defend himself against a murder charge.

It is only when shame affect is tied to too many self scripts that we are likely to get stuck in our shame. The more we experience shame emotion, the more we build our shameful scripts. At some threshold level, a person's core view of self shifts and he comes to view himself as fundamentally defective and unacceptable, rather than simply human. People will do almost anything to avoid falling down that slippery slope.

That desperate urge to avoid it gives shame a particular power to harm intimate relationships, because the stimulus with the greatest power to activate those negative scripts is the negative affect of someone who has access to our self-emotions—our intimate partners. If an individual feels his partner's view of him is pushing him toward that unhealthy view of self, he will desperately fight his partner's view. This is why intimate partners can fight with such intensity over seemingly trivial issues. The content issue may indeed be trivial, but at another level, the partners may feel they are fighting for their very survival.

The Social Emotion

> He remembered the bitterness of his life at school, the humiliation which he had endured, the banter which had made him morbidly afraid of making himself ridiculous; and he remembered the loneliness he had felt since.

W. Somerset Maugham, *Of Human Bondage*, 1915 [1986], p. 256

Shame affect contains no moral judgment. The morality we assign to our feelings does not develop until the innate affects are assembled with scripts and become emotions. The meanings we give to our feelings are heavily influenced by our contact with the world of people. Through our connections with others, we learn to use our feelings to define our sense of right and wrong, fairness, and all the subtle forms of interpersonal sensitivity referred to as emotional intelligence (Goleman, 1998).

Interpersonal situations provoke a great deal of interest and enjoyment, yet dealing with other humans is inherently unpredictable and subject to unwelcome impediments. Thus, shame affect is often activated in interpersonal contexts. Any time a person experiences shame affect in an interpersonal context, he is more likely to activate scripts about the self and produce shame emotion. Individuals with extensive shame are prone to interpret any occurrence of shame affect as being about the self because that is consistent with the nature of their shame scripts. And in an intense interpersonal context—intimacy— all of us are more likely to interpret experiences of shame affect as being about the self because the self is already the object of positive affects—especially when we perceive the positive emotions to be emanating from our partners.

The Shadow Side

A shame-based person will guard against exposing his inner self to others, but more significantly, he will guard against exposing himself to himself.

John Bradshaw, 1988, p. 10

Stuart was a personable man and his wife, Marilyn, was initially happy in their marriage. Yet, over time, she began to complain that something was missing in their relationship. It was hard for her to define. She said their intimacy did not grow, that Stuart was the same when they were alone in the bedroom as when they were socializing at a party. Stuart didn't understand what she found wrong with this; it sounded like she found his consistency to be a bad thing. But what Marilyn was getting at was that she was no more privy to Stuart's private thoughts and feelings than anyone else. Stuart did not seem to have a private self that he shared with her, and Marilyn began to feel uncomfortable around her husband, like he was a stranger that she didn't really know.

Carl Jung proposed the concept of the shadow side, referring to that region of ourselves that contains the more undesirable side of our nature.[9] In his view, the shadow side remains beyond our vision and yet must be explored if we are to become whole. I believe Jung was responding to his awareness of the group of scripts that comprise shame emotion, which, by its very nature, seeks the shadows. It seeks to remain invisible—to ourselves as well as to others. I suspect that Stuart's inability to share himself had to do with his avoidance of his shadow side.

A person's shadow side contains scripts that comprise a view of self as inferior, impaired, and unacceptable. When a person's shame is activated, his subjective experience is that the content of the shame scripts is real and correct—he is inferior, impaired, or unacceptable. This is the power of shame affect. It amplifies its source and motivates the person by imbuing the shame scripts with a feeling of conviction. When shame is experienced in intense proportions, the individual does not simply feel unacceptable; he is unacceptable! People with intensive shame scripts live in fear of their shame being activated. But their subjective experience of their fear is not that their shame will be activated; their fear is that they will be *exposed*, that the reality of their inferiority and impaired nature will be revealed. Intense and excessive shame produces a powerful fear of exposure.

Since intense shame brings this feeling of conviction to the accompanying scripts, the shame-prone person feels helpless to change it. His only alternative is to hide these shameful parts of himself from everyone, including himself. Thus, intense shame generally leads to the development of a powerful shadow side to a person's nature. This powerful force that lays hidden in the human psyche has influenced many of the great theorists. The certainty that one's shame scripts are true is probably what led Alfred Adler (1923, 1931) to propose feelings of inferiority to be a major source of motivation. And the fear of having one's shame activated and one's shameful nature exposed is very likely what led Freud to view anxiety as the hallmark of neurosis.[10]

All instances of neglect, abuse, and abandonment of children will activate shame affect and contribute to the development of shame scripts about the self. But the most damaging kind of abuse is neither sexual nor physical, it is emotional. *The most destructive source of shame is shaming—deliberate attempts to induce shame about the self—that is directed at a person by someone he or she cares about.*

Shaming

Whenever someone becomes significant to us, whenever another's caring, respect or valuing matters, the possibility for generating shame emerges.

Gershen Kaufman, 1992, p. 14

People often try to influence the behavior of others through inducing some emotion. This is usually labeled as manipulation, but it is not always viewed negatively. Whereas the leader who seeks to induce feelings of hatred and racial superiority is seen negatively, the leader who appeals to feelings of loyalty, affiliation, and patriotism is generally seen in a more positive light. In both cases, they are trying to influence the behavior of others through stirring up an emotion. Adults involved with children inevitably try to influence the children through emotional avenues. Seldom do we persuade on a purely intellectual level; the art of persuasion usually involves a significant emotional appeal.[11]

Thus, it is not the act of inducing an emotion that is problematic; it is the nature of the emotion that is induced. Parents who try to influence by inducing fear, anger, and shame raise damaged children. Parents who appeal to feelings of love and caring are more likely to raise loving, caring children. Few parents, however, actually choose to shame their children. They usually resort to shaming when they're at a loss for how to handle a situation. And because shame is such a hidden emotion, we often may not realize what we're doing when we shame someone. Adults who were actively shamed as children are prone to be defensive, argumentative, and hypersensitive to criticism. Any indication that they are being judged is likely to activate their shame.

Toxic Shame

Toxic shame, the shame that binds you, is experienced as the all-pervasive sense that I am flawed and defective as a human being.

John Bradshaw, 1988, p. 10

John Bradshaw (1988) has written extensively about shame and particularly about the most extreme cases of what he terms *toxic shame*. These are cases in which the individual's entire personality comes to be shame based. A shame-based person organizes his life around his need to avoid potential shame-inducing situations and manage his frequent experiences of shame emotion. People with less extensive shame can combat their shame, at least in part, by trying to increase their positive scripts about themselves and replace shame with pride, but shame-based people are more oriented toward fending off the possibility of experiencing their shame. Building pride is like settling down and building a home; the shame-based person is forever on the run and unable to take the time to start building a home.

For an individual to reach the level of toxic shame, there is always a failure in the parenting environment—either in the form of neglect, abuse, or abandonment. The most common example is the abusive parent who ruthlessly shames the child, but this is not the only path to toxic shame. Neglect is equally powerful and often harder to identify and correct in therapy. People who live with toxic shame are among the most damaged members of our society. They can be helped, but they cannot do it alone. To change such a profound negative view of self absolutely requires that another human being be able to see the person's redeeming features.

Shame Reactions

Life is 10 percent what happens to you and 90 percent how your react.

Anonymous

The primary way that shame creates problems in relationships is through the way people react when their shame has been activated. The majority of shame reactions are pretty negative, especially some of the reactions most commonly enacted by men.[12] One of the most common male responses to the onset of shame is to get angry.[13] Spouses and other intimates on the receiving end of the anger may come to understand what will set the shame-prone person off, but they usually don't fully understand why.[14] They just learn to tread very lightly.

The person who is highly shame prone has two levels of difficulty. The first is the ease with which his shame can be activated. He's conditioned to feel shame rapidly and in response to situations that he anticipates will expose his inadequacy. Hence, his reaction can be to what he *expects is going to happen*, rather than to what has already happened. The second level of difficulty concerns how he deals with his shame. His maneuvers at this level—such as getting angry or pulling away—create extensive problems in his intimate relationships. In intimate relationships, a partner's shame reactions are the primary barrier to overcoming shame and achieving emotional safety.

The Role of Fear

When a partner's shame is activated within a relationship, it usually constitutes a threat and the individual experiences fear affect in addition to the shame. The fear is related to the self; the person's underlying fear is that his view of himself is going to suffer. The fear is basically a fear of being humiliated, but it can be as extreme as a sense of losing the self or being destroyed, and many partners will dig in and fight for their survival when the fear is that extreme. The other partner usually doesn't understand the depth of the fear that has been activated, which only makes the fearful partner's reaction less comprehensible.

Most of the time, people reacting to an emotion assembled out of fear and shame cannot even articulate what it is that they fear, but they become aroused and their behavior is shaped by one of the three ways that human beings respond to the kinds of threat that activate fear affect: they either fight, flee, or freeze. The freeze response to shame is one of submission. The individual succumbs to the shame and experiences himself as his shame defines him (to himself). If this happens repeatedly, the individual often moves into depression. Freezing is the passive response to shame; most of the responses that create problems in the relationship are active responses in which the individual either fights the shame or attempts to flee it.

As long as the emotion that is activated contains both fear and shame, the potential for a destructive shame reaction remains high. The fear-based reactions of fight, flight, or freeze do nothing to resolve the shame-related script or the situation that triggers the shame. In order to resolve the reaction, the individual must be able to tolerate experiencing his shame and *act on it*, rather than succumb to it, fight it, or attempt to rid himself of it. We will discuss the process of resolving the shame/fear reaction in Chapter 14; for now we will look more closely at the active reactions (fighting and fleeing) that create so much havoc in the relationship.

The Compass of Shame

It is the four poles of the compass that house all the scripts we know as shameful withdrawal, masochistic submission, narcissistic avoidance of shame, and the rage of wounded pride.

Donald Nathanson, 1992, p. 30

Nathanson (1992) has identified four general strategies that individuals commonly resort to when their shame has been activated. He organizes these strategies into a "compass of shame" with *withdrawal, attack self, avoidance*, and *attack other* at the four poles.[15] As you can see, all of these involve some form of escaping the shame experience, but Nathanson notes how the typical reaction first proceeds: initially, the individual *withdraws* from the connection to escape the pain of his shame, then he feels the pain of being disconnected and so reconnects by *attacking himself* and putting himself in an inferior position, then he seeks to make the feelings go away through *avoiding* them or distracting himself from the source, and finally he resorts to *attacking the other* person so that he maintains the connection but feels better by making the other person feel worse. As scripts accumulate over time, people develop their accustomed reactions and go directly to them in response to the activation of their shame.

Withdrawal

The *withdrawal* pole of the compass of shame occurs when one partner pulls into himself and is not open to the other partner. This is similar to Bowlby's (1969) stage of detachment when the attachment relationship is disrupted, perhaps differing only in degree. However, there are still significant differences between withdrawal and detachment. For one thing, people may resort to withdrawal when they experience shame in any relational context, including casual relationships or even experiences with strangers. Detachment, on the other hand, refers specifically to a significant attachment relationship. Perhaps more importantly, withdrawal can occur on a behavioral level (such as focusing on the television and not listening to one's spouse), but detachment occurs on a deeper emotional level (such as disconnecting so that one no longer cares about what one's spouse feels).

Attack Self

The *attack self* reaction is more common than most people expect. Since a person's shame scripts tell him that he is in some way defective, it is not much of a step for him to get angry at himself and literally attack himself. Most people react this way at times, but it is especially common among people who were treated harshly and not given enough loving acceptance and nurturance as children. The harshness teaches them to control themselves through punishment rather than reward, and the lack of nurturance and acceptance teaches them to be unaccepting of their own shortcomings.

Many children with abusive caretakers learn to get angry at themselves in order to deflect any anger they may feel toward their caretakers. In other words, they are prone to interpret the situation in a manner that leads to shame rather than distrust. This is adaptive when dealing with an abusive caretaker who might be enraged by an expression of anger from the child. Attacking himself allows the child to maintain the connection to the caretaker, while still pulling away from the shame.

People with shame who react by attacking themselves have learned to deal with themselves in a manner similar to that of a child who is given too much responsibility for controlling younger children. The older child may resort to threats and violence in order to force a younger child to behave. The older child is not inherently mean or violent, he simply lacks the more subtle and positive strategies that a competent adult can devise in order to control a young child's behavior.[16]

In an intimate relationship, a partner soon learns to hold back because of the dire effect of his criticism and complaints on the self-attacking partner. Typically, partners of self-attacking individuals learn to tiptoe around difficult issues; they often feel guilty when the self-attacking partner beats up on himself. However, over time, one partner may come to feel controlled by the self-attacking partner's quickness to attack himself, and the other partner often becomes resentful.

In its most extreme form, the attack-self strategy for dealing with shame can lead to suicide. Unfortunately, this is not as uncommon as one might expect. In 1996, the ranking admiral in the Navy killed himself because it had been revealed that he was wearing an undeserved decoration.[17]

Avoidance

The defense mechanism of *disavowal* is the underlying mechanism that allows a person to avoid shame that has been triggered. In disavowal, the person fails to recognize that the potential shame-activating situation has occurred—not just misperceiving it but refusing to appreciate the meaning of it.[18] Nathanson (1992) gives the example of Scarlett O'Hara's reaction to being left by Rhett Butler in the movie *Gone With the Wind*; she will "think about it tomorrow." Disavowal is a component of every shame reaction that fails to recognize the shame-activating aspect of the situation. In that sense, it is also involved in the next strategy to be discussed, when the individual shifts from his experience of shame to a focus on something or someone outside of himself.

Attack Other

To blame is to disavow shame.

Vernon Kelly, 1996, p. 92

The *attack other* response creates the majority of the conflict in intimate relationships. This is the opposite of the attack self response—the attacker tends to interpret ambiguous situations in a manner that results in some variant of distrust emotion. However, this does not necessarily mean that the attacker did not experience any shame emotion; it is often unclear whether shame has been activated in the attack other situation.[19] The attacker feels justified in his attack and the defender is preoccupied with defending, so neither partner is likely to explore the possibility of shame having been activated. Instead, the focus is on blame.

Couples often get caught in cycles of mutual blaming; these cycles are frequently precipitated by a brush with one partner's shame. As in other forms of conflict, each partner adopts a defensive posture when he anticipates being blamed. Once an individual has assumed a defensive mindset, he is usually unable to gain access to feelings of shame. Marital therapists often label such couples as conflictual couples; it seems they will fight about anything. But what they are usually fighting about is their self-esteem. Each partner feels compelled to fight and defend his or her reputation. To lose is to succumb to the humiliation of paralyzing shame; this is absolutely unacceptable. To accept blame in a blaming/shaming relationship feels equivalent to the destruction of one's self, so each partner fights to preserve the integrity of his or her self. In the next chapter, we will look more closely at how negative esteem scripts influence intimate life.

8

How Emotions Operate:
Scripts of Self and Other

There is only one position on the terrain of the emotional relationship in which partners feel completely safe to reveal themselves and grow within the relationship—that is the safe zone, defined by the positive ends of both axes (Self and Other) in both realms (attachment and esteem). The partners can be moved out of the safe zone by difficulties in either realm, but the nature of the emotions that get activated tends to differ. When a partner perceives a threat in the attachment realm, he usually experiences distress, fear, and distrust of the other partner. When a partner perceives a threat in the esteem realm, he experiences shame and inadequacy related to himself and disapproval from the other partner. Occasionally, feelings of shame can be activated by difficulties in the attachment realm, but problems in the esteem realm almost always result in feelings of shame.

Problems in the attachment realm are usually precipitated by a perceived absence of positive attachment feelings in the other (no positive affective tone), while problems in the esteem realm are usually precipitated by the perception of disapproval by the other (negative affective tone). These two affective displays thus become the primary triggers that shift couples out of the safe zone. The display of negative affective tone in the Other Axis of one's partner is perceived as disapproval and activates one's shame, and the lack of positive affective tone in the Other Axis of one's partner activates one's attachment insecurity in the form of distrust.

It is important to note that the most powerful experiences of shame occur when people are in the safe zone. When partners think they are safe and have relaxed their defenses, the sudden experience of shame can be devastating. This is not only because it comes as such a surprise, but because the partners are unguarded and have allowed themselves to experience their positive affects to the maximum extent—thus the shame has to be equally as intense in order to do its job of shutting down the positive affects. That's why it feels paradoxically safer for some people to remain on their guard. Then if their shame is activated, it is not as harrowing. *The most upsetting fights occur when partners start out feeling good!*

Shame-Related Scripts

When the shame affect assembled in a person's shame emotion is activated, the script assembled with it shapes his experience of the current situation. If the script includes other affects coassembled with the shame, then those same affects become activated. His entire response—his perception of the situation, his affective experience, his attitude, and his reaction—is influenced by the script. As people live through a variety of situations that trigger shame affect, they develop an internal library of shame-related scripts. A person's responses are "scripted" to the extent that the individual becomes absorbed into those scripts during current situations (i.e., dictated by his scripts). The more a person is absorbed into a script, the less he is able to relate to the current situation as something novel (similar to, but ultimately different from, his past experiences).

All couple therapists strive to help partners resist responding in a scripted fashion. Our goal is to help them find new and different ways to respond to the current situation.

Shame Affect

Shame affect can be triggered by any situation, but it is only when that situation stimulates a significant script from the person's internal library of historical shame experiences that a fleeting encounter with shame affect turns into something much larger (i.e., shame emotion). The triggering of historical sources of shame creates major problems in relationships. For example, suppose I am looking forward to an activity (going to the movies with my wife) and the activity is impeded by an untoward event (the movie is sold out when we arrive). I may feel mild shame affect as my pleasure is impeded. But if this touches on a script of previous experiences (during childhood, my parents habitually failed to plan adequately and many activities ended in disappointment), then my current experience of shame affect is likely to involve a recycling of more intense shame as well as other coassembled affects (perhaps distress, anger) and my typical reaction (throwing a tantrum, blaming my wife).

Shame affect can be assembled into a wide range of emotional experiences. It can be experienced (a) in varying levels of intensity, (b) with a variety of other affects (each of which can be experienced in varying levels of intensity), or (c) associated with a broad range of situations.[1] For example, a person may have a group of scenes (a collection of memories) about people speaking down to him with a frown, another group of scenes of people speaking down to him with a smile, and another group of scenes of people speaking down to him and refusing to listen to his response. The first situation may trigger moderate shame, while the second situation may trigger only mild shame, and the third situation may trigger greater shame and assemble it with anger. His emotions will differ significantly according to which of these groups is stimulated, but all involve shame affect.

Despite the common nature of shame affect, most people only identify an affective experience as shame when it resembles the particular emotion we typically know as shame. Shame emotion is confined to a rather narrow range of scripts, all of which portray the self as being in some way defective. In this book, I primarily use the word shame to refer to shame emotion that involves those kinds of scripts (i.e., scripts in which the self is the object of shame affect).

The Shame of Failed Attachment

> Since the child is a social being, his strongest motivation is the desire to belong. His security or lack of it depends upon his feeling of belonging within the group.
>
> **Dreikers & Soltz, 1964, p. 14**

Shame emotion is the core experience of the negative self-view in the realm of esteem. I have noted how attachment research with adults has tended to conflate more global aspects of partners' feelings about their relationship with the purely attachment feelings, which can lead therapists to fail to recognize sources of shame that are not attachment related. However, there is overlap: A significant portion of many people's shame experience is derived from the attachment relationship. As the epigraph to this section indicates, being found unworthy to be connected to others is a fundamental source of insecurity in life. The shame associated with believing oneself to be unworthy of love (i.e., unworthy to be in an attachment relationship) extends beyond the realm of esteem and overlaps squarely into the realm of attachment.[2]

This particular source of shame—viewing oneself as being unfit for connection with others—highlights the power of shaming; in essence a shamer is saying "You are not good enough to be with me." This is a more powerful form of rejection than saying "You've done something wrong or bad" or even "I am angry at you for what you have done." The *shame of failed attachment* is one area in which the attachment realm has direct impact on the esteem realm. Viewing oneself as undeserving of love can activate shame emotion and undermine a person's esteem on a more global level.

Shame Severs the Connection

No matter how angry a partner is, expressing anger does not sever the connection. But a shame-inducing remark can; the individual whose shame is activated suddenly feels alone and exposed—cut off from the shaming partner (even if this was not the shaming partner's goal and even if the shaming partner still feels connected to the partner who was shamed). Once a person is primed for feeling shame, it can take very little to trigger it. A simple look of disgust from his partner can be a powerful trigger if a person has extensive shame-related scripts about himself. When his partner conveys even mild disapproval, a shame-prone partner tends to perceive his partner's attitude toward him to be the same as the painful self scripts that have been activated.

This is the nature of powerful shame scripts. When a partner's shame is activated—he perceives the other partner to be viewing him exactly as his shame script portrays him to himself. This process is at the heart of most of the destructive conflict that occurs between intimate partners. He is convinced that she is viewing him in a particular way and he defends himself against that assumed view, often by counterattacking.

Assumption, Not Projection

His assumption that she is viewing him as his shame script portrays him is often regarded as a form of projection—the projected material being his view of himself. However, this experience does not really satisfy the definition of projection as a defense mechanism because it is not an unconscious maneuver to defend himself against his own negative self-view by attributing it to her. The *assumption* that she is viewing him this way occurs because he is in the grip of powerful shame affect and a negative self-script. When an individual is in such a state, he is highly susceptible to assuming that others see him that way as well because the shame affect amplifies the scripted view and brings a feeling of conviction to the scripts with which it is assembled. His experience is not simply that "She sees me this way but I am actually not this way" (disowning the self view), but rather that "I am this way and she sees it and feels the same way about it that I do" (an experience of exposure). The presumed aspect of the self that is exposed (usually some form of inadequacy) is not questioned at the moment of the projection because of the convincing power of shame affect.

However, if his assumption that she now sees him this way is accompanied by his disowning his own negative view of himself, the resulting process would qualify as a defense mechanism. Specifically, he would be utilizing the defense mechanism of disavowal (disowning his own view). When his disavowal is combined with the assumption that she possesses his disavowed view of him, then he might be characterized as utilizing projection. But it is important to maintain conceptual clarity in regard to the role of shame affect in making the negative self-view so convincing that the person feels exposed and therefore assumes that the other sees him this way as well. Thus, the normal experience of severe shame is that one is seen by the other as one is seeing oneself. It might be viewed as projection if it is accompanied by disavowal of one's own view of self, but it is the disavowal that is defending the ego. The assumption that the other sees one in this negative light is the result of the power of shame emotion; it serves no protective function in itself. And it is more likely to occur in an intimate relationship because people already feel more visible to their partners.

Common Sources of Shame

The sources of shame that play the greatest role in developing negative self scripts are those that have significant histories and consequently many shameful scenes. Nathanson (1992) identifies the most common historical sources of shame: (a) issues related to one's size, strength, ability, skill, or physical dexterity; (b) issues related to being dependent on another; (c) issues related to competition; (d) issues involving the self; (e) issues related to personal attractiveness; (f) issues related to one's sexuality; (g) issues related to being exposed; and (h) issues involving one's inclusion/closeness with others. These historical sources, with their well-developed scripts about the self, constitute the various shades of the emotion we know as shame.

Scripts About the Self

[S]hame originates interpersonally, primarily in significant relationships, but later can become internalized so that the self is able to activate shame without an inducing interpersonal event.

Gershen Kaufman, 1992, p. 8

There are two categories of shame scripts: (a) *relational* scripts, which derive from relationships and view the self as unworthy of love, and (b) *adequacy* scripts, which derive from other life experiences and view the self as inadequate. Relational scripts contain scenes from past attachment experiences, and adequacy scripts contain scenes from nonattachment experiences. Within each category, some scripts are less global and view the self as impaired, but the most powerful scripts draw conclusions about the whole self. Obviously, relational scripts derive from attachment failures, but sometimes adequacy scripts are also produced in attachment contexts. This can occur when the individual draws conclusions (beliefs) about his adequacy but not about his worth as an attachment figure. Most individuals have both kinds of scripts and respond differently according to which script is activated.

Individuals who have a lot of shame scripts are easily triggered to feel shame. People who were abused, neglected, or abandoned as children virtually always have significant relational shame scripts. Indeed, any child who is not nurtured properly is likely to develop chronic relational shame. Children have a tremendous tendency to feel responsible for the failures of their caretakers. When their caretakers fail to do a proper job of caretaking, most children assume it is because something is wrong with them. They don't typically consider that it might be something wrong with the caretaker. When those children become adults, they are likely to carry a heightened sensitivity to any indication that something is wrong with them.

Common Shame Scripts

When a partner feels rejected and unloved, his relational shame scripts tell him that he is unacceptable for an attachment relationship. However, if he and his partner have been in conflict, it is often the case that adequacy scripts have been activated, perhaps depending on the kinds of negative comments his partner has made. The following are some common views of self that I have encountered among my clients, but there are surely many more, and none of these may fit any individual exactly. Few people are likely to carry only one type of shame script and fit neatly into a category; most people with extensive shame will fit different categories at different times—depending upon what emotion (script) has been triggered.

Adequacy Scripts ("I am a worthless person.")

>   *Enfeebled Self*: This script emphasizes the person's inability to do anything effectively. "I am weak; I don't do anything well enough."
>
>   *Incompetent Self*: This script emphasizes the person's complete lack of confidence. "I always mess up anything that requires any kind of ability or performance."
>
>   *Victim Self*: This script emphasizes the person's being the recipient of misfortune and/or mistreatment by others. "Everything bad happens to me." Often the victim self occurs in the attachment realm and is focused on relationships.
>
>   *Loser Self*: This script emphasizes the person's failure at strivings. "No matter how hard I try, I ultimately fail at everything."
>
>   *Overwhelmed Self*: This script emphasizes the person's difficulty with emotion regulation. "I get so upset that I just can't function."
>
>   *Just Bad Self*: This script emphasizes the person's inherent badness, which is usually based on misbehavior, or sometimes on the person's awareness of underlying anger. This script is often found among abuse victims. "I am bad." As with the victim self, the identification with badness is frequently a response to attachment failures in early childhood.

Relational Scripts ("I am a worthless partner.")

>   *Destructive Self*: This script emphasizes the person's destructiveness. "I always end up hurting others."
>
>   *Disgusting Self*: This script, which obviously assembles shame affect with disgust affect (and sometimes dissmell as well), emphasizes the person's total reprehensibility to others. "Anyone who really gets to know me will be disgusted."
>
>   *Invisible Self*: This script has the passivity of the victim self but the person does not even feel important enough to be the recipient of abuse. "If I died, no one would even notice."

Needy Self: This script emphasizes the person's excessive neediness. "I am just too much for anyone."

Ugly Self: This script overlaps with the disgusting self script; it emphasizes the person's unattractiveness. "There is nothing about me that would make anyone want to be with me."

Overwhelming Self: This script emphasizes characteristics, such as volatility or excessive need for stimulation, that make the person too difficult for others to deal with. "No one can handle being with me."

There are doubtlessly other common shame scripts, but these scripts give you a feeling for the general appearance of shame scripts in the realms of esteem (adequacy scripts) and attachment (relational scripts). I have encountered each of the above scripts in more than one person. Everyone carries some shame scripts, but people with secure attachment experiences carry fewer relational scripts and are not so easily triggered in intimate relationships. In my experience, the majority of conflicts in intimate relationships are precipitated by the activation of adequacy scripts. This does not mean that shame in the attachment realm is any less powerful or relevant. Rather, it seems to be the case that: (a) partners work harder to avoid saying or doing things that will directly activate the perception of attachment threat, (b) when attachment threats are perceived, shame is not the only possible reaction, (c) shame is almost always the reaction when there is a perception of esteem threat, and (d) most partners prefer to attack in the esteem realm when they fight.

Distrust and Disapproval

There was never any doubt in my mind that William and Kay loved each other. They thoroughly enjoyed themselves when the relationship was going well. But when it went bad, it would turn into a miserable experience for each of them. Most of the time, the shift occurred rapidly and followed a consistent pattern. William would say or do something that appeared inconsistent to Kay and she would begin to question him. No matter what he answered, she was unable to stop her questioning and, after a while, he would get angry at her refusal to accept his answers. Eventually, he would become emotionally withdrawn and that only served to further fuel Kay's interrogation. She was particularly reactive to his withdrawal, and her relentless questioning would focus on whether he was planning to end the relationship. He would grow even more frustrated as it seemed that nothing he said could reassure her. Eventually, they would fight and then separate for a period of time.

In therapy, we learned that Kay had twice been abandoned by men, and both times it occurred without warning. The first and foremost abandonment was by her father. He and her mother did not tell her of their decision to divorce until the day he left. This was absolutely devastating to Kay, a preteen at the time. Later, in young adulthood, a similar event occurred with a boyfriend. In that case, Kay had seen some clues that the boyfriend was losing interest, but when she tried to talk about it with him, he denied there was any problem. Then he abruptly left.

Kay was not a distrustful person; she was a warm, generous person with many friends. But when William behaved in ways that suggested he might be losing interest in the relationship, it stirred her fear that she was going to be abandoned once again. She became distrustful and, worse yet, when she asked about the possibility and received only reassurance that nothing was wrong, her distrust increased. In therapy, they both learned to be more direct and clear when communicating about this issue. William learned to not only reassure Kay; he learned it was much better to answer her questions fully, even to the point of revealing feelings about the relationship that were not positive. That way, she could trust that she truly knew what was going on, even if it was not always what she wished.

What exactly is distrust? Recall that shame affect operates to moderate positive affects; it serves as the governor on a person's affective system. When the positive affect is directed toward another person and some impediment intrudes, shame affect is triggered. *If the object of the shame affect is the person himself, then he has shame emotion. But if the object of the shame affect is the other person, then he has some negative emotion about that person.* The emotion experienced toward the other person could be contempt, jealousy, some variation of anger, or some other specific emotional state, but *I categorize all such emotions as forms of distrust.* Distrust emotion is confined to a range of scripts that portray the other as being unloving, unreliable, untrustworthy, disapproving, contemptuous, or hurtful in some fashion.

Any experience of being mistreated or disappointed by one's partner will trigger shame affect, at least briefly. If a significant distrust script is activated, however, then the person's affective response is extended. Suddenly, the partner's failure takes on much greater meaning. Can he really trust her or will she be forever mistreating him or letting him down? He may begin to question his partner's character, commitment, honesty, and so forth. This is when a partner begins to collect evidence of the other partner's untrustworthiness, finding patterns in the other partner's behavior, often making accusations and supporting his view with absolutes and superlatives ("You always mistreat me and never think about my feelings."). A partner's tendency to cling to his evidence is influenced by his distrust scripts as much as by the realities of how his partner treats him.

Since the person is in the grip of shame affect when he experiences either shame or distrust, the stimulus for the emotion is amplified and the individual has a feeling of intense conviction about the scripts assembled in those emotions. But when he is not in the grip of shame affect, he may regard those same beliefs as irrational. This is why a person can be remorseful or take back what he said during a fight, and mean it, and yet turn around and say or do the same thing again.

Scripts About the Other

Distrust is related to the kind of shame that is composed of relational scripts; they both appear in the attachment realm. Thus, distrust scripts about the other often have some kind of correlating script about the self ("She doesn't love me, and I don't deserve to be loved."). In the esteem realm, disapproval scripts of the other are similarly associated with adequacy scripts about the self, but the link between the self and other scripts does not seem to be quite as powerful as they are in the attachment realm.

Here are some common distrust and disapproval scripts. As with the shame scripts, this is not an exclusive list.

Disapproval Scripts ("My partner makes me feel bad about myself because …")

Critical Other: This is the most common type of disapproval script; it describes someone who is forever finding something wrong with his partner.

Disappointed Other: This is someone who expresses his disapproval by being habitually disappointed in his partner.

Perfect Other: The person who does everything perfectly and denies difficulties of his own can stir up his partner's shame, whether he intends to or not.

Blaming/Shaming Other: This is someone who cannot tolerate his own shame and blames his partner for everything that goes wrong.

Distrust Scripts ("I don't trust my partner because …")

Undependable Other: This is a very common distrust script that emphasizes the other partner's lack of dependability. "I cannot depend upon him to be there when I need him." This script often accompanies scripts about the self being enfeebled (therefore needing someone to depend on).

Abusive Other: This script refers to someone who will purposely hurt his partner, emotionally or physically. This script often accompanies self as a victim script.

Enfeebled Other: This script is similar to the enfeebled self, except that it is about the partner. The individual with this distrust script feels much like the person with an undependable other (the partner cannot be depended upon), but the difference is that the partner is seen as weak rather than unreliable. This script often co-occurs with scripts of the self being overwhelming or overly needy.

Thoughtless Other: The thoughtless other cannot be relied upon to stay attuned to his partner's needs and feelings. The self scripts that tend to accompany this portray the self as powerless and unable to do anything to effectively alter the situation.

Selfish Other: The selfish other not only fails to think about his partner's needs and feelings (like the thoughtless other), but he doesn't care. He is only interested in taking care of himself. The scripts about the self that tend to accompany this script usually portray the self as a victim.

Exploitive Other: The exploitive other script describes an individual who manipulates and uses people for his own ends. It takes a high degree of distrust to have this script; people with this kind of distrust script usually have been involved with some very bad characters.

Needy Other: This script refers to someone who takes more than he gives and consequently drains his partner. The self-script that tends to accompany this usually portrays the self as a victim or an exploited caretaker.

People with extensive distrust scripts tend to avoid dependency; as adults, they usually work at being independent. Their independence can create problems in their relationships if it makes their partners feel unneeded and unwanted, but it is even worse if their partners sense the distrust itself. One partner's distrust is a powerful activator for the other partner's shame.

Distrust Can Feel Safer Than Trust

Harold complained that he always had to prove himself to Elaine. No matter what he did for her, she was able to find some way in which it wasn't quite good enough. He would periodically get tired of feeling constantly tested, and he would lose his temper over some minor incident. Then Elaine would point to his anger and say this was why she still didn't feel like she could trust Harold entirely. She said he was a "powder keg waiting to go off" and she was always expecting it to happen. Consequently, she could never fully relax around Harold. They had been together for over 10 years and this issue had haunted them throughout that time. Twice before, they had tried couple counseling. Both times, they felt a little better but soon reverted to the same dynamics.

In the therapy, we focused on helping Harold develop some alternatives to losing his temper when he got frustrated. He worked with these alternatives and developed better control of his temper. Yet Elaine's distrust persisted. They weren't fighting, but Harold noted how Elaine still felt cool and distant toward him. Elaine acknowledged that she still felt distrustful. As we explored her feelings of distrust, the path led to an area of her childhood that we had discussed several times before.

Elaine's parents divorced when she was very young. She lived with her mother and had a reasonable relationship with her father, who often told her how much he would like her to live with him. When Elaine started high school, her relationship with her mother had become increasingly conflictual, and Elaine opted to move in with her dad when she was a sophomore in high school. She went to live with her father with the expectation that she was not only going to have less conflict but that she would have more of the closeness her father had always professed to want. The reality proved to be very different. There was indeed less conflict but there was no greater closeness. Her father had a busy life and made very little change to accommodate having a teenage daughter living with him. Elaine's disappointment was particularly intense in regard to two or three different episodes in which her father led her to think he would be more involved and then reneged. The most painful was his failure to attend any of her sport activities. He promised to be there but then always ended up too busy to make it.

As I indicated in the introduction to this chapter, for some people, distrust feels like the safer alternative. Initially, in therapy with Elaine and Harold, our explorations of Elaine's distrust focused on Harold's displays of temper, which were reminiscent of Elaine's relationship with her mother. But after the temper problems had abated, the distrust continued. Further exploration revealed that Elaine's life with her father had taught her that it was safer to be distrustful. It protected her from the chance of reexperiencing the painful disappointment she felt when she believed her father was going to come through—only to be let down once more.

Some people react to humiliation and disappointment by developing an extensive library of distrust scripts, and they then go through life protected by their distrust. Ironically, these people often tend to be especially trusting. As a consequence of being hurt by someone they trusted so very much, they learn to maintain their distrust as a way of protecting themselves from getting hurt that badly again. Unfortunately, one partner's distrust is likely to trigger the other partner's shame and vice versa. Whether it is distrust or shame that has been activated, a common response is to focus on the other person. When one partner is focused on distrust scripts, chances are the other partner's shame will be activated and he will often behave in ways that reinforce the first partner's distrust.

The Irrational Nature of Shame and Distrust Scripts

Shame and distrust scripts both involve shame affect, which produces a feeling of conviction regarding the scripted thoughts that are assembled with the affect. The stronger the affect, the greater that feeling of conviction. When a person is absorbed in either shame or distrust and consequently is in the grip of shame affect, he is more prone to believe thoughts that he would regard as irrational at other times (e.g., absolutes like "I am all bad" and "I cannot trust anyone").

Cognitive therapists focus on changing the irrational thoughts and beliefs that accompany certain types of problems (in other words, the scripts in distressing emotions). Irrational thoughts have been labeled with a variety of terms, such as preexisting assumptions, dysfunctional beliefs, automatic negative thoughts, negative self-talk, cognitive distortions, and self-defeating beliefs. Cognitive therapists approach irrational scripts directly, but most forms of therapy address the irrational nature of negative scripts in the process of effecting change. However they are approached, directly or indirectly, the irrational beliefs that compose extreme scripts must be revised and softened if the individuals bearing them are ever to have any lasting emotional safety in their relationships.

This chapter concludes the theoretical description of the emotional safety model. In the second half of the book, we will look at how the model is applied in couple therapy. Application of the model begins with the identification of each partner's perceived threats to either the relationship (the realm of attachment) or the self (the realm of esteem).

Part II
Clinical Applications

9

The Core Components of Relationship Problems

The central measure of the well-being of an intimate relationship is the quality of the attachment bond. A good attachment provides a secure base and a safe haven from which partners can operate in the world. The secure attachment also helps each individual with his or her esteem difficulties; however, individual problems in the realm of esteem can still occur even when the attachment is secure. Unfortunately, problems in the esteem realm, even when they stem from outside the relationship, often precipitate problems in the attachment realm. Similarly, problems in the attachment realm frequently lead to problems in the esteem realm—in part because partners lose the secure base, but also because of the tendency of many insecure partners to attack the other partner's esteem rather than make themselves vulnerable and expose their own attachment needs.

Attachment Needs

No matter what a person's age or how positive his past attachment experiences, he continues to have attachment needs throughout his lifespan. A secure attachment provides individuals with a secure base and a safe harbor for dealing with life's demands. Partners are able to provide each other with a comforting, soothing, contact that makes the task of living so much more bearable. But when an individual's secure attachment is threatened, his shame scripts related to himself (both relational and adequacy scripts) and his distrust scripts related to his partner (both distrust and disapproval scripts) can be activated. He is more prone to severe distress, and his overall ability to regulate affect is diminished.

Attachment Threat

The loss of secure attachment in an adult intimate relationship can be sudden, as with the death of a partner or the discovery of infidelity, but more often it is gradual. She fails to respond to an attachment need—perhaps just being too tired or busy to sit down and chat—and he interprets this as either a momentary frustration that will pass or as an indicator of something possibly wrong in the relationship, in which case his anxiety will be activated. How he interprets her failure to respond to his attachment need is a function of the historical scenes he carries. If he has a history of being let down by attachment figures, then he will have governing scenes of nonresponsive others and he will be more likely to interpret current events in that direction. But if he has historically had secure attachments, he will be more likely to dismiss a momentary failure as having no bearing on the overall security of the attachment relationship.

If he perceives her to have a lack of positive affects (in which he and the attachment relationship are the objects), then he may sense that her investment in the attachment is faltering. Once he concludes that her investment appears to be faltering, he moves out of the safe zone and feels that his attachment is threatened. Now his anxiety about the security of his attachment is activated, and he is likely to behave according to the nature of the scripts he carries. The most adaptive response is to speak directly to the partner, voicing his feelings and his concern about the relationship. If all is well, he will usually be reassured by her response. However, this course requires him to place himself in a position of vulnerability as he reveals how important the relationship is to him. The alternative is to avoid the vulnerability and choose a less adaptive response. In most cases, he becomes either: (a) preoccupied with her feelings about him and anxiously pursues her (in hopes of getting her to reassure him that she indeed does love him), (b) demoralized and depressed and passively waits to see if the relationship will improve, or (c) protective of himself from feeling the potential loss by detaching from the relationship and his dependence on her. In other words, maladaptive responses to attachment threat in adults parallel the three stages of attachment loss among infants identified by Bowlby (1969): *protest*, *despair*, and *detachment*.

Responses to Attachment Threat

The first response, *protest*, is similar to the attachment style referred to as anxious/preoccupied. It occurs along a continuum of intensity: At its least disruptive, it is a minor annoyance to the partner, but at higher intensity it becomes a loud, intrusive cry of protest. If a partner responds to the other's anxious pursuit by pulling away, then pursuit is likely to escalate into a perceived attack. The more he senses her withdrawal, the more critical and attacking he tends to become.

Rene was the angry partner in her marriage. Bob felt he could never please her because she was constantly complaining about things such as how much he traveled, how little he did around the house, and how inconsiderate he was of her feelings. But when the couple therapy advanced to the stage where Rene was finally able to express the feelings of yearning for him that had been fueling her complaints, Bob heard her need for greater connection with him. He was surprised to hear her desire for him. For years, he had been quietly withdrawing from her—his response to the criticism—but now he was seeing how much he had helped maintain her underlying distress. Her loud protest had been a response to her unstated fear that she was losing him.

The second maladaptive response, *despair*, is the response of passivity. In many marriages, one or both partners despair of ever having the connection they wish for. They learn to "settle" for an unsatisfying relationship. Often one or both partners develop a clinical level of depression. Many cases of individual therapy involve lonely, depressed people who have virtually given up on ever getting what they want from their marriages.

Otto and Louise were married for 12 years when he had his first affair. They had two children at the time, and Louise was very fearful that she would lose Otto. Prior to the affair, she had been outspoken and stood up to Otto over a number of issues. But after the affair, she quit speaking up. Her fear of losing him led her to work harder at pleasing him—accommodating to his needs but ignoring her own. She described her behavior after the affair as being more like his girlfriend than his wife. He had a second affair 10 years later, and this time she asserted herself and the marriage ended in divorce. In retrospect, she concluded that she was depressed during those 10 years between the affairs and lived with a level of disconnection that she never should have tolerated. Louise's response to the second affair was one of righteous protest, but for 10 years she lived in despair.

The third maladaptive response, *detaching*, reverses the source of the anxiety. Instead of being the partner who fears losing the attachment, he becomes the partner who is slipping away. Then when she perceives his investment in the attachment to be faltering, she becomes the bearer of anxiety about the attachment. At that point, she will have her own response to the perceived attachment threat.

Ben came to me for individual therapy in his 50s. He was in his second marriage, and it looked like the marriage was not going to make it. What precipitated his coming to therapy was that he had gotten in touch with feelings he had not encountered since childhood. He found himself feeling tearful and emotional in a variety of situations, including when he listened to his pastor preach and when he watched sentimental commercials on television. I asked about his relationship with his wife and learned that Ben had had no investment in the marriage for many years. He talked very disparagingly of women in general, making vulgar jokes about the only things that women were good for and noting that his wife never had anything positive to say.

He showed no embarrassment when he reported that he had run around on his wife for years. He always had sex with other women when he traveled on his job, and he filled his life with other interests when he was home.

I asked what he thought was causing him to come to tears so easily and he said he feared that he was coming apart. He felt an emptiness in his life that he had never felt before. I suggested that the opposite might be the case—perhaps he was coming together. He might be getting in touch with his desire for a real intimate connection, something he appeared to have disdained for the past many years. Over the course of therapy, he did indeed discover that he wanted to feel close to his wife. He ceased all of his carousing and infidelity and made a genuine effort to get close to his wife. They went into couple therapy with a colleague of mine, and it was a very successful therapy. Ben had been living in a state of detachment for years; but now he dared to let himself be vulnerable enough to reveal his longing for secure attachment. To get there, he had to face the possibility of losing that which he yearned for.

The Tone of Attachment Threat

All of these responses are predicated by the perception of attachment threat (i.e., that the other partner's investment in the relationship is diminished). This is his perception of the affective tone of her Other feelings. That tone is expressed in the behaviors she manifests (Is she fully present when she kisses him or is it a polite kiss?), in the feelings she expresses to him (Does she sincerely express her love for him?), in the way she talks about him to others (Does she portray him positively?), and in the way she prioritizes their relationship. If he does not perceive her to have affects of genuine interest and pleasure associated with him, he is likely to feel the attachment is threatened. His perception is also affected by his sensitivity to indicators of an insecure attachment (based on his governing scenes), and his response is influenced by his repertoire of dominant scripts (protest, despair, or detach).

Esteem Needs

The need for secure attachment is universal, and so is the need for positive self-esteem. People need to feel that they are worthy of love (attachment relationships), and they need to feel that they are competent to function in society.[1] Some of these esteem needs are met within the intimate relationship, but many esteem needs are met outside the intimate relationship. Over an extended period of time, a good attachment can change a person's view of self as unlovable (because of previous insecure attachments) to a view of self as lovable. An attachment partner can also help a person feel adequate, but there is a limit to how much the attachment partner can—or perhaps even should—help the other partner to feel adequate. If a person seeks too much of his feelings of adequacy and self-definition from within the intimate relationship, it can place a burden on the relationship and interfere with the individual's sense of autonomy.

The boundary between providing feelings of adequacy ("You are such a great worker") and providing support ("I know you can do the job successfully") is not always perfectly clear, but the general function of attachment is to provide a secure base from which the individual goes out to operate in the world. In most cases, it is his success and positive reception in the world outside the attachment relationship that play the major role in developing and sustaining his sense of adequacy and consequent self-esteem. Providing support is an integral part of every attachment relationship, but relationships vary in regard to how much partners can reasonably expect to have their overall feelings of adequacy shored up from within the relationship. Most partners happily reinforce the other partner's esteem but tend to chafe if they feel too responsible for the other partner's self-esteem. A partner is constricted in his ability to assert his own needs if he is expected to be a completely uncritical audience for the other partner.[2]

Esteem Threat

In most relationships, partners are not expected to be wholly uncritical, but they are expected to be generally supportive. Most relationship problems in the realm of esteem develop when one partner perceives excessive disapproval (usually in the form of criticism) from the other partner (i.e., when he perceives negative affective tone in her view of him). Her capacity to activate his shame with her criticism increases with the importance he places on her view of him. Thus, if he looks to her to provide a great amount of his feelings of esteem, then he gives her considerable power to disrupt his esteem with her negative tone. However, even when a partner does not seek excessive help with esteem issues from the other, he is vulnerable to negative affective tone in his partner's view of him.

The central problem with esteem threats is *shame*—the threat either directly activates the person's shame or it activates his *anxiety* about the prospect of his shame being activated.[3] Whenever a person's personal shame scripts are activated, he will do almost anything to terminate the shame experience. In cases of severe shame, he may even be willing to behave in ways that threaten his attachment bond with his partner—if it will lessen his debilitating shame.

Any threat to a person's esteem is likely to activate his shame, and most of the maladaptive patterns that develop in intimate relationships are the result of shame's power. Nathanson's (1992) compass of shame identified the four responses of avoidance, withdrawal, attack other, and attack self. In the couple context, the attack other response is usually experienced as blaming. Thus, the partner who feels shamed has four potential maladaptive responses: *avoid, withdraw, blame,* or *attack self.*

Responses to Esteem Threat

A partner can *avoid* his experience of shame by disavowing it. This can be adaptive if the shame is minor and the partner has no need to see him experience the shame. (Sometimes, his experience of shame is important to the partner as it reassures her that he cares.) But avoidance tends to become a major problem when the shame is major. Probably the most common of the major problems is when the individual abuses substances (primarily alcohol) to avoid his shame.

Dale was a successful salesman, and part of his success was based on his pleasant personality. It seemed that nothing ever upset him; he took everything in stride. He was always ready with a joke and a laugh—his focus in life was on enjoying himself. Dale went through three marriages and each of his wives ended up complaining that Dale was not emotionally accessible to her, that he would not take anything seriously, and that he made her feel as if she had no impact on him. For his part, Dale was always bewildered when his wives reached the point of threatening divorce. He truly didn't know what the problem was, and his efforts to rectify the situation by downplaying their concerns only heightened their feeling that he didn't care.

When his attachments with his wives were indeed severed, Dale would get depressed and enter individual therapy. I saw Dale briefly at the end of his second and third marriages. Initially, he felt bad about how he had handled the marriages, but as soon as he began to feel better, his focus shifted to the type of women he kept marrying and he soon left treatment with the goal of finding a different kind of woman. My only contribution—other than to help him out of his depression—was to (perhaps) convince him to take his next partner's complaints more seriously and to go to couple therapy if the complaints didn't abate.

Although Dale's problems with his wives probably stem from a variety of sources, one problem was that he never seemed to feel any shame in response to their feelings. If he had, they might have had the opportunity to see that they did indeed matter to him. Unfortunately, because of Dale's fervent avoidance of shame, his wives' importance to him was not visible until after they had left.

Another response to shame in a relationship is to *withdraw* in order to protect one's self-esteem. The person can withdraw on a behavioral level and try to reduce the other partner's power to activate his shame. In that case, he remains fully attached but is less accessible to her (perceived) assaults on his esteem. However, if withdrawal is relied upon excessively, it may reach the point where the person detaches emotionally. But I am not convinced that the relationship between withdrawing and detaching is a simple continuum—I have seen relationships in which individuals remain withdrawn for years yet remain strongly attached. Thus, I think it is prudent to maintain a distinction between withdrawal and detachment, and to think of withdrawal as occurring in the esteem realm and detachment as occurring in the attachment realm.

Gil and Marian, whom we met in Chapter 1, had been married more than three decades, yet there was still a superficial feeling to their interactions. They were each quite sensitive to the other's opinion and had learned to hold back parts of themselves in order to protect their own esteem. They were very close in many respects, spending more time together than most married couples. But they had never had a close physical relationship, and they avoided talking about emotionally powerful topics. Periodically, they would have an intense conflict, and would then remain emotionally distant with each other for days at a time. For different reasons, they each had issues with esteem. It seemed that the solution they had found was to be closely involved without revealing themselves too much, and whenever either of them experienced shame, he or she would pull away from the relationship for a while.

Probably the most common maladaptive response to the experience of shame in the relationship is to *blame* or attack the other partner. This blaming serves the function of shifting the perceived source of the shame. When the blaming response is successful, he activates her shame and escapes his own shame. But if she is not willing to accept the role of being the one to blame, then she usually fights back. The result is conflict.

Phil and Ann had a volatile relationship, and the fight was always about who was to blame. No matter what problems occurred, Phil and Ann ended up arguing about whose fault it was. No issue was too small—whether it involved the checking account or who forgot to buy garbage bags. In therapy, Phil announced that he was not perfect and he knew that he caused many of the problems. Ann challenged him to name one and he was unable to. She then claimed that she was the only one in the relationship who ever took responsibility for her contribution to the problems. Phil then challenged her to name one and the exact same interaction ensued. She came up with several examples, but in each one her contribution was in failing to realize how Phil was unable to do something. When both individuals are unable to stay with their shame, and each blames as a way of disowning the shame, the cycle of conflict never seems to stop.

He may *attack self* as a way of trying to eliminate, control, or punish whatever it is within himself that he perceives to be the cause of his shame. On an interpersonal level, this intrapunitive response often has the effect of causing the other partner to back off.

Stephen grew up with a very abusive older brother and a family that failed to protect him. His brother took every opportunity to attack and humiliate him, and Stephen learned that there was very little he could do to protect himself. If Stephen fought back, his brother only intensified his efforts. So Stephen developed an attack self response to his frequent experiences of shame. He controlled his impulse to fight back by getting angry at himself and chiding himself relentlessly. This kept him from making the situation any worse, but it left him nearly debilitated whenever he encountered shame-activating situations in life.

When Stephen married Marilyn, they discovered how disruptive his attack self response was on his relationship. Whenever his shame was activated, he would get terribly upset with himself, and he would become completely absorbed and preoccupied with his own shortcomings. The result of this situation was that Marilyn's feelings were never a focus of attention, except in regard to their power to activate his shame. He would get upset with himself, and whatever she felt would become invisible. Initially, Marilyn felt bad for Stephen and was understanding. But over time, she grew resentful as his problem so completely eclipsed her own feelings.

The Core Components of Relationship Problems

When an intimate relationship is moved out of the safe zone, one or both partners experience some level of threat in the realm of attachment, the realm of esteem, or both. If the affected partner can be strong enough to tolerate the vulnerability inherent in expressing his concern directly, owning his feelings and not attacking the other partner's esteem, then the partners have the greatest chance of getting the relationship back into the safe zone. However, if either partner resorts to maladaptive responses, then the likelihood increases that the relationship will continue to be unsafe. The longer the relationship remains outside the safe zone, the greater the likelihood that flexibility will decline, maladaptive patterns will be established, and each partner will adopt a more rigid view of both self and other. In the realm of attachment, the most common maladaptive responses are: (a) to aggressively pursue the other partner, (b) to despair and passively submit to the state of the relationship, or (c) to detach from the other partner. In the realm of esteem, the most common maladaptive responses are: (a) to avoid recognizing one's shame and consequently not deal with issues brought forward by the other partner, (b) to blame and attack the other partner, (c) to withdraw from the other partner, or (d) to attack the self.

Table 9–1 Responses to Attachment/Esteem Threats

Partner A's Maladaptive Response	Partner B's Usual Experience
Protest	He feels criticized, Esteem Threat
Despair	He feels a loss of interest from Partner A, Attachment Threat
Detachment	He feels the relationship doesn't matter, Attachment Threat
Avoidance	He feels disconnected and as if the relationship doesn't matter to Partner A, Attachment Threat
Blaming	He feels criticized, Esteem Threat
Withdrawal	He feels unimportant, punished, Esteem/Attachment Threat
Attack Self	He feels unimportant, disconnected, Attachment Threat

When one partner is aggressively *pursued* by the other, he usually feels criticized and experiences the partner's pursuit as a threat in the realm of esteem. The same applies if he feels *blamed* by the other partner. When a partner *attacks* him*self*, the other partner feels helpless and usually experiences the partner's behavior as a threat in the realm of attachment. When a partner *withdraws*, the other partner usually experiences the withdrawal as a threat in the realm of attachment, but it can easily stir esteem issues. When one partner feels the other partner has *detached*, he experiences it as a threat in the realm of attachment. Table 9-1 summarizes the typical experience of the other partner to the maladaptive responses in both realms.

No matter how the unsafe condition is initiated, it is largely the *responses* to the perceived threats in attachment and esteem—and each partner's ensuing responses to the other partner's responses—that comprise the substance of most couples' relational problems. Over time, these responses become organized into the various patterns of conflict and avoidance that are familiar to couple therapists. Here is an example of a couple that came with an array of problems, but when viewed through the lens of affect, the problems condensed down to each partner's perceived threats in the realms of esteem and attachment.

Mario and Elizabeth, a middle-aged couple who had dated for several years, had a rewarding relationship during dating. They had been each divorced and each had two children. Over time, they had get-togethers with their children and found that the blended group got along very well. Everything went well, so they finally decided to move in together. Mario gave up his home, and he and his children moved into Elizabeth's house, which was large enough that each child could have his or her own room. The trouble started almost as soon as the two families began living together.

The kids liked each other and got along very well; the problem was between Mario and Elizabeth. Mario was normally a neat, organized person and had kept his former home in good order. Everything was in its place, and he frequently worked on the house and kept it up. But once he moved into Elizabeth's house, there was insufficient closet space and he had difficulty getting himself organized there. His stuff was all over the place, which was an irritant to Elizabeth as well as him. She complained about the mess and about how little Mario did around the house. Unlike his behavior in his former home, Mario failed to take initiative in caring for the house. He reported that this was because he did not feel a sense of ownership. Within only a few weeks, he fell into a routine of sitting around and watching television. He stopped working out and he made little effort to do the things expected of one of the adults in the household. His mood was depressed and he grew unhappier week by week.

They came for couple therapy about two and a half months after the move. Elizabeth complained that Mario had withdrawn from her and took no initiative in maintaining the household. Mario complained that Elizabeth constantly criticized him, and that he felt he had no real authority in the household. They both agreed that Mario did not like conflict and withdrew from Elizabeth and put up a wall when they had difficulties. Their conflicts focused on myriad daily life issues; I will focus on one particular incident as it captures their underlying emotional dynamics.

On the week of Mario's birthday, his mother talked to Mario and invited them to a party at her house. Mario agreed to the timing of the get-together without checking with Elizabeth. At the same time, Elizabeth knew there was a swimming tournament scheduled for her daughter but had not yet told Mario of the tournament, though she knew that he would want to see her daughter compete. When Mario told her of the planned party, Elizabeth was immediately upset that he had made plans without checking with her. They talked about alternatives, including moving the party to a later time, but Mario made no effort to follow through, and Elizabeth and her children were forced to miss Mario's birthday party, and he missed her daughter's tournament. Elizabeth was very angry and criticized Mario. Mario was also angry and withdrew afterward. He later acknowledged that he had made no effort to move the party because he was so angry at the way Elizabeth had spoken to him (her tone of voice).

In session, we discussed their respective feelings. Each partner had difficulty seeing why the other was so upset. I restated each partner's concerns in terms of the perceived threats to emotional safety. I had concluded that Mario was primarily feeling threatened in the realm of esteem, and Elizabeth was primarily threatened in the realm of attachment, so I interpreted how they each felt in terms that reflected that view. During the discussion, Elizabeth added that she perceived an esteem threat as well. Of course, those are not the words we used at the time; Elizabeth said she was no longer able to see any signs that Mario loved her and she also felt her "self-esteem was taking a beating." Here is how I restated their concerns.

Mario feels humiliated by the way Elizabeth speaks to him. He feels it has occurred so regularly that he is now primed to feel put down by the slightest negative tone from her. He has become depressed living in a home in which he feels like an outsider who is blamed for every problem. Mario confirmed that this was exactly what he felt. For her part, Elizabeth felt devastated when she learned that Mario had made plans for his birthday without ensuring that she and her kids would be part of it. She sees his failure to do anything around the house as a reflection of his lack of commitment, and nothing makes her feel worse than his withdrawing and erecting a wall between them. She can no longer see that he loves her and she needs to be able to see that in order to have something to hold on to through such a difficult time. Elizabeth agreed that this was exactly how she felt.

We ended the session by summarizing their respective areas of sensitivity— Mario's sensitivity to feeling Elizabeth doesn't respect him and Elizabeth's sensitivity to feeling Mario doesn't care about her. I emphasized the need for each of them to: (a) recognize and try to manage their particular areas of sensitivity and (b) be sensitive to the other's area of sensitivity. Elizabeth had some difficulty with this because she felt that Mario's issues were only with himself while she was more concerned about the relationship. It is not uncommon for a partner who is primarily concerned with attachment threat to feel this way when the other partner seems to be focused only on his own esteem. I tried to explain how our priorities can narrow down when we feel the survival of the self is threatened.[4] At this early stage in therapy, partners often show little sympathy for the concerns of the other. But if they have some appreciation of the nature of the other partner's issues, we have a beginning.

I have presented these issues in an abbreviated form, but my goal is not to describe the therapeutic process so much as to help the reader recognize the emotional safety issues inherent in the partners' complaints. The measure of the fundamental accuracy of the model is the way partners respond to having their concerns described in terms of esteem and attachment. I consistently find that partners feel especially well understood when I can identify their perceptions of attachment or esteem threats. It is what is threatened that matters (the self, the relationship, the partner's caring), and when the therapist demonstrates that she understands why the person feels unsafe in the relationship, a strong alliance is formed. Thus, it is imperative to identify the concerns of each partner, thereby forming a strong alliance with each, and to remain in touch with each partner's fundamental concerns (these can evolve through the course of treatment). The couple therapy can then proceed with each partner invested in the process.

Discussing Conflictual Issues

The ways in which partners respond to perceived threats, and respond to each other's responses, have been the subject of research on marital conflict. In one study that quickly became a classic, Sybil Carrere and John Gottman (1999) showed that they could predict divorce among a cohort of newlyweds based on the partners' displays of positive and negative affect in the first 3 minutes of discussion of a marital conflict. Basically, the husbands and wives in the more stable marriages showed less negative affect and more positive affect as the conflict discussion began. Further, the husbands in the stable marriages did not become less positive, even though they did express more negative affect as the discussions heated up. And the wives in the couples headed for divorce tended to open their discussion with criticism rather than a simple complaint.[5] Gottman (1999) refers to this tendency to start the discussion with criticism, rather than a focused complaint, as a harsh startup. He emphasizes teaching partners to use a softened startup when they have something negative to say.[6] An important part of the solution to the harsh startup is for partners to ask for what they want rather than complain about what they don't get.

This study demonstrates the way in which the realms of attachment and esteem are manifested in an interaction between the partners. Criticism is an attack on the other partner's esteem. But maintaining positive affects, even in the midst of a heated exchange, is a way of upholding the positive attachment. When the wives began the discussion with criticism of their husbands, the relationship had already reached the point where they were resorting to attacking their partners' esteem rather than discussing the issue of concern. This was a strong predictor of divorce. On the other hand, those husbands who continued their display of positive affects were demonstrating to their wives that the attachment was not in peril. This was a strong predictor that the marriage would remain stable.

When negative affect is directed at the other person's self, the esteem threat is very real (and destructive). On the other hand, when positive affects continue to be expressed, the attachment is not threatened, thereby allowing the partners to discuss some very difficult issues. Couples can discuss conflictual issues (which all couples have) and maintain relative emotional safety in the process if they can: (a) avoid resorting to esteem threats and (b) continue to express positive attachment feelings (thereby avoiding creating attachment threats). This can be the case even during discussion of some very challenging issues from other realms.

The Relevance of Other Realms

The realms of esteem and attachment are by no means the only areas in which couples encounter difficulty. However, a basic premise of the emotional safety model is that it is the perception of threat in the realms of esteem and attachment that disrupts emotional safety within the relationship and leads to the states of recurring conflict or chronic distance that bring most couples to therapy. Problems occur in other realms, but those problems generally do not threaten the emotional safety of the partners unless the impact ripples into the realm of esteem or attachment.

Other therapy models focus on many of the same maladaptive patterns, but they often focus on the other realms that are present, such as sex or trauma. Often the therapy focuses on visible issues involving things like power/control, communication skills, or problem solving, but the process in which these issues are addressed actually helps the partners with the underlying esteem or attachment issues. For example, virtually all of the skills that are taught to people with communication problems serve to lower esteem threat. The partners learn to listen carefully, speak more respectfully, and avoid making global accusations. Other areas may not be as clearly linked to attachment or esteem, but I contend that issues from those other realms are still secondary to the affective realms of attachment and esteem and, once the central affective issues have been rectified, the couple will be able to solve those other problems.[7]

I will try to demonstrate this contention with two examples, one from the realm of trauma and one from the realm of sex.

Case of Preexisting Trauma

Fred and Linda were both trauma survivors. When she was around 8 years old, Linda was abused by two adolescent boys who molested her and exposed her to sadistic violence. The boys were members of a neighboring family, and Linda's parents refused to believe that the boys were a genuine threat; hence, the parents failed to protect Linda. Fred was physically and emotionally abused by his alcoholic father. He lived in constant fear of his father and learned to suppress any expression of anger. As an adult, Linda spent years in therapy working through her abuse. When she met Fred, he was just reaching the point of seeking treatment, and he went into intensive individual therapy early in their relationship.

Fred had been in treatment for 2 years when he and Deanna first sought couple therapy. They were caught in a cycle of conflict. Fred was avoiding his parents, often asking Linda to make excuses for him, and he was angry at Linda because he felt she was not being supportive and understanding of his trauma-related feelings. Linda was angry because (a) Fred would not tell his parents how he felt and instead kept getting angry at her,

(b) he wanted her to be compassionate but he only showed her his angry feelings and not the vulnerable feelings underneath them (the secondary emotion rather than the primary emotion), and (c) he did not show any concern for how she was feeling. They spent nearly a year in couple therapy that failed to make any impact. Eventually, Fred felt the therapist was siding with Linda.

When they started couple therapy with me, I nearly fell into the same trap as the previous therapist. I thought the problem would resolve if Fred would face up to his parents and if he could show Linda the hurt and fearful feelings he was avoiding. However, this was very difficult for Fred, and he began to become defensive with me until I backed away from his individual issues with his parents. Instead, I tried to unearth the reasons Fred couldn't reveal the underlying feelings to Linda and the reasons she couldn't respond with understanding instead of anger. What gradually emerged were each partner's perceived threats. Indeed, they each described the perception of an esteem threat in its most basic form. Fred said, "She thinks there's something wrong with me just because I don't tell my parents about my angry feelings." And Linda said, "He thinks there's something wrong with me because I don't like his anger."

The issues interfering with this couple's progress were in the realms of attachment and esteem. Fred felt judged by Linda, the ultimate esteem threat that "something was wrong with him." And Linda perceived both an esteem threat—that something was wrong with her—and an attachment threat in his inability to show that he cared about her feelings as well. Gradually, the conflict resided as we began to address these issues. Both partners described a significant shift taking place after Fred's parents had visited one weekend. Linda inquired about his feelings regarding the visit. Previously, such inquiries turned into conflict between them, but this time Fred talked about his feelings (the vulnerable ones rather than the angry ones). In session, Fred acknowledged that he had finally felt safe enough to talk about the vulnerable feelings. They had moved into the safe zone!

This case illustrates how a couple can become bogged down in dealing with a difficult problem, such as Fred's abuse and his ongoing relationship with his parents, because of the way it is experienced in the realms of esteem and attachment. Fred was dealing with difficulties related to a traumatic childhood, but it was his failure to feel safe in the realm of esteem that created the conflict in the marriage. Fred's response created both attachment and esteem threats for Linda. Thus, she didn't feel safe enough to respond with understanding when Fred needed it, and her response then created an attachment threat for Fred. But Fred made a positive step toward creating safety by finding the courage to speak about his vulnerable feelings. Doing so diminished the threat to Linda, who was then able to respond with curiosity rather than defensive criticism.

The development of emotional safety between them did not eliminate the issues Fred was working on in his individual therapy. But it did return his marriage to being a safe haven while he continued with his difficult trauma work.

Case of Inhibited Sexual Desire

Henry and Emily came to couple therapy because they had ceased to have sex by their third year of marriage. Their marriage had evolved into a very distant relationship that continued for approximately 4 years until they came for couple therapy. We explored the problem together. Emily was a quiet, introverted person who seldom complained, while Henry was an extrovert whose career was built on his ability to socialize and connect with his customers. Despite Emily's quiet demeanor, she periodically expressed her unhappiness with the relationship in a burst of upset feelings. At those times, she would complain about a variety of things and eventually threaten to leave the marriage. Henry was unprepared for these sudden outbursts and stunned by her attachment threat. He complained that he never knew that she was unhappy about something until it came out much later. Thus, he felt unsafe because he never knew how Emily was feeling in "real-time."

The need for Emily to express feelings in real-time became one of the initial goals of the therapy. Over a period of weeks, Emily began to express more of her feelings in real-time. Of course, this led to the predictable problem that Henry discovered he didn't exactly like all the feelings he was hearing about, as a lot of what she was expressing sounded critical to him. We worked on Emily expressing complaints without resorting to criticism, and we explored Henry's sensitivities. He had grown up in a critical, disconnected family that rarely had positive things to say about the children. Henry compensated by developing his congenial personality and seeking to win the approval of people outside the family. For her part, Emily came from a family that avoided all conflict and hid everything beneath a surface of superficiality. She acknowledged that she had had considerable problems with self-esteem but had worked hard on her issues and was feeling much better about herself.

Part of Henry's initial attraction to Emily was that she was a very accepting person with whom he could comfortably open up and reveal himself. And part of Emily's attraction to Henry was that she felt she knew where she stood with him and could therefore trust his positive feelings for her. They dated for several years and had a satisfying sex life. However, when they eventually married, their sex life quickly declined.

The therapy did not uncover an original point of departure where their closeness suddenly collapsed, but consistent themes emerged. Henry felt criticized by Emily. This probably started in small ways as the realities of married life punctured the images they had of each other. Despite his seeming confidence and easy-going manner, Henry was actually quite sensitive to criticism and had difficulty with any indications that Emily did not see him as he wished to see himself. His withdrawal was a surprise to Emily as he seemed to be so facile with people and able to deal with ordinary conflicts. But beneath Henry's confident exterior was a sense of shame about never being good enough.

Henry responded to his perceived esteem threat by withdrawing and busying himself with life outside the home. Emily felt neglected, which only accelerated her periodic outbursts at Henry, which only intensified his avoidance of closeness. During their courtship, they had been able to repair the damage from conflicts by reconnecting through sex. After their marital distance developed, Emily continued to try to connect through sex, but Henry always had an excuse why he couldn't participate.

Once Emily began to express her feelings in real-time, and Henry very actively explored his underlying difficulties with self-esteem, the atmosphere of the relationship improved significantly. They began to feel much safer around each other. But emotional safety is a relative experience, each of them was still reluctant to resume a sexual connection. Emily felt she had taken the risk of being the sole initiator for too long, and she was not willing to make herself vulnerable in that way again. Henry acknowledged it was his turn to be the initiator, but he continued to find reasons to avoid it. It was only after Henry talked about his fears related to displeasing Emily—and seeing Emily's accepting response—that he began initiating sex.

Henry and Emily each came to their relationship with preexisting esteem issues. Each of them had developed an adaptation that interfered with intimacy. Henry had cultivated a confident exterior that hid his inner doubts about himself. Emily had learned to disconnect the apparently disagreeable parts of herself in order to avoid threatening the other person.[8] But Emily was unable to keep her disagreeable feelings entirely suppressed, and that fed Henry's feelings of not being safe. He could no longer reside on his pleasant exterior at home, so he withdrew (and became depressed). This constituted an attachment threat for Emily, and her consequent threats to leave the relationship then constituted an attachment threat for Henry.

When Henry and Emily finally opened up with each other and encountered acceptance, they were able to reachieve a level of emotional safety. However, sex remained beyond their grasp for a bit longer because it required even greater vulnerability—they had never had a sexual connection under conditions of such openness. They had to learn to be emotionally safe even at that level of vulnerability.

In this case, the partners considered terminating therapy once they felt close and safe with each other. Each had made individual changes that improved his or her self-esteem, and each felt much better about the relationship. However, their initial complaint concerned their lack of sexual contact. In a sense, they each knew that pursuing greater intimacy could threaten their newfound level of emotional safety as they exposed even more of themselves and experienced greater levels of vulnerability. But their progress had expanded their confidence in their ability to confront their fears, and the more they confronted their fears, the more they were able to create safety. They chose to continue in therapy and resumed having an active sexual relationship surprisingly quickly.

Now that we have a clear grasp of the core issues of perceived threats in the realms of attachment and esteem, we will turn to the many systemic patterns that can develop as partners respond to their perceptions of threat in maladaptive ways.

10
Patterns of Maladaptive Responses

It is my contention that the core components of intimacy problems lie in the maladaptive ways partners respond to perceived threats in the realms of attachment and esteem. When maladaptive responses are not corrected, they tend to develop into rigidified dysfunctional patterns in which each partner takes a characteristic role.

Dysfunctional Patterns

> A big part of marital gridlock is that usually both people feel criticized and unaccepted by their partner.
>
> **John Gottman, 1999, p. 234**

Dysfunctional patterns that develop in relationships are usually characterized by their negative affective tone and rigidified interactions, which largely occur in the realm of esteem. Both partners seek to influence each other in their attempts to meet their respective needs in each of the affective realms, but sometimes a partner will forgo his needs in one realm in hopes of meeting needs in the other realm. Many of these patterns are not conscious; the partners are often unaware of their part in the pattern, though one partner may be aware of what the other partner is doing.

Systemic theorists have shown how relational patterns can take on a life of their own. Each partner's behavior is both a reaction to and a stimulus for the other partner's behavior. From the point of view of script theory, these patterns provide a new series of scenes, and new scripts can develop that are specific to the relationship. Not all of these patterns are destructive; some resemble positive rituals in a relationship. But the less partners are able to influence each other directly, the more destructive their interactional patterns are likely to become. Breaking these negative patterns is a major goal of couple therapy.

This chapter contains some of the most common dysfunctional patterns categorized according to the realm in which the threat is perceived. Many of these patterns have long been recognized in the couple therapy literature.

Responses to Attachment Threat

Attachment threat occurs when one partner perceives a lack of positive attachment affects in the other partner, or when the other partner does something that directly threatens the relationship (such as having an affair or giving a verbal threat to leave). Even when an overt threat has occurred, it will have been preceded by a lack of positive attachment affects. She doesn't call as often, listen as attentively, express as much affection, seek sexual contact, or speak in the same glowing terms. One way or another, he begins to suspect that her attachment is declining, and he begins to experience distress and anxiety. His response to the perceived attachment threat then sets the stage for their particular pattern to unfold.

Anxious Clinging

A common response to the perception of attachment threat is to try to hold on tighter to the other partner. Individuals who pursue this strategy are usually more overtly anxious, and attachment researchers have applied labels such as anxious, preoccupied, or fearful. Although the expression of anxiety about the relationship and increased clinging behavior will often elicit reassurance and more positive attachment behaviors from the other partner in the short run, the long-term effectiveness of anxious clinging is usually limited. Most partners reach a point where they are less willing to keep responding to anxious clinging; indeed, it often produces the paradoxical result of causing the nonanxious partner to seek greater distance.

This is the category that Bartholomew & Horowitz (1991) produced by combining a positive view of the Other with a negative view of the Self. The presence of the negative Self-view suggests that people who pursue this response to attachment threat are more prone to esteem issues. Though that is often the case, the person's esteem issues do not always precede the relationship. The difference between anxiously clinging to the partner and taking a more tactical approach, such as caretaking or protesting (the next two response categories), seems to revolve around a person's sense that he can *influence* his partner. If his experience is that he is unable to influence his partner, then he will be more inclined to intensify his clinging behavior rather than take an action designed to make the partner want to do something different. Many people who resort to anxious clinging are probably with partners who themselves have esteem issues and habitually resist their partners' influence. John Gottman's (1999) research has clearly shown the destructive impact of refusing to accept a partner's influence.

Caretaking Behavior

When a partner is insecure (perceiving an attachment threat), he is less likely to make himself vulnerable and directly ask for his attachment needs to be met. He may do nothing and just hope that his partner will know what he needs (a form of despair response), or he may try to influence his partner to meet his attachment needs through various indirect means. For example, one common approach is for him to intensify his efforts to attend to his partner's attachment needs, presumably in hopes that this will heighten her awareness of his needs.[1] If this approach settles into a rigidified pattern, then the caretaking partner becomes excessively focused on the other partner's needs, while his own needs tend to remain unmet. In the substance abuse literature, this pattern is often labeled as codependent behavior.

Individuals enacting this caretaking pattern are active (rather than passive), but they hide their fears about losing the attachment. Thus, caretaking may be a variation of the despair response (which will be discussed in a few pages). The person avoids direct protest and certainly has not detached. Instead, he tries to fend off his despair by actively focusing on the partner's attachment needs. When it doesn't work, the caretaking partner often becomes depressed and resentful.

In some cases, couples come to therapy when the caretaking partner finally reaches his limit and revolts and asserts his or her needs.[2] The partner who has been receiving the caretaking often does not understand and views the caretaker as going through some kind of breakdown. After all, everything's been just fine up until now, hasn't it?

Critical Protest

A common approach to actively seeking more attachment responses from the partner, but without directly asking for it, is to try to *coerce* the behavior from the partner. The more destructive forms of coercion involve some effort to influence the partner by inducing shame—or one of its variants, such as guilt, jealousy, envy, or depression.[3] The attempt to induce shame as an effort to influence is common among partners, including those who are securely attached. In the best situations, it can be an appeal to the partner's better nature—"You're not going to leave me to wash all these dishes by myself, are you?"—but in less optimal situations it can deteriorate into a perceived attack and create problems in the esteem realm.

Many insecure partners express their unmet attachment needs by criticizing and getting angry with the other partner. A statement of noncritical protest can include anger, but it is focused on the needs of the person making the protest ("I am not getting what I need."). When personal criticism is included ("You are not a good partner."), the protesting partner has shifted from the realm of attachment to the realm of esteem in order to avoid making herself too vulnerable. Needless to say, this strategy is seldom effective. He perceives her protest to be a threat to his esteem, and he becomes defensive. Instead of hearing her protest as a comment on what she needs, he hears it as an attack on what is wrong with him.

How the criticized partner responds to the esteem threat inherent in the critical protest plays a major role in determining the nature of the pattern that develops. Here are four types of responses, all based on Nathanson's (1992) compass of shame. The criticized partner experiences shame, and he may respond by avoidance, attacking self, withdrawing, or blaming (the equivalent of attack other).

The Hostile Disconnected Pattern   If he responds to her *critical protest* with *avoidance*, she feels helpless to make any impact on him. She develops an attitude of hostility that seldom abates, and he regards her hostility as a shortcoming in her, but fails to see that it has anything to do with him. He often maintains a lighthearted view of life that is irritating to her. He doesn't really fight with her, but also doesn't allow her to get close to him. Their relationship falls into a pattern of superficiality. He seems to be okay with the quality of their connection, but she is forever dissatisfied with it. He then views her as simply being someone who is never satisfied. Most people are not able to maintain a consistent avoidance response—effectively disavowing shame—without the aid of substances. Thus, substance abuse is very common in this pattern. What is probably more common is a mixture of avoidance and some other maladaptive shame response, such as blaming. In such cases, he responds by either being unaffected or by blowing up. In either case, his avoidance only serves to heighten the original problem—her neglected attachment needs.

Paralyzed Resentment   If he responds to her *critical protest* by *attacking self*, she feels actively constrained from saying or doing anything. For her, it is the opposite of the situation that occurs when he responds with avoidance. Instead of feeling helpless to make an impact on him, she feels pressured to hold herself back because it seems that whatever she says or does makes too much of an impact. She learns to walk on eggshells around him. This situation can elicit different responses in her. If she has her own esteem issues from past relationships, they are often exacerbated by his attacks on himself. For example, she may interpret his response to mean that she herself is a toxic figure, unlovable and destructive. Whatever her response, she is destined to become increasingly resentful as her needs and feelings must be restrained over and over. This often leads to periodic outbursts, followed by remorse and regret. There is a great deal of pain in relationships that involve a partner who attacks himself in response to shame.

The Pursuer—Distancer Pattern   If he responds to her *critical protest* by *withdrawing*, their relationship develops into the classic pursuer-distancer pattern. She wants him to meet her attachment needs, but she expresses that want in the guise of attacks on his esteem. He doesn't fight back, but continually withdraws in order to protect his esteem. He becomes absorbed in his career, his hobbies, his friends, the kids, the television, or anything but her. His withdrawal only serves to increase her experience of attachment threat, and so she is likely to intensify her pursuit, which intensifies his withdrawal. It is the ultimate vicious cycle.

In therapy, he usually reports that he experiences her needs as overwhelming (some therapists have labeled her as hostile-dependent and him as having engulfment fears). But the view of her unmet needs and his fear of closeness are distorted by the pattern they have developed. When he can be helped to respond to her attachment needs, he usually discovers they are not as overwhelming as they seemed when she was so ardently pursuing him.

Mutual Blaming   If he responds to her *critical protest* with *blaming*, she is faced with an esteem threat in addition to the attachment threat. Although she could respond with any of the shame responses, the most common one is counter-blaming—probably because she was inclined in that direction when she added personal criticism to her protest. These are the couples who are most readily labeled as conflictual; virtually anything can set the stage for arguments over who is to blame. His blaming response has now confronted her with an esteem threat to herself. The mutual blaming both activates shame in each partner and provides an escape from the shame (since that was the original function of blaming, or attack other). However, the actual appearance of shame in these relationships is rare. Very little of the blaming strikes home because each partner is defended against seriously considering anything the other says. For that reason, mutual blaming is sometimes viewed as a kind of collusion by the partners. It is as though they have each agreed to play the role of the bad guy, thereby allowing the partner to avoid his or her internal life by remaining distrustful and focused on the other partner.

When these blaming patterns reach the worst levels, the partners openly try to shame each other. In Edward Albee's caustic play *Who's Afraid of Virginia Woolf?*, marital partners George and Martha are in a relationship filled with pathological shaming. They not only shout and say provocative things to each other, but they also each try to humiliate the other by revealing sources of embarrassment in front of the strangers they are entertaining. Typical of intensely blaming relationships, he is so intent on humiliating her that he is willing to embarrass himself in the process (and vice versa).

Couples caught up in mutual blaming are difficult to treat because it is not safe for either partner to be vulnerable. Thus, the first goal of all couple therapy (to provide a safe environment) often remains the main avenue to successfully helping the couple throughout the treatment. The mutual blaming is presented here as stemming from the *critical protest* of one partner. When that is the case, the partner's original concern about her attachment needs can be very difficult to tease out of the morass of accusations. Many of these couples enter therapy and receive help with communicating more respectfully. This can help to break the blaming pattern, yet the unmet attachment needs that originally precipitated the problem often fail to get addressed. However, not all mutual blaming begins as a result of attachment threat. Sometimes both partners have esteem issues that lead to the mutual blaming. But even then, the vicious atmosphere of the mutual blaming tends to activate attachment concerns as well.

Resolving Critical Protest by Owning Attachment Needs

What leads people to decide to soften their start-up? It has to be an internal dialogue in which what wins is friendship and sympathy and understanding of the other's current life situation.

John Gottman, 1999, p. 225

The problems stemming from critical protest are probably the most common precipitants for couple therapy. His attachment needs are not being adequately met, but he avoids putting himself in a position of vulnerability and asking for his needs to be met and instead attacks her esteem. Her shame is then activated and she responds by resorting to one of the four responses from the compass of shame: avoiding, withdrawing, attacking self, or blaming. The partner expressing critical protest is motivated by attachment concerns, and the criticized partner is motivated by esteem concerns. However, once a maladaptive pattern sets in, additional esteem and attachment concerns can be activated for each partner. Most conflict occurs in the realm of esteem, and, generally speaking, esteem concerns must be addressed before the partner responding to attachment threat can feel safe enough to address the attachment concerns.

Therapists working with couples in which a partner has resorted to critical protest often emphasize the use of "I statements." Typically, the protesting partner starts every statement with "you" because his focus is on the other partner's failings rather than his own unmet needs. The other partner experiences this critical focus as an esteem threat and usually responds defensively. The therapist's emphasis on "I statements" is an effort to get the protesting partner to stop criticizing and reveal his unmet attachment needs.

One of the most important changes that occurs in couple therapy is when a partner shifts from attacking the other partner's esteem to asking directly for his attachment needs to be met.[4] He is much more likely to be heard and receive a compassionate response from his partner when he asks her to meet his attachment needs than when he attacks her for not meeting them. The partner who is attacked generally feels compelled to defend herself, and the interaction is then about her esteem rather than his unmet attachment need. This situation is worsened when the attacking partner generalizes the focus of the attack so that the link to his unmet attachment need is even less apparent.

Despair

A different kind of problem develops when a partner responds to perceived attachment threat with despair. These individuals often feel helpless and sink into depression. The adult behavior of passivity may not be an exact analog to the despair of infants separated from their mothers, but it is a frequent accompaniment to helplessness and depression. Thus, I include passivity (doing nothing and hoping things will improve) under the category of despair responses. In my experience, the despair response has the least impact on the other partner of the three categories of responses to attachment threat. It doesn't really constitute a threat to the other partner's esteem unless he is prone to take anything as a comment on his adequacy. Nor does one partner's despair constitute an attachment threat per se; however, the long-term effect of a partner in despair is usually an erosion of the attachment relationship.

Two patterns tend to develop when one partner has a despair response to perceived attachment threat. The first pattern develops when the other partner also despairs of making the attachment any better; the second pattern is when the other partner does not despair.

Superficiality   When both partners are dissatisfied with the attachment relationship, yet unwilling to protest or to detach, they often learn to avoid conflict by remaining very superficial. Many of these couples are inordinately polite with each other; others may be willing to have some conflict but always about issues that remain on the surface and do not touch either partner's deeper concerns about the quality of the attachment. People in these kinds of relationships do not expose their authentic feelings about themselves and the other; consequently, they are protected from potentially disastrous conflict, but there is always a level of dissatisfaction with the relationship.

I should note that the collusion to avoid the deeper issues is acceptable to some people. They may feel that an unsatisfying, superficial relationship is preferable to a hurtful relationship (full of protest) or no relationship at all (detachment). People who maintain superficial relationships usually do not experience great distress. Rather, they live in a state of perpetual dissatisfaction.

The Symptomatic Spouse   A partner who lives in a chronic state of despair seems to be more vulnerable to developing individual symptoms, most notably depression. In many of these relationships, the other partner is or becomes a caretaker, forever tending to the symptomatic partner. In such cases, the relationship revolves around the symptomatic member's troubles. The helpful spouse gets an esteem boost for being such a selfless helper, so this scenario probably develops more readily when the helpful spouse has esteem issues. In other cases, the other partner does not become a caretaker. Instead, there is usually a gradual drifting apart in the relationship.

Partners who are stuck in despair do not have to stay stuck there. Therapy often helps those individuals to organize and move toward a position of protest (hopefully healthy protest and not critical protest) from which they may successfully engage their partners. It helps to bear in mind that the symptomatic spouse is struggling with an insecure attachment.[5] If the attachment problem is rectified, the individual is frequently then more able to deal with his or her individual symptoms.[6]

Detachment

Responding to perceived attachment threat with detachment constitutes the gravest threat to the relationship. Critical protest generally confronts the other partner with an esteem threat, and threats to the attachment can also develop. Despair makes less of an impact in general, and over time it does come to threaten the attachment; but detachment is a direct threat to the attachment relationship. When he detaches in response to his perception of an attachment threat, she is confronted with an attachment threat of her own. Additionally, she is very likely to view her partner's detachment as an esteem threat and thus have her shame activated. Gershen Kaufman (1989, 1992) contends that the severing of the interpersonal bridge is the central and most powerful activator of shame among both children and adults.[7]

Most partners do not respond with detachment until they feel they have exhausted other avenues. Sometimes a partner will warn the other partner that he feels he is detaching or that he is close to detaching. Many couples do not come to therapy until one partner has reached the point of detaching, and a large proportion of these couples continue to spiral on down until they separate. The patterns these couples develop are usually less conflictual and often resemble the parallel play of children—together physically but not sharing the experience. Affairs are common as partners seek to fulfill their attachment needs outside the relationship. Sometimes these couples stay together for practical reasons, and each partner seeks his or her fulfillment outside the relationship. The most difficult cases are when one partner is detached but the other is not (therefore experiencing intense attachment threat).

When one partner is still attached (insecurely), any of the previously discussed responses is possible. However, the detached partner is relatively unaffected by attachment threat because he is protected by his detachment. Thus, the problems that develop are usually in the realm of esteem—but it is the one partner's detachment that is at the heart of the matter.

Responses to Esteem Threat

Esteem threat occurs when one partner perceives excessive negative affect in the other partner's view of him. It may be relatively subtle; it need not be a highly visible attack. She may speak to him with a different tone, give him a different look, or overtly express criticism, doubt, or lack of confidence in him and his abilities. As with attachment threat, a certain amount of this is inevitable in every relationship. But when it reaches some threshold level, the threatened partner becomes vulnerable to having his shame activated. At that point, he no longer feels safe to openly "be himself" around his partner.

In the preceding discussion of maladaptive patterns that develop as a result of attachment threat, many of the patterns were located in the realm of esteem. This occurs when a partner's response to the attachment threat constitutes an esteem threat for the other partner. In those cases, therapy may start in the realm of esteem but eventually shifts into the realm of attachment. However, there are also cases in which the original threatening perception occurs in the realm of esteem. Often the response to the esteem threat (such as withdrawal) constitutes an attachment threat, and the therapy ends up dealing with both. But sometimes the problem starts in the realm of esteem and does not bleed into concerns about the attachment.

In my experience, most problems that start in the realm of esteem do so because one or both partners have significant problems in esteem that precede the relationship (i.e., extensive scenes and scripts of Bad Self). In some cases, a partner has not sufficiently developed his sense of self-definition and is threatened by the other partner's differences. Or he may seek too much validation from within the relationship and cause the other partner to feel constrained from expressing her disagreeable feelings.[8] Ultimately, the usual cause of problems in the realm of esteem is a partner's use of poor strategies for managing his esteem issues. When he employs these strategies in the relationship, he initiates conflict in the realm of esteem.

The Frozen Partner

One pattern occurs in discrete episodes but may not characterize the overall pattern of the relationship. This is a pattern that occurs when one partner experiences deep distress and the other partner is unable to respond with comforting. Due to societal sex roles, it is usually a woman who expresses her distress and a man who gets frozen and does not respond. This mini-pattern often occurs during couple therapy sessions when she stops complaining or criticizing and instead gets in touch with the depth of her distress (usually over attachment concerns). She breaks down into tears, clearly in need of a simple comforting response that lets her know that he cares, and he becomes totally frozen and unable to respond. Of course, his failure to comfort her in the midst of her distress only serves to intensify her attachment concern.

The reason he is unable to respond to her need for comfort stems from his esteem issues. He perceives her tears to be about him and how he has hurt her or failed her in some important respect. (Indeed, if he perceives her to be crying about something outside the relationship, he is able to comfort her.) Basically, he cannot respond because he feels that comforting her confirms the legitimacy of what she has been saying about him. He may feel compassion for her at some level, but he is completely frozen by his more central need to protect the self. As with many of the esteem battles that develop among partners, to respond with compassion and empathy feels like giving in and taking the blame.

These episodes are especially injurious to the distressed partner. She cannot imagine seeing her partner in such a state of distress and not responding with comforting. To her, his frozen exterior comes across as a cold lack of caring, which may conflict with her previous view of him. It feels to her as if he were refusing to provide comfort; his inner paralysis is invisible to her. He too pays a cost for such interactions. He often feels shame about his inability to respond to her. To avoid that shame, he may resort to intensifying his subjective view of the exchange and insist to himself that she was being manipulative.

Unbalanced Esteem Patterns

The section on critical protest demonstrated the kinds of responses to esteem threat that stem from Nathanson's (1992) compass of shame. These destructive reactions to shame are the most common precipitants for relationship problems in the esteem realm; however, there are other ways in which partners react to an esteem threat. Some of these are not so much *reactions* to shame as relational patterns that develop as a way of minimizing the likelihood of experiencing shame. In these patterns, shame is often not activated per se, instead, the pattern allows the partners (or at least one partner) to structure their lives in such a fashion as to avoid the possibility of shame. The result can still be a dysfunctional relationship pattern.

What these patterns have in common is a persistent imbalance—one partner has greater power or status and the other partner occupies a position of inferiority.[9] Due to the patriarchal bias of our culture, it is usually the male who has the superior position.

The Overadequate/Underadequate Couple

If one person gets the upper hand, that person's beliefs, attitudes, and values become dominant in the relationship. The dominant one gains strength and confidence in what he thinks and feels. ... Meanwhile, his partner loses confidence. ... One becomes the "strong" self (really pseudo-self) and the other the "weak" self.

Michael Kerr & Murray Bowen, 1988, p. 104[10]

One common dysfunctional relationship pattern in the realm of esteem is the overadequate/underadequate couple. Basically, one partner has the role of the less adequate partner, which makes the other partner seem to be even more adequate. There is a payoff for each partner in this pattern, though the costs would certainly not seem to be worth it for most people. The overadequate partner gets to have artificially elevated self-esteem and a sense of competence (leading to the creation of the pseudo-self in the above epigraph), and the underadequate partner gets to remain in the relationship.[11] Thus, the pattern appears in the realm of esteem, but the motivation to accept the underadequate role may stem from that partner's attachment insecurity. In a sense, the overadequate partner has put his need for esteem ahead of his concern for his partner, and the underadequate partner has sacrificed her need for esteem in the service of her need for attachment.

The Controlling Partner   An individual who uses control to manage his difficulties in esteem approaches relationships with rigidity. His goal is usually to ensure that no situations can occur that might activate his shame. As I pointed out in Chapter 7, shame plays a role in the development of our likes and dislikes and how we structure our lives. We all do this to some degree, but the controlling partner extends his likes and dislikes to details of his partner's behavior. People who treat their partners in this controlling way are sometimes overly identified with the partner—he may regard anything she does (or is) as a reflection on him. Whether a partner becomes controlling in response to attachment insecurity or to low esteem, he effectively takes advantage of the other partner's vulnerabilities in the esteem realm. This is a dangerous strategy; it can easily become a form of psychological abuse and, in more extreme situations, lead to physical abuse (as in battered woman syndrome).

The Angry Partner
> Some people actually make a system out of their anger and are notable because they have no other way to approach a problem. They are usually haughty, highly sensitive people who cannot brook a superior or an equal, who must themselves be superior to be happy.
>
> **Alfred Adler, 1923, p. 267**

This whole pattern of achieving a feeling of superiority by making others feel inferior is seen among many individuals even when they do not have partners with whom to adopt a permanent underadequate role. People who put others down in order to achieve a feeling of superiority are fending off the activation of negative feelings in the esteem realm. Alfred Adler (1923) observed this early in the 20th century.[12] In shame-based subcultures, such as prisons and gangs, individuals operate on the assumption that there are not enough good feelings to go around, so they have to obtain good feelings about themselves by dominating someone else and making that person have bad feelings about himself.

When a partner deals with esteem concerns in this way, the resulting pattern is one of dominance and submission. It resembles the overadequate/underadequate pattern but goes beyond it. The submissive partner lives in fear of triggering the dominant partner's shame because she will have to endure his hate, anger, scorn, and contempt (and sometimes violence). Couples who are caught up in the cycle of battering and physical abuse certainly fit in this category, but so do more functional couples who never become physical yet remain stuck in a pattern in which one partner never gets angry and the other partner is regularly angry and scornful.

In the overadequate/underadequate pattern, the overadequate partner does not express scorn toward the underadequate partner for her inadequacy. Indeed, his good feelings often come from helping his less adequate partner. But the angry partner is contemptuous of his less adequate spouse. He obtains his esteem by viewing himself as superior. Women who stay in abusive relationships are sacrificing esteem in order to remain in the relationship. But it is certainly not a secure attachment. The majority of these submissive individuals were traumatized as children, either in the form of abuse or extreme neglect; they usually feel worthless and believe they have little to offer in a relationship. Such women become attached to men whose own extreme esteem and attachment issues have led to strategies of dominance and exploitation.

Mutual Avoidance

I have noted how the use of distancing can appear in either the attachment or esteem realm. Partners sharing despair strategies in the attachment realm will often accept a more distant relationship. The withdrawal strategy in the esteem realm results in a more distant relationship as well. Distancing is a strategy that can easily develop as a response to perceived threats in both realms. And there is one area of intimate relationships that is almost always affected—physical closeness.

Inhibited Sexual Desire

Shame affect, the painful analogic amplifier of any impediment to ongoing pleasure, is more likely to humble sexual arousal than is any other psychological function.

Donald Nathanson, 1992, p. 426

The powerful affects activated by rejection or failure in the bedroom, or the intense vulnerability required to reinstate a sexual connection, lead many couples to avoid any intimate situation that might lead to sex. Over time, both partners tend to quit trying to initiate sex in the relationship. Sex therapists have named this phenomenon inhibited sexual desire. This is a form of avoidance; the partners have developed a tendency to block their interest-enjoyment affect in regard to sex with each other. The partners' fear of activating the negative affects that appear outside the safe zone outweighs their attachment need for closeness and physical intimacy. This reasoning can be applied to many kinds of activities in which partners express no interest.[13]

Walls and Boundaries

Boundaries allow exchange of information across the threshold. Walls do not allow information to cross.

Robert Schwarz, 2002, p. 78[14]

When a partner does not feel safe, he often will put up a wall instead of a boundary. When he puts up a wall, he is no longer simply distancing. A wall allows nothing to cross; it appears in relationships in which one person cannot deal with the other. A boundary, however, is a barrier that allows some things to cross while restricting other things. All relationships involve boundaries, but in problematic relationships boundaries often become rigidified and turn into walls. During periods of change in a relationship, boundaries can become blurred as the partners renegotiate what should and should not be allowed to cross a boundary. Thus, the boundaries in a relationship are not static; they are subject to change as partners negotiate their differing wishes and needs. It is important that partners be both flexible enough to change boundaries and stable enough to maintain them when they have become clear and accepted.

Identifying Threats, Responses, and the Pattern

This chapter has identified several common patterns that develop in response to how partners manage perceived threats in the realms of attachment and esteem. As with most descriptions of psychological phenomena, real-life people often do not fit so easily into a particular pattern. There are surely other patterns that I have not captured here, but more than that, many couples simply do not fit as cleanly or operate as predictably as our models might suggest. But that should not pose a problem for the working clinician; the clinician does not really need to be able to categorize couples according to a particular preexisting pattern. The patterns described in this chapter are only examples; they are intended to help the clinician be better prepared to recognize issues involving attachment and esteem. Ultimately, the clinician seeks to identify three things: (a) the attachment or esteem threat(s) that underlies a partner's behavior, (b) the ways in which the individual is managing that threat, and (c) the way in which each partner's style of managing his or her particular threat(s) affects the other partner, thereby establishing a pattern.

Over the course of therapy, Will and Barbara each have identified significant issues from childhood. Will's primary concerns are in the realm of esteem, and he uses a lot of withdrawal and attack-self strategies in response to his extensive shame. Barbara's primary concerns are in the realm of attachment; she was abused and neglected and has difficulty trusting that her partner will really be there for her. At the end of our most recent session, I summarized what we were working on in terms of safety. Will has been avoiding closeness with Barbara because he fears she will judge him; he does not feel safe being fully open with her. Barbara is hurt and angry but most of all frightened because she is close to detaching. When Will promises to try harder she is skeptical; she does not let herself trust him. She has been disappointed too many times and doesn't feel safe allowing herself to expect more.

I pointed out their safety concerns and how each of their respective ways of dealing with those concerns interact: He fears being judged so he holds back, which feeds her fear that he won't come through for her, so she expresses her expectation that he will let her down, which feeds his fear that she will judge him harshly. You can start at any point in circular patterns like this and describe the sequence; there is no beginning or ending point. They both agreed that this is the pattern in which they are caught. *It is very important to identify the pattern because it is conquering the pattern that becomes the goal and removes the issue of one individual being held to blame.* Individually, they each work on changing the way they manage their respective areas of threat—Will needs to work on not withdrawing when he fears being judged, and Barbara needs to work on expressing her attachment needs (without being critical) when she fears being let down.

Barbara is easily able to activate Will's shame because he cares so much about what she thinks of him.[15] When he withdraws from her, he is trying to alter his view of her and the way he feels about her. He wants to focus less on what she thinks of him, so he tries to make her into someone who no longer matters to him. At its most extreme, withdrawal can become a wall and no longer just a boundary. Gottman (1994a) has identified stonewalling as the final stage of marital breakdown.[16] When a partner maintains a wall for more than a brief period of time, it constitutes the ultimate attachment threat to the other partner. This is the danger for Barbara; she responds to her perception of attachment threat with hostile protest, but she can only maintain that for a limited time in the face of stonewalling. Then she moves toward detachment.

In typical systemic manner, Will relents in his stonewalling when he perceives Barbara getting close to detachment. He realizes that the relationship is at stake (attachment threat), and that usually provokes him enough that he is able to break out of his own paralysis. Gradually, they are getting better at not overreacting to the other's worst reactions. Will turns his withdrawal around before it reaches the point of stonewalling, and Barbara has softened her protest and is able to express her attachment needs more directly. But each of them feels vulnerable (they have each given up their more extreme defensive reactions), and the change process is periodically disrupted by setbacks.

In the next chapter, we will look at how to engage a couple like Will and Barbara in the work of therapy. The initial step of identifying the problem is critical in determining how the therapy process will unfold. Despite the seeming complexity of the various ways people respond to perceived attachment and esteem threats, the actual moment-to-moment experience of the therapist is very clear once she has determined the realms in which each partner is perceiving threat. Those realms may change as the therapy evolves, but the therapist simply continues to use the lens of affect to determine what the partners are experiencing (perceiving and reacting to) at any given moment.

11
Identifying the Problem

Couples come to therapy with complaints. When the couple is caught in the cycle of repetitive conflict (whether expressed in overt fighting or in perpetual distancing), those complaints are about each other. Correctly identifying and understanding those complaints is key to having a successful therapy. This is not always as simple as it might appear. Some partners avoid directly identifying what is really bothering them. Instead, they may allude to it, embed it in a description of a less threatening problem, or avoid it altogether and perhaps hope that the therapist will notice when it occurs in the session.

The therapist's capacity to recognize underlying problems is greatly aided by her ability to view the couple through the lens of affect, especially the affective realms of attachment and esteem. If he complains that his partner has an annoying habit, is it simply the habit that is bothering him or is it that she might not seem to care enough about him to address his concern? If she complains that he is always late for dinner, is she concerned about scheduling or is she concerned about his commitment to the relationship? If he says he is always late because he is working, is he avoiding her? If so, is it because he has withdrawn (from her disapproval) or has he detached? These kinds of questions should occur to therapists as they discuss the partners' complaints. Additionally, therapists have direct access to the couple's affective communication as it occurs in the consulting room.

Injuries/Hurt Feelings

Underlying most conflict in intimate relationships is the feeling that one has been hurt, though many people skip the hurt (the primary emotion) and go to anger (the secondary emotion) so quickly that they fail to notice the hurt. Viewing oneself as hurt by one's partner is the most common excuse offered for retaliatory attacks, raised voices, name-calling, threats, and other displays of anger. When my clients describe themselves as hurt, I usually seek specifics. Exactly how were they hurt? What is it in them that has been hurt? If they explain that their feelings are hurt, I seek to determine what particular feelings are hurt. Needless to say, most people are initially perplexed by these kinds of questions. They assume the answers to be self-evident; they have lived in a world in which proclaiming oneself to be hurt is evidence enough that one has been hurt. But I am interested in determining what feelings have been hurt because it will make a difference in how I choose to intervene.

So what do we mean when we say that someone's feelings are hurt? Why don't we just say that the person is hurt? I believe it is because we are literally talking about feelings that have been damaged, specifically feelings about the self or the significant other. *What is hurt is the positive feeling that the person has about either the other person or himself.* Since the hurt involves a positive emotion being interrupted, shame affect is involved. The positive emotion about self or other is replaced by one of the two emotions that involve shame affect—shame or distrust—and the person's capacity to hold on to his view of himself as worthy or of his partner as trustworthy is diminished. This is what is hurt when one's feelings are hurt. Figure 11-1 illustrates the two types of hurt feelings.

Identifying the Threat

The first goal of the couple therapist is to identify the exact nature of the attachment or esteem threat for each partner. This usually takes the form of talking with each partner about the ways in which he feels he has been mistreated, injured, offended, or had his feelings hurt. Of course, many individuals (especially men) do not relate to the notion of being injured or having had

Hurts to Feelings about the Self

(Pride is diminished and Shame is activated)

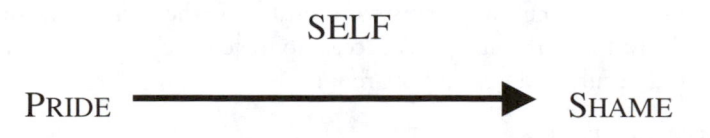

Hurts to Feelings about the Other

(Trust is diminished and Distrust is activated)

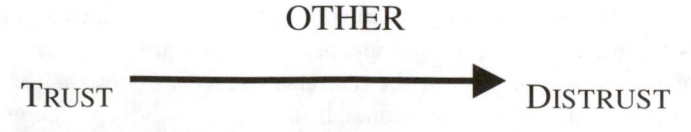

Figure 11-1 Hurt Feelings

their feelings hurt, because they long ago learned to block their awareness of those kinds of feelings. However, those people usually still have complaints about their partners' behavior. The therapist's task is to listen for the perceived esteem or attachment threats contained in those complaints.

Of course, partners may have legitimate complaints about a multitude of very difficult problems that do not reflect an underlying perception of threat in the esteem or attachment realm. The premise of the emotional safety model is that these problems are not responsible for the repetitive conflict or distancing, and the couple will be able to address such "normal" problems if they can move back into the safe zone where the relationship and the esteem of the partners is not at risk.

Susan Johnson (1996/2005) refers to this process of finding the threats as identifying the attachment injury. In my experience, there is virtually never only one injured partner—though there may be a partner who denies his own hurt feelings and claims he is only there to help the other partner. This partner may not perceive the same level of threat, but it is usually the case that he too has been moved out of the safe zone and is operating cautiously. Any partner who has moved out of the safe zone has the perception of some threat in either attachment or esteem.

The therapist starts with the presenting complaints, a process that often requires the therapist to help the partners articulate their grievances. The therapist seeks to find the perception of threat (either in the realm of esteem or the realm of attachment) that lies at the heart of each partner's complaints. There is no reason that a partner cannot have concerns in both realms. Indeed, there are usually layers of concerns that unfold as the therapy develops, but most of the time each partner is focused on one initial area of concern. *The therapist must work with the partners' areas of immediate concern; to get ahead of the clients will disrupt rapport and cause the therapist to lose credibility.*

The Core Intervention—Identifying the Problem

One of the things that highlights the relevance and applicability of this approach is what occurs when the therapist is able to correctly identify a partner's concern and restate it in attachment or esteem terms. Clients typically respond enthusiastically, conveying a feeling of finally being understood! Indeed, it is often the case that the therapist is able to state the client's concern better than the client can, because the therapist's understanding of the realms of esteem and attachment, combined with her capacity to see the murky affective messages, gives her a much keener grasp of the subtleties of the partners' emotional relationship.

Once the therapist has identified the issue from the client's point of view—and received confirmation from the client—it becomes easier to comment on the client's reaction (to the perceived threat in attachment or esteem). Partners are more willing to acknowledge unseemly behavior when it is stated in the context of the threat that precipitates it. "So when she shrugs her shoulders and says that you're never around anyway, you start to feel like she doesn't really care about you or appreciate how important the family is to you, and that's when you're more likely to make one of those 'nasty' remarks that she finds so upsetting."

Thus, the identification of the problem begins with identifying: (a) the realm of each partner's concern or hurt feelings, (b) the specific nature of the complaint (stated in terms that reflect the affective realm), and (c) how the partner reacts to the injury/threat. However, the description of each individual's affective experience and ensuing reaction only sets the stage for the complete description of the problem. Once these factors have been identified for each partner, the therapist must describe the basic cycle of conflict or distancing in which the couple is caught. The cycle is a systemic description of how each partner's behavior is, at least in part, both a reaction to, and a stimulus for, the other partner's behavior. The description of the cycle should be as short and simple as possible (I often illustrate the cycle for the partners to see). The description of the cycle should include each partner's perceived threat and his or her reaction. In most cases, it is the partners' reactions that then constitute the threat for the other partner.

Problem identification is the core intervention because it dictates everything that follows in the therapy. It shifts the focus from what people are doing wrong to what they are hurting about (their emotions). What they are doing wrong is now seen as a reaction to what they are hurting about (or what they fear might happen). When the therapy has effectively identified each partner's perceived threats, their reactions, and the way the partners' reactions interact to create a vicious cycle, then it can proceed in a variety of ways. Different therapists will work on these issues according to their own strengths and background. But whatever the therapist's approach—it could emphasize homework tasks, communication skills, insight, irrational beliefs, behavioral change, or a variety of other avenues—the proposed tasks of the therapy should always make sense to the clients as a way of doing something about the core problem.[1] Within that framework, there is room for a lot of latitude.

It is important to note that this basic intervention structure (empathizing with each partner's experience of threat and describing how their reactions then constitute threats for the other partner, thereby creating a cycle that keeps them out of the safe zone) is not restricted to the early stage of therapy, nor is problem identification something that is only done once. Problem identification is generally repeated many times throughout therapy, usually with different events providing the details. Often, however, there is a central overt event that produced a major injury, and that event may need to be discussed many times before it is fully resolved. Also, there may be more than one pattern or the couple's core problem may evolve over time, thus each event must be understood individually. Sometimes identifying the problem will just take a few moments because it fits a pattern that is familiar to both partners and the therapist. Other times, identifying the problem may consume the entire session or even multiple sessions.

In the following example of a brief discussion that occurred in my office, a pattern had been identified in previous sessions, but in this session, I saw the entire cycle unfold in less than a minute.

Hank had been notified that he was being let go from his job. He was a professional, was going to receive a good severance package, and there were no immediate financial concerns. Still, he was depressed and his wife, Gwen, had been trying to be supportive.

Gwen: I just want you to know that I am okay with whatever you decide. We are okay financially and my job is still solid.

Hank: I appreciate that. It's just a blow to my ego. But you don't need to keep reassuring me, it makes me feel like you don't think I can hack it.

Gwen: I know you can hack it; I just don't want to put more pressure on you. I realize I take it personally when you get irritable with me and lately you've been irritable, but I know it's just that you're feeling the pressure.

Hank: (his voice gets louder) That's exactly what I've been trying to tell you. But you sound like you just figured it out. I said that a dozen times on Saturday. Why didn't you ... never mind, I'm frustrated; I'm just frustrated.

Gwen: (her voice gets quieter and she looks down) I'm sorry. I just can't get it right. I won't ever bring it up again.

Hank: (glaring, throws up his hands) Great, that'll fix everything. (glares at me)

At that point, I intervened and asked Gwen how she felt right then. She said she wished she'd never brought it up. I checked in with Hank and he felt angry and frustrated, like he'd done something wrong and he didn't know what it was. We then discussed what had happened and how each of them had dealt with it. Gwen was trying to be supportive, felt Hank only got angry in response, got her feelings hurt, and withdrew. Hank recognized she was trying to be supportive but then felt she was telling him what he was always trying to get her to see (that his frustration was not about her), and he got frustrated even though he should have been pleased that she understood. When she lowered her head and withdrew, he became angry because now he had hurt her feelings and that made him feel like the bad guy.

They both agreed that this little episode was representative of what goes on between them much of the time. Invariably, Gwen gets her feelings hurt and withdraws; Hank gets angry about it, which only hurts Gwen more; that only makes Hank angrier and they end up very distant from each other. Gwen feels hurt because she usually starts out by trying to reach out, show support, or otherwise connect positively with Hank. Hank gets angry and frustrated because she seems to be forgiving him for something he doesn't feel he's done, and yet he always ends up looking like he has done something bad because she gets hurt by his anger. He goes away and stews in his anger; she withdraws and feels unloved. This pattern occurs, to a greater or lesser degree, on a regular basis. These two people love each other and want it to work, but they keep running into this conflict, and each feels helpless to do anything to stop it.

Let's reexamine the interaction between Hank and Gwen in terms of the affective realms of esteem and attachment. To begin with, Hank has lost his job. This is clearly an esteem injury and one that derives from events outside the relationship. Gwen's initial comments are intended to reassure Hank that the trauma of the job loss is not too great. She is trying to provide an attachment need, to soothe and comfort her mate when he has taken a beating at the hands of the external world. Hank is touchy about accepting her soothing; his esteem issues are very sensitive at the moment. Then the interaction turns in a negative direction. In one sentence, Gwen goes beyond the job loss and both comments on Hank's irritability and owns her tendency to "take it personally." She is trying to tell Hank that her own esteem is affected when he is irritable with her. Hank's response is to get irritated, purportedly because this is what he has been telling her (i.e., that she should not take his irritability personally because it is not about her).

Although Hank's focus is on the fact that he has already told Gwen that his irritation is not about her, his irritated reaction is precisely about her. I believe he heard Gwen to be saying that he continues to hurt her with his irritability, and that when she says she is "trying not to take it personally" she is indirectly criticizing him for being irritable with her and requesting that he stop. In short, he felt criticized because he heard an affective tone of hurt in her remark. This struck him in his esteem realm, and his angry response was his reaction to the activation of his shame. Gwen then announces her withdrawal (I believe Gwen often suffers an esteem injury when she perceives herself to have failed at an attachment task). Of course, this only heightens Hank's shame because he feels blamed by her withdrawing.

Describing the Affective Realms to the Couple

In this example, Hank is dealing with an external esteem injury (outside the relationship); Gwen tries to respond with attachment soothing and then brings up her internal esteem injury (inside the relationship), which he experiences as a further assault on his injured esteem, which she experiences as an assault on her esteem. The result is that she withdraws and he feels guilty and angry. Hank typically deals with his esteem injuries by directing anger outward, and Gwen typically deals with her esteem injuries by withdrawing.

I can add to our understanding of this particular interaction from what I know about each partner. Hank is in his 50s and has lived alone until the past year. He had a critical mother and learned to disavow or disown many of his attachment needs a long time ago. My guess is that part of what led this interaction astray was his failure to embrace the attachment soothing that Gwen offered. Gwen has been in many relationships; she always focuses on the other person's needs and is very indirect about asserting her own needs. She has a legitimate complaint about how Hank directs his frustration at her, but she avoids complaining directly and instead inserts her complaint in a comment that is intended to appear innocent and positive. Hank feels ambushed when he hears the affective tone of the disguised complaint, and that activates his shame.

My goal was to restate what happened in terms of the affective realms. I observed to Gwen that I could see that she was trying to be supportive in light of Hank's job loss. Then I noted that she seemed to also be trying to find a way to tell him that she understands his irritability is not really about her but that it is still hard for her because she still tends to look at herself critically when he gets upset with her. I suggested that Gwen begins to feel bad about herself whenever Hank is unhappy with her, and that maybe he should not take that personally, because Gwen has a long-standing tendency to not feel good enough about herself and so looks to her partners to confirm that she is okay (something she had already discussed in the therapy). I suggested she has the tendency of a people pleaser, seeking her own positive feelings about herself by pleasing her partner, and that this has the unfortunate side effect of increasing the power of her partner's irritability to cause her distress. Gwen glumly agreed and noted how this problem had intruded on all her previous relationships. I added that being a people pleaser also interferes with her being able to express her own frustrations and disappointments, and that she may find herself sneaking in indirect criticisms rather than complaining openly. She acknowledged that she knows she does that as well, although she often doesn't realize it until well after she has done it.

I then spoke to Hank. Since we were on the subject of self-esteem, I noted that he was managing his job loss pretty well, but that it was still a sensitive area and a challenge to his good feelings about himself. He agreed. Then I delved into his reaction to Gwen's comment about his irritability. He reiterated that he was just frustrated that she seemed to only now be recognizing what he had been telling her. I commented that it seemed the most frustrating part was that he seemed to be making Gwen feel bad despite his obvious desire not to do so. He said that was true, and it seemed to be what happened over and over. I asked him how it made him feel when he made her feel bad. His voice grew louder as he emphasized how crummy it made him feel about himself, "I'm always the bad guy, no matter what happened."

At this point, I felt Hank was squarely in his esteem feelings, and so I identi-
fied his reaction. I said, "It looks to me like your contribution to the problem
is that you get angry when you feel you're being seen as the bad guy. Then
that just seems to confirm that you are indeed the bad guy, even though your
anger may not have anything to do with what led to your being seen as the
bad guy in the first place." Hank was nodding and nearly shouted, "Yes! And
then no matter what has happened, I AM the bad guy."

I had not identified Gwen's reaction yet, but at this point I noted how
Gwen typically responds by withdrawing. She nodded and agreed. I sug-
gested to Hank that her withdrawal always makes him feel like the bad guy.
He agreed and Gwen said that she saw that as well. I wondered if her reluc-
tance to express negative feelings might even play a role in her withdrawing
because some part of her wanted him to feel like the bad guy. She didn't
think so, and I did not pursue it. This was a suggestion that went beyond the
emotions that Gwen was aware of, and I had no reason to believe it was the
case. I returned to the emotions that she was aware of. I observed that their
cycle of conflict ends with Hank feeling like the bad guy and Gwen feeling
she can't do anything right. Both agreed.

I then summarized the entire cycle, but stated it in nonspecific terms
so that it didn't apply to only this one instance. Gwen does something to try
and show Hank her love and support, but inserts a complaint and tries to
surround it with positives. Hank reacts to the complaint by getting irritated.
Gwen reacts to his irritation by feeling that she's done something wrong
(her shame has been activated) and she withdraws (her common reaction to
shame). Hank then feels that he has injured her and he feels like the bad guy
(his shame has been activated), which only makes him more angry (his com-
mon reaction to shame). Now they are stuck in a distant position until one or
the other reaches out (usually with a positive attachment behavior). Gwen's
perceived threat is Hank's anger (his shame reaction), and Hank's perceived
threat is Gwen's getting hurt and withdrawing (her shame reaction).

The foregoing discussion of the dynamics occurring in the session may sound complicated, but the actual experience of the session—and application of the model—is much simpler. The therapist's primary focus is on identifying the threats to each partner. The partners' respective reactions to those threats are hard to miss. As long as the therapist knows what the partners are responding to, and how they are responding, she is able to construct the interactive pattern. The final aspect of identifying the problem is to note that each partner brings sensitivities to this interactive pattern, but that the pattern takes on a life of its own after a while. The goal is to remove the onus of responsibility for the problem from an individual partner and to get the two of them allied in an effort to break the pattern. This usually leads to a discussion of what they can each do differently.

Heightening the Partners' Awareness

After the partners' core affective threats have been identified, a significant part of the therapy involves their dealing with these emotions differently. This generally requires each partner to increase his personal awareness of his emotions and how he is reacting to them. This dimension of therapy is often described in terms of insight or psychological mindedness, but I prefer to describe this process in terms of *increasing awareness*. Insight is sometimes viewed as a fixed characteristic that some people have and some do not, but I believe that any adult in an intimate relationship is capable of increasing his level of awareness of his emotions. Unfortunately, many people do not increase their awareness; it is a task that requires courage and a willingness to examine undesirable or unpleasant aspects of experience.[2]

The failure to be more completely aware is a contributing factor to most couples' repetitive conflict. For example, a partner may be dimly aware that he has feelings he is not expressing, that he is allowing his partner to believe he is feeling something—or not feeling something—rather than acknowledge the full range of his feelings, because some of those feelings will not help his case in the couple's arguments. At some level, he is aware that he is exaggerating or minimizing certain feelings (in order to influence his partner), or that he is flitting past his primary emotions and allowing his focus to fix only on his secondary emotions.

To begin to explore the feelings that lie on the periphery of awareness is a difficult choice—albeit a courageous one—because it feels like one is giving up one of the few advantages one may have in the recurring conflict. I emphasize the word *awareness* because this process does not require the individual to think in an entirely new and unfamiliar way. It is not a paradigm shift such as might be required for a person to suddenly recognize the existence of an unconscious thought. Nor is it an ability per se, though it does improve with effort and practice. It is simply a move toward greater openness to the possibility that one is feeling more than one has recognized and the willingness to explore that territory.

Hank and Gwen came to their couple therapy with different levels of awareness. From her previous experiences in therapy, Gwen was already aware that she was a people pleaser. She tended to ignore feelings that related to her personal needs and desires and focused on feelings that related to her partner's needs and desires. She was able to become more aware of the ignored feelings only because she *chose* to expand her awareness of all that she was feeling. Similarly, Hank thought he was only irritated by Gwen's failure to grasp what he had been telling her, but further discussion revealed that he was primarily upset that their interactions typically resulted in his being viewed as the bad guy. He was not unaware of this feeling but tended to focus more on Gwen's seeming failure to grasp what he told her (probably because this seemed to give him an advantage in the argument). Later in the therapy, he also was able to identify the esteem feelings (shame) that preceded his flight into anger (his secondary emotion). Hank's acknowledgment of the breadth of his esteem emotions came as a result of his willingness to explore what he was feeling rather than insist that what he had already identified was the entirety of his emotional experience.

Once They Get It

The therapy generally doesn't have much leverage in the realms of esteem and attachment until the partners accept the relevance of their perceived affective threats and associated reactions. It is the effective identification of the problem that establishes that relevance. Once each partner is aware of his or her perceived threats and associated reactions, sees how his or her reactions constitute a threat for the other partner, and sees how the two of them are caught in a repetitive cycle leading to conflict and/or distancing, then the therapist has a mandate to work more directly in the realms of esteem and attachment.

Identifying the Solution

Once the partners accept the definition of the problem and understand their respective threats and how their reactions constitute threats for each other (that culminates in the repetitive cycle), the therapist can outline what needs to happen in order to solve the problem. *In the emotional safety model, the therapist explicitly identifies the exact behaviors each partner must work on.* This identification of individual partner goals often bears repeating from session to session. This can be challenging because some goals are clearly active ("You need to do more of this or that.") compared to others ("You need to do less of this or that."), or some may seem to emphasize one partner's contribution to the problem more than the other partner's. This is why it is so important to have acceptance of the problem definition before focusing on what each individual partner must change. The therapist always seeks to balance this focus—addressing each partner's part—as it can so easily feed into blame fears.

Al and Lynn came to therapy because Lynn discovered Al was having an affair. He had become intensely involved with the other woman, and the therapy initially focused on ending the affair and reestablishing some minimal level of trust. Al had considerable difficulty ending the relationship, and Lynn was put through several pseudoendings before it was actually over. Over this period of time, she grew increasingly angry and her trust was damaged further. Al moved out of the family home, and it was questionable whether they would remain married at all, but somehow they hung in there through this difficult period. By the time the affair was genuinely over, the distrust and bad feelings between Al and Lynn had reached very high levels.

Throughout the focus on the affair, Al had insisted that the problems in the marriage preceded the affair, but this was difficult for Lynn to see while she was continuing to deal with ongoing infidelity. When the affair finally ended and moved into the background, we began to focus more directly on their relationship. Things began to improve a bit and they had a successful vacation. Lynn reported she felt closer to Al, and so, after the vacation, Lynn wanted Al to move back into the family home. Al resisted, saying that he didn't feel they were ready. This set off a very angry reaction by Lynn and the following occurred in the session.

Lynn expressed her anger, and Al got defensive. I tried to get Lynn to talk about what she was angry about—rather than simply venting the anger. (Getting partners to focus on explaining what they are angry about often helps them move back to the primary emotion.) This took some therapeutic prodding, but she finally began to talk of the pain she had experienced over the past year. Al smiled and shrugged his shoulders at some of the things she said, and Lynn reacted by shifting back into intense anger. (His affective tone was apparently stimulating Lynn's shame, and she reacted to the shame with an attack other response.) Again, I tried to focus her on what the anger was actually about. She said his attitude made her feel that he didn't really care about her. I confronted Al about what was going on behind the smiling, and he eventually recognized that it was a way of not taking in Lynn's feelings and could even be an expression of contempt for her (he was only mildly aware of being angry at her). Once Al could see how he was fending her off, I directed him to listen to Lynn's feelings without smiling, and instead to focus on taking in what she was telling him.

As Lynn talked about what the whole affair experience had been like for her, she began to get angry again. I inquired what had precipitated the anger this time and, after some focused exploration, she was able to pinpoint a "glazed-over" look that Al had to his eyes. This led to our identifying how Al avoided Lynn's feelings by withdrawal (listening to Lynn's pain was stimulating Al's shame). Lynn's shift from pain to anger seemed to be a product of their mutual responses to shame—he would feel shame and distance from her pain, and she would then feel foolish for expecting him to care enough to listen in the first place. As soon as Lynn shifted to anger again, Al would get defensive and they would argue. Lynn would then leave the interaction, feeling foolish for continuing to try to make it work with Al, and he would leave the interaction viewing himself as the victim of Lynn's anger.

At the end of this session, I identified what each of them must work on. I emphasized the powerful negative effect Al's withdrawal and glib looks have on Lynn when she is trying to reveal how much she hurts. I directed Al to work very hard on staying engaged and not withdrawing, and we discussed some of the many other ways in which he withdraws or tries to dismiss Lynn's feelings. I also emphasized the powerful effect of Lynn's pain and anger on Al. Throughout the therapy, and especially in this session, I had focused them on telling each other about themselves rather than about each other. I used that intervention several times with Lynn as I kept her focused on telling Al about her pain (rather than telling him about what a schmuck he was for causing it). I emphasized to Lynn that she must tolerate staying with her pain rather than escaping into anger (shame affect was a definite component of that pain) and that she must work at telling him about herself rather than focusing on him. Finally, I again stressed their reactivity—Al to her pain and anger and Lynn to his withdrawal and dismissive responses. Once more, I noted the systemic quality of their reactions—each reacting to the other's reactions—and how easily the entire pattern can be triggered. I tried to increase the likelihood that each partner would focus on his or her own area marked for improvement and not on the other partner.

In this example, I am trying to show how explicit I am about what each partner must do to change the destructive cycle. The other thing that this example highlights is a central tenet of the emotional safety model. *The behaviors targeted for change are defined by the other partner's experience of emotional safety.* This is one of the primary ways in which this model differs from many others. The therapist is not concerned about preexisting psychopathology, family structure, system rules, levels of individual development, and the like. The model is focused on emotional safety. *If one partner is doing things that disrupt the other partner's emotional safety, that is what must change.* Some people might argue that this gives a partner too much power; he can insist she change because she is making him feel unsafe. But if what she is doing is indeed making him feel unsafe, then they are not going to achieve emotional safety without addressing her behavior. Of course, the same applies to him, and invariably the couples with problems have fallen into patterns in which each partner is doing (or not doing) things that make the other partner feel unsafe.

In the next chapter, we will examine what needs to occur in the realms of esteem and attachment and the obstacles typically encountered.

12
Establishing Safety

Once the problem in a relationship has been clearly identified, the thrust of the therapy is directed toward achieving and maintaining emotional safety. Just as proper identification of the problem sets the course for the entire therapy, the goal of safety establishes the parameters of the therapy and informs everyone involved when it is progressing and when it is not. An initial goal (a sort of "working safety") is to make the therapy sessions safe enough to work in and, for the more conflictual couples, to implement a structure outside the sessions that can protect them from dangerous escalations. But the ultimate goals of the therapy are for the partners to achieve a state of emotional safety in their relationship and acquire the ability to recover and reestablish that state of safety when it gets disrupted.[1]

A Clearly Defined and Achievable Goal

Emotional safety means that each partner needs to feel that the other is securely committed to the relationship and not harboring significant feelings of disapproval. If the partners can achieve and maintain this state of safety the repetitive conflict or emotional distancing becomes unnecessary. Of course, this does not mean that the partners will now develop exceptional closeness, engage in great sex, or have the relationship they have always longed for. It only means that the major affective impediments to these outcomes have been reduced.

The goal of this model is emotional safety; it is not enhanced intimacy per se. The model is oriented toward helping partners correct the conditions that caused the loss of emotional safety within the relationship. The loss of that safety is usually what led to either the repetitive conflict or excessive distance that caused them to seek therapy. Further enhancement of the relationship is up to the two individuals involved; the extent to which they pursue that enhancement will depend upon their personal values and feelings for each other. Many couples maintain emotional safety by *not* pushing for greater intimacy; they find an acceptable distance that satisfies both partners.

Some couples will want to continue to expand their capacity for intimacy or otherwise enhance their relationship. They may or may not choose to use therapy in the course of that pursuit. To the extent that issues in the realms of attachment and esteem continue to be relevant, so too will the emotional safety model continue to be helpful to those couples, helping them to maintain or reachieve emotional safety while they implement other changes in their relationship.

The Benefits of Positivity

Positive affects help maintain emotional safety. One of the strongest findings from research on marital relationships and on individual and group functioning concerns the value of positive affect. John Gottman's (1994a) startling discovery that those marriages that last can be distinguished from those that don't by the ratio of positive to negative affects was a turning point for many couple therapists.[2] It became clear that we not only must work to stem the tide of the negatives, but we must help couples build their positives. Similar findings have come from research on individuals and groups. Barbara Fredrickson and Marcial Losada (2005) have shown that a positivity ratio similar to Gottman's applies to individual and group functioning.[3]

Gottman's threshold ratio of positive to negative affects (for stable, satisfied couples) is 5 to 1. Couples who maintain an effective level of emotional safety have at least five times as many positive interactions as negative ones. Part of what this finding indicates is the power of negative affect. It takes a lot of positive affect to counter the effects of a little negative affect. Of course, all the emphasis on positive affect should not be taken to mean that simply being positive creates emotional safety, but it sure helps to have positive affect.[4]

Past Versus Present

Emotional safety is established by eliminating perceived threats in the realms of attachment and esteem. Ultimately, safety depends upon how partners deal with each other in the here and now. However, many partners come to couple therapy with significantly damaged relationships as a result of past interactions. The therapist is then faced with the twin tasks of addressing the ongoing obstacles to safety and healing the damage wrought from past interactions. Ironically, it is usually not possible to address past damage without some minimal level of safety in the here and now, and it is difficult to achieve safety in the here and now without healing past damage. This is a perpetual problem in many couple therapies. The best way I have found to work through this dilemma is to conceptualize different levels of safety.

The initial goal must be to achieve a *minimal level of safety* in which the partners can interact without reflexively reacting to each other. The clearest measure of this minimal level of safety is that one partner can express a negative affect without the other partner either responding in kind or withdrawing from the interaction. At this level of safety, the partners may begin to be able to explore the damage wrought by previous actions (or inactions, such as one partner's failure to respond to the other during a time of heightened need). However, it is seldom the case that the partners simply discuss the previous situation and resolve their feelings about it. Instead, the therapy tends to oscillate between discussion of the earlier situation and discussion of current perceived safety threats. Some of the current threats will inevitably remind a partner of the earlier situation, and discussion of the earlier situation will remind a partner of behaviors that suggest that the underlying dynamic has not changed. Thus, it seems that progress in each sphere is, to a degree, dependent upon progress in the other sphere. Complete healing of previous damage usually does not occur until the partners have achieved a *maximum level of safety* in which each partner feels secure attachment and fundamental acceptance.

Once the initial goal of minimal safety is achieved and the therapy begins to address the esteem damage and attachment injuries derived from earlier actions and inactions, *healing* from these past events becomes a significant goal. The process of healing in these two affective realms is discussed in greater detail in Chapters 14 and 16. Even when past events have healed, there is a significant danger of problems reigniting as long as either partner has low esteem. Many partners come to their intimate relationship without ever having established and maintained good self-esteem. This places undue stress on the relationship—low-esteem partners may try to use the relationship to bolster their sagging esteem (which generally produces problems) or they may have heightened sensitivity to esteem threats and therefore be unable to stay in the safe zone. The subject of maintaining positive esteem is discussed in Chapter 13.

The establishment and maintenance of *emotional safety* is the overarching structural goal of the therapy. The therapist strives to make the therapy setting a place where the partners can safely delve into a discussion of their perceived threats. Part of how the therapist makes the therapy setting safe is through enforcing rules of interaction and interrupting and preventing behaviors that make the relationship unsafe. The therapist addresses safety issues in the discussion of past damage both by helping the partners to interact safely in their present discussion of past interactions and by highlighting the safety issues in the actions that created the earlier damage. Even when the partners have effectively healed damaged esteem and attachment injuries, the therapy is not finished until each partner feels safe in his or her present interactions, especially in interactions outside the protective influence of the therapeutic setting.

Emotional Safety

Emotional safety was defined in Chapter 5 as the quadrant of the terrain of the emotional relationship that was defined by the positive ends of the Self and Other Axes. In the esteem realm, this means *pride* in the self and the perception of *acceptance* by the other. In the attachment realm, this means *pleasure* related to the self and *trust* in the other. The goal of couple therapy is to remove the impediments that can prevent the partners from achieving these affective states. As you know, the primary impediments come in the form of perceived *threats* in the realms of attachment and esteem (and, of course, how the partners react to those threats).

In order to *maintain* emotional safety, partners must be able to eliminate or defuse threats as they occur. In order to *achieve* emotional safety, many couples have to return to earlier threats and resolve hurt feelings or injuries that have gone unaddressed. Subsequent chapters will address the process of resolving earlier threats and injuries in each realm. This chapter will focus on the establishment of emotional safety in the here and now, that is, on the conditions that allow a couple to conduct their relationship in the safe zone.

The main issue in creating emotional safety is to eliminate or defuse threats in the realms of attachment and esteem. This is accomplished primarily through expression of positive attachment and curtailment of expressions of disapproval. These are not new concepts to couple therapists, of course; most conjoint therapies have long focused on building positive feelings and teaching individuals how to express their unmet needs and negative feelings without attacking the partner.

Eliminating Attachment Threats

A core element in making any intimate relationship safe is the elimination of attachment threats. I have already noted that attachment threat is more often perceived in the lack of positive attachment affects. However, sometimes there are overt attachment threats, such as affairs, separations, or stated intentions to separate. Such overt threats must be adequately addressed before there can be any hope of safety in the attachment realm. Additionally, partners must learn that they may not attack the sanctity of the relationship as a tactic in their arguments.

Partners who threaten to leave the relationship may initially find that they get an apparently positive response, but the seeming effectiveness of such a tactic is misleading because they have also contributed to the other partner's insecurity about the relationship. Threatening abandonment *as a tactic* is a certain way to keep the relationship unsafe, but that must be distinguished from the situation in which an individual is truly approaching the point of detaching from the relationship and chooses to reveal that fact to the partner. Actual feelings of detachment should be revealed, not as a tactic in a fight, but as an opportunity for the other partner to know how far the partner's feelings have gone.

Promoting Positive Attachment

John Gottman's research has highlighted the importance of positive interactions. He and his team of researchers have shown that couples can maintain a stable relationship when the ratio of positive to negative interactions is at least 5 to 1. From the perspective of the affect model, this means that each partner sees ample evidence of the other partner's positive affects related to the relationship. The result is that each partner is reassured that the attachment is secure.

A related research finding is that it is a bad sign when one partner's displays of negative affect elicit a negative affect response from the other partner. One way of interpreting this finding is that the immediate negative response creates doubt about the depth of the other partner's positive feelings about the relationship. Gottman recommends that therapists teach partners to be able to hear an expression of negative affect without having to respond in kind. If they have a negative comeback, they should suppress the urge and wait to discuss it later. A partner's capacity to hear a negative without responding in kind reassures the other partner on multiple levels: (a) he has a reserve of positive affect that can allow him to hear her negative feelings without losing all of his own positive feelings, and (b) his failure to respond with an attack indicates that he has not tried to instantly reject what she said and therefore she will be more likely to feel heard. The attachment is thus more secure both because he has positive affects and because he can hear negatives, which may lead to improvements in the relationship.

This last item leads to a third piece of Gottman's research: the importance of *accepting influence*. When a partner sees that he is able to influence the other partner, he is reassured that it may be possible to improve even those parts of the relationship that he may not care for. He does not feel powerless in the relationship, and it is because his partner cares enough to allow him to influence her. Again, this contributes to a more secure attachment.

Avoiding Esteem Threats

Positive change in the realm of esteem means either learning to deal with esteem threats in less destructive ways or removing esteem threats altogether. In general, I do not consider it one partner's job to build the esteem of the other partner.[5] In Chapter 13, we will examine ways in which partners can help each other maintain good self-esteem or provide an environment that facilitates the development of better esteem, but the job of building better self-esteem ultimately belongs to the individual. The very nature of self-esteem requires that the individual be responsible for building his own positive self-esteem. Although it is not his responsibility to build her esteem, it very definitely is his responsibility to not undermine her esteem!

As I have suggested already, the vast majority of conflict occurs in the realm of esteem. In order to achieve safety, partners must learn to interact without creating esteem threats. This means (a) each partner must be sensitive in how he deals with the other partner, especially in areas where the other partner is vulnerable to esteem threats (this especially includes developing more adaptive reactions when a partner's shame has been activated), and (b) each partner must endeavor to reduce his sensitivity to having his shame activated. Thus, the mantra for the partners is one of both increasing and decreasing sensitivities: Be sensitive to your partner's capacity for shame, and learn to reduce your own sensitivity to shame triggers.

Improving Communication

Many couples reach sufficient safety when they improve the way they communicate with each other. The increase in safety that occurs as a result of communicating differently accounts for the popular belief that the problem is communication, as reflected in the numbers of couples who come to therapy saying, "We just don't communicate" or "We just need to learn to communicate." The problem is not that couples are not communicating, but that the partners are resorting to attachment and esteem threats rather than (a) exposing their vulnerability by expressing their own needs and feelings and (b) maintaining respect for each other's vulnerabilities and sensitivities.[6] Couple therapists have long been teaching partners to listen and not interrupt, to quit speaking for each other, to stay specific and not make overarching generalizations, to make "I" statements instead of "You" statements, and to stop escalations, attacks, labeling, withdrawal, and so forth.

When couples report "improved communication," they are usually saying that they have learned to speak in a manner that is more direct, respectful, and sensitive. Basically, they stop behaving in ways that stir up esteem and attachment threats. A good proportion of couples reach a satisfactory level of emotional safety when they have effectively changed the way they communicate, and they will usually terminate therapy at that point. Other couples must continue therapy until they have resolved the safety threats that linger from past interactions.

The Tyranny of Living for Approval

Kerr and Bowen (1988) observed families in which the members were highly reactive to one another and labeled them as emotionally fused. Bowen (1978) developed his hypothetical scale of differentiation to describe this dimension of functioning. More highly differentiated people were able to remain closely involved without being excessively reactive to their differences. Less differentiated people seemed to require others' approval so badly that they either sacrificed their individuality for it or they had to be excessively distant in order to retain their individuality. Less differentiated people could not get involved in an intimate relationship without becoming either overly reactive or excessively distant. Bowen's poorly differentiated families can also be characterized as those who have adopted the strategy of managing shame by avoiding differentness and focusing on shared approval ("We're all okay because we all agree that this is the proper way to be.").

The problem with this shame avoidance strategy is the reliance on others' approval. It creates a family environment in which one family member's differentness and individuality cannot be accepted because it is likely to activate another member's shame. All family members must endorse—and perhaps compete to influence—the prevailing view of how a person should be. If an individual rebels against this requirement of conformity, he then becomes the recipient of everyone's disapproval. Individuals who grew up in such families go through life highly sensitive to others' approval. Of course, this doesn't mean that they always seek approval, though that is the more common response. Some individuals go out of their way to behave in ways that express their scorn of others' approval, but even that antiapproval response reflects their excessive concern with approval.

Since family members typically vary in regard to their personal power in the family, some members inevitably have more influence than others on the family norms. Those members usually become more invested in maintaining the status quo, while less powerful members are often relegated to assuming antithetical roles, such as the family rebel. Ironically, excessive concern with approval ultimately breaks up the cohesion of many families. When adults bring an excessive concern with approval to their intimate relationship, it interferes with authenticity and consequently dampens intimacy.

We all need to be accepted in our important relationships, but acceptance is not the same as approval. Acceptance means recognizing the reality of how someone is. As long as we refuse to accept that reality, we will not be able to deal with it. Pop psychology has highlighted the importance of self-acceptance, but it has also confused the concept of acceptance with approval in many people's minds. Acceptance is the opposite of denial. When the parents of a sociopathic criminal finally accept the reality of what their child is, that is when they call the police. In relationships, acceptance includes the person's affective life. When we deny that someone is hurt or angry or spiteful, we are failing to accept that person.

Partners in conflictual relationships usually express considerable disapproval of each other, which, of course, constitutes an esteem threat. One strategy to avoid this unpleasant situation is to seek approval. In relationships in which both partners are approval seeking, there is an inevitable squelching of authenticity and a tendency toward superficiality. If only one partner is approval seeking, a power imbalance is likely to develop. I label the positive end of the other esteem continuum as acceptance, rather than approval, to emphasize that the goal of a healthy relationship is mutual acceptance. As long as partners are seeking approval, they are still not accepting themselves, and they are creating a situation in which another person controls their self-esteem.

Flooding

The capacity to reduce one's own sensitivity (and reactivity) is most challenged when an individual is flooded with emotion. Being flooded is an emotional state that is accompanied by clear indicators of physiological arousal, such as elevated heart rate and blood pressure. Gottman's research suggests that individuals lose the capacity to function thoughtfully (and sensitively) as the state of flooding increases. The actual condition of flooding may involve a variety of affects; however, I am sure that shame is frequently involved—whether initially or in reaction to being flooded.[7] Since intimate relationships tap into a greater breadth and depth of affective experience, the potential for flooding is high, and some partners develop a pattern of protecting themselves by frequent reliance on distancing.

Partners who are more susceptible to flooding (and the research tells us these are primarily men) have to learn to deal with themselves differently. As long as one partner is prone to flooding and unwilling to curtail his reactivity when he is flooded, neither partner can feel completely safe. Partners who get flooded have to learn to either monitor themselves internally and control their reactivity by pacing themselves, or they must learn to disengage when they recognize they are escalating. Since most flooding involves shame or a secondary response to the activation of shame, the process of getting control of these tendencies is greatly enhanced by therapeutic work targeting their shame and shame reactions.

Working on Shame Reactions

Threats in the realm of esteem can come from a variety of sources, but one of the primary sources is the other partner's reactions to his own experience of shame. The four reactions identified in Nathanson's compass of shame—withdrawal, avoidance, anger at self, anger at other (blaming)—each have the power to activate the other partner's shame. A major part of establishing safety involves changing these shame reactions. This can be challenging work; shame reactions are usually heavily scripted and very long-standing. Most individuals do not recognize that they have any choice about how they will react when their shame is activated. They view their reaction as simply a feeling that has a life of its own, something over which they have no control ("I just get angry whenever she speaks to me that way.").

The therapist's job is to help partners recognize the shame itself and learn to stay with the shame, rather than flee into a secondary emotion. I characterize this process as *owning one's shame*. When a partner is able to own his shame, rather than react to it, the other partner will experience an enormous increase in safety—as it usually marks the end of blaming. This is frequently a major turning point in the therapy.

Bringing Shame Into the Relationship

We own our shame by recognizing, acknowledging, and accepting the reality of it. When we own our shame, we do not blame anyone because we have shame; it is simply an emotion that we experience. It is only when an individual is able to own his shame that he can delve into what it is about. The process of exploring one's shame may require the person to go into his dark side, the parts of himself that he tries to hide—from himself as well as from others.

Once a partner owns up to his shame, many of the problems with the other partner begin to fade. What he is left with is just his own humanity. A central tool for helping partners accept their shame and bring it into the relationship (as opposed to continuing to try to keep it out of the relationship, which often occurs with a partner who is in individual therapy) is identifying each partner's *shame story*. Once a person truly knows, and accepts, his own shame story and shares it with his intimate partner, he will be less easily triggered. Of course, sharing one's shame story makes one more vulnerable in the relationship. Thus, like many other elements of increasing safety, the thing that helps to increase the safety is also the very thing that results from increased safety.

Relationships are much safer when partners experience their shame as their own and not something the other partner has made them feel. He is more able to own his shame when he understands that she doesn't *make* him feel it—what she does is trigger or activate his shame (specifically, she triggers a process that activates his existing shame script). She can help him to transform his shame, but her help will only feel like criticism if he has not accepted the reality of his own shameful views of himself. Ultimately, *delving into an individual's shame cannot be initiated by anyone but that individual.* Accepting shame as one's own is the first step toward greater self-acceptance and self-respect.

Increasing the Safe Zone

When a couple's safe zone grows, they find more opportunities for connection. Each partner can be more vulnerable, and that leads to greater intimacy and more secure attachment.

Some people try to avoid esteem threats by controlling their partners. Their goal is to avoid the possibility of ever having their shame triggered. That path leads to the endless fight; it never increases the safe zone. The only effective way to increase the safe zone is to: (a) decrease each partner's sensitivity to being triggered by the other partner (mostly by increasing their empathic walls), (b) reduce the power of each partner's shame by developing pride scripts and disassembling shame scripts, and (c) learn more adaptive ways to deal with shame when it is triggered. *The most adaptive way to deal with shame when it appears in one's intimate relationship is to go into it and act on it rather than avoid it and react to it.*

When partners aspire to have a safer relationship, they must do what feels counterintuitive. They must bring their shame *into* the relationship instead of trying to forever keep it out. This frees them to experience their healthy shame, which largely remains blocked as long as they're trying to fend off their pathological shame. Ironically, healthy shame plays a major role in helping partners to heal the myriad little injuries that are an inevitable part of all relationships. When he openly experiences his healthy shame, she can see that he truly cares.

Individuals cannot escape pathological shame but they can overcome it and open up their capacity for healthy shame. Every person with significant shame is carrying some distorted views of himself. These distorted views (Bad Self) can change only if he can be vulnerable enough to take in his partner's view of him. If his shame is based on genuine shortcomings in his character, then he can work to overcome those shortcomings. If he has unhealthy shame reactions that are creating problems in the relationship, he can change those by staying with his shame and owning it rather than fleeing from it. And if his life is twisted as a result of his efforts to avoid his shame, that too can change with self-acceptance. Of course, change does not come easy; it requires two things: (a) the courage to confront oneself and (b) a partner who is willing to hang in there and not add to the person's shame while he delves into the forbidden reaches of his worst feelings about himself.

In the remaining four chapters we will examine what is specifically required to restore and maintain safety in the realms of esteem and attachment.

Maintaining Esteem

Positive self-esteem is one of the most valuable things a person can possess, yet parents cannot will it to their children, and intimate partners cannot bestow it upon each other. Unfortunately, in most intimate relationships, a partner's power to diminish the other's self-esteem is much greater than his power to enhance it (though even that has its limits). Positive self-esteem is not an innate trait; it is acquired as the result of self-evaluation. Our esteem grows primarily from facing challenges, managing to do the things that we regard as difficult but valuable. We each have to earn our own respect! Although a parent or a partner cannot give positive self-esteem, there are things they can do to facilitate its growth.

It is very difficult to keep a relationship in the safe zone as long as either partner has poor self-esteem. So partners owe it to each other, as well as themselves, to maintain an environment that is conducive to the development of positive self-esteem.

Self-Esteem

The realm of esteem, including both self and other dimensions, is fundamentally the realm of self-esteem—the emotions we have that reflect our valuing of ourselves. The dimension of other is important because of the impact of each partner's view of the other partner's value and competence. His view of her adequacy as a person can have a powerful impact on her self-esteem. But that doesn't mean it is his job to shore up her self-esteem! *In an intimate relationship, it is each partner's job to maintain his or her own self-esteem.* When both partners have good self-esteem, each individual is less vulnerable to esteem threats and more likely to respect the other's sensitivities.

Although mental health professionals are usually aware of the level of their clients' self-esteem, many still underestimate the extent to which self-esteem influences their clients' daily experiences. The quality of a person's self-esteem is one of the key factors that determine the quality of his life.

Self-esteem is not simply about feeling good about oneself; it is about feeling competent to manage the demands of life and valuable to oneself and to others. The psychologist Nathaniel Branden, who has devoted his career to the study of self-esteem, describes self-esteem as a fundamental sense of efficacy and worth, "the integrated sum of self-confidence and self-respect" (1983, p. 4).

People with high self-esteem possess an inner conviction that they are competent to deal with life, and that they deserve to be treated with respect. They may lack skills in specific areas, but they are confident that they can readily acquire whatever skills may be required to meet life's demands.

The acquisition and maintenance of genuine high self-esteem is a major achievement in life, and it is less common than external appearances might suggest. The high rates of substance abuse, divorce, dependency/codependency, depression, and anxiety among our society's apparently successful segment belies the face of good self-esteem that they try to show the world. In psychotherapy, it is only when people begin to value themselves that they dare to change such behaviors. One of the most helpful things that therapists do is simply remind people that they are worth the effort it takes to improve their lives. Indeed, therapists like to point out that the valuing of self and the process of change have already begun when the client has taken the momentous step of seeking therapy.

The focus of this chapter is on positive self-esteem—how individuals establish it in themselves and how they can help their partners establish it for themselves. When individuals do not have positive self-esteem, they often resort to compensatory strategies that provide them with the appearance of good self-esteem. Unfortunately, these compensatory strategies tend to create problems in their intimate relationships. Before we look at how individuals successfully maintain positive self-esteem, we will examine some of those compensatory strategies. One of the most common is when partners try to use the relationship to bolster their self-esteem.

Seeking Esteem From How One Is Seen

> Monarchies, aristocracies, and religions are all based upon that large defect in your race—the individual's distrust of his neighbor, and his desire, for safety's or comfort's sake, to stand well in his neighbor's eye.
>
> **Mark Twain, *The Mysterious Stranger,* p. 667**

One of the unfortunate byproducts of modern mass media is that it seems to support the illusion that self-esteem can be derived from how one is perceived by others. The cultural emphasis on physical beauty, for example, has contributed to huge industries—from cosmetics to cosmetic surgery—that convince many people (mostly women) that they will feel good about themselves if they are viewed as more attractive by others. Many of the people whom we have elevated to the status of celebrity have bought into this myth, yet they behave in ways that indicate they have poor self-esteem. The public tantrums and lurid behavior intended to attract the media spotlight are ample evidence of a population of people who do not value themselves very highly. It should not surprise us that many of those celebrities have difficulty with long-term relationships.

The erroneous belief that self-esteem can be obtained from how one is seen by others may be more common among celebrities, since this group of people is clearly invested in managing how they are viewed by others, but the belief is also widespread throughout our culture. We all work to manage the impression we make on others. It is a short step from that to being more concerned with how others view us than how we view ourselves. Or perhaps it would be more accurate to say that we hope to use how others view us to change how we view ourselves. If he can convince her to view him as competent, then perhaps he can feel that he is competent.

Misrepresenting ourselves to others is a mark of shame, but it can take different forms. Many people try to hide those aspects of themselves they regard as shameful. They live in fear of having those parts exposed. But others go beyond hiding their shameful parts; they create a false exterior and seek to generate feelings of pride by getting others to view them as something other than who they actually are. A person who creates a false exterior lives in fear of not only being exposed but of being found to be an imposter. Furthermore, he finds it even more difficult to develop genuine, positive self-esteem.

The seemingly good feelings he might glean from exaggerating his accomplishments—from leading others to think that he is more honest, courageous, or intelligent than he actually is—are not the foundation of positive self-esteem, because he knows that they are not true. The more invested he becomes in trying to feel good about himself by misleading others, the further he gets from genuine self-acceptance. And in his intimate relationship, his fear of exposing his real self is even greater.

The illusion of high self-esteem that comes from the way one is perceived within the relationship is an aspect of many of the problems discussed in this book. People who appear to have high self-esteem yet are brittle and easily triggered into shame are struggling to hide an underlying negative view of self (Bad Self). The positive self-esteem they appear to manifest is superficial; it is not grounded in their core view of themselves.

Pseudo Self-Esteem

Many people function very well in some spheres of their lives but not in others. Some people with poor self-esteem compensate by trying to overidentify with the successful spheres of their lives and deny, minimize, or otherwise avoid the unsuccessful spheres. They may act as though they have high self-esteem, but their good feelings about themselves are limited and brittle; the good feelings collapse if the individual is exposed. Nathaniel Branden (1983) has applied the label of *pseudo self-esteem* to this strategy.

One of the most common splits in the ability to function is the person who functions very well in his work life, perhaps in his leisure activities, and casual relationships, but who does not function well in an intimate relationship. Such people frequently appear in therapists' offices. For me, there is an immediate indicator of how effective I am likely to be in providing help to such a person—and that is his willingness to acknowledge his difficulty. Does he express confusion and a failure to understand why he has such a problem, does he suggest that he just has poor judgment regarding people and blame the partners he has chosen, or does he acknowledge that he does not function well in the arena of intimacy and knows that he needs to change something about himself?

As a rule, the more honest an individual is in recognizing and taking responsibility for his shortcomings, the higher his self-esteem is—or soon will be. The more the person seeks to make excuses and evade responsibility for his difficulties, the more likely he is struggling to preserve a view of self that is not based in reality.[1] If his self-esteem is based on a need to deny his own contribution to his difficulties, then that need actually creates much of the difficulty. He will approach relationships in a rigid manner, needing his partner to agree with his view of himself, and he will be especially vulnerable to esteem threats. In many cases, the person may go so far as to completely disown aspects of himself.

Disowned Aspects of the Self

Ann was a strong, competent woman who ran the family business and got things done when others failed. She had long played this role in her family of origin, and it was one of the things that Phillip found very attractive about her. Yet, despite her personal strength, one of Ann's greatest sources of shame was the way she always submitted to her elderly father. Ann ran the family business better than her father ever had, yet he constantly criticized and humiliated her and she never stood up to him about it. Phillip was disgusted by Ann's inability to stand up to her father, and he was often attracted to other women whom he perceived to be stronger than her.

When I pushed Phillip to examine his own ability to stand up for himself, he realized that he too had avoided certain kinds of conflict all his life. His parents had fought throughout his childhood and he was always called upon to settle their disputes. When he grew up, he became a fierce litigator and created an image of himself as a man not to be trifled with, yet in his own way he had avoided conflict in his marriage and was forever getting emotionally involved with other women. As Phillip examined his negative reaction to Ann's shame, he came to see that his rejecting response was dictated by his own shame.

An old piece of folk wisdom posits that the things we most dislike in others are really things that we most dislike in ourselves. Usually we have blinded ourselves to the fact that we ever possessed a similar attribute because we regard it as a source of shame. Gershen Kaufman (1989) says that disowning aspects of the self is a common strategy for dealing with potential shame. Unfortunately, this strategy tends to create difficulties in intimate relationships.[2]

Many perceived esteem threats stem from situations in which a partner is reacting to a disowned aspect of himself. He conveys an affective message of disapproval whenever she does "that thing," and that thing might be any number of behaviors—she might always run late or she might insist on punctuality; she might bite her nails or she might take particular care of them; she might procrastinate or she might be highly disciplined; she might always leave a mess or she might clean obsessively, and so forth. I give examples of opposites to make the point that there is nothing inherently disturbing about the traits that bug him. Rather, the traits that he reacts to have some personal meaning for him. Often the meaning is that he has a history involving these traits (whether in himself or in an intimate other, such as a parent), and he has *composed a view of who he is that explicitly excludes those traits.* Thus, those traits become disowned aspects of himself.

A view of self that is specifically focused on what the person is *not* is probably always a signal that the person is reacting to some painful past experience. This view will play a central role in the person's pride scripts, and, since it is based on the need to see the self as never manifesting certain characteristics, it leads to rigidity. People who are invested in seeing themselves as never manifesting particular characteristics are especially vulnerable to experiencing shame if they should recognize those characteristics in themselves.

Until a partner can recognize that he is reacting to things he continuously tries to eliminate from his view of himself, he will remain focused on the other partner. Partners are controlled by their inner voice of shame or their need to disown aspects of themselves as long as they remain unaware of the underlying emotions that drive these processes. The primary affect that drives these processes is fear—the fear of experiencing shame (fear is the affect; the resulting emotion is anxiety). Some people learn to criticize themselves relentlessly as a way of anticipating and forestalling any possibility of activating their shame. But others may pursue a different strategy. They learn to rid themselves of potentially shameful aspects of their selves by burying those parts and disavowing the feelings associated with them. This disowning of aspects of the self not only leads to rigidity in the person, but can cause him to be very judgmental and disdainful when he encounters those parts in others, especially his partner.

For example, if he grew up around overly aggressive adults, he may have hated it and promised himself that he would never be like that himself, which could cause him to feel deep shame if he encountered aggression in himself. Over time, he cultivated his nonaggressive attitudes and suppressed any impulses to be aggressive until he developed a consistent view of himself as someone who never experiences aggressive feelings. If he enters a partnership with someone who is comfortable with her aggressive feelings, then he may be especially reactive to her displays of aggression (whether directed at him or others). Her displays of aggression may or may not be appropriate, but his response is likely to be judgmental and disdainful (even contemptuous if their repetitive conflict reaches the level where respect vanishes).

Disowning aspects of the self is an esteem issue; it revolves around the person's need to maintain a view of himself as not possessing the unwanted characteristic. Since it is a bit artificial for most of us to believe that we are completely free of undesirable feelings (envy, hatred, fear, aggressiveness, greed, and so forth), a partner's need to maintain a distorted view of himself makes him more vulnerable to the other partner's view of him. If she views him as aggressive, this not only threatens to activate his shame, but it clashes with his long-standing defense against that particular source of shame. The result is that he is likely to dig in and fight harder to maintain his view of himself and work to persuade her to change her view of him as well.

Or, instead of struggling to resist, he could choose to *go into his shame* and expand his awareness to include the fact that he too is capable of feeling aggressive. Perhaps the only difference between him and her is that he is more motivated to avoid behaving aggressively. Being able to go into his shame is liberating; he will no longer be terribly concerned with whether or not she is aggressive.

Building Esteem—The Value of Pride

In general, people feel better about themselves—and are less sensitive about how others view them—when they have sources of pride. People who lack sources of pride typically are more sensitive about how they are viewed by others, are usually defensive, and have difficulty accepting responsibility for their failings. However, focusing exclusively on one's sources of pride does not in itself produce good self-esteem. A singular focus on sources of pride, if combined with ignoring significant problem areas, can lead to pseudo self-esteem. So it is important to develop sources of pride, but it is also important to maintain a comprehensive view of the self, including those parts of the self that one might prefer to deny.

Sources of pride vary: for some, it is a good golf game, for others, a meaningful career, and for others, it is all about treating people with dignity. Though many people derive apparent pride from possessions and innate characteristics, the most meaningful sources of genuine pride are personal accomplishments—especially when those accomplishments involve overcoming personal challenges. What constitutes a challenge for one person may not be one for another, so what matters is what the individual must overcome.

Some partners rely upon sources of pride that lack much depth, such as their personal attractiveness or experiences that do not really require much effort. The pride derived from these kinds of sources tends to break down much quicker than the pride gained from hard work to overcome personal challenges. And pride is something that we have to continue to create in our daily lives; it is not something that is established once and then requires no further attention. But it is certainly true that success at facing challenges builds confidence and makes the individual less vulnerable to the perception of threats in the realm of esteem.

This is an area that some couple therapists refrain from pursuing—the individual's feelings about himself and what he might do differently to improve those feelings. Sometimes a partner may feel that he is being identified as "the problem" and that his complaints about the relationship are not being accepted as valid. Consequently, many therapists shy away from exploring personal issues in couple therapy. But those issues bear on the relationship. A partner who is lacking in legitimate sources of pride is much quicker to perceive esteem threats and to blame the other partner. Delving into the partners' feelings about themselves can be a tricky proposition, but it often can prove helpful—especially if esteem threats dominate in a relationship.

Helping a partner to build sources of pride is almost always helpful (it may be more accurate to think of it as "challenging" the person to build sources of pride). But increasing sources of pride is only a building block toward positive self-esteem; a better measure of whether the person has made it to positive self-esteem is authenticity.

Authenticity and Awareness

So what does it mean to be authentic (at least, as I am using the word)? Obviously, it is about being honest in one's expression of oneself, and from the point of view of affect theory, that means affectively honest. Authentic people are congruent in what they say and what they feel. But the key word here is authenticity, not just honesty, because it is possible to be honest about what one is aware of feeling yet quite wrong because of the limits of one's awareness. The person whose feelings are hurt but who denies the hurt feelings because he always rushes to the secondary emotion of anger may be honest, but he is not being completely authentic. Thus, *expanding awareness* is a key step in becoming more authentic and maintaining high self-esteem.

There are two aspects to authenticity: the first is knowing what one is feeling; the second is about how one presents oneself to others. Years ago a supervisor told me the story of a famous artist who asked his psychoanalyst, "Is it narcissistic if I sign my paintings?" The analyst's response was, "If you're narcissistic, then it's narcissistic if you sign your paintings and it's narcissistic if you don't sign your paintings." I assume the analyst meant that what matters is the motive behind the act. The artist might pump up his self-esteem by signing his paintings or he might feel he is special because he doesn't sign them. In either case, he is trying to present himself to others in such a way as to make a particular impression. Thus, either way could be inauthentic.

In a similar fashion, we are all capable of distorting the way we present ourselves to others. We may emphasize certain traits ("I am very organized."), always make sure that certain data get mentioned ("Yes, that reminds me of when I was elected president of the student body."), or deny certain aspects of ourselves ("I am never late."). We may distort our image as being bigger than life ("Oh yeah, I played football in high school; I probably made half the tackles on my team.") or smaller than life ("Yeah, I played football in high school; I didn't make a single tackle all year."). Whether the distortion is an exaggeration or a minimization, the goal is the same—to manage how we are viewed by others and avoid our particular avenues to shame.

Being authentic means presenting ourselves to others exactly as we are—neither greater nor less than that. It means acknowledging our shortcomings and not trying to deny them, but it also means acknowledging our strengths and not trying to hide them either. Humility is not about denying our strengths and accomplishments; it is simply about keeping them in perspective and remaining conscious of our defects along with our strengths. When two partners are each authentic, there is very little opportunity for esteem threats to occur.[3]

Branden's Pillars of Self-Esteem

> Do not say untruthful things for the sake of personal interest or to impress people. … Do not criticize or condemn things that you are not sure of. Always speak truthfully and constructively.
>
> **Thich Nhat Hanh, 1992, p. 129**

Nathaniel Branden (1971) has identified six central principles for maintaining good self-esteem. He calls these the six pillars of self-esteem. First, he advises people to *live consciously*. By this he means to be fully present in the moment and aware of the choices and decisions they are making.[4] Second, he emphasizes the importance of *self-acceptance*. We cannot change until we accept the reality of what we are dealing with. Branden's emphasis on acceptance is not the same as approval; it is closer to self-honesty. Third, he advises that people must *take responsibility for their experiences*. As long as people avoid responsibility for their experiences, they give the power over their lives to others. The fourth principle is for people to *assert who they are*. Pretending to be something other than what they are only keeps people in hiding (and controlled by their fear of activating their shame). The fifth principle is to *live purposefully*. This is a step beyond taking responsibility for one's life; Branden is emphasizing that people must take charge of their lives. The final principle is that people must strive to *maintain their integrity*. If people abide by their own principles and live up to their own standards, they will feel good about themselves—regardless what others may think.

These six principles are so brief and succinct that it can be easy to skim through them and not take in the depth of their wisdom. Working on improving one's self-esteem has been parodied in the media and portrayed as some kind of blind self-approval. It is anything but that! Building self-esteem begins with fearless self-honesty—scrutinizing oneself and accepting the reality of what is really there. Until a person accepts what is actually there and takes responsibility for it, he has no chance of ever changing it. Branden emphasizes the importance of asserting oneself as being exactly who one is. This is not easy if the person does not like who he is, but it opens the door to change. Self-esteem that is based on pretending to be someone else is a form of pseudo self-esteem that is perpetually vulnerable to collapsing into shame.

Self-Esteem in a Relationship

The Shame-Pride Axis describes the affects that underlie the continuum of self-esteem. But self-esteem is not just the affects directed at the self; it is a composite view of the self that is contained within a coherent set of affect-laden scripts. Self-esteem is a set of emotions related to the self. In an intimate relationship, partners have a very high level of access to each other's self-emotions. This gives them a degree of influence over each other's self-esteem. Ultimately, high self-esteem comes from within the individual, and a negative view from the partner does little damage to someone who has a sound, positive view of himself that is based in reality and his own willingness to look at himself critically. Unfortunately, many people do not have a positive, reality based view of themselves. Their positive feelings about themselves are precarious, and a negative view from the partner can activate their own negative views of themselves.

Similarly, people with moderate self-esteem may be able to find a temporary boost from their partners' positive views of them. But such boosts in self-esteem are transitory; a momentary positive view from anyone cannot change an individual's fundamental view of himself. A lasting positive view from someone the person respects can be a helpful influence, but a dependence upon the partner's positive view is a recipe for the kinds of problems discussed in this book. Improving one's self-esteem is ultimately the job of the individual—a job that every one of us faces in life! However, this does not mean that the partner cannot help. First and foremost, the partner can cease doing the kinds of things that activate the other partner's shameful views of self. The partner also can help in other ways, as long as both partners clearly understand that changing one's self-esteem is ultimately the responsibility of the individual.

Preserving Self-Esteem in Social Situations

The primary challenges to preserving esteem occur in social situations, where shame can be activated by a perception of disapproval from others.[5] Shame and poor self-esteem are not the same thing, but frequent activation of shame in social situations has a corrosive effect on self-esteem. To the extent that an individual is sensitive to criticism and disapproval from others, he needs to work on preparing himself for these situations. Here are some tools that help.

The Right Attitude. The essential attitude to be fostered is to learn to not take things personally. Admittedly, this is much easier said than done, but it is the goal that shame-sensitive individuals should strive to achieve. It may help to recognize that anyone who directs much disapproval toward others is dealing with some internal issue of his own (usually involving shame) and externalizing it. The shame-sensitive person must remind himself that objective criticism is useful, but an excess of affective messages of disapproval is more about the person sending the message.

Sensory Focusing. Self-consciousness is a major component of shame in social situations.[6] People who have had many bad experiences in social situations are prone to be more self-conscious. Unfortunately, thinking about how he must appear to others only primes a person's tendency to enter a shame state. The solution is to change his focus. In social situations, the shame-prone person should focus on the other people, the task at hand, or the immediate sensory experience. Changing one's focus becomes easier with practice. A good forum for developing this capacity is mindfulness meditation, which teaches people to focus on their senses and allow their thoughts to fade into the background.[7] Simply shifting the self from foreground to background can eliminate self-consciousness and give the shame-prone person a greater chance of success in social situations.

Energy Bubble. Hypnotherapist Robert Schwarz (2002) has developed a useful device for people who work well with visual imagery. He teaches his clients to imagine a bubble of energy surrounding them, a shield of sorts. The client learns to intensify the shield when needed in social situations. The shame-prone person can use an imagined energy shield to filter out and repel messages of disapproval, while allowing accepting messages to pass through untouched. This is a form of boundary; the visual imagery gives more substance to the person's goal of maintaining a boundary with others.

These are just some of the kinds of techniques that people use to maintain their self-esteem in social situations. Many therapists have their own repertoire of techniques. *The shame-prone person must contend with two challenges in social situations: affective messages of disapproval and his own anxiety about encountering those messages.* Simply having some mechanisms to withstand disapproval messages can reduce the anxiety about encountering them.

Changing one's self-esteem takes place in small steps over time, the same way that a person changes his view of himself in acquiring a skill or ability, such as playing a musical instrument. At any given point, he may not be able to see any progress, but over time the difference is discernable. And, just as with acquiring a new skill (or any other form of personal growth), it is critically important that the person feel free to make mistakes in the process.

Other-Esteem

This section is about the things people can do to facilitate the development of their partner's positive esteem, but I am going to begin with a discussion of the use of shame in healthy relationships. I just noted that partners can help by not doing the kinds of things that activate the other partner's shameful views of self. But this does not mean that partners must take tremendous care to never activate each other's shame! Shame is an inevitable part of every intimate relationship. Indeed, shame is part of what holds the relationship together. Virtually all partners utilize shame in their dealings with each other.

I never see the professional literature acknowledge this important aspect of shame, and I think it needs to be recognized because we are so prone to view all attempts at instilling shame as destructive. I have never encountered a couple in which the partners did not attempt to influence each other through inducing shame.

Inducing Shame

Almost everyone is aware of the destructive consequences of shaming, but the fact is that almost everyone tries to induce their partners' shame at times. The attempt to activate another's shame is a common means of trying to influence others—especially in an intimate relationship. When he calls and says he's going to be late and her voice takes on that hurt tone, she is aiming to influence him through his shame whether she realizes it or not. If she complains and he comments that nothing satisfies her, he is trying to shame her into silence. When he says he's going to play golf for the tenth Saturday in a row and she says that's fine, she'll clean his car for him since he's so busy, she may be trying to induce his shame or she may be just showing her love. When he asks if she's going to wear *that* dress to his parents' house, he may be trying to activate her shame and get her to wear something else. The primary trigger in these inducement situations is, of course, affective tone, but the result—that is, whether the recipient changes his behavior in a positive manner or whether he goes into a destructive shame state—depends upon what scripts are activated from the person's internal library of shame scripts.

Using Shame to Influence

One reason that shame so often becomes a weapon in relationships is because it is also a tool in relationships. Like any tool, the use of shame inducement can be productive or destructive. If what the person wants is only to make himself feel superior or to win a fight (or any other unsavory reason), the outcome can be the activation of the partner's scripts of Bad Self. But often a partner appeals to the other partner's capacity for shame in hopes of bringing out the best in the partner. Remember, our capacity for shame is a significant part of our ability to be honest, good citizens. For example, consider a situation in which Rob and Gwen were alone in a part of the world that they will never see again.

They were camping in a beautiful national park. They had accumulated trash and were thus faced with a choice to bag up the garbage and carry it to a place where they could dispose of it properly or to just litter the ground at their campsite where they would never have to look at it again anyway. There was no one around to enforce the rules and Rob knew they would never get caught if they just left the garbage. It is our capacity for shame that prevents us from leaving a pile of litter for strangers to encounter. Rob was tempted to ignore what he knew was the proper choice when Gwen appealed to his capacity for shame. "You're not planning to leave that for someone else to clean up, are you?"

Gwen was trying to influence Rob by inducing his sense of shame. She was not doing this to further her own goals or obtain self-esteem or pride at Rob's expense, she was simply trying to help him do the right thing and be able to feel good about himself. In this case, Rob took that twinge of shame in stride and carried their trash out. However, if this couple had a history of destructive shame inducement—for instance, if Gwen often tried to make Rob feel guilty—then he might have experienced this particular episode differently. It could have activated some of his Bad Self scripts and led to trouble between them, and the nature of that trouble would primarily be determined by Rob's manner of reacting to the activation of his shame.

How do we induce shame in others? The healthy direction is to appeal to the person's own standards, as in the above example. Problems come when one partner induces the other's shame for his own personal benefit, whether to make himself feel better or to establish control over the other partner.

Negative Forms of Inducing Shame

Partners can help each other to develop better self-esteem by striving *not* to induce the other partner's shameful views of self. Since the inducement of healthy shame is an inevitable component of most relationships, I will identify the most common forms of destructive shame inducement. *The essence of a shame-inducing interaction is that the shame-inducing partner says or does something that reveals or seems to imply a view of the other that contains a negative affect.* A variety of different emotions can be conveyed in that view, but some aspect of the emotion will touch on the disapproval end of the Disapproval-Acceptance Axis. A destructive inducement process leads to the activation of a shame-laden view of self (Bad Self). For example, if he shows fear of her, he may trigger one of her Bad Self scripts in which she views herself as an angry person whom others wish to avoid.

In the example, fear is the inducing affect and it *implies* a negative view of the other person. However, the more common route to inducing a partner's most shameful views of self are direct revelations of a negative view possessed by the other partner. The most common emotions used to reveal these negative views are *anger, disappointment*, and *disgust*. And, of course, the context and behaviors surrounding the emotions influence the message as well. Here are some of the ways that intimate partners influence each other (consciously or unconsciously) by inducing shame. Many of these may not always result in the activation of destructively shameful views of self, but they each have that potential.

> *Getting Hurt*: This is probably the largest category. Partners often induce shame in each other by indicating that the other partner has hurt them in some fashion. Sometimes, partners can fall into a pattern of overacting when they are hurt. When they do this, the goal is to make the other partner feel bad for doing something hurtful, whether the hurt partner is conscious of this goal or not.
>
> *Implied Disapproval*: These are usually behaviors that imply that the other partner is *not* something (i.e., considerate, a hard worker, smart, and so forth). There are many variants on this behavior, such as the guilt-induction attributed to parents who induce shame by playing the martyr ("Go on out and have a good time, I'll just sit here in the dark alone."). Some people become very talented at the insidious technique of implied disapproval, and they can be very difficult to confront as they claim innocent motives. Indeed, confrontation often seems to make things worse because the partner being confronted claims innocence and *implies* that the offended partner is just too sensitive.
>
> *Killing With Kindness*: Individuals who have difficulty being directly aggressive will often influence their partners by being so self-sacrificing that the partner will hopefully feel bad for getting away with so much. If the partner doing the sacrificing is conveying some negative affect about the other partner, such as anger, then the sacrificing takes on the tone of martyr behavior and the partner is usually wise to it. However, if the sacrificing partner is not angry, then he is simply relying on her to feel compelled (by her shame) to correct the imbalance in the relationship. Thus, this strategy can be positive or negative, depending upon whether the negative affect is present.
>
> *Sarcasm*: Most sarcasm in an intimate relationship is an attempt to make the partner feel shame. For example, profusely thanking the partner for minor or expected contributions can be a comment on how little they do. Being patronizing has a similar effect.

Refusing Help: Another way of conveying that the partner is not contributing enough in a relationship is by refusing their help when it is offered (especially if there is an angry tone to the refusal). When a partner's help is clearly needed yet not accepted, he generally feels shame.

Making Unkind Comparisons: He generally induces her shame when he compares her to people whom he knows she dislikes or toward whom she has negative feelings ("You're being just like your mother/father/boss.").

A Look Loaded With Affect: A look that conveys disgust or anger is a common shame-inducing tactic between partners. Due to affective resonance, partners are highly attuned to nonverbal messages from each other. They may recognize and react to those messages when others might miss them entirely.

Feigning Shame for the Partner: He reacts to situations that might cause her to feel shame as though the situation has caused him to feel shame. This is a common shame-inducement strategy in families that are not well differentiated and is frequently employed by parents trying to influence their children. The implied message is that the source of the shame is so powerful that she certainly should feel shame about it because it is so shame-laden that he feels it simply as a result of his connection to her.

Direct Attacks: A more direct route to inducing shame in one's partner is to accuse him of behaving shamefully ("You're being insensitive" or "You only care about yourself."). Sometimes this is accomplished by putting the shameful accusation in other people's mouths ("Everyone thinks ..." or "Your sister always said ..."). In any case, the direct attack is always accompanied by powerful affect—usually anger, disappointment, or disgust—and usually occurs within the context of a fight.

Criticism, Stonewalling, and Contempt: Three of John Gottman's "Four Horsemen of the Apocalypse" (the other is defensiveness) are shame-inducing mechanisms. The most common is criticism. When one partner criticizes the other, the goal is to influence, and the mechanism is the inducement of shame. Of course, most of the time it provokes defensiveness rather than accommodation. Though the partner who stonewalls usually justifies his behavior as a means of avoiding conflict, again it is at least partially an attempt to induce shame in the other partner. But the most lethal effort to induce shame in an intimate relationship is the expression of contempt (usually containing disgust affect). This is often the death knell of a relationship.[8] Unlike criticism, contempt leaves no room for the partner to correct his behavior and become acceptable once more.

Needless to say, this is not an exclusive list of the destructive ways in which partners resort to trying to influence each other. Indeed, the ways in which partners can induce each other's shame seems to be limited only by the bounds of their creativity. Now we will look further at the ways in which partners can help each other in their efforts to develop better self-esteem.

Approval Versus Recognition and Acceptance

> When a baby finds that her signals are validated and responded to appropriately—that troubles are soothed and pleasures enhanced—she begins to sense that her feelings, expressions of her very being, are of value and important.
>
> **Holinger & Doner, 2003, p. 82**

When a child's affective life is generally accepted, he grows up generally accepting himself. If the adults are adept at recognizing the variety of the child's emotional states, then he learns to recognize the range of his emotions. Adults can (and should) accept all facets of a child's affective life, while still distinguishing behaviors that are not acceptable. The recognition and acceptance of his affective experience facilitates the development of the child's authentic self.

Many parents try to banish negative feelings in their children ("You're not really angry at your brother."). The child then grows up without access to part of himself. If the breadth of his emotional life is not recognized or accepted, a child can grow up feeling invisible.[9] No one sees who he is, they only tell him who he should or should not be. In order to fit the approved model, the child usually disowns part of his affective experience. Indeed, without the aid of an empathic adult, the child not only disowns but fails to recognize many aspects of his affective experience. At best, the richness of his affective life lies on the periphery of his awareness.

To accept someone is to acknowledge the reality of who and what they are. I once treated a couple in which the wife had led a very active sexual life before the marriage, but the husband had not. He always said that he did not want to know anything about her life before they got together. He was a gentle and accepting husband, but the wife still did not feel accepted. She felt that his refusal to hear about her earlier life indicated that he disapproved of it, and, consequently, she did not feel emotionally safe in the marriage. He thought he was being accepting by never talking about her earlier life, but to her, his avoidance of the topic was a kind of denial of who she was. She had a need for him to know about her background, even though she knew he would not approve of some of it. She wanted acceptance more than the appearance of approval.

Sometimes we emphasize how people try to change their partners rather than accept them. This may be a slightly different use of the word acceptance, but it still differs from approval. People who try to change their partners seldom, if ever, succeed because people resist being changed from the outside. Real change comes from the inside—the same way that positive self-esteem develops. Most therapists would agree that few people change until they feel accepted. But we are not saying that people do not change until they feel approved! We simply accept people for who and what they are, and we acknowledge that we cannot change them. It is only when the emperor accepts that he is indeed naked that he can recognize his need to get into some clothes.[10] *Partners help each other to develop better self-esteem when they accept each other for who and what they are.*

Managing Self-Emotions

Intimate partners have such power to trigger each other because of the phenomenon of affective resonance. Yet some individuals remain close despite the appearance of negative affect from their partners by strengthening their empathic walls and reducing their sensitivity to their partners' affect displays. Most people do have some ability to erect their empathic walls—so why do some couples remain in almost continual conflict? Surely it would be preferable to simply put up a stronger empathic wall, even if it meant a less satisfying experience of closeness in the relationship. The answer involves the mechanisms by which many people learn to manage their emotions.

Our capacity to manage our emotions is quite limited when we are infants and young children. Since there is social pressure on us to quickly learn to moderate our affective display, we employ whatever mechanisms can help. For example, a common mechanism is to tense up and fight the display of affect. This is referred to through euphemisms such as gritting your teeth, biting your tongue, or keeping a stiff upper lip (these euphemisms all capture our physically constraining expression via the mouth). But it is the management of negative emotions about the *self* that poses the greatest problem. Infants and young children do not have adequate mechanisms to help manage their feelings about themselves, they must rely upon their caretakers to help them. The child's view of self is primarily determined by the caretaker's view of the child. In a sense, the child might be said to be channeling his view of himself through his perception of the caretaker's view of him.

Healthy emotional development entails a decreased reliance on the other's view and an increased reliance on one's own view of self. The primary obstacle to healthy development in this regard is when the adult caretaker has failed to make this fundamental step himself. In such cases, the caretaker still cannot manage his own feelings about himself without using another person. When an adult caretaker relies upon a dependent child's view of him in order to maintain positive feelings about himself, the child is not free to have negative feelings about the caretaker!

When the parent is emotionally immature, the child is prohibited from experiencing distrust-related feelings. When the child experiences distrust, he is punished by the parent's reaction. It is the equivalent of the marital fight, but it occurs in a relationship in which one party has all the power. A child being raised by immature caretakers must tread very carefully—if she displays negative affect toward the caretaker, she will trigger the caretaker's shame and the caretaker will react negatively, often doing something that will activate the child's shame.

This channeling of one's view of self through others will predominate in a family if the adults resort to it. However, if the adults are effectively able to tolerate the child's displays of distrust without being triggered, then the child learns to regulate her affective states and increasingly learns to evaluate herself according to her own internal standards. But if the adults are overly reactive to the child's distrust—meaning their shame is triggered—the child cannot relinquish an excessive concern with the other's view.

Emotional Fusion

Bill and Jennifer described one of their fights. They were planning their weekend and Jennifer commented that Bill never gets up before nine on Saturdays. Bill felt the comment was a jab and began to argue with her about it (in our session, Jennifer insisted the comment was completely inno-cent; she was simply making an observation). Bill argued that he used his time more efficiently than Jennifer and brought up how much time is wasted on cleaning up Jennifer's messes. Jennifer was hurt; she felt Bill was inten-tionally attacking her, and she tried to convince Bill that she was not that messy. In making her argument that she was not that messy, she compared herself to Bill and noted several messes that he had created. They launched into a recurring argument about Jennifer's messiness and never got around to planning the weekend. Indeed, they were each angry and spent the week-end avoiding each other.

Psychiatrist Murray Bowen (1978) developed the concept of *differentiation* to refer to a continuum of emotional separation that ranges from one's ability to view oneself objectively to one's complete subjectivity (which always includes reactivity to the other's view). Kerr and Bowen (1988) used the term *emotional fusion* to describe relationships in which each individual is highly reactive to the other's affect. The most common conflict that occurs in emotionally fused relationships is the closeness-distance struggle, in which "one partner presses for greater involvement, intimacy, or closeness while the other strives for more disengagement, separateness, or distance" (Pistole, 1994, p. 147).[11] From the point of view of the emotional safety model, the underlying problem in emotionally fused relationships occurs in the esteem realm. Each partner is unable to maintain good self-esteem if he perceives the other partner to be experiencing disapproval.[12] This excessive concern with the other's view is invariably the case with highly conflictual couples.[13]

The underlying problem is emotional immaturity. These people have diffi-culty maintaining a good feeling about themselves (i.e., activating pride scripts rather than shame scripts) and are highly reactive to the feelings they perceive their partners to be having about them.[14] They are easily triggered into their shame, which causes problems in their relationships, but the bigger problem is when they try to solve their shame proneness by attempting to control how their intimate others see them. This both creates conflict in the relationship and reinforces a feeling of helplessness in the shame-prone individual because he experiences his feelings as being controlled by others.

All intimate relationships involve some level of emotional reactivity. The healthy end of the continuum of emotional fusion is not indifference (the stonewalling defense is an effort to be indifferent). Rather, a healthy distance is a combination of affective resonance and empathic wall (i.e., being able to remain emotionally close without being excessively reactive). Individuals who have a preponderance of shame and are too reliant on the other person's posi-tive regard in order to feel good about themselves are seldom able to do this. But even people with strong pride scripts have a certain amount of emotional reactivity in their intimate relationships. *Partners help each other to develop better self-esteem when they operate from the clear understanding that they are separate and different people, each with his or her own unique standards.*

Preoccupation With Approval

Since less differentiated people are more concerned with their partners' views of them, they are quick to have their negative self scripts (Bad Self) activated if they perceive disapproval affect in the partners' views of them. To protect themselves from the power of the partners' disapproval, they either *remain distant, fight to change the partner's view,* or *sacrifice their individuality* in order to receive approval. We have focused on those who either distance or engage in repetitive conflict because they come for couple therapy, but the ones who sacrifice their individuality pay an enormous individual price (espe-cially in the realm of self-esteem) and often seek individual therapy. They have adopted the strategy of managing their potential for shame by avoiding dif-ferentness. Often they come from families in which the members cope with potential shame by focusing on shared approval ("We're each okay because we all agree that this is the proper way to be.").[15]

The need for approval stifles the development of individuality among fam-ily members; anything one member says or does can be perceived as a poten-tial comment on the other members. A member's assertion of his individuality is easily interpreted as a statement of disapproval of the other members. For example, everyone in one family drove American-made automobiles. When the oldest daughter purchased a foreign car, the other members demanded to know what was wrong with American cars, as though her personal choice was an expression of disapproval of their choices.

Sometimes these families sacrifice the esteem of one member by treating his differentness as bad (thereby reinforcing that the rest of them are good). Or, in many cases, no one gets singled out as bad, but everyone grows up unable to maintain their self-esteem without the approval of others. They live in fear of being exposed and never have the satisfaction of feeling fully accepted. Generally, their capacity for intimacy is stunted.

People who base their good feelings about themselves on their partner's positive view of them inevitably become highly reactive to any indication that the partner has a negative (disapproving) view. And partners who encourage each other to be overly concerned with the disapproval of people outside the relationship ("What will the neighbors think?") are undermining each other's growth toward better self-esteem. The latter is a popular parenting message, but the distance from the necessary socialization of children to an unhealthy preoccupation with the possibility of disapproval is not large. *Partners help each other to develop better self-esteem when they operate from the clear understanding that they only require acceptance, not approval, from each other.*

Boundaries

Therapists often emphasize the importance of boundaries with couples. Appropriate boundaries are a central component of what keeps relationships safe and prevents couples from becoming fused. But boundaries are often misunderstood, particularly when employed by people who tend toward fused or enmeshed relationships. Some people erect walls, which are not boundaries, and some people employ rigid rules, which are not boundaries, and some people try to control their partners, which are not boundaries. One way of thinking about boundaries is that they involve maintaining freedom of choice. A partner may choose to tolerate some things and refuse to tolerate other things from his partner. As long as those things (which he is or is not tolerating) involve him, then he is exercising his right to establish a boundary. However, if those things only involve his partner, then he is trying to control his partner. Thus, he is exercising his right to impose a boundary if he refuses to attend certain activities with her, but he is trying to control her if he forbids her to attend those activities without him.

Mickey and Fiona had a mismatched marriage. Fiona was terribly concerned with displeasing Mickey, and Mickey was overly concerned with Fiona's personal choices. Mickey did not like the clothes that Fiona wore because the colors were too bright and attracted too much attention. Early in their marriage, he objected to her behavior at a party because she was too outspoken and got into a heated exchange with one of her colleagues. He gave her disapproving looks when she disagreed with him over issues that were ultimately only a matter of taste or opinion. Over time, Fiona quit wearing bright colors, became quiet at parties, and grew progressively more submissive in her relationship with Mickey. She also became increasingly more unhappy.

Mickey insisted that what he was doing was applying appropriate boundaries by not tolerating Fiona's "inappropriate" behaviors (Mickey was a mental health professional). In my opinion, Mickey was upset by their differences and responded by trying to control his partner. Rather than manifesting "appropriate boundaries," Mickey was intruding into Fiona's personal choices, her ways of expressing who she was. Fiona also manifested poor boundaries by submitting to Mickey. Over time, this led to a diminishment in her feelings about herself.

The essence of good boundaries is the ability to say no. People who have difficulty saying no (such as Fiona) become increasingly restricted in their ability to maintain closeness in their relationships. Since they can't say no, they must maintain distance in order to protect themselves. Without that distance, they are vulnerable to giving up too much of themselves. People who can say no are free to get as close to their partners as they wish, secure in the knowledge that all they have to do is say no if the partner tries to steer them in a direction that they do not want to take.

Wanda was forever trying to please Wayne. She went so far as to have extensive plastic surgery because Wayne wanted her body to be different. Unfortunately, no amount of change seemed to satisfy him. In couple therapy, he revealed that one of the things he most wanted her to change was the way she deferred to him about everything. He felt he never got to see the real Wanda. This created a dilemma for Wanda, because she came to see that she too had never seen the real Wanda. She had spent her life trying to be what everyone else wanted her to be, and she really didn't know "who she was." She eventually found that the path out of her dilemma was not located in figuring out "who she was" but in what she wanted. Gradually, she began to focus on her choices, including saying no when she objected to a choice that Wayne wanted her to make.

This process took a long time. Wayne discovered that he wanted her to be more real with him, but he didn't really want her to disagree with him. And Wanda discovered that holding on to her own sense of what she wanted was not easy. She would have periods of feeling she finally knew what she wanted, only to have her sense of clarity collapse all over again. But over time, Wanda became more real, and Wayne found that he preferred this Wanda.

It was to Wayne's credit that he ultimately supported Wanda in her efforts to make her own choices, even when he disagreed with some of those choices.

At times he tried to coerce her into choices that he thought were best for her, and sometimes his coercive efforts produced feelings of shame in Wanda. But she persevered in taking charge of her life, and she needed to make her own mistakes in the process. Helping people take control of their own sense of choice can be difficult. It can appear to be a move toward selfishness, especially if the partner is threatened by the change and attacks the assertion of choice. Sometimes the person acquiring his or her sense of choice overdoes it and says no to everything.[16] This can be very disheartening to the partner. The intimate relationship is truly strengthened when each partner can *choose* to overrule his or her own wishes in order to please the other partner, but this only works if the person freely chooses to overrule his or her own wishes, rather than doing so because the person feels compelled to please the partner.

Acquiring good boundaries does not mean saying no to everything that the person doesn't like; it means having choice. The person can choose to say no, or the person can choose to accommodate the partner's needs.

Respecting Differentness

I like to sleep with the window open and you keep the window closed, so goodbye, goodbye, goodbye.

Paul Simon, "You're Kind"

Having good boundaries is important in relationships because people have so many differences. Individuals differ in their views of childrearing, adequacy of lifestyle, financial priorities, choice of friends, allegiance to family of origin, political and religious beliefs, and many other arenas that come up in intimate relationships. Some people come from families that are very emotionally expressive, while others come from families in which no one ever raises his voice or sheds a tear. The range of conceivable differences is immense, and all have the potential for relationship-ending conflict, whether it is about a decision to have children or to sleep with the window open. None of these differences are about shame. Yet people can have shame about all of these differences.

There are solutions to many, but not all, conflicts and differences in intimate relationships. For the couple that is heavily influenced by their shame and their need to avoid it, a difference like wanting the window open versus closed can lead to relationship-ending conflict. Another couple may choose to sleep in different rooms and accept the consequences without it making an appreciable impact on the relationship. Some conflicts, such as two people who are adamantly opposed about having children, can only be resolved one way or the other. And some issues are so profoundly important that people will break up a relationship because they cannot accept the only solutions their partners can tolerate. But the majority of issues can be resolved, even though one or the other partner may have to accommodate, sacrifice, or otherwise not get his or her way.

There is no shame in one partner "giving in" to the other, as long as there is some kind of fair balance in the big picture, and as long as the partner doing the giving *chooses* to do so. Chrys Harris (2004) has written about the positive value of sacrifice in a relationship. When one partner chooses to sacrifice for the other, there is no giving in. The real issue is respect. Most of the problems in the realm of esteem disappear in an atmosphere of respect. *Disrespect activates shame in a partner, but respect counters shame.* When one partner shows respect for the other, it is a way of relating to the other partner's pride scripts and ignoring the shame scripts. When he fails to relate to her as a whole person, responsible for herself and her actions, or when he fails to be a whole person himself, then he is being disrespectful. When he deals with her openly and honestly, not pretending that either of them is without shame, then he brings respect into the relationship.

End the Use of Criticism to Influence

Many partners who are caught in negative cycles have fallen into patterns of using negative affect to influence each other. They initially resort to expressions of disapproval because they feel powerless to influence each other. After a while, the reliance on negative affect becomes the norm. Gottman (1999) emphasizes the value of learning to complain instead of criticize (i.e., to clearly convey what it is that one finds objectionable without making it the other partner that is objectionable). This is similar to Haim Ginott's (1965) classic advice to parents to find fault with a child's behavior but not the child's character.

When partners have fallen into the habit of trying to influence each other via criticism, their needs tend to get ignored. Critical comments are frequently a result of one partner wanting or needing something from the other, as with the hostile protest response to attachment threat. Most of these sentiments can be expressed as a request rather than a criticism. "You're not paying enough attention to me" has a negative impact; "I need more attention" has a greater likelihood of producing the desired response. John Gottman (1999) and Susan Johnson (1996/2005) both emphasize the importance of softening the tone and language of such requests.

The Value of Being Valued

> To love someone is not first of all to do things for them,
> but to reveal to them their beauty and value,
> . to say to them through our attitude:
> "You are beautiful. Your are important. I trust you. You can trust yourself."

Jean Vanier, 1992, p 16.

It is not one person's responsibility to make another adult feel good about himself, but the emotional safety model emphasizes the influence partners have on each other's self-esteem. They each have a responsibility to convey messages that activate pride rather than shame in each other. In general, partners can provide each other with the *perception of being positively regarded*. One of the fundamental tasks of loving someone is to see the best in that person—especially when the person cannot see it in him- or herself! This is not a form of denial in which a person refuses to see his partner's shortcomings. Rather, it is a choice to focus on positives instead of negatives in order to help the partner be his best self. Each partner should strive to relate to the other partner's best self, not his shameful self!

There is a body of research that supports and explains the value of regarding the partner positively.[17] People who have a sense of being positively regarded by their partners have better relationships and are better partners themselves. When conflict arises in their relationship, those people who feel valued respond by drawing closer to their partners. They do not respond by increasing the conflict and distance in the relationship. They are less easily hurt, less reactive to minor indications of disapproval, bounce back from difficulties, and are more resilient.

In the next chapter we will look at how partners help each other to overcome problems with shame and low self-esteem. Part of overcoming Bad Self views of self involves being held in positive regard by someone that matters. When one partner relates to the other's best self, she helps him to be more of that self. A loving mother sees the good child that deserves love, despite whatever surface behaviors exist that might make the child appear undeserving. A loving partner does not lose sight of who the other partner is capable of being.

Shame and the Safe Zone

The esteem realm of the safe zone is marked by respect. When a couple's safe zone grows, they find more opportunities for connection, because each partner can be more open and vulnerable. Some people try to avoid esteem threats by controlling their partners. Their goal is to avoid the possibility of ever having their shame triggered, but that path leads to the endless fight; it never increases the safe zone. The only effective way to increase the safe zone is to: (a) decrease each partner's sensitivity to being triggered by the other partner (mostly by increasing their empathic walls), (b) reduce the power of each partner's shame by developing pride scripts and disassembling shame scripts, and (c) learn more adaptive ways to deal with shame when it is triggered. *The most adaptive way to deal with shame when it appears in one's intimate relationship is to go into it and act on it rather than avoid it or react to it.*

When partners aspire to have a safer relationship, they must do what feels counterintuitive. They must bring their shame *into* the relationship instead of trying to forever keep it out. This frees them to experience their healthy shame, which largely remains blocked as long as they're trying to fend off their pathological shame. Ironically, healthy shame plays a major role in helping partners to heal the myriad little injuries that are an inevitable part of all relationships. When he openly experiences his healthy shame, she can then see that he truly cares. Finally, for the individual to both improve his self-esteem and keep his intimate relationship in the safe zone, he must relinquish his need to change his partner's perception of him.

14
Repairing Damaged Esteem

The vast majority of repetitive conflict in intimate relationships occurs in the realm of esteem. Partners clash as they try to defend their honor and either change the way they are being portrayed or avoid the person who portrays them in an undesirable way. When shame is activated and a person's self-esteem is threatened, many people move into a survival mode in which preserving their self-esteem takes priority over everything else. As important as relationships are, as powerful as attachment is, some intimate partners will go so far as to destroy the attachment relationship itself in order to protect their self-esteem. Such is the power of shame emotion and the desperate feeling that can be activated by perceived threats to the self.

Attempting to escape pathological shame is a never-ending task, but shame-burdened people can engage their shame, gradually disassemble the shame scripts, build pride scripts, and open up their capacity for healthy shame. Every person with significant shame is carrying some distorted views of himself. These distorted views (Bad Self) can change only if he will dare to be open enough to take in his partner's view of him. If his shame is based on genuine shortcomings in his character, then he can work to overcome those shortcomings. If he has unhealthy shame reactions that are creating problems in the relationship, he can change those by staying with his shame and owning it rather than fleeing from it. And if his life is twisted as a result of his efforts to avoid his shame, that too can change with self-acceptance.

Of course, change does not come easy; it requires two things: the courage to confront oneself and a partner who is willing to hang in there and not add to the person's shame while he delves into the forbidden reaches of his worst feelings about himself.

Sources of Shame

There are two sources of shame scripts in an intimate relationship: those that precede the relationship and those that develop within the relationship. Scripts that precede the relationship predominate, though they may be modified and reinforced by events within the relationship. Less frequent are scripts that develop solely within the relationship, but they do occur at times. However, most of the significant shame scripts that populate the realm of esteem stem from childhood, often with revisions and refinements developed throughout the person's life.

Healing Shame

There are two dimensions to healing shame: revising and overcoming the shame scripts, which is an individual task that is facilitated by a sensitive partner, and getting control of the partner's interactions that activate those scripts, which is a shared task with specific work for each individual. In some cases, simply getting control of the negative interactions is enough to allow a couple to move into the safe zone and live comfortably. But in severe cases, no amount of interactive change is sufficient; partners with extensive shame scripts must work on themselves to overcome their legacy of shame. The second task always applies: All effective treatment of shame in couples involves the shared task of getting control of the negative interactions. The first task depends upon the severity of each individual's issues with shame: In cases of severe shame, individuals must work to revise and overcome their legacy of destructive shame scripts. And even when an individual must work on his personal shame scripts, the partner helps there as well—not only by avoiding negative interactions but also by providing healing interactions.

This chapter will focus on each aspect of healing shame—the interactive and the individual. However, the focus on individual work should not be interpreted to mean that an individual partner can cure himself on his own. When an individual is attempting to revise and overcome his personal shame scripts, he requires a relational context. Shame cannot be overcome in a vacuum. If a person cannot do that work with his partner, then he must seek some other relationship. *Whether it be a professional therapist, a men's group, or an Alcoholic's Anonymous sponsor, the individual who chooses to confront his shame must do so before the eyes of another human being.* Only then can he be liberated enough to truly live without fear of being exposed.

Relating to the Individual With Shame: The Therapist's Role

Shame emotion disconnects us from the people around us, and healing shame requires connection with another. This is the most fundamental and essential aspect of healing shame; there is no substitute for a human connection. Shame cannot heal in isolation! The shame scripts can only change when the individual engages in an intimate connection with someone who can both see his shame and also see beyond it.

Sometimes it helps to talk through the early events that spawned the shame scripts; other times it seems to help more to focus on current life.[1] In either case, therapists must continually help the person experiencing shame to see that although he has a problem with shame, that does *not* mean there is something fundamentally wrong with him. His shame scripts say that something *is* fundamentally wrong with him (and that is his reality when he is in the grip of shame affect); it is only through a sustained connection with someone who absolutely believes otherwise that this belief can ever change.

When we relate to the shame-prone person, we have to relate from the perspective that we are all human beings and subject to difficulties in life, including our personal sources of shame. Psychologist Carl Goldberg (1991) says that the therapist has to be in touch with her own shame in order to connect to the shame-prone person. We cannot hide behind a professional facade and help someone with shame. When I first encountered Goldberg's assertion, I wasn't exactly sure what it really meant to be in touch with my own shame, much less how that would help me connect with the shame-prone person. The more I have worked with people who are struggling with shame, the more I have come to appreciate the essential truth of that assertion. For me, it means maintaining a shared understanding with my clients that experiencing shame is an inevitable part of the human condition, and no one is immune, including me. I may not share the chronic, disabling shame that some of my clients experience, but I can still understand and relate to their experiences because I too experience moments of intense shame.

Some people have developed techniques for dealing with shame, but I have had limited success with techniques in this area. Instead, I repeatedly find that the most important variable in helping someone with shame is the quality of our relationship. The essence of that healing connection is that I must never lose touch with the fact that I am dealing with a person who *has* shame, not a person who *is* shame, not a person who has something fundamentally wrong with him or her.[2] The person with severe shame cannot make that distinction when he is in the grip of shame affect. But *repeated contact with someone he trusts who sees him in his shame and yet maintains a view of him as being fundamentally okay as a human being*—this is how lifelong scripts are altered. This is also the power of an intimate relationship and why a partner will fight like his very survival depends upon it if he feels he is being seen as not okay as a human being.

The Inner Voice of Shame

For experience to become meaningful requires that bodily excitations, including the archaic affects of infancy, be given mental representation by a transitional parental figure.

Donald Kalsched, 1996, p. 37

People who were seriously abused or neglected in childhood typically have very severe shame scripts. Often they have learned to protect themselves from this severe, disabling shame by developing an inner voice whose job is to anticipate every possible activator of shame. This voice criticizes the person, predicts the worse, and does everything possible to anticipate trouble (in the form of shame) before it happens.[3] Donald Kalsched (1996) notes how this personalization of affects leads to a powerful internal tormenter among people who were traumatized as children. In a monumental display of irony, the internal voice of trauma protects the person from further fear by terrorizing him. Similarly, the internal voice of shame protects the person from further shame by constantly wielding the threat of intense shame. Both kinds of internal voice utilize negative affects to influence the person for purposes of protection, and both usually result from experiences in early childhood before the person developed more adaptive coping mechanisms.

Many authors have described this powerful inner voice, though they do not link it to shame. But they always describe the voice as extremely critical. Several authors have developed techniques for dealing with this negative form of self-talk, and the techniques are very similar—they give the voice some form of external manifestation in a fashion similar to the gestalt work of Fritz Perls (1972, 1992). Hal and Sidra Stone (1993) have developed an approach they call voice dialogue, in which the client is induced to speak from the inner critic's point of view (as well as others). Richard Schwartz (1997) has developed a theoretical model that employs a similar approach, inner family systems therapy (IFS), in which the critical inner voice is encouraged to speak. As with voice dialogue, the IFS approach also addresses other inner voices and emphasizes the protective function of the critical inner voice. Peter Thomas (2003) has identified many of the same components of self-talk in his internal protection model, but his theoretical focus is on the internal working models proposed by Bowlby (1969). Thomas (2005) also gives voice to the internal critic and has suggested role playing with the therapist adopting the inner critic's role. His model emphasizes the lack of emotional safety as a key factor in the development of the critical inner voice.

It may be that we all have inner voices of shame, and most of us just don't recognize that we have such internal voices because our internal voices are not as pronounced as those of people with pathological shame. However, for many people with chronic shame, the inner voice is a very real and distressing experience. Worse yet, the voice has authority (based on the person's fear of shame affect), and the person learns to believe what the voice says. Most authors report that the critical inner voice usually sounds like the parent who was most critical.

In therapy, we must educate these people about the fact that this inner voice is only expressing a point of view, and *its power comes from the person's assumption that what the voice says is always right* (that assumption is magnified by shame affect). As the person learns to recognize the voice and understand that its goal is to protect, then the individual can challenge its authority. Ultimately, however, the shame-bound person must be able to prove to himself (and therefore to his critical inner voice) that he can protect himself without the need for the harsh self-criticism.

The existence of an inner voice of shame has a profound impact on an intimate relationship and will often surface in couple therapy if the therapist is inclined to look for it. But it is not easily swayed. For that reason, individuals with harsh inner voices of shame usually require intensive individual therapy. Sometimes this kind of work can be accomplished in the conjoint context of couple therapy, but only when (a) levels of conflict are low, (b) the other partner can tolerate taking a more subordinate role, and (c) the shame-bound partner can feel safe enough to submit to the process with the other partner present. More often, the shame-bound partner will need to pursue this work in an individual therapy context.

The Outer Voice of Shame

> Whenever we experience shame in the presence of another person, we experience that person as holding all the beliefs about us that shame has already created within our personal psychology.... . When it is in the presence of another person that we have been shamed, it is to that other person that we attribute the pain of shame and against that person that we must defend ourselves.

> **Donald Nathanson, 1992, pp. 250, 255**

Examining human interactions through the lens of affect illuminates the extent of the common human concern with how we are viewed by others. Nowhere is this concern greater than with the people who see our most private selves—our partners, our parents, our therapists. A person's shame emotion can be activated by simply experiencing a moment of shame affect in the presence of his partner. As the epigraph above from Nathanson notes, he will then expect that his partner shares the shameful view of him. Or his shame can be activated by his perception of negative affect—especially some piece of shame affect assembled with a distrust script—in his partner's view of him. In either case, *he perceives his partner to be viewing him in the same fashion as that defined by his own shame scripts.*

Of course, his subjective experience is that his partner caused him to have the bad feeling. So he blames his partner for making him feel bad and engages in behavior intended to either change or distance him from his partner's perception. But such maneuvers are not necessary when he understands that his partner did not "make" him feel bad; she only triggered a negative view of himself that he already possessed. *What needs to change is not his partner's perception but his own scripted view of himself.*

Some adults are easily influenced by others' views; their shame is more easily activated. This is generally due to either the person's shame-related scripts or the person's manner of avoiding shame, or both. The individual may be a shame-prone person with extensive scripts of Bad Self. Such individuals are more easily triggered than people without so many negative scripts lying in wait. And, of course, no one can trigger those people more readily than their intimate partners. Many people with such chronic shame either avoid relationships altogether or maintain distant relationships with rigid limitations on their interactions with their partners.

The other group of people especially susceptible to the shame-activating power of others' views is comprised of those whose primary strategies for avoiding shame rely heavily upon their relationships. They use their partners' views of them to supplement, even to counter, their own negative views. This strategy of shame avoidance interferes with self-development—especially in the areas of individuation and autonomy—and makes those individuals very reactive in relationships.

People who rely upon their partners to help them maintain a positive view of self usually come from families that heavily censured individuality and differentness. Such families can provide members with a feeling of being okay as long as they conform to the family's norms, but the avoidance of shame is obtained at the sacrifice of more authentic expressions of self. When people cannot tolerate expanding their awareness to the parts of themselves that they have disowned, buried, disavowed, or otherwise avoided, they can avoid activating their shame by being with intimate others who confirm and validate who they are and how they are. When parents establish this kind of relationship, it is practically impossible for the children to explore the full range of their potential. In such families, it is considered a betrayal when a member is too different. Some people rebel in such families and go to extreme lengths trying to establish their individuality; others conform to the family definition of who they must be and live their lives according to the narrow definition of self tolerated in their families.

Partners from such backgrounds, whether they rebelled or conformed, often have difficulty in their intimate relationships. The conformers are not comfortable with differentness and often react in a manner that interferes with their partners' autonomy. The rebels have usually mistaken differentness for a more authentic experience of self. Thus, whether they rebelled or conformed, they are still restricted in their capacity to fully connect with another person. In both cases, the path out of this problematic background is *expanded awareness*, which creates the possibility for each partner to accept all aspects of himself and the other.

Repairing Damaged Esteem: The Individual's Responsibilities

The solution to being too easily influenced by the outer voice of shame is self-acceptance, but it must be an acceptance that is based in reality. When the individual truly accepts himself, other people's opinions of him lose their sting. Achieving genuine self-acceptance is not an easy task; it requires self-scrutiny, self-honesty, and courage.

Self-Acceptance

Wendy was never athletic. She always felt very vulnerable when she had to engage in any kind of physical activity. As she grew up, she learned to avoid physical activities and focused on her intellectual and interpersonal talents. Nevertheless, there were times when physical activity was unavoidable. At such times, she felt she was at her worst. When she married Peter, she was able to keep her difficulty with athleticism out of sight, until they went on a skiing trip. She warned her husband and the other members of their group that she was not very athletic, but she planned to avoid making a fool of herself by finding some pretext to spend most of her time in the lodge. The only reason she consented to try skiing was that neither she nor Peter had ever skied before, and so she felt no one would expect her to be any good. Other members of the group assured her that her first ski trip would be spent just mastering a few basics.

Unfortunately, the ski trip turned into one of the worst episodes of her marriage. Peter picked up skiing very quickly, while Wendy struggled with being able to do virtually anything. After the first day, Peter wanted to leave the beginner's slope and ski on some of the more demanding slopes. Wendy wanted him go on without her; she intended to find an excuse to give up on the skiing and return to the lodge after she was on her own. However, when she encouraged Peter to go on without her, he insisted on remaining with her. She was petrified at the thought of leaving the beginner slope, and so he remained there with her. She then couldn't abandon the skiing as she had planned. From that point on, Wendy felt she was a constant drag on his fun and he became increasingly irritated with her. By the end of the trip, they were barely talking to each other.

A year or two later, Wendy ended up being pulled into another physical activity, a company softball game. Memories of the horrendous skiing trip filled her head. But this time, it went differently. Wendy told everyone she was "a total klutz" and would never be able to hit or field the ball. The group encouraged her to play anyway and made clear that they were not at all concerned with her playing well. They simply wanted her to have fun. When it was Wendy's turn at bat, all the outfielders sat down and a coworker helped her swing at the ball. When she got a hit, they all cheered for her as she ran the bases. She noted that this could have been extraordinarily embarrassing, but it wasn't because she felt everyone genuinely liked her and didn't care that she was not athletic.

Wendy's lack of athletic ability was a perceived source of shame. When she stopped trying to hide it and simply accepted it, she no longer lived in fear of experiencing shame if others discovered how unathletic she was. It became just another aspect of who she was, rather than a terrible secret. She had never claimed to be athletic, but neither had she ever openly claimed the title of "total klutz." Of course, this may or may not have worked with her husband. His response on the ski slope (yelling at her when she made mistakes and fell down) suggests that her difficulties were triggering some of his own shame issues. I did not hear these stories until long after the marriage had ended, but one thing was clear: Wendy was no longer terribly concerned about her lack of athletic ability. She had accepted it and moved on.

Healing Self-Alienation

When a person has disowned significant aspects of his self (sometimes the entire experience of self has been disowned), he becomes numb and loses touch with his emotions, his needs, or sometimes even his personal thoughts. This can be seen as a form of dissociation, and it generally begins on a physical level—the person literally loses touch with his own body.[4] To lose touch with one's body can show itself in a variety of ways: from not recognizing feelings of hunger or satiation (e.g., the person who keeps eating long after he is full), to misinterpreting affect states as physical problems (e.g., the depressed person who keeps thinking he is coming down with a cold), to not even feeling physical sensations (e.g., the person who is numb and pursues extreme experiences, or even cuts his body, in order to feel something). Being alienated from one's self typically produces a feeling of emptiness, but that seems preferable to the intolerable feeling of intense shame that precipitated the original disconnection.

Many people are not disconnected from themselves until something activates their shame. The partner says something that reveals or implies an affect-laden view of the person that is negative, and it activates a Bad Self script. Then the person reacts by becoming cut off from his own internal experience, which is sometimes experienced as going numb but other times as a very painful experience.

To remain connected to the self is a challenge if a person tends to automatically respond with disconnection. Even when people change this mechanism, it usually does not change overnight, and there are moments of progress and regression. But the first step is the pivotal one and is generally more pronounced. For many people the most crucial step is learning to *stay in the body*, especially when shame is activated. Fundamentally, this comes down to keeping one's awareness focused on one's bodily sensations in the present moment, which the therapist can facilitate by asking about physical sensations if the client seems to be disconnected.[5] However, remaining fully conscious of one's bodily experience is even trickier in the context of the following recommendation for dealing with the immediate experience of shame affect.

Functioning in the Face of Shame Affect

Learning to deal with the immediate experience of shame affect comes down to two things: not avoiding the shame through some problematic reaction, such as getting angry, and, at the same time, finding a way to function through the experience of shame affect. Most people who are haunted by chronic shame cannot conceive of being able to function despite the shame. Shame affect is debilitating when it is intense. By its very nature, the function of shame affect is to shut down the behaviors that were motivated by the positive affect that preceded the shame. No matter how excited, how joyfully, we might be pursuing something, the activation of our shame will overwhelm those positive affects and put an end to the behaviors they were driving. Most people describe a loss of cognitive abilities in the midst of shame affect. It is part of the experience that occurs where someone embarrasses us and we are struck dumb, only to think of a snappy comeback later after our ability to think has returned. So how can a person learn to operate in the midst of such a disabling state?

An enormously helpful tool was identified by Gershen Kaufman (1989, 1992). He observed that the experience of shame was accompanied by a state of *intense self-consciousness*. At the moment of shame, we see ourselves as we believe we appear to others, and we assume that those others are viewing us similarly. So Kaufman taught his clients to focus outside themselves at that perilous moment. His goal was to remove the focus on the self, and it worked! The target of his intervention was the self-consciousness that maintains the shame, rather than the shame itself. If a person intensifies his focus on the rest of the world, his focus on himself diminishes—and the moment of shame passes. Remember, shame affect is fleeting; it is our recycling of the shame scripts that turns a moment of shame into an endless state of distress.

Focusing externally is a common technique in performance situations; most people just never thought about it in terms of shame. Athletes are taught to focus on the ball, not on how they will look to others as they handle the ball. Musicians focus on their music; students focus on the exam questions; actors focus on the other actors. Years ago some experts recommended that public speakers could overcome their anxiety by visualizing their audience naked, and it seemed to help some people. I think the operative mechanism was not simply the ludicrousness of the image but the image's power to get the speaker's focus off himself. Focusing on the self can easily interfere with performing. An old golf joke suggests that one way to interfere with someone's game is to ask him whether he continues to breathe or holds his breath on his backswing. The answer doesn't matter; the point is that the question tends to shift the person's focus from his shot to himself, thereby increasing the likelihood that he will mess up his next shot.

As I noted at the end of the preceding section, this recommendation (focusing outside the self) gets trickier when the person is also trying to remain aware of his shame and not flee from it. But shifting focus does not mean denying the shame, and it is different from launching into one of the reactions from Nathanson's (1992) compass of shame. Shifting focus is primarily a perceptual task—the individual intensifies his focus on his sensory input (what he sees, hears, smells, tastes, touches). This is essentially what is achieved during mindfulness meditation—an intensified focus on the surrounding world.[6] In the process, the self moves into the background. It is a perceptual shift between figure and ground so that the self is no longer the figural focus.

There is another danger in using this technique within a relationship. Focusing outside the self can contribute to a tendency to focus on the other person, and thus can augment a tendency toward blaming the partner. Some people rely on this strategy in their approach to their careers or other activities, maintaining an aggressive, external focus to avoid being intimidated in confrontations or competitive situations. They accomplish this feat by entering a state of intense (though often hidden or silent) anger and relentlessly focusing on the other person throughout the interaction, like a predator that is preparing to pounce on its prey. I have heard this technique described by both a professional athlete and an aggressive litigator. Such people have probably learned to unconsciously recycle their anger scripts and use that anger to help them maintain a focus outside themselves. As long as their focus never dwells on the self, they cannot be intimidated. I believe a similar process occurs for many soldiers during battle; they reach a point where their only goal is to destroy the enemy and their concern for their personal well-being fades into the background.[7]

Shifting focus to outside the self is an adaptive means of dealing with the momentary intensity of shame affect. Within an intimate relationship, individuals can certainly use it, but they must be careful not to fall into blaming their partners as a way of escaping their own shame. The larger goal is still to be able to stay with the shame, the focus shift simply helps the individual to maintain functioning in the heat of the moment.

Overcoming Shame Reactions

Daniel and Michelle had a busy lifestyle, especially Daniel who had a very busy career. Consequently, he did not get to spend very much time with their young son and Michelle did the majority of the parenting. One evening, Michelle was out with their son when he announced he would like to go skating, which happened to be an activity that Daniel did much better than she. Michelle saw it as an opportunity for Daniel to get some quality time with their son and called him, suggesting he come home and take their son skating. Daniel was supposed to attend a meeting, but he came home and took the boy to the rink. However, when they got there, the boy balked and said he did not want to skate after all. Daniel was very angry. He took the boy home and spoke very sternly to him about how he had made his father miss a meeting and should never behave this way again. Michelle was uncomfortable with the way Daniel was speaking to their son, and she finally interrupted him. When she interrupted him, Daniel lost his temper and said and did things that injured Michelle's ability to trust him and feel safe with him.

When they later tried to discuss what had happened, Daniel emphasized how he felt Michelle kept him from having a relationship with their son. She emphasized how she had been fearful since the blowup and kept a wall between herself and Daniel.

In therapy, Daniel was able to recognize how rejected he had felt when his son didn't want to skate. Basically, Daniel felt that his son did not want to skate because he was with his father. This activated Daniel's shame, apparently a view of himself as unlovable. His reaction to his shame was to attack the other—first his son and then his wife, whom he blamed for his difficulties with his son. After he had attacked his wife, she was more fearful about being with him. He could sense her distrust; it made being around her a constant reminder of his unseemly behavior and hence a ready trigger for further shame. He had been dealing with this problem by distancing from her and trying to reduce her impact on him.

No relationship is safe as long as either partner reacts very negatively when his shame is activated. Any individual working to overcome his shame must strive to first become aware of his particular shame reactions and then to learn to do something different when his shame is activated. The four poles of Nathanson's (1992) compass of shame comprise the common negative reactions. As I indicated in Chapter 7, I view these reactions as influenced by fear affect as well as shame. Basically, the script assembles the two together, as the individual learns to fear experiencing his shame because it leads to a diminishment in the self.[8] All four reactions are problematic in a relationship, but the reactions that are based in anger are probably both the most common and the most destructive to emotional safety. Anger, whether directed at the self or at the partner, quickly severs the interpersonal bridge, but avoidance may be the most basic shame reaction and the logical starting point for change.

Managing Avoidance Reactions   The avoidance reaction generally allows the person to diminish the experience of shame affect or to miss it altogether. One of the most common forms of avoidance is substance use, especially alcohol. Needless to say, changing this particular form of avoidance can be a major life task. But whether the avoidance is something as deep-seated as an alcohol problem or as superficial as a partner immersing himself in a television show, the first step in managing the problem is awareness. People are not always aware that they have shame about something. When he becomes highly invested in an argument, when he insists that it is the principle of the thing, when he feels his dignity is somehow on the line, when he feels he is being made to be the "bad guy," when he feels his very self is at stake, these are usually times that the person is fighting against his own propensity to feel shame. When an individual becomes aware that he is avoiding the experience of shame, he must then consciously choose what he will do. As I noted in Chapter 7, the defense mechanism of disavowal is at the heart of avoidance and is probably involved in all of the shame reactions. Thus, *expanding awareness* is a crucial first step in changing any destructive shame reaction.

Managing Anger Reactions   There are two kinds of anger reactions—one directed at the self and one directed at the partner. The scripts in these two reactions are consequently quite different, but the process of thwarting the anger reaction is fundamentally the same. Since anger affect alone is fleeting, the target for change is the script that recycles and perpetuates the anger. These scripts generally take the form of things that the angry person tells himself, sometimes referred to as self-talk. Since he tells himself these things when he is in the grip of shame affect and/or anger affect, these internal thoughts carry a sense of conviction and achieve the status of beliefs (at least when the person is experiencing them).[9] The kinds of things the angry person says to himself were cataloged in Chapter 8 under the headings of "Adequacy Scripts" and "Relational Scripts" about the self and "Disapproval Scripts" and "Distrust Scripts" related to the partner. All of these scripts usually involve shame affect, but only the self scripts typically result in the emotion that we would recognize as shame. However, as we saw in Chapter 8, there is often a linkage between scripts of an inadequate self and disapproval by the partner and between negative relational scripts about the self and distrust of the partner. Anger can be activated in situations involving any of these scripts, and it is then directed either at the self or at the partner. Wherever the anger is directed, it serves to shift the person's experience away from the shame affect that preceded it. Thus, the person must become aware of the shame that precedes the shift into anger, as well as the irrational nature of the scripts assembled with the anger. Finally, the person must make a decision to deal with his shame differently. Such decisions are not made at the moment when shame is activated; the decision is made earlier—when the person is rational and not in the grip of shame affect. Making this decision in couple therapy—in the presence of both the therapist and the partner—increases the individual's will and ability to follow through on the decision. But he will still have to face the power of shame affect, which makes those irrational scripts so real. I have seen many partners overcome their anger reactions to shame, but it is a monumental achievement every time.

Managing Withdrawal Reactions   Obviously the solution to the withdrawal reaction is to not withdraw, but it helps to think about what happens when a partner withdraws in a relationship. If the person is responding to an attachment threat, the analog to withdrawing is to detach. But withdrawal in response to an esteem threat is different because the attachment usually remains intact. Instead, the person pulls into himself and refuses to allow the partner to have access to his inner self. The detached partner can truly stop caring, but the withdrawn partner usually continues to have considerable feelings about the other partner. So the solution is not simply to stop withdrawing, it includes addressing—and expressing—the feelings that are being held back. The couple and family literature often characterizes the withdrawn partner as withholding, which implies not expressing positive attachment affects to the other partner. In addition, he is protecting himself from esteem threats. Thus, the withdrawal reaction usually constitutes an attachment threat to the other partner and, if the other partner is sensitive to the disapproval inherent in the withdrawal, an esteem threat as well. John Gottman (1999) has identified the behavior of *stonewalling* as the final response in the breakdown of marital connection. When stonewalling, the partner is deliberately nonresponsive to the other partner. Often individuals make a conscious decision to stonewall their partners. Thus, it may not be an immediate reaction to the activation of shame per se. But it is a form of withdrawal and is surely a reaction to earlier experiences of shame. Although the behavior of stonewalling can reflect detachment, most of the time it is a response to an esteem threat. It occurs among couples who are locked into cycles of destructive conflict. The primary way to help an individual stop stonewalling his partner is to develop emotional safety, and that usually starts in the immediate experience of the therapy session.

Intervening with Shame Reactions   As long as either partner continues to respond to the activation of his shame by reflexively launching into one of the four reactions from Nathanson's (1992) compass of shame, it will be very difficult for the couple to maintain emotional safety. It is the responsibility of each partner to work on these destructive reactions, and it is the responsibility of the therapist to make the therapy setting a safe place for both partners to do this kind of work. When a partner reacts from the compass of shame in session, the therapist should intervene. The nature of the therapist's intervention will vary with the therapist's style, but it will usually involve exploration of the person's feelings and interruption of the movement inherent in the reaction. Each of the four reactions involves a sort of movement, the directing of affect toward or away from self or other (the object of the affect). In the anger-out- or blaming reaction, the affect is directed toward the partner. In the anger-in reaction, the affect is directed toward the self. In the withdrawal reaction, the affect is directed away from the partner. And in the avoidance reaction, the affect is directed away from the self. The goal of the therapist, as well as the partner experiencing the reaction, is to interrupt this movement and increase the person's awareness of the shame precipitating it. When a partner does get control of a previously destructive shame reaction, it is a major step toward emotional safety in the relationship and toward repairing his individual esteem.

"The Only Way Out Is Through"   The common solution for dealing with shame is to avoid, deny, and disavow its existence. But avoiding shame instead of confronting it leaves the person more susceptible to being triggered, especially in his intimate relationships where affective resonance with his partner is so great. If a person tries to avoid being easily triggered without confronting his shame, he ends up constricting the very thing that drew him into the relationship with his partner—their intimate emotional connection. But when he confronts his shame he becomes harder to trigger, and he is then more able to maintain a stronger connection with his partner—without fear of her power to trigger him. To overcome destructive shame reactions, the person must discover that he can tolerate the feeling of shame! If he has lived all his life fleeing from his shame and avoiding every potential shame-producing circumstance in life, he has not had the opportunity to discover that shame affect can be tolerated. This can be a startling discovery. The more the person has oriented his life around getting away from negative feelings, the less confidence he will have that such feelings can be tolerated. Instead, he tends to feel that he has no choice but to react the way he does; it seems to go without saying that he must stay away from such feelings at all costs. *The solution to fleeing shame is for the shame avoider to go into his shame instead of away from it.*

Talking About the Shame   Going into one's shame is a lonely enterprise. But that lonely feeling that is a central part of the shame experience can be diminished by talking about the shame itself. When the person talks about his shame with someone who understands, he is no longer alone. It is very hard for a shame-prone person to talk about his shame while he is in the grip of shame affect, but the more he talks about it, the easier it gets. At the lower levels of intensity, he simply acknowledges the moment of shame affect, "I feel foolish." At the higher levels of intensity, he may be unable to put words to his experience until the affect state has diminished (remember, affects are brief; it is the recycling of scripts that keeps affects going). The guideline is clear: Partners must not run from the feeling; they must stay with it until they can talk about it. The encouraging thing about a person's acknowledging shame affect when he feels it is that it tends to lessen his tendency to get caught up in shame emotion. Instead of staying in his head and reverberating through the scripts about himself or his partner, he brings it out between them where a script's irrational nature is harder to ignore.

Maintaining the Interpersonal Bridge   If the therapy setting is especially safe, the individual is more able to face the fear component of his response. The goals are to stop his fear from determining his response and to stay with his shame and explore it rather than surrender to it. If he surrenders to his shame, he accepts the correctness of the shame-based view of self. But if he explores it, he tolerates feeling the shame while also seeking to examine the basis of it. This can be intensely unpleasant for the partner exploring his shame, but it is possible! The fear component is significantly lessened when the therapist maintains a solid empathic connection throughout the experience. Since shame has a powerful tendency to disconnect the person and superimpose his Bad Self view on the other (as in projection; he assumes the other sees him this way), it behooves the therapist to be especially active in expressing an empathic understanding and maintaining the connection. Through active empathy, the therapist fights to hold on to the connection.[10] In the midst of the shame activation, if the therapist can help the individual to resist doing as the fear dictates (and not fight, flee, or freeze), then he is less inclined to lose the interpersonal bridge. At that point, the view of the person held by the other (either the therapist or the partner) can remain an active part of the person's consciousness. In a sense, it is like activating a nonshame-based view of self (Good Self emotion) alongside the shame-based view.

Overcoming Shame Emotion

In order to permanently overcome shame, the emotions containing particular shame scripts must be disassembled. This does not mean that the individual will be completely free of shame, but this is how he can overcome the deep-seated, irrational scripts that control his experience when shame is activated. To understand the process of disassembling shame, recall that our emotions are constructed out of an assemblage of affects, scenes, scripts, and reactions. We overcome emotions—change them—by disassembling those components. In order to disassemble the components of shame, at least one of those components must change first. We see this happen all the time in psychotherapy. People change primarily because their emotions change, and the emotional change is predicated on change in one of three components:

1. Some people first succeed at changing their reactions to shame affect. When they can experience shame affect without reacting so negatively, they feel better about themselves. This helps them to build pride scripts that further diminish the power of their shame.
2. Others diminish the intensity of the shame affect in their shame scripts by "working through" the painful memories, the scenes. Sometimes these people experience a powerful emotional release (an abreaction) that helps them separate the affects from the scripts about the self.

3. Still others initiate change through rational examination of their shame-related scripts. These people are able to change the irrational thoughts that stem from their self-shame beliefs. This is the explicit goal of cognitive therapy and is a frequent outcome in insight-oriented therapies.

Working through painful memories and challenging irrational scripts often occur together, especially in psychodynamic treatment. The individual receives validation of the emotional experiences that spawned the scripts and is better able to separate the past from the present. This increases the possibility for new experiences and the further amending of old scripts. Indeed any combination of improvements among the components of shame has a synergistic effect on the overall goal of disassembling.

Learning to react differently when shame is triggered is usually the most accessible goal. Even to pursue this goal, however, requires a clear grasp of the person's common reactions to shame. Working through painful memories and learning to react differently when shame is activated often occur together in couple therapy, especially if the therapist's orientation leads her to probe for the original scenes. Working on both of these at once brings momentum to the process of change. And both are practically impossible without a caring, tolerant connection with at least one other person. This is the unique healing power of an intimate relationship.

The third element to disassembling shame emotion, examining the irrational self scripts, is often the focus of individual therapy. Through a process of self-examination, the person is able to identify the various shame scripts that he carries. Then he is more able to recognize their irrational nature at those moments when he is in the grip of shame affect. Basically there are two kinds of shame scripts—those that are valid and those that are not.

Valid Self Scripts. We all have some valid scripts! These are the scripts that are based on our genuine failures and shortcomings, such as a person's tendency to behave in a domineering or infantile fashion. But just because the initial source of a person's shame has some validity does not justify the noxious state of extended distress that characterizes pathological shame.

Invalid Self Scripts. Invalid self scripts generally develop from situations in which the individual was neglected or abused (i.e., situations in which the child developed shame almost purely because of parental failures). These are people who concluded that they deserved their parents' mistreatment because something must have been wrong with them (the child, not the parents). The process of revising these scripts is associated with the person's developing recognition that his painful childhood was truly not his fault. This process can take years if the individual has strongly absorbed the identity of someone who has something wrong with him.

It is critical for every person with extensive self shame to examine the validity of the scripts composing his shame because the path out of shame requires explicit self-honesty. If a person fails to accept his actual shortcomings and limitations, his very escape from shame creates new sources of shame. The goal is for a person to identify exactly who and what he is, and then to strive to be the best he can be.

An Objective Self-Assessment

The problem with shame is not that people have scripts that portray them negatively to themselves; the problem is that they believe them! At least they believe them when they are in the grip of shame affect—which causes them to recirculate the scripts, which activates more affect and reinforces the scripts. People have conflicting beliefs about themselves. Right alongside a person's view of himself as worthless is an awareness of those things about him that make him worthwhile. But the positive view loses all credibility when he's in the grip of shame affect.

The goal of helping a partner to examine his scripts when he's not in the grip of shame affect is to help him achieve greater objectivity about himself. Though total objectivity about the self may not be possible, people who are controlled by their shame are not even close to being objective about themselves—they're either excessively positive or excessively negative, either inflating themselves or putting themselves down.[11]

Self Confrontation

For a person to really look at himself objectively is a form of self confrontation—he has to include all the big and little ways in which he may not be what he seems to be. This is very hard, especially in the world today. As a society, we are consumed with concern about how we present ourselves to the world. Girls are not supposed to be seen without their makeup, and boys are not supposed to show pain. Everyone is exposed to media personalities whose public selves are all bigger than life. From cosmetics to fashion to cosmetic surgery, our consumer economy has created whole industries that function just to help people conceal their shameful ordinariness. In the late 20th century, we developed new categories of mental disorder (the eating disorders and body distortion disorders) that are driven by people's concern with not looking good enough. Clearly, for someone to try to confront himself on not being what he seems to be goes against many of the lessons of our daily lives. Still, there are people who successfully confront themselves every day. And many of them were once among the most ardent of those who try to fool everyone (especially themselves).

The shame-sensitive person becomes so averse to having his shame activated that he distorts his view of himself to protect himself from what seems to be the true view (his shame scripts). Being objective does not mean accepting that "true" view—which only feels true because of the power of shame affect—it means being *accurate*. Most people exaggerate in one form or another. Either the fish was bigger, the job was harder, or the pain was more intense. Or they may insist the fish was smaller, the job was easier, or the pain was nothing. Whether exaggerated to make themselves seem bigger or smaller, better or worse, the underlying goal is to misrepresent themselves in order to minimize the chance of their shame getting activated.

As a partner becomes more objectively aware of the nature of his shame scripts, how they are usually activated, and what he usually does in response to that activation, he begins to develop more choice. The first choice point is to do something different at the moment his shame starts to get activated. Instead of fleeing from how he feels, he can confront himself.

Self confrontation is a key element in overcoming debilitating shame in a relationship and achieving emotional safety.[12] It often occurs during those pivotal moments when core affects shift in the relationship. It may be as simple as a partner finally acknowledging a kernel of truth underlying the other partner's criticism. On occasion, self confrontation is a large, dramatic exploration filled with emotionality and new insights. But more often, it is a subtle shift in tone and a willingness to look at oneself in a less-than-flattering, but more realistic, light.

Building Pride Scripts

Self-control and will power are almost synonymous. It is precisely the establishment of long-term goals or the setting of difficult tasks which brings the will into play, and strengthens it … this determines the amount of effort a man can put forth, and thereby what he accomplishes and what he may think of himself.

Wolfgang Lederer, 1964, pp. 40–41

Confronting oneself and facing one's shame not only help the person to change his negative scripts, they provide an additional payoff, a potential source of pride. The shame-bound person feels good when he overcomes something that previously held him back. Will power is strengthened by the power of the tasks we set for ourselves. Many men overcome shame about their uncertain masculinity by joining male fraternal organizations that put aspiring members through demanding ordeals.[13] Nothing increases a person's confidence like discovering that he can handle more than he thought he could.

The person's will is strengthened by taking on his shame—thereby allowing him to take on even more shame—and his pride grows as he takes on his shame. The result is that the seesaw balance of the Shame-Pride Axis shifts—shame shrinks and pride grows. The person feels good about himself just for daring to confront his bad feelings about himself. And this empowers and encourages him to confront himself even more. He replaces shame with pride by taking responsibility for the valid shame scripts and correcting them.

The partner who truly has turned the corner on facing his shame is able to tolerate being confronted by the other partner. Instead of defending himself, he focuses on the kernel of truth in what his partner is saying—even if some of the facts are wrong and he could seize on those to make a grand argument on his behalf. He has learned that facing the truth about himself actually reduces his shame, whereas in the past he always fought against it because it seemed it would only increase the shame.

Final Thoughts on the Individual's Role in Overcoming Shame

A partner begins to overcome his shame when he comes to recognize that what needs to be revised is not his partner's perceptions of him but his own emotions about himself. If his shame scripts have a certain amount of validity, as many do, then he must face that fact if he ever hopes to improve the way he feels about himself. As long as he struggles against any validity in the scripts, he will keep himself—and his shame—in the darkness. When he comes to truly know and accept the sources of his shame, his partner will then have less power to trigger him. What he is left with is just his humanity.

Problems in the realm of esteem fade when each partner experiences his shame as his own and not something the other partner has made him feel. Although his partner can help him to transform his shame, her help will only feel like criticism if he has not accepted the reality of his own shameful views of himself. Ultimately, *confronting the self and delving into the sources of one's shame cannot be initiated by anyone but oneself.* A person's acceptance of his shame as his own is a major step toward greater self-acceptance, self-respect, and self-esteem.

Repairing Damaged Esteem: The Partner's Role

As I noted earlier, the one essential ingredient for overcoming shame is a genuine connection with another person. Whether it occurs in individual therapy or the partners' intimate relationship, it is only within an interpersonal connection that a person can ever truly learn that his shameful self scripts are distortions. Of course, the relationship must be emotionally safe for this to happen. Open, honest communication will not occur if emotional safety is lacking. When the relationship is safe, it is possible for each individual to be sensitive to both his own and his partner's shame. The deepest intimacy occurs when partners can go into their shame (rather than flee it) and share themselves with each other. When she sees him in his shame and still accepts him, when he sees her make no effort to hide herself from him, then they can have the deepest intimacy and the greatest prospect for repairing esteem and relinquishing distorted views of self.

Theologian/philosopher Martin Buber (1970) conceived of two different ways in which we relate to our world: I-It and I-Thou relations. In the mode of I-It relations, one person considers the other as an It and views him from a distance, like a part of the environment. In the mode of I-Thou relations, both individuals relate with their innermost, whole beings. Each person influences the other and is influenced by the other. The theorists at Wellesley College's Stone Center (Hartling, Rosen, Walker, & Jordan, 2004) refer to a similar aspect of relating when they emphasize the need for mutuality in order to create safety and overcome shame in relationships. Authenticity in an intimate relationship is founded on the I-Thou mode of relation. When partners refuse to hide from their shame, they bring a new level of respect into their relationship. *In the realm of esteem, it is ultimately the presence of genuine respect that makes the connection emotionally safe.*

The Partner as Listener

The partner who is attempting to overcome his shame and change his shame scripts has to examine the negative beliefs he has about himself and their impact on others. He may be able to recognize the irrational nature of the beliefs when he looks at them objectively, but when he is in the grip of shame affect, he either completely believes his own worst beliefs about himself or he at least fears that they are true. However, the experience of considering his own worst views of himself can be very different when he is in the presence of someone who knows him well. When he is emotionally connected to his partner, he is then influenced by his partner's affects. Thus, when he himself is the topic, his partner's affective response influences his own affective experience of himself.

If he reveals something about himself that he regards as shameful, the shame can be heightened or lessened according to the affect he perceives in his partner. If his partner conveys disgust, his shame will likely increase; but if his partner conveys interest and acceptance, his shame will likely decrease.

This is a difficult process, even though an atmosphere of nonjudgmental openness helps to move it along more rapidly. The person is not sharing his shame with someone who is uninvolved, but the involvement is essential for the person to actually take in a different view. Even a professional therapist has little impact if there is no emotional connection between therapist and client. The listening partner must be involved on an emotional level to have any impact, and among partners, the listener will almost certainly have been hurt by some of the ways the sharing partner has dealt with his shame.

Finally, the listening partner has his or her own shame and sensitivity to being triggered by the sharing partner. So even as she listens to his shame, she is very sensitive to his feelings about her. Yet, ironically, it is precisely in those moments of heightened vulnerability that the capacity for growth is the greatest![14]

How the Partner Facilitates Self-Confrontation

An alcoholic businessman is said to have approached the psychiatrist Carl Jung and asked why he (the businessman) could not overcome his problem with alcohol. Jung replied that he had never seen a chronic alcoholic successfully recover. But, he added, there were exceptions. Once in a while, some alcoholics have "vital spiritual experiences. ... They appear to be in the nature of huge emotional displacements and rearrangements. Ideas, emotions, and attitudes which were once the guiding forces of the lives of these men are suddenly cast to one side, and a completely new set of conceptions and motives begin to dominate them."[15]

Jung was describing profound emotional change, the kind of change that has occurred for thousands of men and women who participate in Alcoholics Anonymous (AA). AA is a perfect example of the kind of social environment that facilitates self confrontation.[16] The structure of the AA meeting creates an atmosphere of emotional safety, a setting in which people can confront themselves without fear of disapproval. What makes it safe is that everyone there is confronting themselves and owning up to their shortcomings—and their humanity.[17] No one hides behind the illusion that they are above the problems that the others have. The nonjudgmental acceptance displayed by the members of AA allows each individual to explore his shame without *being* his shame.[18]

Relating Through Shame

Hank and Ann sought couple therapy about 6 months after Ann had begun individual therapy for her depression. She had been depressed for a couple of years, but it had reached an intolerable level in the previous year. They were a picture of opposites. Ann was overweight, tearful, and apologetic. Hank was fit, upbeat, and sure of himself. They described some conflict, but they agreed the primary problem was disconnection. They described a history in which Ann had made a series of accommodations to Hank's career. Several times, she gave up valuable jobs so that they could move with his job. Both partners emphasized that this was always Ann's free choice. They felt the sacrifice was worth it because Hank's career had taken off and they were well-off financially. They had two children and Ann had tried to keep up her career while also doing parenting. Hank was an active and involved parent as well, although Ann put in more time parenting.

Ann described herself as struggling in many areas, from childrearing to her job to daily living. She was clearly hampered by her depression, and her esteem had declined noticeably over the years. Hank, on the other hand, described himself as flourishing over the same period. He had overcome a weight problem and become devoted to maintaining his fitness. His career had moved ahead steadily. He attributed his advances to his driven, goal-oriented nature. He constantly worked on self-improvement and was confident he could learn to do anything better than anyone else. He acknowledged he was fiercely competitive.

A pattern had developed in which Ann would talk about a variety of problems and Hank would tell her what she should do to correct the problems. She agreed that his suggestions always made good sense, but she had difficulty implementing them. When she failed to follow through on his suggestions, Hank would get frustrated and eventually get angry. He acknowledged that, over time, he reacted to the entire situation by withdrawing. He no longer felt connected to Ann and did not even have the desire, though he said he was still committed to the marriage. Ann was pleased to hear that he was still committed to the marriage; she had not known that he still felt committed.

Hank understood that it was important for Ann to resolve her problems herself and that his unsolicited advice only served to remind her of her lack of competence. But he had difficulty restraining himself to the role of listener, because he was such a solution-oriented person. Consequently, he gradually distanced from Ann. Both agreed that Ann did not feel needed by Hank in any way.

Hank and Ann's relationship is an example of the unbalanced esteem patterns discussed in Chapter 10; their's is a cross between the overadequate/underadequate couple and the symptomatic spouse. They probably started out in the overadequate/underadequate pattern and then moved toward the symptomatic spouse pattern as Ann got depressed. This case illuminates the role of shame in these patterns. Ann's life had slipped into a slump of shame as her opportunities for maintaining esteem kept getting thwarted. Obviously, other spouses often make similar sacrifices without the same impact, so it seems likely that Ann had some significant shame scripts hanging on from her earlier life. But a major factor in Ann's slide into shame and depression was Hank's complete inability to relate to her shame!

At the beginning of their marriage, Ann was quite functional and happy, and Hank was having some struggles of his own. The route that Hank found to deal with his own sources of shame was complete avoidance of the shame itself and an aggressive orientation toward anticipating and rooting out all potential sources of shame. This worked well for him individually, but it destroyed the interpersonal bridge between him and his wife. He was unable to relate to her shame (it probably would have felt intolerable to him), and she ended up feeling that there was something wrong with her. For Ann to overcome her depression, she needed to connect with someone who could relate to what she was feeling, thereby normalizing it and making it possible for her to examine her shame scripts more objectively.

When an individual confronts himself about the sources of his shame, he is perilously close to the activation of his shame and consequently very vulnerable. A person in this state is highly attuned to any affective indicators of disapproval from others. Yet for his self confrontation to have any lasting impact, it must occur in the presence of another human being. Ultimately, it must occur with his partner if the couple is to fully heal from the ravages of shame-inspired conflict and hurtfulness.

What the partner can do to facilitate this process of self confrontation is to accept the shame-prone partner without judging. The other partner must convey an attitude similar to that of the members of AA—that she is in touch with her own capacity for shame and knows there is no superiority in her not having an immediate problem with shame herself. More important, she must openly acknowledge her own shame when it arises and be willing to examine it just as her partner is doing with his shame. If either partner insists on hiding his shame, it will not be safe for the other partner to engage in self confrontation.

People with severe shame issues are extraordinarily attuned to the slightest affective messages of disapproval from their partners. When they are trying to explore the validity of their shame scripts, the perception of disapproval can sting like a slap in the face. For most couples, the perception of disapproval is going to happen from time to time, even when the partners are doing their best to be nonjudgmental. When it does occur, emotional safety will be interrupted, at least temporarily. The challenge then is to be able to recover emotional safety, and the path to recovering safety is primarily through the partners' shame.

When his shame has been activated, his reaction is likely to activate her shame as well. But she may not be as affected by the activation of her shame and may appear to be functioning okay. If so, this will heighten his feeling that he is the one with the problem, that he has something wrong with him. Chances are that she will react to the activation of her shame with something unhelpful from Nathanson's (1992) compass of shame. She may become distant or get defensive, and that will tend to reinforce his distorted perception. Thus, the activation of his shame (during the course of his trying to confront himself about that shame) often leads to a loss of emotional safety and the activation of shame in both partners. However, if she can stay with her own shame—explore it and reveal it to him—then they are likely to have the remarkable experience of emerging from their shame together. The interpersonal bridge between them is restored.

Self Confrontation, Acceptance, and Change

A person's self confrontation—recognizing his shame and talking about it in the presence of his partner—can loosen the grip of shame affect if the partner's affective response is accepting. The revealing partner is usually very sensitive to any indications of disapproval from the other partner when he is in the process of confronting himself. The therapist often can diminish some of that sensitivity by helping both partners maintain clarity about the difference between acceptance and disapproval. Disapproval of a partner's behavior need not be disapproval of the partner as a person. Partners must distinguish their disapproval of behavior from their acceptance of the person.

Just as acceptance is not the same as approval, neither is another person's acceptance the cure to shame (though some people seek it thinking that it is). Another person's acceptance does not eliminate a person's shame or build pride scripts, but what it can do is open the way for the person to confront himself. In the process of self confrontation, the person has the opportunity to earn his own acceptance. Nor does transforming shame mean that it will be eradicated; it may just be lessened, and the person may have to talk about it many times before he notices any lessening. Also, the process of bringing the source of shame out into the open will sometimes diminish the shame but still leave the person with other emotions, perhaps new emotions that were not there before.

There is a big difference between a partner who expresses remorse but doesn't change his behavior toward the other partner and one who demonstrates his desire to improve his behavior. For emotional safety to develop for both partners, the revealing partner not only acknowledges his shameful behavior, he takes responsibility for changing it. And if both partners don't take the revealing role at times, there is probably an imbalance and emotional safety will still be precarious.

A lot depends upon a partner making a *decision* to explore and reveal the sources of his shame. Being made to talk is not the same as making a decision to talk. In research on adult survivors of child sexual abuse, survivors who had not voluntarily chosen to disclose their abuse showed significant signs of shame, while those who had chosen to disclose their abuse expressed greater disgust when recalling the abuse.[19] Clearly the decision to disclose made an important difference in transforming the shame. And it is interesting to note that the shame feelings about the self were replaced with feelings of disgust about what was done to them by the perpetrator.

The most important requirement of the partner (to facilitate self confrontation by the other partner) is that he be in touch with his own capacity for shame. Together, both partners maintain an atmosphere of self confrontation. This means that each partner is focused on him- or herself and what needs to be done, not on what the partner needs to do.

A Shared Focus on Self-Change

[C]hange occurs only as we begin thinking about and working on the self—rather than staying focused on and reactive to the other.

Harriet Lerner, 1989, p. 86

One of the most common interventions in couple therapy is the focus on "I statements." This is a basic communication skill in which each partner is encouraged to talk about his own experience and quit making assumptions, mind-reading, criticizing, or otherwise focusing on the other partner. "You statements" usually interfere with emotional safety and produce defensiveness in the other partner. A partner can offer valuable observations and insights when requested, but unsolicited or unwanted observations tend to feel like criticism.

Focusing on the self is a simple, yet profound, intervention; it is particularly relevant in establishing an atmosphere in which partners can safely confront themselves. Scripts of Bad Self cannot be safely examined and repaired if the individual feels he is constantly being scrutinized by the other partner. A focus on the other person perpetuates an emotionally unsafe atmosphere, while a focus on one's own experience is liberating to the other partner. It goes hand in hand with the goal of relating through shame.

Example of Self Confrontation

[T]aking the focus off the other does not mean silence, distance, cutoff, or a policy of "anything goes." Rather, it means that as we become less of an expert on the other, we become more of an expert on the self.

Harriet Lerner, 1989, p. 87

Kurt and Sally, whom we met in the first chapter, had a much briefer course of therapy their second time around. Though they reentered couple therapy in a state of considerable conflict and distrust, they didn't remain there for long. Our initial goal was to stabilize their relationship and limit the conflict. They agreed to several limits on their interactions, and they saved their biggest complaints to discuss in our sessions. Soon, each partner began to acknowledge difficulties that he or she was contributing to the situation. Although these admissions might be viewed as concessions the partner is making in the relationship, I prefer to emphasize their role in each partner's relationship with him- or herself. Kurt and Sally were each exploring and recognizing unpleasant things about themselves; they were either unaware of these things about themselves or had failed to appreciate the significance of the thing for the relationship. Many of these revelations concerned issues they had learned about in our earlier course of therapy but then ignored when their relationship began to decline again.

Sally talked about the roots of her difficulties with self-esteem and how she needed a visible response from others to reassure her that she was okay. She described her interactions with her critical mother, a woman who was never satisfied that Sally had done enough. Kurt also had difficulty in that area; he had long ago learned to prove his worth by performing. This made him especially vulnerable to Sally's barrage of criticism. Her criticism was mostly a response to attachment threat. When Kurt felt too much disapproval at home, he intensified his involvement at work and in other activities outside the home. This made Sally feel insecure about the attachment, as well as stirring her esteem concerns, especially the relational component of her esteem feelings (i.e., that she might not deserve the relationship).

In session they agreed about the nature of the pattern they were caught in, and they formed an alliance to overcome it. In the course of that work, there were several instances of self confrontation on both sides. The more each partner explored and acknowledged his or her sources of shame, the safer the relationship became. Here is a description of some of the work that involved self confrontations by each partner.

Sally talked about her need to be perfect, going back to being a perfect student in high school. She had difficulty relaxing and felt there was always something she should be doing. Consequently, one of her frequent criticisms of Kurt had been about his watching television when he was with the kids, rather than focusing exclusively on the kids. Sally acknowledged that she felt guilty if she was not constantly doing something productive. She felt her mother was not particularly critical when Sally was growing up, but for some reason, her mother became extremely critical of Sally's mothering when Sally had children (just as Sally tended to do with Kurt). Sally went on to describe how she always craved more attention than she received in her large family, and she acknowledged that she brought that need to her relationship with Kurt. Though Sally had been aware of much of this, she said that she was realizing that she took advantage of Kurt's gentle nature by directing the kind of criticism at him that she otherwise reserved only for herself.

Kurt went into his background in greater depth than he had the first time they were in couple therapy. His parents were immigrants, and Kurt described how difficult it had been for him growing up in an American neighborhood. He was picked on by the other kids for being different. They attacked his ethnicity, his appearance, and his use of the English language. He reported that he felt very inadequate during those years and learned to keep to himself. He revealed feelings of sadness that elicited compassion from Sally in the session. When he became an adult, he found success in his industry and was able to shed his view of himself as inadequate. But he acknowledged that he was secretly very sensitive to criticism; he just covered it up and acted like nothing bothered him. Sally's criticism was the most devastating, and Kurt acknowledged that he responded by withdrawing from her, just as he did as a child. This led Sally to talk about the impact his withdrawal had on her, and Kurt vowed to quit withdrawing and instead talk about what he was feeling when he felt criticized.

Although the content of the self confrontation in the example involves shame-related material, there was never any discussion of shame per se. Sometimes self confrontation involves material that can be explicitly labeled as shame; other times the topic of shame never arises. Much of the above discussion could be classified as family of origin work or resolving transference issues. But from the perspective of emotional safety, the part that leads to change is each partner's looking at him- or herself objectively, acknowledging something unpleasant that was previously denied or minimized, and seeing how he or she is bringing these issues into the relationship and affecting the other partner.

Although partners often try to get each other to see these kinds of things about themselves, their efforts are rarely successful if the relationship lacks emotional safety. This is why delving into the sources of one's shame basically must be a confrontation with oneself. A person generally only sees and acts on painful insight into his shame when that insight is the result of a personal decision to examine himself. It just doesn't work if the person feels the decision was foisted upon him by his partner.

The Necessary Encounter With the Despicable

The kind of discussion that includes self confrontation generally occurs when both partners are in the safe zone and each is able to listen nonjudgmentally. However, some aspect of the discussion may still trigger a partner's shame or his distrustful view of the other. For example, if she is confronting herself and says something that activates his shame and causes him to feel unsafe, his ensuing reaction is likely to trigger her shame and feelings of unsafety as well. If this occurs, the partners may have to suspend her self confrontation while they resolve the hurt that has arisen in the course of the discussion. And the hurt can be very powerful if it occurred when either partner was in the process of confronting and facing his or her shame. But, ironically, it is in the process of resolving that hurt that partners can often make the greatest progress in confirming their positive views of each other. When shame or distrust arises during an interaction and the partners confront it together, major steps in healing and growth can occur.

Being accepted nonjudgmentally is obviously a key to closeness among partners, but a shame-prone partner may have difficulty trusting it completely. He may not feel that she has really seen his true self, so her acceptance may feel superficial to him—not because she put conditions on her acceptance, but because he knows she has not really seen his most undesirable parts. Ironically, *he may not feel that she has truly seen his most shameful parts (his shadow side) until he sees her react with some variant of distrust affect.* Only then does he know for certain that she has seen what he sees in himself. If she does react with an affective response that convinces him that she sees his shadow side and *yet she still maintains her positive view of him,* he has the opportunity to feel both seen and accepted. This is the essence of the interpersonal healing of shame.[20]

This is why an individual cannot overcome shame in isolation. The shame-prone person is able to change his worst views of himself when he feels that the other person truly sees the person in his shame scripts (his Bad Self), and yet does not lose sight of the good person in his pride scripts (his Good Self). The partner experiencing the shame is unable to hold on to his view of Good Self when he is in the grip of shame affect, but his capacity grows stronger as he sees and resonates with the other partner's positive view of him. When she shows that she sees both sides of him (Good and Bad Selves), then he can dare to see the positives about himself even as he is aware of the negatives.[21]

The revealing of the shameful partner's shame (which often feels like the exposure of the true self) is usually accompanied by a lot of distress. If it is mishandled, it can turn into a fight as he tries to convince her that he is not what she thinks he is (his "projection" of his own shame script). But even when it is handled well, he will usually experience distress. He may not feel that his shame has really been seen unless his partner reacts with some form of negative affective tone. At this point there is hurt and a disruption in the attachment bond. But it is in the process of repairing that disruption that his view of himself can finally improve.[22]

When he can tell that she really sees his shameful aspects and yet does not sever the connection, when she can tell that he really sees her shameful aspects and yet does not sever the connection, when they can take in each other's reaction to their shameful aspects and yet remain connected, then healing occurs and there can be a profound shift in the experience of shame for each partner.

The term *affect regulation* is often used to refer to the capacity to manage emotional upheavals, especially the ability to remain constructively engaged with another person despite the presence of negative affect (McDonough, Carlson, & Cooper, 1994). In learning to manage a powerful negative affect, such as shame, it is critical to be able to stay involved with the other person. Couples dealing with shame frequently break that interpersonal bridge, thereby creating additional problems in the realm of attachment. In the next two chapters we will examine how to maintain that bridge and repair it when it is disrupted.

15
Maintaining Attachment Security

There are two sources of attachment threat. One is a behavior that overtly threatens the security of the relationship. This can be anything from an affair to a verbal threat of divorce to accepting a job position that will entail more time apart. The other source is when one partner perceives a diminishment in positive affects from the other partner. This can be anything from calling less often to leaving a mess for the partner to clean up to not noticing when the partner needs a hug. The lack of positive affects usually precedes the more overt threat and thus is an issue in practically all cases involving attachment threat. Overt threats often produce an attachment injury, which is his conviction that she no longer cares about him, or she would not have been able to do what she did (or what she failed to do when something was needed). To reacquire the belief that the other partner cares (a necessary component of trust) requires an additional dimension to the healing. We will address the healing of attachment injuries in the next chapter.

In this chapter we will focus on the behaviors and affective messages that maintain a secure attachment. When attachment security is threatened, these behaviors and affective messages are a necessary component of the process of recovering attachment security. There are a variety of behaviors that serve to maintain a secure attachment. When these behaviors begin to disappear from a relationship, a partner can experience attachment threat.

Increasing Positive Attachment

Secure attachment is founded on the positive affects of interest-excitement and enjoyment-joy. Each partner needs to see that he and the relationship are sources of these affects for the other partner, at least at times. The positive affects are assembled in the emotions representing each partner's attachment to the other. When those emotions clearly exist, partners feel secure and emotionally safe, at least in the realm of attachment. However, perceptions of a partner's attachment are not based purely on emotional expression; partners perceive the existence of those attachment emotions in a variety of behaviors, all of which are motivated by the affects assembled in those emotions. The emotional safety model breaks those attachment behaviors into three categories: *attunement*—behaviors that represent one partner's attunement to the other partner's feelings and needs, *positive affects*—behaviors that represent one partner's interest and pleasure in the other partner and the relationship, and *reliability and commitment*—behaviors that represent one partner's commitment to keeping the relationship viable and the other partner's life pleasant and manageable.

Category A: Attunement Behaviors

Infant research suggests that the modulation of infant affect by an attuned and responsive mother is the essential precursor of secure attachment.

Jeremy Holmes, 1996, p. 55

Being attuned is based on the affective resonance that underlies all intimate relationships. The best example is the one used in Chapter 2, the attunement of a mother to her child. At times, she may seem to be telepathic because she seems to know what the child needs or feels even before anything has been expressed. However, this is not really something supernatural. It is primarily a case of *familiarity* (knowing the child really well) and *interest/orientation* (thinking about the child's needs and feelings even when they are not being expressed).

A well-attuned mother knows the rhythms of her child's life. She knows when he has his periods of high energy and when he is depleted. She knows when to expect these kinds of changes and quickly recognizes them when she sees them. She knows her child's basic temperament, his energy capacities, his interests, and his fears. Thus, even without knowing the child's specific mood on a given day, the mother can often predict what will be difficult and what will go well for the child.

Add a keen interest in the child's well-being to this high level of familiarity and you have a mother who expends a lot of energy thinking about and anticipating her child's needs and feelings. When a mother performs at this level, she is able to provide an environment that contains minimal frustrations and maximal opportunities for the child to develop.[1]

Partner Attunement

A well-attuned partner, like a well-attuned mother, knows how the other partner is doing and often can infer what he needs. This provides a warm, secure feeling in the cared-for partner. But when there is a lack of attunement, he can feel unseen or unimportant to the unattuned partner.

In my experience, failures in attunement are the most common complaint that women express about their male partners. When a husband makes a decision without consulting his wife—or, worse yet, when the nature of a decision indicates that he did not consider its impact on her needs and feelings—the wife experiences it as a failure in attunement. I have tried to avoid stereotyping the sexes in this book, but the fact is that men generally have to work harder at being attuned.[2] Women tend to be more attuned to the emotional states of others, particularly those states that indicate unhappiness, need, and the like.[3] It is possible that the female propensity for attunement is based on some genetic difference between men and women, but it also seems likely that their role training is a factor. Consider the play of little girls when they are pretending to be mothers; they often practice hearing their babies and knowing what is needed.

Communicating Effectively

The partners' ability to communicate effectively is a component of attunement. Many kinds of difficulties get subsumed under the heading of communication problems, especially esteem attacks that take the form of disrespectful messages. Thus, respectful communication is an element of emotional safety in the realm of esteem. But I choose to emphasize the role of effective communication in the realm of attachment, specifically as a component of attunement, because truly effective communication does not occur in an intimate relationship unless the partners are attuned to each other. Effective communication is not about using I statements and paraphrasing the other's words—those are techniques to overcome breakdowns in communication.

Effective communication means the partners understand each other. Partners who are well attuned to each other can often communicate volumes in a few words, or even a look. They may not always agree, but they know when they disagree and what it is that they disagree about.

Accessibility

Partners often describe the feeling of being connected in terms of being able to "be themselves" with each other. It is a liberating experience when both people in a relationship are fully, genuinely themselves. When neither person keeps important parts of himself out of the connection, then each person feels connected and more fully alive. The theorists at the Stone Center say the more people are connected to others, the more fully they become themselves.

Our culture tends to encourage people to regard certain aspects of themselves as unacceptable. Revealing those unacceptable parts can activate shame, but hiding them leads to isolation and loneliness.[4] Many people become so adept at hiding certain kinds of feelings that they themselves do not know when they're experiencing those feelings. They block their awareness of unacceptable feeling states, either ignoring them entirely or converting them into some other feeling they regard as more acceptable. Thus, distinctive parts of a person's emotional life are often blocked and inaccessible, even to the individual himself.[5]

Partners are able to be highly attuned to each other because of the extent of their accessibility. They allow each other to see parts of themselves that they typically hide from public view. When a partner begins to hide parts of himself, the other partner is likely to perceive an attachment threat.

Interference With Attunement

[A] further difficulty turns on the fact that a mother can be physically
present but "emotionally" absent.

John Bowlby, 1973, p. 43

Once a person begins to feel that his partner is not attuned, he may react more
readily to seemingly minor manifestations. He may get upset that she does not
handle his things the way he likes or know to leave him alone when he is tired.
He feels that she is not considering him and his needs, and he may complain
that she is misreading his feelings, perhaps mistaking his sadness for anger.
This kind of tuning out is usually the result of the intensification of the partner's empathic wall as part of her withdrawal or detachment. But some partners have difficulty with attunement because they are emotionally blocked.

Anyone who is emotionally blocked is going to have problems tuning in to
the emotions of others. A rule of thumb is that people who are emotionally
blocked will have the most difficulty tuning in to other people who are experiencing those specific emotions the blocked individual cannot access in himself. For example, many men have difficulty tuning in to vulnerable feelings in
their partner, while many women may have difficulty tuning in to aggressive
feelings in their partners. If the obstacle is emotional blocking, the obstacle
involves the individual's difficulties with certain emotions in himself. But if
the obstacle is withdrawal or detachment, then the breakdown in attunement
is a reaction to a perceived threat in esteem or attachment.

Reinstating attunement is often a specific goal in couple therapy. Sometimes it is helpful to assign a check-in task to help the partners have a safe
structure at home for them to learn more about each other's feelings.[6] During
the course of the therapy session, the therapist may ask one partner what the
other might be feeling when affect is displayed, especially if it is an affect that
is going unnoticed or may be misunderstood. This gives partners an opportunity to revise their assumptions about each other (of course, it is important
to do this in a nonshaming manner). As the mothering example shows, good
attunement requires a high degree of familiarity with the partner's life. Many
partners (usually men) have the unrealistic expectation of maintaining intimate relationships with their spouses and children without spending significant amounts of time together. Then they don't understand when problems
spring up.

Attunement is not a static phenomenon; it typically waxes and wanes with
the rhythms of people's lives. When partners talk about feeling connected, they
are usually referring to their sense that they are attuned to each other. However, it is frequently the case that one partner is more attuned than the other,
and it is typically the partner who is more attuned who will describe greater
feelings of disconnection.[7] John Gottman (1999) describes the phenomenon of
"turning toward" a partner, demonstrating a receptivity toward, and interest

in, the other person. The partner who is less attuned needs to turn toward his partner, seeking opportunities to connect and rediscover her feelings and needs.

Category B: Positive Affect Behaviors

[I]t is the absence of disclosing and responsive interactions that begins the process of relationship distress.

Susan Johnson, 2005, p. 35

Throughout this book I have argued that the primary source of attachment threat is the lack of *positive attachment behaviors*. Certainly, there are overt threats to attachment—the affair, the threat to separate, the failure to provide support during a crisis—but these overt events typically do not occur until an erosion in attachment has already begun. And that erosion is evident in a diminishment of the kinds of behaviors that tell a person that his partner is attached. Since a diminishment in positive behaviors is much harder to pinpoint than an outright negative behavior, the gradual development of attachment threat can be difficult to articulate and hard to prove. A partner who repeatedly seeks reassurance from the other partner is often dismissed as insecure or neurotic, the things he is responding to are difficult to pinpoint and easy to explain away.

The emotional safety model recognizes that the insecure partner is responding to his perception of attachment threat. If there is no overt threat, he may be responding to something that is *not* occurring, which puts him in a position in which he may be challenged to justify his feelings. The other partner can have difficulty acknowledging the validity of the insecure partner's concern when all the insecure partner can articulate is that there seems to be less of the kinds of things that indicate all is okay.

The emotional safety model treats a partner's feelings of attachment threat as legitimate. Though he may be distorting some things, he is usually responding to something real that is occurring (or which has stopped occurring) in the relationship. More important, the threat is real to him and is playing a central role in determining his stance in the relationship.

The behaviors that tell a person the partner is attached occur in the three categories discussed in this chapter—attunement, positive affects, and reliability/commitment. A diminishment in attunement is a frequent source of conflict, and failures in the area of reliability/commitment often reach the stature of overt threats to attachment. But it is in the area of positive affects that the subtle development of attachment threat is most often first perceived and is hardest to establish or prove.

There is a natural ebb and flow of these positive affect behaviors; they vary with how stressed and busy people are. When a partner begins to express concern in this area, the other partner typically explains away his lack of attentiveness on the basis of being stressed and preoccupied with other demands. But the real measure of the other partner's response is whether he responds to his partner's expression of concern by making an effort to intensify his positive affect behaviors. If he does, then the perception of affect threat usually fades away and the couple returns to the safe zone.[8] If he does not, then the insecure partner's perception of attachment threat does not abate, and further problems are likely to develop.

At times, attunement and reliability/commitment each can feel like work. They are driven by positive affects, but they often involve behaviors that are not intrinsically rewarding. Instead, the partner performs these behaviors because the relationship is important to him—so the experience of interest or pleasure may be indirect at best. Unlike attunement and reliability/commitment, the category of positive affects refers to behaviors that are more directly and obviously rewarding; these are the behaviors that help to remind partners of why they value being in the relationship. Thus, these are behaviors that can quickly resuscitate a failing relationship—as long as the partners feel safe enough to engage in them. Couple therapists have developed many techniques and homework tasks that prescribe actions that reveal and develop positive affects, things like gift giving, caring days, positive exchanges, and reading aloud together.[9] The behaviors that represent positive affects soothe the anxiety of attachment threat.

Shared Time and Activities

Perhaps the most central of all positive affect behaviors in an adult attachment relationship is the simple act of doing things together.[10] This is where most relationships begin. Partners often express their sense of loss in this area of attachment by complaining of not having fun together anymore. As with all of the areas of positive affect, couples go through periods when they have less shared time and activities. This is not a problem as long as they are able to resume their shared activities. But many couples get into trouble in this area because of what they typically refer to as "growing apart," meaning they no longer share the same interests. Growing apart is a real phenomenon in some cases, such as partners who get together at an early stage of development and literally grow in new directions. But, more often, partners grow apart because they fail to address other attachment or esteem threats in the relationship.

Some partners lose their shared interests because they are not prepared for the inevitable changes that accompany the process of maturing. The demands of children, mortgages, and changes in physical capacity force most couples to evolve their shared activities to fit new demands and capacities. If a partner cannot engage in that kind of change, then a serious attachment threat develops. For example, if he is not prepared to give up partying on Friday nights and replace it with investing more time in conducting children's birthday parties together (or shopping together or cooking together or working on the home together or almost anything that ends with "together"), then she is likely to complain about their not doing things together. From his point of view, he is happy to continue engaging in the kinds of things they always enjoyed in the past, so he may complain that she is no longer any fun.

When shared activities have declined because of a failure to adapt to the process of maturing, it sometimes helps to confront the partners with the realities of change and challenge them to experiment with some new, shared activities. However, a failure to adapt can reflect deeper individual problems in at least one partner, suggesting a need for intensive individual treatment. The more common reason that partners suffer a decline in shared activities is because of esteem or attachment threats in the relationship. In that case, the therapy will be addressing those threats, and the partners can be encouraged to separate their work on the relationship from their enjoyment of shared activities. If it can be done safely (i.e., if the couple is not too conflictual), the therapist may encourage the couple to go out on dates and to abide by a rule that they focus on enjoying themselves and refrain from discussing their relationship while on dates. If the couple is too distant, the therapist might suggest daily check-in talks. Overall, the goal is to reestablish a satisfying level of shared time and activities.

Shared Goals and Childrearing

A large part of what brings people into an adult intimate relationship is the existence, and development, of shared goals. Certainly one of the most common shared goals is the desire to have a home and a family. Other common shared goals include financial security, health goals, maintaining religious/ spiritual involvements, and other quality of life issues. Such goals emerge from a matrix of positive affects and play a major role in shaping the two individuals into a partnership, a team that works together to achieve a shared vision. But if either partner perceives the other to have become less invested in the achievement of the shared goal, an attachment threat can develop.

When goals or values have shifted in a relationship, the partners often fail to talk about it directly. The safe setting of couple therapy makes it possible for the partners to acknowledge and address such undiscussed differences. Simply being able to acknowledge and discuss such issues directly is often a major step for the partners. Sometimes the development of differences can be resolved; sometimes the differences are simply understood and tolerated; and sometimes the surfacing of significant differences can end a relationship. The latter usually occurs around major differences, such as the decision to have children, which are normally resolved before the relationship evolves into a long-term commitment. In such cases, the perception of attachment threat was quite accurate. And in all cases, directly addressing the development of potential differences in shared goals must occur in order to manage the perception of attachment threat and reestablish emotional safety.

Sex and Affection

Sex and affection play an important role in providing avenues for positive affects to develop and maintain the attachment relationship. Partners obtain tangible pleasure from each other and each gets the satisfaction of serving as a source of pleasure for the other. Some individuals place greater importance on sexual contact. For them, it serves as a sort of gateway to the achievement of attunement and other shared activities. For others, sexual contact is meaningless unless attunement already exists. A popular stereotype portrays men as needing sex to feel close and women as needing to feel close in order to have sex. This is not the case with all couples, and the respective positions are not confined to the sexes as defined in the stereotype, but such pronounced differences in connecting do occur and can create an attachment threat for both partners.

Most couples experience a decline in sexual contact over time. Particularly among couples who have children, the bonds of affection are increasingly expressed through other avenues, such as shared activities and investment in the home and family. However, as sexual contact declines, additional avenues of expressing affection open up as partners come to know each other better and the relationship evolves. Partners express affection and please each other through activities as diverse as cooking, gift giving, performing chores, and making sacrifices for each other. Thus, when one partner perceives the other to be doing less of these kinds of activities, a vague sense of attachment threat can develop. As with spending time together, a partner can easily dismiss the other partner's concern on the basis of real-life impingements, such as a busy work period. Vacillations in sex and affection are a normal part of life, but it is important that a partner be responsive when the other partner expresses concern about sex and affection (including the many derivative forms of expressing affection).

Sometimes sexual contact increases in response to a partner's perception of attachment threat. One of the most common responses to the overt attachment threat of a revealed affair is for the betrayed partner to suddenly take a renewed interest in sex. This typically surprises both partners, but it makes sense from an attachment perspective. Increasing sex and affection is an adaptive response, a way of intensifying one of the positive bonds in the relationship.

For many couples, sex and affection are among the first things to go when the attachment falters, but for many others, sex and affection may persist long past other areas of positive affect. When the failure to connect is confined to the arena of sexual contact, the more behavioral forms of sex therapy are often effective in addressing the problem. Sometimes, however, the breakdown in sexual function is the beginning of an attachment problem, and purely behavioral treatment of the sexual dysfunction will not be sufficient. If the sexual dysfunction stems from physical problems, a behavioral focus can sometimes lessen the likelihood of a partner experiencing the problem as an esteem threat.

But whether the problem originates in the realm of attachment or is simply a physical problem, therapists must be on the lookout for the development of esteem difficulties. Indeed, esteem difficulties are a common concomitant of sexual dysfunctions, either spawning the problem or developing secondary to some other source. And, of course, the sexual problem can become an attachment threat regardless of how it originated.

Category C: Reliability and Commitment Behaviors

Crying for parents, mainly for mother, was a dominant response especially during the first three days away.

John Bowlby, 1973, p. 27[11]

The third category of positive attachment, *reliability and commitment*, refers to those behaviors that play the central role in providing a safe haven and a secure base. This is the component of attachment that Bowlby's studies revealed when he observed infants who were separated from their mothers (see the epigraph for this section). The attached infant needs to know that his mother is there; if he discovers that she is not there, he experiences the anxiety and distress of attachment threat. In infancy, the infant's need is fulfilled by the mother's immediate physical availability and responsiveness in the face of the infant's distress. She helps the infant to manage his affect states first by being attuned and second by being responsive when he enters dysphoric states. Her responsiveness to his needs provides a barrier against impingements from the surrounding world. Her consistency in caring for him and taking care of him helps him to develop a working model of the other as reliable.

The adult correlates of reliability and commitment extend beyond the manifestations seen between mothers and infants (though they still have their roots there). *Some adult forms of reliability and commitment can go for an extended period of reduced expression without creating a noticeable problem. But other forms cannot, most especially the need for support, which becomes increasingly cogent with the immediacy of the need.*

Providing Support

Whether it is a mother caring for her infant or an adult responding to her partner, the provision of support is an essential part of an attachment relationship. What it means to provide support is defined differently at different times, but it centers on what the person needs. Sometimes, he may need nothing more than comforting or for her to stay with him or listen to his concerns. Other times, support can take a physical form, such as performing errands or assuming responsibility for tasks, especially if the behavior is responsive to the partner's needs. Still, the main element in support is emotional, most commonly manifested in a willingness to tune in when someone is experiencing distress.

Like most of the areas of positive attachment, the provision of support can wax and wane with the vagaries of life's demands. However, support differs from the other forms of reliability and commitment in one very important respect: *The failure to provide support at a moment of intense need can cause a major attachment injury.* This goes beyond the creation of a vague attachment threat; a major attachment injury can destroy trust and possibly end a relationship if it is not repaired. Among some clinical populations, the provision of positive support has been found to play a relatively minor role compared to the power of negative support (a failure to respond with support when the person needed and expected it), which can quickly cause a worsening of symptoms.[12] Thus, the ongoing provision of support is a sign of positive attachment, but the failure to provide support when it is needed and expected can create an attachment injury, resulting in an even greater impact.

The need to increase support is a usual part of responding to a partner's perception of attachment threat, but the appearance of an attachment injury in this area is a signal that more is required. Simply increasing support does not adequately address an attachment injury. We will discuss what is needed to repair an attachment injury in the next chapter.

Managing Conflict

[O]ver time most marital problems do *not* get solved at all; instead, they become what we call "perpetual" issues. What turns out to be important is the *affect* that surrounds the way people talk about … these perpetual marital problems.

John Gottman, 1999, p. 16, [*sic*]

Couples must be able to resolve conflicts, or live with the unresolved ones, for an attachment to thrive. People in intimate relationships do not find a resolution for every conflict, but they must be able to live with the unresolved ones. Some couples get into heated exchanges over their differences, while others avoid such exchanges. Gottman's research indicates that it is not the presence or absence of overt conflict that determines a stable marriage.[13] Every couple has their unresolved conflicts. These perpetual conflicts are usually based in fundamental differences between the partners. Gottman emphasizes the importance of the partners being able to acknowledge these unresolved conflicts and periodically have a dialogue about them. Insecure partners are heartened when the other partner makes an effort to respond to expressed concerns. That is a sign of a positive attachment in the other partner, even when that partner remains limited in his capacity to change in the particular area of concern.

Many of the conflicts that occur in relationships do not have solutions in which each partner's needs can be accommodated. In those conflicts, no satisfactory compromise exists; one partner may get what he wants but the other partner will not. The best solution to this kind of conflict of needs is for one partner to sacrifice and allow the other partner's needs to predominate. Sometimes this occurs in an alternating pattern ("We'll see a chick flick this week and a sci-fi monster movie next week."), and sometimes one partner simply volunteers to sacrifice. Of course, this can lead to a different problem if there is not some balance between partners in regard to sacrificing. The central factor, though, is that the sacrifice is made voluntarily by one partner so that the other partner can have her need met.[14] Therefore, *sacrificing is not "giving in" or losing, it is a loving behavior that all partners perform in successful intimate relationships.*

Tolerating Negative Affect

The capacity of the caregiver to recognize and accept protest is as much a foundation of psychological health as the absence of major separation.

Jeremy Holmes, 1996, p. 6

The ability to listen to a partner's concern, even when that concern is expressed with anger, is an important component of reliability and commitment. This is an area that frequently breaks down and brings partners to therapy. Listening to a partner's anger does not mean agreeing with what she is angry about; a partner can accept the other partner's anger without diminishing his own position in a disagreement. But accepting a partner's anger is a challenge, and it is especially difficult if the listening partner is sensitive to esteem threats. When he cannot listen to her anger (because of his difficulty with esteem), his consistently defensive response can stir her sense of attachment threat.

His refusal to hear her anger makes her feel like she can't rely upon him to hang with her through tough times in the relationship. That constitutes an attachment threat. Unfortunately, the partner who is the recipient of the anger often has difficulty grasping that his refusal to listen makes her feel like he is not committed to the relationship.

Helping Manage Extended Family

Pediatrician and psychoanalyst D. W. Winnicott (1963) emphasized the infant's need to be protected from impingements by the surrounding environment. Winnicott believed that the infant needs to maintain an internal state of equilibrium in order to effectively develop a sense of self, and impingements on that state interrupt the development of self.[15] In a sense, adult intimate relationships are similar to the infant's self—the relationship must be protected from emotional impingements, especially in its more vulnerable early stages of development. One of the most common potential impingements is the intrusion of a partner's relatives, whether in the form of in-laws who want to influence the couple's relationship or children from an earlier marriage who resent the relationship and the new stepparent.

When an adult enters into an intimate relationship, he expects his partner to help him manage the new relationship with his partner's kin. If a partner fails to provide that help, it is often experienced as an attachment threat. Therapists frequently encounter this issue and sometimes struggle with boundary questions related to it. Is it appropriate to expect him to intercede when she has a problem with his mother, or is that a violation of her autonomy and likely to interfere with her ability to establish her own relationship with her mother-in-law? There doesn't seem to be one single answer to this kind of question; what works for one couple may have a different effect with another. But if there is a perception of attachment threat, it must be addressed.

Accepting the Partner's Influence

Within the rules of Monopoly, there's no way for players to cooperate so that all benefit. … The same is true for boxing, football, hockey, basketball, baseball, lacrosse, tennis, racquetball, chess, all Olympic events, yacht and car racing, pinochle, potsie, and partisan politics. … If we revere the Golden Rule, why is it so rare in the games we teach our children?

Carl Sagan, 1997, p. 187

Though our success as a society depends upon our ability to cooperate with one another, our society is still enormously competitive. But one place where people expect to cooperate and not compete is in their intimate partnerships. Yet a common problem in troubled relationships is that one partner, almost always a male, will not accept the other partner's influence. In this age more than ever before, adults enter into intimate relationships with the expectation that they are forming a partnership. Perhaps there was a time when adults did not have such expectations of their attachments, but it is hard to imagine. An attachment without mutual influence would not be a relationship between two adults; at best, it might resemble the relationship between parent and child.

When a person discovers she has no influence with her partner, she experiences a threat in the realm of attachment. How committed is he if he will not engage in a partnership? Cooperation requires partners to give up a certain amount of control and accept influence from the other partner. The willingness to engage as full-fledged partners is another aspect of reliability and commitment. When it is lacking, the therapy must uncover why the resistant partner is resisting. Most of the time, this leads to difficulties in the realm of esteem.

Fidelity

A final aspect of commitment is the expectation of fidelity. Though some people enter attachment relationships with an understanding that the relationship will not be exclusive, that seldom works. As partners become attached, they become less comfortable with the possibility of infidelity. The prospect of other relationships increasingly stirs the feeling of threat in the realm of attachment, and the relationship loses emotional safety. In most relationships, fidelity is a given; it is when infidelity occurs that trust is disrupted.

Many people view infidelity as the force that destroys relationships, but it's more often just the final straw.[16] Infidelity is an indication that something is seriously wrong in the relationship; but other problems usually precede it. What is wrong may have started in the realm of esteem, but the partner who diverts his needs to a third party has clearly escalated the problem and created a major threat in the realm of attachment. Most of the time, the appearance of infidelity constitutes an attachment injury and requires a lengthy process of atonement before the injured partner can recover feelings of trust and confidence that the other partner is being faithful.

In the next chapter, we will examine the process of healing attachment injuries, when simply eliminating attachment threat is no longer enough.

16
Healing Attachment Injuries

Partners can get into trouble if they approach their intimate relationship with the goal of using it to heal historical problems with esteem (those that precede the relationship), but an intimate relationship is the *only* place where they will ever heal attachment injuries—either historical or those that arise in the relationship. Many couple therapists have described the healing power of intimate relationships. That healing does not refer to the realm of esteem, though many people may try to use their relationships for that purpose. The healing possible in a healthy intimate relationship refers to the healing of old attachment injuries. Some theorists have even suggested that a potential mate's capacity to provide such healing is one of the prime factors that determines a person's choice of a life partner.[1]

The most fundamental difference between repairing damaged esteem and healing attachment injuries is in the respective power each partner has to influence the process. In the realm of esteem, only the individual himself has the power to change his self-concept (through self-confrontation), but he requires an intimate connection in which to do this. But in the attachment realm, it is the partner who possesses the healing power (though she too requires an intimate connection in which to do it). The partner with the attachment injuries has to have courage in order to trust and be vulnerable; he may have to overcome his impulse to detach or to protect himself from getting hurt. But it is the other partner who provides the healing love. And, of course, since both partners may have historical attachment injuries, in many relationships each partner serves as a healer even while being healed.

Healing Preexisting Attachment Injuries

> Through marriage or other long-term committed relationships, an individual may learn to trust, to share vulnerabilities, to be more self-reliant, to be softer, to be clear about beliefs and feelings, indeed, to be more certain about his or her boundaries, limitations, and strengths.
>
> **Jerry Lewis, 1997, p. 24**

Issues of personal shame and damaged esteem can occasionally be healed without the participation of both partners, but the healing of attachment injuries occurs exclusively within the relationship. From the perspective of script theory, the change that occurs is fundamentally the same as that which occurs in the esteem realm—old irrational scripts of self and other are relinquished or revised. But in the realm of esteem, the negative self scripts are often hidden from the individual, and uncovering them can be a major achievement. This is less often the case in the attachment realm—the negative scripts of self and other are usually accessible. Even if those scripts remained buried while the person was on his own, they surface quickly when he gets into an intimate relationship.

These script-based issues that people bring to relationships are the same issues that emerge in the transference in intensive individual therapy.[2] These issues are most pronounced with people who have been abused, neglected, abandoned, or otherwise traumatized in early life. Some of these issues overlap into the realm of esteem, particularly when a child has concluded that he is unlovable (a relational source of shame rather than a competence source), but most of these issues involve scripts of distrust of the other. It is a new experience with a loving and reliable partner that can finally lead to the dissolution of these harmful scripts and their replacement with scripts of trust. *Healing old attachment injuries is about the power of love.*

Revealing Old Injuries

It is important that partners know about each other's historical attachment injuries. For most people, revealing these aspects of each partner's personal history is a part of the bonding process that occurs when they first develop their attachment relationship. But occasionally, partners will not have talked enough about their histories and need to learn more about each other. Sometimes a partner will try to minimize the extent of his historical attachment injuries for fear it will frighten the other partner off. And some partners will insist that they do not need to know about the other partner's past. It is usually significant if the partners have not talked about their pasts with each other. It often means that at least one of the partners is fearful about dealing with this kind of material, perhaps fearing that the feelings will be overwhelming or that someone will learn something that can't be tolerated.[3] In either case, it limits the emotional safety in the relationship and prevents the kind of whole person acceptance that makes for a strong, secure attachment.

To be clear, a failure to share significant attachment injuries from the past does not lead to repetitive conflict. It can contribute to a general wariness and distance, but even the excessive distance discussed in Chapter 1 is more often a reaction to previous brushes with conflict. Avoiding discussion of earlier attachment injuries is not in itself a threat to emotional safety; it just tends to limit the intimacy and hence the tools available to the partners for dealing with threats to their emotional safety. The partners do not know each other to the depth they might, and so the security of the attachment is not what it could be. In such cases, couple therapy may be able to provide a safe enough setting for the partners to reveal themselves more fully.

The Intrusion of Old Injuries

When people have old attachment injuries, they tend to bring them into their adult relationships. People with old attachment injuries are generally going to have greater insecurity in current attachment relationships. They will be prone to perceive attachment threats more readily than partners from more secure backgrounds. Many clinicians have observed that people with unresolved attachment relationships from childhood often seem to choose marital partners whose personalities resemble those of the earlier attachment figures. These people may be trying to master or repair the original relationship, but what it generally does is confuse both partners about the source of the injured partner's injuries. The idea that these problems represent unfinished business with parents is a popular therapy hypothesis and is well known among many laypeople. Hence, many people dismiss their partners' attachment-related concern by contending that it has nothing to do with them, it is just their partners' childhood issues being manifested.

In my experience, *a partner's perception of attachment threat in the current relationship is almost always based on something that has actually occurred in the current relationship.* This is not to say that the existence of earlier attachment injuries is irrelevant, because it most certainly is not. But it does not lead to the transference of earlier perceptions onto the current partner (or therapist) without some current stimulus. In other words, the person with old attachment injuries does not simply superimpose his former reality onto his current relationship. It is more accurate to say that he is highly sensitive to the perception of attachment threat, and he may react to behaviors (especially affective expression or its lack) that might be regarded as minor by someone with a more secure background. On occasion, he may misperceive a behavior, but even that occurs much less often than most partners want to believe.

This is not an easy situation for the partner (or for therapists working with these people individually). The offending partner must be willing to examine his own behavior and accept the legitimacy of the injured partner's perception. The threatening behavior may indeed be something that the offending partner considers minor, but it is a mistake to argue that the behavior was minor or irrelevant. Instead, he must accept responsibility for the threatening behavior, however minor it may seem.[4] This is particularly difficult for the offending partner to do if he has esteem issues. He does not want to view himself as someone who would hurt his partner, so he argues that it is not his fault; the injured partner was hurt because her perceptions are distorted. Yet to help her to heal, he must rise above his own esteem concerns and acknowledge how he has hurt her, even if unintentionally.

It is every partner's job to be sensitive to his partner's sensitivities. When a partner is unable to be sensitive, that becomes a focus for the therapeutic work, which often leads back into that partner's esteem issues. But whether the injured partner has preexisting injuries or not, the work of healing attachment injuries from within the relationship remains the same. And, as with repairing damaged esteem, shame plays a central role in the healing—but in a very different manner.

Current Attachment Injuries

Sue Johnson and her colleagues (2001) define attachment injuries as a violation of the expectation that the partner will provide caring and comfort at a time of need. Many attachment injuries occur when a person is in a vulnerable state of danger, distress, or need and the partner fails to respond with appropriate caring or comforting. But there are times when the injured partner is not so obviously in a vulnerable state. Some attachment injuries occur when the injured partner is not feeling particularly vulnerable or needy. But there is a degree of vulnerability inherent in being in the safe zone—the individual is trusting the other partner implicitly. Thus, overt threats to the attachment relationship, such as an extramarital affair or accepting a job that requires a separation, can yield attachment injuries even when the injured partner was not in a state of acute need or vulnerability.

When an attachment injury occurs, the problem has gone beyond a perception of threat in the realm of attachment. A partner's feelings of trust have been damaged, and simply correcting the threatening behavior is no longer enough to repair the damage. Now repairing the problem involves a process of emotional healing, which entails relinquishing distrust scripts and developing or rebuilding new scripts of trust. This process takes time, and the noninjured partner is an essential part of the process.

Healing Attachment Injuries

Healing attachment injuries that occur within the relationship is different from healing preexisting injuries. The healing of preexisting injuries focuses on the distrust scripts that the person carries in order to protect himself. The current relationship provides a new, more trustworthy experience, and the individual gradually relinquishes the old scripts as the new experiences build more scripts of trust. In the process, the vulnerable feelings that preceded the old scripts gradually emerge. Distrust scripts also exist in the case of injuries from within the relationship, but there is a different order to the process of healing when the current partner is also the person who betrayed the injured partner's trust.

The process of healing attachment injuries from within the current relationship usually does not proceed until the injured partner can expose the vulnerable feelings that were occurring at the time of the betrayal of trust. As long as the injured partner only expresses the distrust feelings that followed the betrayal (often containing a lot of anger), the offending partner is likely to experience the exchange as an esteem threat and consequently try to justify his actions or otherwise defend himself. He is unlikely to be able to access his feelings of concern for his partner or express the kind of remorse that shows his partner he really cares.

When the offending partner resists participating in this process because he experiences it as an esteem threat, the therapist usually must address the offending partner's perception of esteem threat before the couple can effectively work on healing the attachment injury. This is a frequent point of impasse in those therapies that fail to ever achieve safety; the offending partner's esteem issues prevent him from being able to accept any responsibility for the injuries he has inflicted in the realm of attachment. Unfortunately, if he cannot accept any responsibility for hurting her, then she will not be able to heal her attachment injuries. A concomitant step is usually to help the injured partner soften her expression of her complaints so that they do not constitute an esteem threat as easily. But *the essential feature of the healing is the expression of concern by the offending partner, and this concern is most vividly communicated through affective messages containing healthy shame.*

Apologies: The Essence of Healing

Regrets, but No Apology, in London Subway Shooting

New York Times **headline, July 25, 2005**

Foreign Minister Says Japan Must Show War Remorse

Chicago Tribune **headline, December 8, 2005**

The above headlines appeared in articles respectively about the London police shooting a man whom they mistakenly believed to be a terrorist and the Japanese government's acknowledgment of its atrocities in China and Korea during World War II (prompted by the anniversary of the attack on Pearl Harbor). These headlines highlight the often subtle distinctions people make when they offer an apology, whether as individuals or nations. There is a world of difference between "I'm sorry your feelings were hurt" and "I'm sorry I hurt your feelings." The former looks like an apology (it starts with "I'm sorry"), but it is really just an expression of sympathy. The latter is an apology because the person is acknowledging responsibility in causing the hurt feelings. It is that dimension of taking responsibility that people typically avoid. In legal and political situations, people are concerned about liability. But in intimate relationships, partners are worried about how they will be seen if they acknowledge themselves as being responsible for hurting the other person. They may be blamed or seen differently or see themselves differently as a result of a true apology. In other words, *genuine apologies often constitute an esteem threat for the apologizer, which only makes the apology even more meaningful when expressed.*

In order to be effective, an apology has to be more than mere words. The words alone don't mean much, it is the sentiment that they convey that matters. When a person says he is sorry, he is saying that he feels something. If a partner says he is sorry but there is no affect supporting his words, the apology rings hollow and the other partner is not comforted by the words alone. But if the words are accompanied by an affective tone that says the same thing, the difference can be phenomenal! Suddenly, the other partner's hurt and anger can evaporate into thin air. What is the nature of that affective tone that can cause it to have such a profound impact? It is the presence of shame affect, the healthy variety that promotes positive change. If his tone conveys that he truly feels bad that he has hurt her, then she can see that he does care about her, and he cares enough to feel bad about himself for causing her pain. There may be other affects present in an apology, and we would seldom identify the feeling as shame emotion, yet it is the presence of shame affect that makes all the difference.

Forgiveness: The Essence of Repair

> All sustained relationships depend to some extent on forgiveness. Successful marriage means an inevitable round of disappointment, anger, withdrawal, repair.
>
> **Robert Karen, 2001, p. 5**

Intimate relationships cannot thrive without forgiveness. It is an important part of every successful relationship, although it often appears in such low levels that it goes unnoticed. All relationships have their moments of irritation, frustration, disappointment, and hurt that can produce lingering resentment. Yet in successful relationships, that resentment is eventually left behind, though sooner in some relationships than others. What does it mean when he relinquishes his resentment toward her? It probably means he has forgiven her, but if that is the case, he has relinquished more than just resentment. The dictionary defines forgiveness in terms of letting go of resentment and any claim of requital. This latter part of the definition means that the person doing the forgiving relinquishes any expectation that he is owed something because of the other person's transgressions.

Many partners make genuine attempts to forgive, yet they continue to carry the belief that the other partners still owe them. That is incomplete forgiveness, if it can be viewed as forgiveness at all. Sooner or later, the other partners begin to sense that the first partner may not appear resentful, but he still feels he is an aggrieved party and deserves some kind of reparation. *True forgiveness returns the ledger to a zero balance—neither partner is considered to be more deserving, or less deserving, than the other.* Every interaction is to be weighed in terms of its intrinsic merits—not on the basis of what either partner did or didn't do in the past. Needless to say, this is not an easy level to reach, especially if one partner feels seriously injured by the other.

I have used the metaphor of a ledger, a device introduced by Boszormenyi-Nagy and Spark (1973). But I hasten to add that couples who keep careful track of their interpersonal ledger are almost always living outside the safe zone. Partners who are truly able to forgive each other usually do so with a spirit of generosity. They are not keeping track of who makes more sacrifices because they each do so willingly.[5]

Forgiving Major Injuries

Overcoming unforgiveness can be conceptualized, at least in part, as overcoming the negative view of the self implied by the transgressor's behavior, namely, that the victim is not deserving of better treatment.

Frank Fincham, Steven Beach, and Joanne Davila, 2004, p. 73

The everyday ability to let go of minor sources of resentment in a relationship often goes unnoticed and is seldom identified as even involving forgiveness. Yet if that ongoing form of forgiveness is missing, the relationship will lack emotional safety, and intimacy will be severely limited. Ultimately, the relationship will probably collapse under the accumulated weight of minor resentments. Still, the need for forgiveness is prone to be invisible in situations involving minor resentments. Instead, the partners remain focused on their grievances, each feeling that he or she has never received a fair hearing. But the process is very different when the resentment stems from a major attachment injury. When these major injuries occur, the need for forgiveness is usually quite explicit.

Forgiveness of a major attachment injury is most often an excruciatingly slow and arduous process. Kristina Gordon and Donald Baucom (1998, 2003) have compared the process to that involved in recovery from trauma, suggesting that the injured partner goes through stages of recovery that are comparable to the stages of recovery from traumatization.[6] When a major injury has occurred, it is rare that the injured partner can simply forgive. Instead, he almost always needs to see something from the other partner before he can enter the process of forgiving. What he needs to see is: (a) some expression of shame, (b) often combined with acts of reparation, and (c) a clear statement of intent to prevent such injuries from happening again.

Even when the offending partner does all of the above, it can be difficult for many injured partners to forgive. The injured partner seems to fear relinquishing his resentment and letting the other partner off the hook. Instead, he clings to his resentment (and his feeling that she owes him) as a sort of shield to protect himself. Unfortunately, he tends to bring up this shield in too many interactions, which makes her feel that she is constantly being judged on the basis of her past behavior. This usually constitutes an esteem threat for her, so she cannot feel emotionally safe, and the conflicts are likely to continue. The therapist might wonder what it is that the person fears so badly that he cannot give up his shield of resentment. The obvious answer is that he fears it will happen again if he relents and opens his heart to her once more. But there may be more to it.

When a partner carries a grudge and clings to his resentment, it is generally the case that shame is involved. Just as shame affect serves to squelch positive affects that have encountered some impediment, the fear of experiencing deep shame leads many partners to surround themselves with a wall of resentment. The key to this situation lies in the humiliation aspect of the injury. When the injury was purely in the attachment arena, the injured partner is fearful of allowing himself to care too much again. He may move toward depression or detachment. But when resentment plays a dominant role in his stance, it is usually the case that the attachment injury also constituted a threat in the realm of esteem. Shame can play a role in the forgiver's experience as much as that of the apologizer.

Unhealthy Shame Impedes Healthy Shame

To become a more forgiving person, to decrease the hold of powerful and ingrained psychological factors, requires a confrontation with oneself.

Robert Karen, 2001, p. 38

Pathological shame creates problems on top of problems—not only does it make the bearer miserable, but it interferes with his capacity to have a fully satisfying intimate connection with his partner. People need to be able to experience their healthy shame—the shame affect that is a normal part of life—if their intimate connection is to be truly satisfying. People with too much unhealthy shame have great difficulty experiencing their healthy shame, because it is so likely to activate the unhealthy variety. For the shame-bound person, genuine apologies are terribly threatening.

When she can tell that he feels shame related to his (mis)treatment of her, and especially if it is the healthy variety of shame that motivates him to make things right, then she is reassured that he cares. However, it almost never helps for her to try to induce that shame if it is lacking. Efforts to make him feel bad are likely to activate his unhealthy shame, which usually will lead to all the unhealthy reactions in his repertoire. The same is true if the therapist tries to induce his shame. Instead, we must focus on removing the obstacles to healthy shame. And the primary obstacle to healthy shame in a relationship is excessive shame about the self.

Paul and Collette had been together for 5 years and married for 4 when they sought marital therapy. They explained that they argued too much and each felt criticized by the other. They agreed that their arguments were about trivial things, so there must be something more than the immediate issue at stake. When asked to identify when the arguing had started, they disagreed. Collette felt it started during their first year, whereas Paul felt it didn't start until some time later. I asked Collette about that first year and she referred to the big issue that had occupied them at that time. Paul's previous girlfriend had gone through a very difficult period and Paul had devoted considerable time and attention to helping her through that experience. Collette had been accepting of the situation at first but grew resentful as it went on for months. They both agreed that Paul had been clear that Collette was his girlfriend, and Collette did not feel that Paul had wanted to renew his romantic relationship with his old girlfriend. Still, he was unable to limit his involvement with the old girlfriend, and Collette began to feel that she was not as important to Paul as the old girlfriend was.

Collette talked about how warm and complimentary Paul had been when they were first together. She felt this came to a stop by the end of that first year. When they married, she expected the warmth to return but it did not. Paul's view was that Collette had become increasingly critical and angry since they married. He felt misunderstood regarding his former girlfriend; he had helped her out of a sense of responsibility for her, not because of any deeper interest. Since the focus of all the more recent arguments seemed to fall in the trivial category, we all agreed that the damage that occurred early in their relationship still needed to be repaired. We talked about what had happened, and what eventually emerged was that each of them was hurt by what had happened. Collette felt Paul emotionally abandoned her for someone else, and over time she came to feel resentful. Paul felt Collette had not appreciated that his efforts to help the former girlfriend came from a really good part of him. When she came to resent him for his involvement with the former girlfriend, he felt she was rejecting a very important part of him, and he began to shut down around her.

Paul was in a bind because of his desire to respond to the needs of both Collette and the former girlfriend. He was someone who took care of people, a trait he had manifested all his life. Collette was aware of this side of Paul and was drawn to him because of it. But when it led to her feeling of secondary importance to him, she became resentful. When they had the helpful context of therapy, they were able to talk about these issues without arguing. Paul, who was usually very controlled, became emotional as he talked about how bad he felt for the pain he had caused Collette. When Collette saw Paul's tears and heard how bad he felt, it made a difference. For the first time, she was able to let go of her conviction that he didn't care. This made it easier for her to let go of her anger and resentment.

People with excessive shame go through life constantly on the lookout for reminders of their inadequacy. Feeling any kind of shame is likely to trigger their severe shame scripts so they are compelled to avoid all experiences of shame. In their intimate relationships, acknowledging that they have been hurtful with those they love can trigger massive amounts of shame, so shame-based individuals learn to disavow their hurtful behavior. The way this is most commonly done is by treating the partner's hurt as an indication of something that is wrong with the partner. This allows the shame-based partner to maintain his view of himself as not hurtful and thereby keep his shame from getting triggered. Shame-based individuals seldom show their partners that they feel bad about hurting them; their partners are thus denied the feelings of security that can come from truly knowing (seeing) that one's partner cares. Basically, *the severe shame of the shame-based individual feels so terrible that he will stifle his caring feelings and sacrifice his partner's sense of security in order to avoid his deep shame (though this is seldom a conscious choice).*

Owning and Acting on Shame

The power of shame is greatly decreased when the shame is acknowledged. It is *hidden* shame that fuels conflict and constitutes such a destructive force in a relationship. When shame is acknowledged, then the healing power of a positive attachment relationship can be brought to bear on the injuries (and distorted scripts about both self and other) from earlier attachment relationships. When partners can acknowledge their shame, conflict declines. There is less need to fight about who caused the bad feeling because both partners know the shame was already there and just got activated.

Intimate relationships have the greatest power to produce shame, and they offer ample opportunities to actively disown shame. It is surprisingly easy, and unfortunately common, for a partner to disown his shame and not be held accountable for actions that may hurt the other partner and make her feel insecure. Yet the damage of disowning his shame comes back in myriad ways and interferes with intimacy. *The primary measure of the health of an intimate relationship is how shame is managed within the relationship.*[7] There are a number of psychological models that describe healthy versus unhealthy ways of relating; virtually all of them address how people deal with shame affect (though it is seldom named as such).

The healthy management of shame involves owning it and taking responsibility for making things better—acting on it instead of reacting to it. After what you have read on the destructive nature of shame, it may be somewhat startling to hear that shame helps us to connect.

Connecting Through Shame

I have tried to show how shame interferes with intimate connections. Partners twist and turn to find ways to avoid their shame, and in the process, they limit their intimate connection. But when partners stop trying to avoid their shame and instead own up to it and stay in it when they encounter it, the possibility for much greater connection becomes open to them. How can this be so?

We know that partners can trigger each other's shame through a variety of routes, many of them destructive (contempt, disgust, rage, and so forth), but when shame is triggered in a nondestructive fashion, perhaps unintentionally, then the possibility is created for deeper emotional connection. One of the most common examples is when one partner is disappointed with the other. If she expresses her disappointment and he is able to remain with his shame and not sever the connection, she then has the opportunity to see how much she matters to him, how much he really cares.

When he can allow her to be disappointed in him, stirring his shame, without his trying to escape it by being defensive or turning it on her, their emotional connection will deepen. If he tries to make the disappointment impersonal and not about him in order to avoid his experience of shame, it will disconnect them. An example: My wife tells me she is disappointed that I didn't think about her when I made plans for the weekend. I have a choice. I can try to avoid my shame by being defensive ("I didn't do anything wrong; all I did was plan this one little thing."), by discounting her disappointment ("Look, it's only a couple of hours; why do you have to make such a big deal out of it?"), by turning it on her and blaming her ("You usually have plans anyway; you didn't tell me when you were going out last week."), or by making it impersonal ("Hey, I didn't know you wanted to go out."). Or I can stay with her disappointment and own my shame ("I'm sorry; I didn't think about you. I'm sorry I let you down."). The result of the latter choice is that she feels understood, cared about, and we become closer.

One of the principles for effective marriage derived by John Gottman's (1999) research is his concept of "turning toward" the other rather than turning away. He provides various examples of turning toward, but I believe the fundamental element is for a partner to remain with his shame or his willingness to experience his shame while he tries to hear what the other partner has to say, even if hearing his partner's thoughts and feelings is likely to activate his shame. His capacity to remain connected to his partner when she is activating his shame with her feelings of disappointment is a powerful measure of emotional maturity.

Apologies and Esteem Threat

Every person in an attachment relationship wants his partner to understand and show that she cares and feels bad (healthy shame) if she's done something to hurt or disappoint him. And he can tell whether her apology is real or only done for appearances because he is highly attuned to the affective tone of the apology. The need for an apology is a major mechanism in repairing attachment injuries, yet that same need ends up fueling a lot of conflict in intimate relationships. Most of the time this is because one or both partners regard some aspect of the apology process as an esteem threat.

The act of apologizing can activate the apologizer's shame; hence, many people avoid genuine apologies because they are trying to avoid their shame. This is the most common source of conflict around the need for an apology. The injured partner doesn't receive a genuine message of concern and desire to heal any hurt feelings, so the injury remains unhealed. But the intrusion of an esteem threat does not stop with one partner's inability to apologize.

Often the injured partner's esteem concerns get involved as well. Some people become indignant when they do not receive a real apology, and they go on the warpath in their righteousness. The appearance of indignation generally means that the injured partner has experienced the lack of an apology as an esteem threat and is now attacking the perceived source of the threat.

Of course the attempt to force an apology is doomed from the outset. The partner who feels he is being forced to apologize generally feels the injured partner is trying to shame him, and he resists with all his might. When no genuine apology appears, the partners remain disconnected to some degree. *A partnership that lacks real apologies is a partnership of two people whose fears of experiencing their shame outweigh their concern for each other's feelings.* This does not mean that they don't love each other, but it does mean that their capacity for loving is limited by their esteem concerns.

People who cannot apologize usually have too much shame and feel they are debasing themselves if they genuinely apologize. They justify not apologizing with the argument that they would be taking all the blame and that would be unfair since the other person is also at fault.

Viewing apologies in terms of blame moves the process into the realm of esteem and erases the real need for the apology. If the need for an apology involves an attachment injury, it is crucial that the therapist remain clear on why the apology is needed. Apologies about attachment injuries are not about deciding who is at fault. Apologies are: (a) an acknowledgment that one has caused emotional pain, (b) an expression of concern, and (c) an expression of remorse. The apology shows the injured partner that the offending partner cares. Apologies stem from healthy shame and a partner's awareness that he can hurt those he loves. Until a partner can face his shame, he will have difficulty apologizing.

Long-Term Intimacy

[I]t is a rare person who can cut himself off from mediate and immediate relations with others for long spaces of time without undergoing a deterioration in personality.

Harry Stack Sullivan, 1953/1997, p. 32[8]

Many partners describe the long-term satisfactions of their intimate relationships in terms of *companionship*. They want someone to talk to and do things with; they don't want to be alone. Of course, companionship is not limited to sexual relationships or love relationships, but then, neither is *intimacy*.[9] Both terms connote an atmosphere of openness and mutual acceptance. People connect through interacting—they talk together and do things together. In their intimate relationships, they don't just interact in a flat, unemotional manner; they communicate on an affective level as well and reveal themselves by exposing their feelings. This allows affective resonance to develop, which motivates them to hold on to the relationship (become more attached) and sets the context for their feelings about themselves to enter the relationship to a greater degree.

The next step is personal growth or interpersonal conflict, whether they signed up for it or not.

Personal Growth

One can acquire everything in solitude—except character.

Stendahl (Marie Henri Beyle), quoted in Seldes, 1985, p. 399.

I have emphasized how intimacy is necessary for individuals to grow and transform themselves into the kinds of people they want to be. Most people probably don't think of themselves as looking for a relationship that will help them to grow emotionally, but continued growth seems to be a hallmark of health and maturity. Obviously there are a variety of reasons that impel people to seek intimate relationships. Although popular culture often seems to emphasize the role of sexual pleasure, the need for a secure attachment relationship is surely the primary factor driving most people's desire for intimacy. Affect theory reveals how that attachment need recruits affects that stir feelings of passion powerful enough to motivate the individual to endure the risks of painful disappointment and rejection.

Interacting and talking openly in an accepting relationship is good for people. There is research evidence indicating that people pay a physical cost for inhibiting their thoughts and feelings and derive physical benefits from expressing their thoughts and feelings. People who habitually inhibit themselves are at greater risk for problems with their immune, cardiac, vascular, and nervous systems.[10] A relationship in which we can confess our deepest thoughts and feelings is good for our health!

Courage and Intimacy

It appears that the benefit of partners opening up and revealing themselves with each other is derived less from the content of what is revealed than from the process of revealing themselves. Yet the content matters a great deal because the more personal and private the content is, the more powerful the revelation. This is why *it is an act of courage for a partner to reveal the depth of his need or go into his shame with the other partner!* The process has the potential for producing greater closeness but also poses the danger of rejection and pain. What if he reveals something about himself that he considers to be truly awful, something he fears can never be accepted, and his partner responds with disgust and distance? Or what if he hears something from his partner that he finds repellant? These are the kinds of dangers that keep people from revealing themselves in the first place.

The couple therapist cannot eliminate the danger that marks the path to greater intimacy. In fact, it is important that she maintain a healthy respect for that danger. If she denies it or minimizes it, then the therapy is not safe. Her job is to serve as a guide, but it is the partners who must take the risks. If one partner reacts negatively to the other partner's revelations, the therapist can try to make the setting safe enough for him to examine his negative reactions. Just examining one's negative reaction to the other partner's revelations is in itself an act of courage because genuine self-examination requires the person to be willing to be vulnerable and reveal himself.

Truly confronting themselves and going into their shame, expressing remorse when they've hurt each other and distress when they've been hurt, and revealing how much they want and need each other's acceptance and caring and respect—these are the kinds of risks that partners must be willing to take if they want greater intimacy. Emotional safety is their barometer along that path, and the achievement of emotional safety changes with the levels of intimacy. Some partners are satisfied with lesser levels of closeness and openness; others want more. The couple therapist's job is to help them achieve emotional safety at whatever level of intimacy they choose to pursue. The rest is up to the couple.

17
The Emotional Safety Model of Treatment

The emotional safety model begins and ends with the issue of emotional safety. Couples who are caught in cycles of repetitive conflict and/or distancing lack emotional safety in their relationships. From the first session and throughout the entire course of the therapy, the therapist's most basic intervention is to be attuned to the specific realms in which each partner feels unsafe. The therapy is not successfully completed until the couple has achieved emotional safety and has the ability to reachieve it in the wake of the occasional threats to safety that characterize intimate relationships.

The therapist's capacity to identify the sources of each partner's feelings of unsafety plays a major role in the formation of a strong working alliance, which is a key factor in working with couples. Each partner feels understood, which strengthens the bond to the therapist. The goal of the emotional safety model is to achieve and maintain emotional safety in the relationship. This goal is readily grasped by most partners, particularly as it is operationalized in terms of each individual's specific concerns. The tasks the therapist then proposes in order to achieve that goal make fundamental sense to the partners.[1] There is rarely any question about why the partners are being asked to do this or that because the therapist chooses tasks that have an obvious relevance to the goal. The entire process of identifying the goals and tasks of the therapy is transparent; the therapist makes no effort to disguise her efforts and readily explains what she is doing and why.

Treatment proceeds in stages, as with other models of couple therapy. Most couple therapies describe an initial stage of stabilization, particularly with couples in conflict. What the emotional safety model emphasizes in that initial stage is the development of a clear understanding of each partner's emotional experience. Most models include assessment in the beginning of therapy, but that term is insufficient to capture the rich, interactive process that constitutes this intervention. The therapist is not just assessing the partners, she is actively exploring her understanding of each partner's fundamental concerns and engaging each partner in correcting her and guiding her to a fuller and more complete understanding. The result is that each partner feels understood and the therapist has the foundation for strong rapport with each partner.

The power of helping each partner feel truly understood should not be under-estimated. The emotional safety model and the lens of affect give the therapist a unique advantage in grasping the dynamics of the partners' emotional relationship. She is frequently able to identify and articulate a partner's concerns more clearly and succinctly than the partner himself. The result is not just that the partner feels understood by the therapist; it is very often the case that the partner ends up with a better understanding of himself and what he is reacting to. And, of course, since this is occurring in the presence of the other partner, the development of the partners' understanding of each other begins to grow.

As I indicated in the Preface, this model is not restricted to a particular school of therapy. It should enhance most couple therapy approaches, some more than others. It will probably appear somewhat different in the hands of different practitioners. Here is a summary of the general form of the therapy as I use it.

Identifying the Problem

The initial goal is to determine the realm (or realms) in which each partner perceives a threat to his or her emotional safety. Once the perceptions of threat have been accurately identified, the therapist seeks to determine how each partner is reacting to this perceived threat. Usually, one or both partners' reactions are a significant factor in creating a perception of threat for the other partner. Once the relevant threats and reactions are identified, the interactive cycle is described to the couple, and each partner is told exactly what he or she needs to do in order to break the cycle. This responsibility for changing is balanced; it is never focused on only one of the partners.

Working Phase

The therapy then moves into an ongoing (usually weekly) process of identifying what has been stimulated and how the partners have responded. The partners' perceptions of threat may evolve over time, but the overall process remains the same. Gradually, the partners begin to recognize the cycle, as well as their individual concerns, on their own.

Within each partner's areas of perceived threat, the therapist seeks to both validate the partner's concerns and help the partner overcome them. When the partner's primary concerns are in the realm of esteem, the therapist seeks to: (a) teach the other partner to be more sensitive to his power to stimulate esteem threat, (b) teach the afflicted partner to recognize his sensitivity to esteem and explore its roots, and (c) challenge the afflicted partner to improve his esteem. When the partner's primary concerns are in the realm of attachment, the therapist seeks to: (a) teach the other partner to be sensitive to the afflicted partner's attachment sensitivities, (b) teach the other partner to respond better to the afflicted partner's attachment needs, and (c) make the relationship safe enough that the afflicted partner can allow himself to be vulnerable with the other partner. *Whether the perceived threats are in the realm of attachment or esteem, a prerequisite for effective therapy is that the sessions be emotionally safe. This is a central priority throughout the therapy and supersedes other priorities any time emotional safety is lost in the sessions.*

Concerns in either realm can lead to exploration of the roots of a partner's sensitivity. Exploring early painful attachment experiences usually increases: (a) the other partner's empathy and compassion for the afflicted partner and (b) the afflicted partner's ability to be more vulnerable in the other partner's presence. Exploring early painful esteem experiences usually increases: (a) the afflicted partner's self-knowledge and (b) the other partner's understanding of the afflicted partner's sensitivities.

It is important to keep exploration of early life roots of esteem and attachment concerns in perspective. Some partners may seize on such explanations to blame the afflicted partner and argue their own innocence in current problems. The therapist must block any effort to treat a partner's past as a source of blame. It is each partner's responsibility to be sensitive to the other partner's sensitivities; understanding the roots of a partner's sensitivity does not relieve the other partner of responsibility. In fact, it produces the opposite effect; it increases the other partner's responsibility to be sensitive in that area. Ultimately, an understanding of the past only serves to help partners better understand the present. It is usually best to end explorations of the past by bringing both partners back to their current relationship before finishing a session.

During this phase of the therapy, each partner is instructed to make specific changes. Negative reactions (to perceived threats) are usually the initial target. Partners who are reacting from Nathanson's (1992) compass of shame elements are taught to recognize their shame and stay with it rather than react to it. Partners who are dealing with an attachment threat by attacking the other partner's esteem are taught to soften their protest. Both partners are taught to listen without automatically reacting negatively.

When a partner perceives attachment threat, the other partner is directed to increase the behaviors that represent positive attachment. These directives are usually fairly specific (e.g., the poorly attuned partner is directed to focus on attunement, the unreliable partner is directed to being more supportive, and so forth). When a partner's attachment concerns are diffuse, both partners are directed to perform activities that reintroduce positive affects into the relationship.

When a partner has experienced an explicit attachment injury, the therapist seeks to uncover the offending partner's shame so that the injured partner can see the other partner truly cares. The usual impediment to this process is the offending partner's difficulty accessing his shame. That difficulty is most often the result of his perception of an esteem threat ("I'll be taking all the blame."), but often the process of working through major attachment injuries reveals that the offending partner also perceived an attachment threat at an earlier point. The process of working through major attachment injuries often continues into the third phase of the therapy.

The course of therapy in this middle phase often starts with mutual esteem concerns and then shifts into attachment concerns in one partner as he gets past his focus on esteem. Many partners can state attachment concerns from the outset, but others do not recognize their attachment concerns while they are battling for their esteem.

Ending Phase

If the therapy is working, each partner begins to change his reactions (to perceived threats) so they are less threatening for the other partner. If either partner was dealing with an attachment threat, the appearance of positive attachment behaviors brings feelings of renewed connection (though this can be a very slow process in the case of major attachment injuries). This phase of therapy is where partners may go into their shame and connect at a level of vulnerability that brings greater intimacy. I do not mean to imply that all couples do this kind of work; many (perhaps most) do not. When couples are satisfied to resume their life without therapy, then the therapy is completed. The decision to probe deeper and pursue a more intimate connection is the couple's, not the therapist's.

In addition to the work just described, two distinct kinds of sessions often occur during this phase of therapy. One is when the couple comes in feeling good and has nothing to talk about. The therapist can use these sessions to review what each partner is doing differently and to discuss how the couple will repair the loss of safety when it inevitably occurs. The other kind of session is when everything blows up and they feel they have made no progress. Sometimes it helps for the therapist to point out that progress may only be visible in the decreased frequency of such blowups, and that when there is a blowup (meaning a complete loss of emotional safety) the partners may feel just as bad as they ever did. In fact, if they have actually been feeling safer with each other, then a sudden blowup can feel even worse than in the past. The real measure of progress is not whether the partners ever lose their emotional safety, but whether they can repair the relationship and reestablish safety when they do lose it.

Ending therapy varies with the couple. Some couples reachieve emotional safety rapidly and end cleanly. Others take longer to achieve safety and longer to give up the safe haven of therapy. With couples in the latter category, it is helpful to decrease the frequency of sessions over time and allow the partners to gradually gain confidence in their ability to manage on their own.

Structured Tasks and Homework

Couple therapists commonly employ therapeutic tools and structured tasks as part of the therapy. I am distinguishing therapeutic tasks from the tools that we teach our clients, but sometimes the two overlap. We provide tools for partners to use when particular situations arise. Probably the most common tools are mechanisms to use in order to stop conflict escalation[2] and communication tools, such as paraphrasing what the other partner has said.[3] Whereas *tools* are techniques to use when situations arise, *tasks* are specific, structured exercises that couples are asked to perform either in or out of session.

Tasks can be used to reduce threats in the realms of esteem and attachment, but since delving into these realms increases the potential for activating those threats, it is very important to structure tasks in such a fashion as to maximize the likelihood that they can be performed safely. There are a variety of tasks currently employed by couple therapists, and many of these tasks address aspects of the threats identified in the emotional safety model. For example, positive attachment affects can be enhanced by structured tasks in which the partners do little things for each other.[4] There is one particular structured task which I have found to be especially useful in the emotional safety model.

A common task employed by couple therapists is "checking in." Basically, the partners are instructed to talk to each other regularly about how they are doing as individuals and as a couple. I found a variant of this task that was developed by Maggie Scarf (1988), and I began using this task with partners who were having difficulty bringing their shameful parts into the relationship.[5] I renamed it (at least in my mind) as the shame and pride task.

The task is a way of helping partners stay in touch with both themselves and each other. On a regular basis, the partners sit down and check in on how they are feeling about themselves. Specifically, they must each identify the sources of shame and pride they encounter in their daily lives. To do this, each must tell the other two things about his or her day: at least one thing that made the partner feel good about himself and at least one thing that made him feel bad about himself.

This simple task can be profoundly helpful—or it can accomplish nothing at all. It depends upon whether the partners remain superficial or whether they use the opportunity to probe more deeply into their feelings about themselves. The most common error is to talk about what made them feel good or bad—rather than good or bad *about themselves*. Here is what happened when Dan and Darla began to check in with each other.

For years, Dan and Darla kept their relationship at a superficial level. Dan became increasingly unhappy with the relationship, yet he never said anything. Although he still loved Darla deeply, he found their time together to be boring and found himself drawn toward other women. In therapy, we worked on what prevented him from speaking up with his feelings. An overly simplified explanation is that he feared she would not sustain her interest in him if he complained. Among other things, they began to use the check-in task.

Initially, Dan had considerable difficulty distinguishing between good/ bad feelings and good/bad feelings about himself. He was literally unaware of most of his feelings about himself. However, he caught the difference very abruptly during one session. He suddenly realized that he had never fully revealed himself to anyone in his life. As a child, he felt his parents' approval was only forthcoming if he did something extraordinary. So he became a performer and received accolades throughout his adult life. But he always had a vague awareness that no one was getting the real Dan. Because he felt the real Dan was not interesting, not someone who could keep anyone's attention. This highly accomplished man felt very small and unimportant deep inside.

Darla was dismayed by Dan's interest in other women. It confirmed her own inner belief that she had little to offer. Indeed, her belief was not news to her; she was well aware of her feeling. She had greater difficulty identifying the things that made her feel good about herself. As she reported on those, Dan observed that they always involved her doing things for other people. He began to spontaneously point out other kinds of things that made him feel good about her. These were hard for Darla; she was quick to discount the things that Dan suggested. But, gradually, she began to take in more of Dan's positive view of her.

Over time their relationship changed and they held back less from each other. Dan saw the vitality that Darla displayed with others return to their own interactions. And Darla found Dan to be coming out of himself, more alive and happy with her. They also had more conflict, but it was never disrespectful or destructive. It was just two adults managing their differences.

Safe Enough

I have discussed some of the ways in which therapy may address preexisting problems with esteem and attachment. The adult attachment relationship offers a unique opportunity to redress problematic views of self and other that haunt the person who grew up in an atmosphere of abuse or neglect. The partner with long-standing esteem issues can become less easily triggered by confronting himself, strengthening his empathic wall, and going into his shame. Through such means, the emotional safety model allows for both personal and relational growth. However, *the achievement of emotional safety does not necessarily require that preexisting issues be resolved.*

For example, an esteem threat may be eliminated by a strengthened empathic wall on the part of the partner feeling threatened, or it may be attenuated by greater sensitivity and a softened protest on the part of the other partner. An attachment threat must be resolved before partners can achieve emotional safety, but resolution of the threat can come from efforts by the other partner without resolving the threatened partner's long-standing sensitivities.

The emotional safety model is not oriented toward healing past attachment injuries or overcoming negative self scripts *unless the partners are unable to achieve emotional safety without addressing these preexisting problems.* Many couples achieve satisfying levels of emotional safety even though individual partners continue to carry long-standing sensitivities based on problematic views of self and other.[6] In this respect, the emotional safety model is structured like Pinsof's integrative problem-centered therapy (1995; IPCT). In the IPCT model, the first goal is to establish consensual agreement between the clients and the therapist regarding the problem to be worked on. As long as the tasks of therapy are demonstrably linked to the resolution of the consensually identified problem, the therapist has a mandate to pursue those tasks. In the emotional safety model, the lack of emotional safety is the problem, and the therapist is mandated to pursue those tasks that will restore emotional safety. Any work that exceeds that mandate is outside the model.

Long-Standing Individual Issues

The emotional safety model allows for work on long-standing issues when work on the more immediate sources of threat proves to be insufficient. When work on more remote sources of threat is required, the model directs the therapy into the historical aspects of attachment and esteem. The work on these preexisting issues is similar to other kinds of individual-focused work, but there are some important distinctions.

Structural Models

The script theory view of emotions differs markedly from the views of emotions implied by various structural models of personality, including object relations theory, self psychology, and Freudian drive theory, as well as most cognitive models of mental functioning. From the point of view of script theory, most of the enduring traits that constitute personality simply reflect an abundance of particular kinds of scripts and the emotions in which they are assembled. Change is largely about disassembling the emotions containing those scripts and developing a different repertoire of emotions. It is the emotions themselves that shape personality, and it is the emotions that must change. This is a very different view from that implied by models that treat emotions as products of cognitions, drives, or structural elements in the personality. Tomkins's (1962, 1963, 1991, 1992) insight that affects provide the majority of motivation is an essential component in understanding the importance of emotion in personality functioning.

The view of emotions derived from affect and script theory is so radically different from traditional views of personality that this will surely remain an area of controversy for many years to come. Yet there is already a developing base of research that lends some support to this view of emotion as a structural component of personality. Research on negative emotionality has shown it to be consistently predictive of a variety of mental health problems and vulnerabilities, while positive emotionality appears to confer a degree of resilience to stressors.[7] Krueger, McGue, and Iacono (2001) have shown how negative emotionality consistently underlies personality disorders, but that the nature of the particular personality disorder may differ according to the amount of positive emotionality and capacity for constraint. Clearly, the combination of an abundance of negative emotions and a lack of positive emotions constitutes a serious risk factor for emotional problems, while an abundance of positive emotions and a relative dearth of negative emotions contribute to psychological resilience.

Internalization Models

A focus on the attachment and esteem realms of a partner's internal working models of self and other differs from a focus on processes of internalization. The difference has to do with the partner's experience of his emotions and the scripts assembled in those emotions. The emotional safety model emphasizes the individual's *personal construction of his emotions* based on his unique experiences; it avoids conceptualizations that suggest the irrational nature of the scripts is based on a lack of ownership.

For example, negative views of self that rely on the concept of internalization imply that the individual is adopting another person's view (Person A is adopting Person B's view of Person A). This way of thinking leads to misunderstanding. It would be more accurate to say that negative evaluations of the self may *develop* in response to perceived negative evaluations by the other. The negative self-evaluation remains one's own, and therapeutic growth occurs when the individual confronts his *own* feelings about himself. Viewing such emotions as internalized can seem to imply that the developing self is some kind of passive container for the attitudes of others. Script theory emphasizes that it is the meanings that an individual derives from his affect-laden experiences that determine the nature of his emotions.

The idea of internalization of others' attitudes and feelings toward a person leads to an awkward theoretical view of that person's emotions. For example, Greenberg and Paivio discuss the role of contempt and disgust in the experience of shame, stating that "Contempt and disgust … when internalized and directed at the self … produce maladaptive feelings of shame and self-loathing" (1997/2003, p. 230). Their formulation is consistent with that of many traditional theorists, and it certainly acknowledges the importance of contempt and disgust in triggering shame; but the emphasis on the internalization of the contempt and disgust of others can lead the therapist on a course of trying to remove foreign attitudes (e.g., "You're not really disgusting and contemptible."). If, instead, we recognize that the individual's experience of being the object of others' contempt and disgust triggered his shame, then we seek to help him confront himself about why *he* feels he is disgusting and contemptible. What was it about himself that he concluded justified the poor treatment? He may conclude the treatment was unjustified or he may reveal the characteristics about himself that he has tried to disavow and hide from the world. In either case, the path to overcoming his shame is to confront his own views of self, not to support the idea that his views were planted by others.

Transference Models

Transference models of treatment help partners separate the current relationship from past relationships, which helps partners treat current interactions as unique. However, the transference model emphasizes the individual's feelings toward someone else (that which is being transferred or displaced) and can contribute to a defocus from the self. A focus on the other in the attachment realm is consistent with the emotional safety model, but a focus on the other is counterproductive when the individual has esteem issues, as it shifts the locus of the problem to the person's feelings about others rather than himself.

A central facet of the emotional safety model is its recognition of the importance of the realm of esteem, in which a negative view of self is a much greater impediment than a negative view of the other. Of course it is not simply the negative view but the negative affects assembled with that view. When shame affect is directed at the self (not to mention disgust and dissmell), shame emotion results, and people burdened with excessive shame pay an exorbitant price. The toxicity of high levels of shame can be so lethal that partners will do virtually anything to escape their shame—including sacrifice their attachment relationship.

The popularity of interpreting transference feelings about the other probably stems from the power of shame to fool us and remain hidden. Focusing on the Bad Other is a common defense against recognizing and experiencing one's most shame-producing views of self. But viewing couples through the lens of affect makes it easy for us to distinguish between perceptions of the other as untrustworthy (attachment realm) and perceptions of disapproval from the other (esteem realm).

The implication of focusing on the other when the issue is actually esteem is that transference can be a defense. It is the same type of defense as his fighting with her about what she thinks and feels about him. In both cases, the focus on the other person is a defocus from his shame and an attempt to eliminate the stimulus triggering it. A focus on transference can easily lead to a focus on the other in the childhood relationship and still fail to get at the person's self scripts.

Deficit Models

It is an error to characterize shame proneness as some kind of deficit in the self or in one's ability to feel good about oneself. Script theory suggests that the shame-prone person does not have an incomplete self or even necessarily lack good feelings about himself; he is just acutely sensitive to feeling bad about himself because of his extensive shame scripts. His shame is easily triggered. The typical early life environment that contributes to the development of such extensive shame is unlikely to provide people with the resources to regulate such affects. So the shame-prone person is usually emotionally immature and prone to seek help from others to manage his feelings about himself. This makes him highly reactive in a relationship. Furthermore, his life choices are shaped by his avoidance of potential triggers of his shame. Thus, when two individuals with significant shame become intimately involved, they form a relationship that is dominated by their shared need to avoid shame. Any differences between them have the potential to trigger shame so they avoid bringing those differences into the relationship. This results in the picture of the undifferentiated system. They are highly reactive to any potential triggers, and their fights focus on changing each other's perceptions.

The concept of growth of the self is tricky as it might be interpreted to mean that the self was deficient. An alternate view to the self-deficit model is that the deficiency refers to pride scripts. It is not necessary to posit pathological development of the self. Those people who lack confidence, are self-conscious, oriented toward pleasing, or who seek mirroring do not necessarily have incomplete selves; rather they may simply have well-developed shame scripts and insufficient pride scripts.

Empathy Models

Many approaches to couple therapy emphasize the development of empathy between the partners as both a goal of therapy and a means of helping the couple work out their problems. Sex therapist David Schnarch (1991), who uses Bowen's differentiation model with couples, says that couples do not achieve empathy until they are well differentiated in their relationship. Viewing couples through the lens of affect leads to some different conclusions about the role of empathy. If affective resonance is the core of empathy, then intimate partners are not lacking in empathy. Indeed, what they often need is to be able to employ their empathic walls more and empathize a bit less.

People often talk about empathy as though it were a form of sympathy informed by some kind of deep understanding of the other person's feelings. The deep understanding is part of empathy, but the sympathetic feeling is not necessarily part of it. *Webster's Unabridged Dictionary* defines empathy as the intellectual identification with or vicarious experiencing of the feelings, thoughts, or attitudes of another. This may lead him to have a sympathetic feeling when she is feeling bad, but it can produce quite a different response when she is conveying a negative feeling about him, the empathic listener. When he identifies with her negative feelings about him, he might be said to be experiencing empathy, but his experience will not resemble the model of compassion so often represented by clinicians. Empathizing with her disapproving feelings toward him can activate his shame. And if he is disavowing his shame, then he is likely going to react negatively.

Differentiation Models

Couples (and families) characterized as poorly differentiated are hypersensitive and overreactive. Autonomous behavior by one person typically elicits a negative response from other members of the system. The emotional safety model views these people as controlled by their inability to manage shame. Partners are either shut down and emotionally dead or endlessly maneuvering to shift shame (blame) away from themselves. As I suggested in Chapter 12, the partners in these kinds of couples come from families in which the mechanism of *external approval* has been substituted for genuine self-esteem. The worst possible actions are acts of disloyalty, because disloyal actions challenge the *approval mores* that provide every family member with a sense of approval. When a family member operates in a manner that indicates that he doesn't agree with the family's conventional definition of approval, it creates anxiety in everyone and they react by trying to make him wrong so they can feel right. This is essentially the same situation that occurs with couples who fight over esteem.

No argument is contained within these families; everyone gets pulled in because everyone is concerned about approval (being right). Triangulation (bringing a third person into a conflict) is always an effort to leverage the opposing person's thinking and prove oneself right. "If I bring Mom into it and she agrees with me, then I am right and you are wrong and I do not have to feel shame." Individuals, families, and couples characterized as well differentiated are people who are able to acknowledge their shame and act on it rather than react to it. Bowen (1978) contended that the central issue that defines differentiation is balancing the competing pulls for autonomy and togetherness. But these are simply the arenas in which the family's mechanism for providing approval encounters the greatest difficulty—it's hard to be different (autonomous) if the other members withdraw approval (togetherness). People who are well differentiated can safely be individuals (i.e., people with differences) with each other because they are not dependent upon one another's approval to help them avoid being triggered into shame.

Developmental Models

The emotional safety model differs from models that focus on individual development in how the responsibility for change is determined. In the emotional safety model, the need for a partner to change is determined by the other partner's perceived safety. If she perceives an attachment threat, he must change by increasing his positive attachment behaviors. If he perceives esteem threat, she must change by decreasing her esteem attacking behaviors.[8] Also, she must change by improving the behaviors that constitute her reaction to her perception of an attachment threat, and he must change by improving those behaviors that constitute his reaction to his perception of an esteem threat.

The emotional safety model contends that *each partner is responsible for whatever he or she is doing that creates threat for the other partner, and those are the behaviors that must change.* This emphasis is a radical departure from models that focus on each individual's level of development. The emotional safety model emphasizes acceptance of each partner, and significant individual psychopathology is not viewed as a problem unless it is specifically involved in creating a threat to emotional safety. This point of view assumes that individual pathology was present before the partners lost their safety, and that they can re-achieve that safety without necessarily having to correct all aspects of individual pathology. *Mutual acceptance can make a relationship safe, even with the presence of individual psychopathology.*

The Emphasis on Shame

Concerns about attachment can produce significantly distressing emotions without necessarily activating shame. But concern about esteem always involves some variant of shame, and attachment concerns often do so as well. Additionally, I have emphasized how the capacity to go into shame can play a role in achieving greater openness and connection in an intimate relationship. Therefore, I should point out that shame is not the only affect that makes relationships difficult.

Emotions containing any of the three negative affects can be problematic. Fear-terror has the power to paralyze partners if it is not understood. It frequently enters relationships as a sequela of one partner's exposure to trauma. The traumatized partner's fear is a problem in the relationship, but it doesn't lead to cycles of conflict or distancing unless it activates a partner's perception of threat in the realm of attachment or esteem. For example, if her fear is triggered in his presence, he may respond with understanding or he may take it personally. In the latter case, he has probably perceived her fear as an esteem threat. The emotional safety model can be used to help keep the relationship safe while individual work occurs with the traumatized partner. Depending upon how safe the relationship is, that work can occur in conjoint sessions or, if the relationship is not safe enough, in individual therapy sessions.

Emotions containing distress-anguish are difficult when they appear in any relationship. A partner's depression is the most common way that these affects enter an intimate relationship, and it is a challenge for the nondepressed partner to be able to remain connected and yet block out enough of his resonance to the distress affect so that he can continue to function. Depression is even more challenging for the relationship when it includes significant aspects of shame (indications are that shame plays a role in a large proportion of depressions).[9] However, as with fear, the presence of distress does not lead to relational problems unless it activates a perception of threat in the realm of attachment or esteem.

The third negative affect, anger-rage, can be a major problem when it appears in an intimate relationship, but this varies with the people involved and the intensity of the affective expression. The emotional safety model is usually well suited for dealing with anger problems since anger is almost always a secondary emotion when it appears in an intimate relationship. In most cases, the anger is a reaction to shame.

So shame is not the central problem in every relationship, but as I said in the Preface, shame is a factor in every relationship. I regard the way in which shame is handled as the most important factor that distinguishes healthy from unhealthy relationships. Unhealthy relationships are marked by frequent shame, reactions to shame, and shaming of others. Healthy relationships are marked by infrequent shame, the ability to tolerate occasional shame (especially healthy shame), and a lack of shaming-based behaviors. A major goal of the emotional safety model is to make the couple's relationship safe enough for partners to openly acknowledge and act on their shame.

Therapist Use of Self

When it comes to dealing with issues of shame, the therapist's personal stance is critical. For the partners to safely acknowledge and act on their shame, they must be in therapy with a shame-aware therapist who herself is not inhibited by her fear of activating her own shame and is willing and able to act on her shame if it is activated. Therapists who utilize techniques that address shame-related issues tend to come to recognize the importance of their relationship with their own shame. Dealing with our clients' shame is unlikely to succeed if we therapists are unable to access our own shame. When we make therapeutic failures that create pain for our clients, our capacity to go into our shame and act on it plays the key role in healing—just as it does between intimate partners. It is only in making that interpersonal connection as imperfect human beings engaged in a cooperative task that we have any hope of offering our clients a realistic path to emotional safety.

Applying the Model

I have emphasized that this model can enhance any approach to couple therapy. When therapists view couples through the lens of affect, paying particular attention to the partners' perceptions of threat in the realms of esteem and attachment, the therapists will have incorporated an appreciation of their clients' emotional safety into the treatment. This does not mean that the emotional safety model cannot stand on its own—I myself work exclusively within the model. But an appreciation for emotional safety issues is not inconsistent with the goals of most, if not all, couple therapy approaches. Thus, I believe this model will prove useful to all couple therapists, not just those in search of an approach. I hope you and your clients find this helps you to achieve greater emotional safety.

Notes

Preface

1. There are several models that hypothesize specific mechanisms of change, of course, but there is no body of adequate research studies that supports a specific model. What has been shown is that several therapy approaches work: Behavioral Couple Therapy (BCT), Emotionally Focused Couple Therapy (EFCT), and Insight-Oriented Couple Therapy (IOCT) have the most research support (Chambless & Hollon, 1998; Snyder, Castellani, & Whisman, 2006). Additionally, several other approaches appear to be relatively effective when examined from the perspective of metaanalytic studies. These include cognitive behavioral, systemic, and eclectic/integrative approaches (Shadish & Baldwin, 2003). EFCT is fast emerging as the leading approach in couple therapy research, and it has been researched in a variety of contexts. It has been examined as an overall approach compared to nontreatment controls, as an overall approach compared to other approaches, and as a treatment for specific populations (Johnson, 2005). There is also a growing literature on the specific interventions employed in EFCT.

2. The emotional safety model has not been subjected to empirical investigation. Thus, it remains to be seen whether my view that this constitutes a common factor (or the only factor) will find empirical support.

3. Susan Johnson's Emotionally Focused Couple Therapy is a specialized approach to couple therapy that has its roots in Emotionally Focused Therapy for individuals, which Les Greenberg developed in concert with Susan Johnson in 1988. Johnson has written two major books on EFCT (1996, 2002, and a revised version of the original, 2005), as well as numerous articles and chapters.

4. Some of the shared components include paying particular attention to: (a) the partners' internal views of each other, as in Harville Hendrix's (1988, 1993) Imago Relationship Therapy; (b) the partners' historically determined emotions, as in Scharff and Scharff's (1991) object relations approach to couple therapy; (c) the partners' irrational beliefs as in Albert Ellis's (2001) Rational Emotive Behavior Therapy; (d) the partners' level of emotional fusion and differentiation as in Bowen's (1978) Family Systems Theory (Schnarch, 1991, 1998); (e) the partners' entrapment in circular interactions, as in the systems theory of the Palo Alto Group at the Mental Research Institute (Bodin, 1981); (f) the congruence and affective tone of the partners' communications, as in the family work of Virginia Satir (1967, 1988); (g) the partners' reactions to the activation of shame, as in Nathanson's (1992) individual model of shame; and, of course, the preeminent importance of (h) attachment processes, as in Susan Johnson's (1996, 2005) Emotionally Focused Couple Therapy; and (i) self-esteem, as in the work of Nathaniel Branden (1971, 1983).

   I'm sure many theorists would characterize the emotional safety model as an integrative approach because of these elements from so many different schools of therapy (and more), but I do not view it as such. I would say it is an *affective* model. It identifies and explains what is happening in a couple's emotional relationship, thereby allowing therapists to use it with a variety of interventions and approaches.

5. In a review of attachment and conflict studies, Lin Shi states: "Typically the wife demands change and emotional closeness and the husband avoids or disengages from this process. The husband's level of withdrawal is positively related to the wife's level of demand" (2003, p. 144).

Chapter 1

1. No theoretician came closer to the emotional safety model's view of esteem processes in a relationship than the father of interpersonal psychiatry, Harry Stack Sullivan (1953/1997). In the middle of the 20th century, he introduced the idea of a self system containing

"good me" and "bad me." He posited that people invested huge amounts of energy in "security operations," which were basically behaviors and attitudes intended to prevent the activation of "bad me." The notion of fighting to preserve one's being seen as "good me" rather than "bad me" by the partner is consistent with Sullivan's thinking.

Chapter 2

1. Tomkins's studies were published in a series of four volumes (1962, 1963, 1991, 1992). Some of the specifics of his theory evolved over the 30 years spanning those publications. I have tried to present his ideas in their final form. Of course, what little I have said about Tomkins's theory is vastly simplified, and I refer the reader to his original works for an appreciation of the true depth of his thoughts.

2. "The drives … are built-in mechanisms that sense a need, indicate how that need may be satisfied, and initiate the activity required. Affect … provides the sort of amplification that makes any information urgent and important, whether from drive, cognition, memory, perception, or any other source" (Nathanson, 1996b, p. 386). Nathanson gives the example of the hunger drive responding to blood levels of glucose or the drive to urinate responding to stretch receptors in the bladder. But these drives must recruit affects to bring a sense of urgency and motivation. We influence and manipulate people by triggering affects, just as we motivate ourselves by finding ways to generate our own affects. And we control ourselves by finding ways to dampen our affects.

3. Needless to say, many theorists do not agree with Tomkins's view that we are born with innate affects. See chapter 1 of S. B. Miller's (1996) book for a summary of the major criticisms of Tomkins's assertion that human infants are born with a set number of neurologically hard-wired affects. She refers to his theory as the theory of basic affects. It can also be argued that there may be more or less than the precise nine affects identified by Tomkins (he himself changed his mind about the number of innate affects over the course of his career). For the purposes of this book, it is not terribly important that the affects are exactly as he describes them. What does matter is: (a) the idea that affects provide motivation, (b) the observation that affect gives meaning to verbal and nonverbal communication, and (c) the idea that shame plays a special role and has the power to overrule the other affects.

4. Broucek (1991) argues against Tomkins's notion that shame affect is activated in any situation in which a source of interest or pleasure is impeded. He notes there is no experience of shame if a person is watching a sports event on television and the power fails. This is an excellent example because it is precisely the kind of situation that Tomkins views as certain to activate shame affect. The reason this doesn't make sense to Broucek and other theorists is because they are still thinking of shame as an emotion rather than the pure affect. Shame affect would show itself in the bad feeling that comes as a result of the power failure, but shame emotion would occur if the person felt it was somehow his fault that the power failed.

Chapter 3

1. See Holmes (1996) for a discussion of the psychoanalytic community's two-decade-long rejection of Bowlby's theories about attachment. He notes that when Bowlby first showed his film *A Two Year Old Goes to Hospital* at the British Psychoanalytic Society, Wilfred Bion is said to have insisted that "the little girl's misery was a manifestation of her envy of her mother's pregnancy, rather than a response to the separation itself" (1996, p. 43). This is a graphic example of the view prevalent at that time that mental pain primarily stems from the subjective inner world rather than from actual experiences in the external world.

2. The quote is from Johnson, 2005, p. 32. It is probably no coincidence that the lasting impact of attachment injuries and traumatic events were each known in small enclaves of the professional mental health community but neither took hold in the mainstream until posttraumatic disorders were finally acknowledged and accepted.

3. Bowlby's description of the infant's "listless turning away" is precisely the biological pattern that Tomkins describes as the infant's experience of shame. This illustrates the essential role of shame affect in the detachment of the infant that has been separated from mother for too long. As you will see in later chapters, the same mechanism is at work among adults.

4. Ainsworth, Blehar, Waters, and Wall (1978) identified several different styles of insecure attachment. She and her colleagues made similar observations to Bowlby's, but they created a situation for research purposes (Bowlby relied on actual separations). They exposed babies to a strange adult and studied the ways in which the babies were able to use their mothers as a source of security. Their observations led them to create different categories of attachment along a continuum from secure to insecure. They found some babies were able to effectively separate from mother and explore the new situation, but they avoided mother when she returned. The behavior of the babies was similar to the detached stage identified by Bowlby, even though these babies had only been separated from their mothers for a few moments.

5. The four-category model of attachment developed by Bartholomew (1991) and developed into an instrument by Bartholomew and Horowitz (1991) has become the template for the most successful of the adult attachment scales (Brennan, Clark, & Shaver, 1998).

6. Research linking attachment security with the ways in which adults approached their romantic relationships began with a self-report method developed by Hazan and Shaver (1987). This was a new approach to studying attachment, a simple questionnaire designed to assess adults' conscious evaluation of their attachment relationships. It led to other questionnaires, all designed to allow adults to rate their relationships (Stein, Jacobs, Ferguson, Allen, & Fonagy, 1998). This line of research has since blossomed into studies linking attachment security with a vast array of factors—ranging from individuals' attitudes toward relationships in general (Carnelley & Janoff-Bulman, 1992) to the ways in which individuals rate their marital satisfaction (Feeney, 1996; Tucker & Anders, 1999), to measures of personal commitment to relationships (Pistole & Vocaturo, 1999), effective communication within relationships (Feeney, 1996), general stability of relationships (Hill, Young, & Nord, 1994; Kirkpatrick & Davis, 1994; Kirkpatrick & Hazan, 1994), and expectations regarding future relationships (Whitaker, Beach, Etherton, Wakefield, & Anderson, 1999). Overall, the studies of attachment security show that individuals with more secure attachment styles are more likely to (a) be in long-term relationships, (b) maintain more stable relationships, and (c) experience fewer difficulties in their relationships (Mikulincer, Florian, Cowan, & Cowan, 2002).

7. Self-report questionnaires used to assess adult attachment have been criticized on the basis that they confound more global feelings about the relationship, such as liking versus disliking a partner, with specific attachment feelings. Recently, a group of researchers developing a measure of attachment queried a group of expert judges on the appropriateness of various items. They found a significant variance among the experts regarding what constituted an attachment item or a nonattachment item. The researchers' conclusion was that the expert judges were overinclusive regarding attachment (Allen, Stein, Fonagy, Fultz, & Target, 2005). I view this observation as representative of the way the field has tended to approach the concept of attachment when it is applied to adults.

8. There are, of course, other realms of significance, and sometimes considerable work is required in those realms. Trauma and sexuality are common examples. Problems certainly occur in other realms, but it is my contention that those problems alone seldom threaten emotional safety and lead to repetitive conflict or chronic avoidance. Instead, it is when the impact of problems from other realms is filtered through the realms of attachment and esteem that couples truly lose their emotional safety. Chapter 9 ends with examples of how problems in the realms of trauma and sexuality can activate concerns in the realms of attachment and esteem.

9. This description of an emotion is very similar to what some analytic authors have referred to as an ego state. In a discussion of how borderline patients shift between contradictory ego states, Otto Kernberg stated that "these ego states represented an affect linked with a certain object-image or object representation of the patient while in that affective state" (1976, p. 28).

10. The term "Other-esteem" was used by Philip Hwang to refer to our treatment of, and attitudes toward, all other people. "Other-esteem is the respect, acceptance, caring, valuing and promotion of all human beings, without reservation" (Hwang, 2000, p. 16). I am using the term to refer to the same qualities of respect, acceptance, and so forth as directed at the partner. I am specifically interested in the impact of one partner's other-esteem emotions on the other partner's self-esteem emotions.

11. The area of esteem most often discussed by attachment theorists is self-worth, specifically whether the individual feels worthy of being loved. This particular aspect of esteem is strongly influenced by the partner's attachment emotions. However, many more aspects of esteem fall under the rubric of adequacy or competence. In those areas of esteem, the individual is less attuned to whether the partner is attached and is much more attuned to the partner's Other-esteem emotions. Does my partner view me as adequate?

12. Affect theory views the drives as the biological needs all organisms have. Thus, there is a drive to have sufficient water, to obtain food, to reproduce, and so forth. Strictly speaking, drives are essential to life. From that point of view, attachment may not qualify as a drive per se, but I have treated it as fundamentally the same as the drives. In any case, the profound insight of affect theory is that the drives provide little in the way of motivation. It is the affects that motivate; the drives must recruit an affect in order to assign any urgency to the need.

13. Again, this description of an emotion resembles what others have tended to view as ego states.

14. Defining the self is an ambitious enterprise, and my approach to it is certainly limited in scope. My goal is not to develop a new metapsychology, but simply to clarify the use of the concept in the practice of the emotional safety model. Hartmann's (1939) ego psychology approach to viewing the self as an internal structure that results from the organization of self-representations has always influenced my view of the self. From the perspective of affect theory, the various scenes containing the self coalesce into relatively stable views of self (and other), and these views are activated at various times, resulting in different emotional states. The working model of the self is thus composed of different emotions/views of self that constitute the immediate belief about the self, depending upon which view is activated.

15. The idea that infants are beginning a long road of development toward ever greater levels of separateness is reflected in theories such as Mahler, Pine, and Bergman's (1975) separation-individuation model. The whole idea of striving toward separateness is also reflective of the Western valuing of individuality.

16. Stern (1985) noted that infants actively participate in the relationship with mother. From early in life, they exercise the power to make and break interpersonal connections through initiating and terminating eye contact. This capacity to place boundaries on the connection reflects the beginnings of the development of the empathic wall and the infants' developing capacity to regulate their affect state. Over time, they develop more and more of a presence, a personality, a self.

17. D. Nathanson, personal communication.

18. The development of the empathic wall is probably also a component in the development of the ability to regulate one's own affect states.

19. The theorists at the Stone Center have taken a strong stand in favor of the idea that the fundamental direction of growth in the self is toward being able to connect with others. They are adamantly opposed to the idea that greater separation from others is the natural course of development (Jordan, Kaplan, Miller, Stiver, & Surrey, 1991).

20. I switched to the female gender in this sentence because the Stone Center theorists refrained from applying their model to both men and women. They only apply their theory of development to women, refusing to do what so many men did in the 20th century and arrogantly tell the other sex what they are about. However, I believe the Stone Center's view of the development of the self applies very well to both sexes.

21. The Stone Center model has evolved over time and the name of the model has changed from self-in-relation to relational to relational-cultural. Regardless of the name, the underlying idea that self growth only occurs in a full connection with another person has remained a foundation of their approach (Jordan, 1989, 2000).

22. I'm sure many traditional theorists will blanche at this assertion, but in my view, it logically follows the premises of affect theory. We do not think about the self without having an affect (usually interest affect).

23. Les Greenberg and Susan Johnson (1988) made the distinction between primary emotions, the initial emotional response, and secondary emotions, the learned emotional response that the person shifts into experiencing. They also noted a third category, instrumental emotions, which are generated in order to influence the other person.

Chapter 4

1. Freud reduced everything down to two basic drives. Affect theory takes the view that virtually everything associated with our survival has a drive, but the drives are inherently weak and need to recruit the power of affect to bring a sense of urgency and immediacy to the goal of the drive.
2. People can maintain feelings of self-worth during an insecure attachment relationship if they had earlier secure attachments. However, even people with a strong sense of self-worth are affected if they remain too long in a poor relationship.
3. Being able to tolerate the differences and still remain closely connected would mean he is very high on Murray Bowen's scale of differentiation. Bowen (1978) contended that the highly differentiated person was able to balance the drive for autonomy with the drive for closeness without sacrificing too much from either realm. Perhaps because of Bowen's emphasis on autonomy, many people have misconstrued differentiation as being the same as individuation and viewed it as opposed to closeness. Instead, it is about being able to be *both* close and autonomous.
4. Attachment style has been a very meaningful construct for research purposes, but it refers to an average style, and most people do not fit into a single category of attachment style. Their views of self and other vary across time and are subject to being activated by events. In the first research study of Bartholomew's categories (beyond the research done for Bartholomew's dissertation), Bartholomew and Horowitz state, "None of the subjects in this project uniquely fit any one attachment prototype. Instead, most subjects reported a mix of tendencies across time and within and across relationships" (1991, p. 241).
5. Reber (1996) notes that the extreme negative end of the attachment continuum results in a syndrome which he terms reactive attachment disorder (RAD). This extreme disorder is usually attributed to abuse or neglect in early childhood. It is not what we see with normal child-rearing practices. Rather, to the extent that the dependent bond between child and mother (or other primary caretaker) is severed prematurely but still survives, then those children grow into adults who may be insecure about forming attachments, but they do still have the ability to do so.
6. The three attachment categories of secure, anxious-resistant, and avoidant were derived from the work of Mary Ainsworth, who extended Bowlby's research into situations requiring children to separate from mother in order to actively explore a new environment (Ainsworth, Blehar, Waters, & Wall, 1978).
7. Bartholomew's Good/Bad schemas of Self and Other refer to the four specific working models that derive from positive and negative views of self and other. Their emphasis on models of Good Self and Bad Self is the latest in a history of formulations of this sort. Possibly the earliest identification of these competing views of the self was Harry Stack Sullivan's "self-system." He proposed three fundamental modes of personification: good-me, bad-me, and not-me (1953/1997).
8. Bartholomew continued to expand on the four-category model, including breaking down more of the emotions and other characteristics within the four quadrants (Griffin & Bartholomew, 1994). But the foundation of the model is the bivalenced poles of self and other. As you will see, affect theory supports the idea that these are orthogonal poles, propelling people in one direction or the other, depending upon whether a positive or a negative affect has been activated.
9. I refer to this attitude as the Groucho Marx syndrome because of his famous response when offered membership in an exclusive club—that he would not be a member of a club that would have him for a member. Through the use of humor, he seems to be saying that anyone who would accept his Bad Self must be a Bad Other.

Chapter 5

1. Both the Self and Other Axes are influenced by shame affect. When shame affect is combined with a view of self, it becomes *shame emotion*, and when shame affect is combined with a view of the other, it becomes some variant of an *unaccepting emotion*. Of course, it is unlikely that shame will be the only affect involved when an individual has negative emotions about the other. Any of the negative affects can be involved. However, when the other is an attachment figure in an intimate relationship, negative feelings usually involve

a disruption of previously positive feelings about the other, thus shame affect is probably always involved, but often it will be assembled with other negative affects.

2. Sandra Murray and her colleagues have studied "perceived regard." They found that individuals who feel less positively regarded read more negative meaning into minor events, are more hurt after difficult interactions with their partners, and behave more badly toward their partners when they feel hurt. People who feel less positively regarded tend to distance when they feel hurt, but people who feel more positively regarded draw closer to their partners when they feel hurt (Murray, Bellavia, Rose, & Griffin, 2003). On the other hand, people with low self-esteem were more likely to read negative meaning into minor events and to treat their partners poorly (including distancing) after such events. The partners with high self-esteem were less sensitive to feeling rejected (Murray, Rose, Bellavia, Holmes, & Kusche, 2002; Murray, Holmes, & Griffin, 2000).

3. I used the verbal form, loving, rather than the noun, love, to emphasize some of the activities that represent attachment. Actions of love provide comfort, care, and protection; it is not just about having interest and pleasure in the other person's presence. The presence or lack of these kinds of attachment behaviors produce security versus insecurity about the other's love or commitment. Susan Johnson's beautiful quote captures the tone of the human need for an attachment relationship.

4. The reason the majority of esteem and attachment emotions are not neutral but cluster into positive or negative groups is because the underlying affects that provide motivation are generally either positive (impelling towards) or negative (pushing away). If the emotion is neutral, that usually means the person has no emotion. Generally speaking, when emotion is activated, we are being motivated toward one pole or the other.

5. There is increasing evidence that couple therapy is effective not only with relationship problems but with many individual disorders, but there is little evidence that individual therapy does much for relationship problems (Byrne, Carr & Clark, 2004; Gilliam & Cottone, 2005; Johnson & Lebow, 2000; Snyder & Whisman, 2003).

6. Researchers examining attachment have labeled many survivors of early trauma as having a disorganized attachment style (i.e., best described as an approach-avoidance dilemma in which the attachment figure is viewed as both a threat and a secure base) (Holmes, 2004). Recent research suggests that most children who develop disorganized attachment patterns are responding to parents who have unresolved loss or trauma, which disrupts their capacity to provide a consistently secure base (Green & Goldwyn, 2002).

Chapter 6

1. People in intimate relationships are acutely attuned to the affective tone in the other person's view of them; however, this does not mean that their perception of the other person's view is accurate. Research on perceived regard tells us that people who are secure and feel good about themselves tend to overestimate their partner's positive regard of them, and people who are insecure and do not feel good about themselves tend to underestimate their partner's positive regard of them (Murray, Holmes, Holmes, Dolderman & Griffin, 2000; Murray, Holmes & Griffin, 2000). Better yet, the positive illusions predict better relationships, in the form of greater satisfaction, love and trust, and less conflict (Murray & Holmes, 1998). So if you're going to misperceive your partner's feelings about you, it is best to misperceive them in a positive direction.

2. I suspect that Freud's view of the infant as fused with the mother stemmed from his encounters with this phenomenon, in which our views of ourselves are so caught up with our perception of the other's affective view of us. Many people in a state of psychosis seem to lose all sense of there being a boundary between their own view of themselves and others' views of them. This phenomenon also may have played a role in leading Heinz Kohut (1971) to construct a model of the self in which the other is experienced as an extension of the self and provides soothing and stabilizing functions that the self is considered to be lacking. Kohut's model operated on the traditional premise that development is toward separation, and it posited that people with such difficulties had not developed a cohesive self. An understanding of the nature of affects, especially shame affect, can lead to a different interpretation of self-soothing in a relationship. Self-soothing may have more to do with the amount of, and access to, scripts in which the self is viewed as competent and

resilient (pride scripts). If the person views himself as competent and resilient, then his fears quickly diminish.

3. Bear in mind that all self-scripts are based on interpersonal experiences. The affective tone perceived to be felt by the other toward and about the self is a major factor in the original formation of our self-scripts. Our emotions are derived from all of our life experiences, but our emotional views of ourselves are fundamentally social views. The concept of a self only acquires meaning within an interpersonal context. This is why shame emotion is different from the many other emotions in which shame affect is assembled. It is in those relationships that are the most important to us—our attachment relationships—that we are most concerned with the other person's affective view of us. Those are the views that exert the greatest influence on our views of ourselves.

4. The psychiatrist Jerry Lewis (1998) concludes that it is the intensity of the affective bonds that determines the success of marriage and, in turn, individual well-being in such seemingly unrelated spheres as immune competence.

5. Robert Sternberg (1987) has described the concept of love in long-term relationships in terms of three key variables: intimacy, passion, and commitment. Over time, intimacy and commitment increase but passion declines.

6. Her disapproval scripts activate his shame and his view of self switches from Good Self to Bad Self. The Bad Self scripts are very powerful. Researcher have found a strong relationship between negative view of self and psychopathology, a relationship that is much stronger than the relationship between negative view of other and psychopathology (Muller, Lemieux, & Sicoli, 2001). Similarly, a negative view of self was a very strong predictor of posttraumatic stress symptoms, but negative view of other was not (Muller, Sicoli, & Lemieux, 2000).

7. Mary's response of self-disgust and subsequent anger at herself is a common reaction to shame, which we will examine in detail in the next chapter.

8. Professional therapists will recognize this interaction as heavily laden with transference. That is one effective way of describing and understanding what happened, and working with the client to recognize that her husband is not her father would be a perfectly appropriate approach. From that point of view, affect theory adds an appreciation of the mechanics of the transference process (i.e., the role of affective resonance in triggering her transference reaction). However, what a focus on transference may sometimes miss is the powerful shame about the self underlying her response.

9. One distinct source of fears is earlier trauma in the person's life. This is a distinctly separate realm that is primarily composed of fear affect and those affects that are recruited to counter fear affect (such as anger).

10. The distinction between anxiety being about possibilities and fear being about perceptions occurs at a neurological level (Catherall, 2003).

11. This is the strategy marital researcher John Gottman (1999) has labeled as "stonewalling." In effect, it is an intensification of the empathic wall in order to reduce the partner's capacity to activate one's shame affect. It virtually always indicates that the stonewalling partner perceives a significant esteem threat.

12. Sex therapist David Schnarch (1998) refers to the ability to remain close while not being pulled into the other person's anxieties as "holding on to your self."

Chapter 7

1. Eight years younger than John and 10 years younger than Joe Jr., Bobby Kennedy was physically small and dwarfed even further by the dynamic, competitive personalities of his father and two older brothers. Steel's quote (from *In Love With Night*, 2000, p. 38) captures the approach to overcoming shame that Robert Kennedy pursued throughout his life.

2. The level of the individual partners' shame has been found to predict their levels of perceived intimacy (Owens, 1995).

3. Most, if not all, of the emotions evoked by situations that go bad will include some shame affect. When it is co-assembled with other affects, and especially when the self is not the object of the affect, then we do not experience that emotion as shame. But if shame affect is part of the emotion, we are affected by it. Donald Nathanson said, "No matter when

and how triggered, shame [affect] damps and impedes and reduces and makes painful everything with which it is co-assembled" (1992, p. 413).

4. There are several reasons why it is difficult to recognize when our shame affect has been triggered:

An affect knows no master. Shame affect is not restricted to situations that produce the emotion we call shame. The affect itself—accompanied by some or all of the physiological response of flushing, lowering the eyelids, turning the face away, losing muscle tone in the neck and shoulders, and temporarily losing control of cognitive powers—potentially can be assembled with any other affects and scripts. Shame affect is neutral in regard to the meaning of the events triggering it, but we quickly come to attach meanings to the events, and those meanings become associated with the affects they trigger.

An emotion is more than its affects. Once that neutral affect has been recruited into a particular situation, it is coupled with its typical script and its typical other affects, and it takes on the quality we call emotion. The emotion is no longer just the affect; it is a greater thing, especially because every emotion is fraught with meaning.

Shame the affect is not the same as shame the emotion. Thus, the emotion of shame is much more than the simple affect of shame. The emotion has a particular meaning for us, one that has its own subtle shades and nuances that cause it to be different from what may seem to be the same emotion in someone else. Your shame is not my shame.

Shame the affect is short-lived. The experience of shame affect, as with most affective experience, is short-lived. It is over within seconds, having performed its job of amplifying the power of some impeding event in order to cause us to back off on our pursuit of the interesting or enjoyable thing that is being impeded. However, often our experience of shame emotion continues because, although the original affective experience is over, the script is much harsher and causes us to continue to view ourselves in the context of the shame experience. In effect, we continue to replay our shame script, retriggering the affects and our responses.

Shame the emotion is assembled out of scripts and affects. Our own version of shame is shaped by the nature of our scripts and by the other affects that we co-assemble with it to form the particular emotion being experienced. The example of the two men late for a meeting illustrates how different proportions of the various component affects can lead to very different emotional states. Though shame can be co-assembled with any other affect, it becomes particularly strong when co-assembled with disgust and dissmell. The three together have a very powerful ability to motivate us to back away from anything in which we might have been interested. When individuals grow up in an atmosphere of intense shame, they often assemble these three affects with negative scripts about the self ("I stink and I am disgusted with myself.")

5. The triad of moderator affects (shame, disgust, dissmell) so often associated with negative scripts about the self is frequently followed by a reaction of anger directed at the self. When the shame is intense enough, some people with chronic shame may express this anger through self-injurious behavior, such as cutting themselves. Self-injurious behaviors are commonly believed to be attempts by dissociative individuals to break free from the numbness of dissociation (by piercing the numbness with pain). That may well be the case; however, in my experience such behaviors frequently follow the activation of intense shame.

6. Nathanson (1993, 1996a) describes the act of drawing attention to sources of pride as a way of avoiding shame.

7. Donald Nathanson, personal communication.

8. Memory is composed of different types of systems. There are varying views regarding the subtypes of memory but general agreement on the distinction between (a) explicit memory, which contains facts, words, ideas, and the kinds of things we learn in school, and (b) implicit memory, which contains things we learned without either realizing we were learning something or things that we cannot put into words, such as the bodily sensation involved in riding a bicycle.

9. Jung (1968) discussed the shadow world in the first of five untitled lectures at the Tavistock Clinic, delivered in 1935.

10. Freud (1923) viewed anxiety as originating in the ego and stemming from dangers from the external world, the superego, and the libido of the id. He did not view anxiety as restricted to neurosis but did note its existence in all forms of neurosis (Freud, 1926). He referred to all anxiety as "an expression of a retreat from danger" (1923, p. 46), a view that would certainly include the fear of shame being uncovered. Helen Block Lewis has referred to shame as the "sleeper" in psychopathology. She believed it is a key factor in the irrational guilt underlying neurotic and psychotic symptoms (1987a). She also believed shame plays a central role in the low self-esteem that accompanies depression (1987b).

11. Robert Pinckert discusses the role of emotional appeals in the art of persuasion in his book *Pinckert's Practical Grammar*. Among his examples, he includes the appeal to shame, "Everyone on the block gave; won't you?" (1986, p. 187).

12. Krugman (1995) contends that it is the male's difficulty integrating shame effectively that accounts for male emotional vulnerability and such negative behaviors as social withdrawal and violence.

13. The link between shame and anger or aggression in men has been noted by numerous observers. Shame proneness has been linked to anger arousal and a tendency to blame others in men who assault their wives (Dutton, van Ginkel, & Starzomski, 1995). Some theorists believe shaming in families is related to aggression in adulthood (Lansky, 1993).

14. Those involved with the shame-prone person usually come to regard him (or her) as hypersensitive and unable to handle criticism. Therapists often use labels like narcissistic, infantile, and controlling.

15. Since the interpersonal experience of shame has such dire implications for the individual's view of self (and the consequent impact on functioning), fear affect is usually assembled in the reaction script, a fear of being personally diminished by the shame experience.

16. Similarly, many abuse survivors do not have enough self-loving/accepting strategies. When they feel they have let themselves down, by being inadequate and feeling shame, they punish themselves. This is likely both an expression of anger at themselves and a way they have developed of controlling themselves.

17. When Admiral James Borda was a junior officer, he was stationed on a destroyer off the coast of Vietnam and he received a decoration. When certain decorations involve combat, they are adorned with a "V" device. Since Admiral Borda received his decoration in a combat theater, he mistakenly thought he was entitled to wear the combat "V." Apparently he learned of his error later but continued to wear the "V." He killed himself upon learning that this was about to become the subject of a television news story. Considering the immense value placed on combat experience and decorations in the military, misrepresentation of a combat decoration can be the worst kind of humiliation for a senior military officer.

18. Michael Basch (1996) notes how Freud conceived the concept of disavowal to capture the process by which people disconnect the affective meaning (significance) from their perception of troubling external events. He stated: "Disavowal defends against anxiety-provoking external perceptions and is the counterpart of repression, the latter being directed toward similar demands from the inner world of the instincts" (p. 260).

19. Because our emphasis is on the other person, it is tempting to interpret these situations as triggering distrust scripts. Indeed, there are times when that is all that has been triggered and no shame has been activated. But shame scripts are frequently co-assembled with distrust scripts, and the focus on the other may easily obscure the shame that is being disavowed. One clue often can be found in the stated reason for the attack. If the attacking individual justifies the attack on the basis that he or she has been injured in some fashion, chances are that the injury involved the activation of shame. Aaron Beck's (1999) work on the cognitive component of anger reactions identifies a perception of an attack on self-esteem as the usual precipitant for the train of thoughts that culminates in an anger reaction.

Chapter 8

1. This gives a sense of the breadth of emotional experience that can contain shame affect. Some of the blends of that range of experience would never be subjectively viewed as falling anywhere near the group of emotions that would be grouped under the heading

of shame (such as embarrassment, humiliation, and so forth). Some theorists criticize affect theory because they consider it to have too limited a view of affective experience. Susan Miller wrote, "If all affect experiences fell neatly into one of nine classifications, one would think that designating the appropriate label for a feeling would go farther than it does in conveying the essentials of an experience" (1996, p.13). I believe such a view misconstrues affect for emotion, a common error. Affects are a component of emotion, and the affects can be combined—both with each other and with various scenes and scripts (all to varying magnitudes)—to create an immense range of emotional experience. Indeed, if three primary colors can be mixed to form all the colors of the rainbow, what is possible with the nine affects?

2. Wurmser's classic text, *The Mask of Shame* (1981), identified the infant's experience of being unlovable as a core component of lasting shame. This idea has influenced many theorists since, and its widespread acceptance has probably contributed to the tendency to regard failed attachment as the sine qua non of shame.

Chapter 9

1. Feeling worthy of love is that part of esteem that comes directly from secure attachment. Feeling competent and adequate to function in the world mostly comes from experience outside the attachment relationship. I was tempted to categorize these as different types of self-esteem (such as relational esteem and adequacy esteem), but that would be misleading. Self-esteem is a unitary phenomenon; relational and adequacy scripts both contribute to a person's general feelings about self—they just stem from different sources. In my view, the term self-worth refers to the relational component—we derive feelings of self-worth from being valued by others. The more general concept of self-esteem includes both feelings of self-worth and feelings of competence.

   Self-esteem develops in concert with the development of the self in an attachment relationship, but the sources of self-esteem expand as the individual matures (especially in regard to adequacy scripts). Recognizing self-esteem as a unitary phenomenon helps us to understand how an individual may increase his efforts to enhance his esteem outside the relationship if he feels his esteem is diminished within the relationship.

2. This issue of relying excessively on the partner to supply esteem needs frequently appears in modern life when one partner (usually the woman) ceases working outside the home and devotes herself to raising children. It is helpful if she has sources of esteem outside the relationship as she will already have an increased need for her partner to validate her parenting. If her esteem needs become exclusively focused on her partner, it can interfere with her sense of autonomy and make her feel as though she is competing with the children for Daddy's attention.

3. Both attachment threats and esteem threats can activate anxiety (fear affect). The difference is in what is feared—the possibility of not getting what one wants from the other (positive affective tone) or the possibility of getting what one does not want from the other (negative affective tone).

4. Explaining why the partner focused on esteem can seem indifferent to the relationship is a challenging task, and it does not always go well. It sometimes helps to describe it in terms of Maslow's (1987) theories of self-realization and his hierarchy of human motives, noting that when the self is threatened, less fundamental priorities receive little attention.

5. The researchers defined criticism as a comment that suggests the problem is with the other person's overall personality.

6. Susan Johnson (1996/2005) also relies on the goal of softening the injured partner's requests for support (which are stated in terms of criticism of the other partner). In the language of the emotional safety model, the harsh startup is usually an expression of hostile protest by the partner experiencing attachment threat. Unfortunately, the attacking style of making the "request" for support constitutes an esteem threat to the other partner.

7. My contention that many of the traditional problems focused on in therapy are secondary to the realms of attachment and esteem—and can be relatively easily resolved once the couple is in the safe zone—is shared by Susan Johnson's *Emotionally Focused Couples Therapy* (2005). She takes this same explicit position, though she defines the central underlying problem only in terms of attachment. But her view of attachment clearly

includes the realm of esteem. I have simply introduced a further distinction between the two realms.

8. Emily's disconnecting part of herself in order to be accepted in the relationship is what Irene Stiver and Jean Baker Miller (1994) call a strategy of disconnection.

Chapter 10

1. This pattern usually has its genesis in early childhood. Many children of neglectful parents become caretakers and do not learn to assert their needs in relationships.

2. In my experience, caretakers are more often women. This is probably due to social roles learned in childhood; however, there are plenty of male caretakers around as well.

3. John Gottman's research illuminated the importance of partners being able to influence each other directly. When individuals feel they have little, if any, influence over their partners, they are likely to resort to shaming. Destructive efforts to induce shame are highest when the capacity to exert direct influence is low.

4. John Gottman's (1999) research has identified the importance of a "softened startup" and Susan Johnson (1996/2005) regards the development of "blamer softening" as a pivotal aspect of emotionally focused couple therapy. Most couple therapists are seeking this change when they ask partners to make "I statements." The "I statement" approach can apply to a variety of issues, such as assuming the other's feelings, but the most important change is usually from attacking or criticizing the other to requesting what one needs and desires from the other. Asking for an "I statement" prods the partner in this direction, but it helps if the therapist can identify the need to ask for what one is wanting from the other partner (and most especially in the attachment realm). Making such a request is also the essence of vulnerability.

5. The symptomatic spouse is one pattern that develops when that individual is unwilling to protest, or has given up on protesting, problems with the attachment relationship. This certainly does not mean that all individual symptoms reflect attachment problems—only that some people who despair of improving their attachment develop individual symptoms, especially depression.

6. An analog to the symptomatic spouse might be the school-phobic child. Children who are school phobic are generally insecurely attached and therefore lack the confidence of a secure base that facilitates their exploration of a new environment.

7. Kaufman (1989, 1992) emphasizes the severing of the interpersonal bridge with another as the central activator of all shame.

8. Murray Bowen (1978) developed a scale of differentiation of the self, referring to an individual's capacity to be fully himself (therefore different from others in a variety of ways) while simultaneously maintaining closeness in a relationship. Bowen would view a failure to develop sufficient self-definition as a lack of differentiation. Sex therapist David Schnarch (1991) has emphasized the destructive impact of seeking excessive validation from the partner in an intimate relationship, and notes that it is a manifestation of a lack of differentiation.

9. A related pattern might be triangulation, another term coined by Murray Bowen (1978). It refers to the recruitment of a third person into a conflictual relationship. If you and I disagree, I may speak to another person and get him to agree with me and share or validate the feelings I am having about you. This can aid me in reestablishing my self-esteem. Triangulation may serve more purposes than shoring up esteem issues; getting an ally helps in decision-making and unbalanced power situations. But don't underestimate the power of shame and the importance of esteem concerns in these kinds of interpersonal dynamics.

10. Kerr and Bowen (1988) use the concept of a "strong" self and a "weak" self in reference to Bowen's scale of differentiation of the self. In this context, Kerr and Bowen are using the term "strong" to refer to a pretense of strength. In their view, a solid self is not artificially inflated by the "lending, borrowing, trading and exchanging of self" that occurs in less differentiated relationships. Actually, when they refer to the systemic patterns that people get into, they talk of functioning positions and use the terms overfunctioning and underfunctioning to describe the overadequate-underadequate system.

11. David Kerr and Murray Bowen (1988) labeled the artificially elevated sense of competence of the overadequate partner as "borrowed functioning."

12. In his classic text *Understanding Human Nature* (1923), Alfred Adler discusses how the feeling of inferiority drives a striving for recognition that can result in aggressive character traits, including vanity, ambition, jealousy, envy, avarice, and hate. Modern affect theory helps us to recognize the role of shame in the feelings of inferiority and the role of shame avoidance in an aggressive orientation toward others.

13. Avoidance is a particularly resistant defensive strategy because it tends to be inherently self-reinforcing. Whether it is the mutual avoidance of a couple who has learned to dodge conflict or the isolated avoidance of an individual who believes he is happier when he doesn't have to deal with the anxiety-provoking aspects of life, avoidance is one of the most powerful strategies therapists ever encounter. Indeed, the only reason avoidant people come to treatment is because it's not working. Consequently, the therapist must maintain a focus on how the avoidance is not working—or the clients may forget why they came for help in the first place.

14. Robert Schwarz (2002, p. 78) provides an excellent example of the difference between walls and boundaries by observing the difference between the Iron Curtain (a wall) and the border between the United States and Mexico (a boundary).

15. "For shame to occur there must be an emotional relationship between the person and the 'other' such that the person cares what the other thinks or feels about the self" (Lewis, 1971, p. 42).

16. John Gottman (1994a) noted four behaviors that were particularly destructive to a marriage—criticism, contempt, defensiveness, and stonewalling. The stonewalling is the ultimate in withdrawal (i.e., putting up a wall and being unresponsive to whatever the spouse says or does). Gottman noted what a powerful destructive force this is in a relationship, perhaps all the more so because the person doing it (85% of the time, it's a man) is often able to regard himself as being merely neutral and inoffensive.

Chapter 11

1. The definition of the core problem sets the stage for the development of the therapy. William Pinsof's *Integrative Problem-Centered Therapy* (1995) is founded on this principle. Pinsof emphasizes the importance of being able to demonstrate the connection between the problem and the interventions being employed. Once the clients accept the therapist's formulation of the problem, the therapist then has a mandate to intervene in or explore areas that can be linked to the problem. Without that demonstrable link, those areas might otherwise be resisted.

2. Nathaniel Branden (1983) discusses this same issue specifically regarding the realm of esteem. He uses the term *focusing* to describe the choice to consciously think about the exact nature of one's emotional experience.

Chapter 12

1. John Gottman's (1999) research has led him to emphasize the importance of the partners being able to repair the relationship. Successful therapy is when the couple is able to repair the relationship effectively on their own. From the point of view of the emotional safety mode, I would say that what is being repaired is their loss of emotional safety.

2. Gottman (1994a) found that partners in marriages that are stable and satisfying express approximately five times as much positive affect as negative affect, while partners in marriages that eventually failed expressed negative affect more than positive affect. Clearly, an abundance of positive affect is a factor in making partners feel emotionally safe in a relationship.

3. In a recent study of positive affect at the University of Michigan, Barbara Fredrickson and Marcial Losada (2005) cited studies showing the benefit of positive affect on cardiovascular health, frontal brain asymmetry, immune function, resilience to adversity, happiness, psychological growth, and longevity. In their own research and in Losada's research on groups (Losada, 1999; Losada & Heapy, 2004), they found a positivity ratio similar to Gottman's, except that the ratio was lower (2.9 to 1, as compared to Gottman's ratio of 5 to 1 in intimate relationships).

4. Richard Heyman (2001) reviewed the research on couples and notes several "stubborn facts": "Distressed partners, compared with nondistressed partners (a) are more hostile, (b) start their conversations more hostilely and maintain it during the course of the conversation,

(c) are more likely to reciprocate and escalate their partners' hostility, (d) are less likely to edit their behavior during conflict, resulting in longer reciprocity loops, (e) emit less positive behavior, (f) suffer more ill health effects from their conflicts, and (g) are more likely to show demand-withdraw patterns" (p. 6). More positive affect is clearly associated with a more satisfying relationship, but that could be the effect of a better relationship as much as cause. However, Gottman's research, taken as a whole, paints a compelling picture that partners who give each other more positives create an entirely different atmosphere to the relationship, an atmosphere with momentum in the direction of greater growth and safety. This is essentially what Barbara Fredrickson's (2001) research has led her to conclude about positive emotions in the lives of individuals in her "broaden-and-build theory of positive emotions."

5. It is the responsibility of parents (and teachers and other adults) to build the positive esteem of children. We encourage their growth by mirroring their successes and embedding our observations in positive affective tone ("Great job, you took a step!"). We express pride in their accomplishments. Sometimes a similar situation is required between adults, such as when an adult has been disabled and is recovering. However, the more one adult takes the role of cheerleader for another, the more difficult it is to maintain a balanced relationship of two autonomous, independent individuals who choose to engage in a mutually fulfilling relationship. This must be kept in perspective. It is good for the relationship and promotes positive attachment for the two adults to support each other, have positive feelings for each other, and to be pleased and take pride in each other's successes. But if one partner is always the supporter and the other partner is always receiving the support, an imbalance develops. Or if either partner is unable to function without the other partner's support, then autonomy has been sacrificed and the relationship can become a form of disability.

6. Indeed, as Watzlawick, Beavin, and Jackson (1967) point out, it is impossible to not communicate.

7. Indeed, I suspect that the experience of flooding that is being measured in the laboratory is primarily an experience of overwhelming shame affect. Since many people move from the shame to a secondary emotion, especially anger, the emotions reported may not appear to be shame related. However, at this stage of the research, we cannot say with certainty what emotions are primary, especially if they are not accessible to the subject.

Chapter 13

1. Branden (1983) notes that people with "pseudo self-esteem" distort reality in order to maintain a positive view of self. He emphasizes that true self-esteem is based on the ability to face reality and make changes as needed in order to deal with it.

2. The act of disowning aspects of self is an individual process. It is not really the same as the experience of losing one's self in a relationship. Losing one's self in that way is a relational process in which some people with poor esteem give too much control to the partner in regard to defining their lives. It would probably be categorized as more of a form of emotional fusion than disowning of the self, even though it may involve elements of disowning.

3. The talented family therapist Virginia Satir (1967) was acutely sensitive to the triggering of shame and worked to help families be authentic and communicate forthrightly. She conceptualized her work in terms of self-esteem, but the result was that family members would not be imprisoned by their fear of shame. Satir was especially valuable as a therapist because she herself was not easily triggered. She was quite willing to speak the unspoken, even as she so sensitively dealt with the shame-proneness of her clients.

4. The goal of living consciously has received increased attention in recent years. Popular books, such as *The Power of Now* (Tolle, 1999) and *Wherever You Go, There You Are* (Kabat-Zinn, 1995), counsel readers on the value of remaining focused on the present moment. This has also been emphasized in spiritual traditions and is taught in classes on mindfulness meditation. John Kabat-Zinn (1990) has been a major proponent of the health-related value of mindfulness and has demonstrated its positive effects with cancer patients.

5. Social situations are the core challenge for children who are especially shame sensitive— long before intimate relationships become the issue in adulthood. There is evidence to suggest that some people may be temperamentally or genetically more sensitized to the

potential shame-activating properties of social situations (Markway & Markway, 2003). Shyness is the word we give to people with this sensitivity (Markway, Carmin, Pollard, & Flynn, 1992). Many, if not most, of these people continue to be sensitive to social situations into adulthood and have to learn to manage their anxiety whenever they are going to be thrust into a social situation. If their shyness is combined with high anxiety, their reticence to expose themselves to social situations can become disabling and they may qualify for the diagnosis of social anxiety disorder or other phobias (Beidel & Turner, 1998).

6. The role of self-focused attention in maintaining social anxiety is leading to the development of attentional strategies in the treatment of social phobia (Bogells & Mansell, 2004). There is also a growing literature on the role of self-focused attention in depression (Watkins & Teasdale, 2004). In depression, there may be a link between self-focused attention and over-general biographical memory, which has a tendency to recall categoric summaries of events rather than specific memories. Needless to say, a categoric summary easily lends itself to a distorted view of self (e.g., "I failed at everything I tried to do in high school" as opposed to "I tried out for the tennis team but failed to make it."). Watkins and Teasdale (2001, 2004) have emphasized the difference between ruminative forms of self-focus, in which the individual tends to analyze and evaluate himself, and experiential forms, which are more similar to mindfulness. Melanie Fennell (2004) is extending this work from the focus on depression into the realm of self-esteem.

7. John Teasdale and his colleagues have brought mindfulness meditation into the field of cognitive therapy (Teasdale, Segal, & Williams, 1995; Segal, Williams, & Teasdale, 2002). Rather than trying so hard to change self-defeating thoughts, which is the traditional approach of cognitive therapy, Teasdale et al. focus on changing the person's relationship with those thoughts. They contend that meditation can increase *metacognitive awareness*, which is the ability to experience one's thoughts as simply transient events, not necessarily objectively true, and not manifestations of the self (Teasdale et al., 2002). This is the basic attitude cultivated in mindfulness meditation training.

8. John Gottman's (1999) research revealed that stable, satisfied couples almost never express contempt. When it appears, it is a strong predictor that the relationship is headed for dissolution.

9. Nathaniel Branden (1983) describes the impact of growing up without appropriate recognition of one's emotions and describes the experience in terms of feeling invisible.

10. For anyone who doesn't understand this reference, it is referring to the fairytale of the emperor's new clothes. The emperor is told that the clothes are made of such magnificent materials that they can only be seen by people who are good/superior/pure of heart. The emperor doesn't want anyone to know that he himself cannot see the clothes, so he walks around naked until an innocent child calls out that the king is not wearing any clothes.

11. Many authors equate severe closeness-distance struggles with psychopathology. Gunderson (1996) suggests the essential underlying problem for people with borderline personality disorder is an intolerance for being alone, the result of insecure attachment experiences. "Being alone is often intolerable to borderline patients because it is associated with a profound sense of being bad or evil—a self-image distortion accompanied by such intense feelings of guilt or shame that the question of worthiness to live often follows" (p. 756). His description of what is activated is remarkably consistent with what I have labeled as Bad Self scripts. His formulation suggests these Bad Self scripts are activated when borderline patients are alone, and that these individuals depend upon their interpersonal connections to fend off the activation of those scripts.

12. People who are unable to maintain an independent view of themselves have long been a subject of study in the psychiatric world. The labels and explanations attached to them vary with the theories applied. They have been described as lacking a cohesive self, lacking a positive introject, fixated at an early stage of object relations, fixated at an early stage of separation/individuation, insecurely attached, enmeshed in their family of origin, undifferentiated, or characterologically impaired—to name just some of the more common explanations.

13. I have chosen to focus on Bowen's concept of differentiation because I think it best describes the dilemma created by the competing needs for closeness and separateness. However, the same issue has been addressed by other authors, and this discussion could be transposed into the terms utilized in other theoretical models. The psychiatrist Jerry

Lewis (1997) has a well-developed theory of marital systems that is founded on the competing needs for separateness-autonomy and connectedness-intimacy. I simply prefer Bowen's term because it captures the ability to balance these two needs into one term.

14. People who do not feel good about themselves and who are highly reactive to their partners' views of them are exactly the people whom Sandra Murray et al. were referring to in their studies of low self-esteem partners (Murray, Holmes, & Griffin, 2000; Murray, Holmes, Griffin, Bellavia, & Rose, 2001; Murray, Rose, Bellavia, Holmes, & Kusche, 2002). This was discussed in Chapter 5.

15. Bowen did not say that poorly differentiated people are controlled by their concern about receiving approval; Bowen talked about anxiety providing the motivation, but he never probed into the source of the anxiety. I think the anxiety is a manifestation of their fear of having their shame activated via disapproval. In a recent piece of research that supported Bowen's theory—the anxiety of college students was found to be inversely related to their parents' levels of differentiation (Peleg, 2005). The anxiety manifested by the students was specifically social anxiety. A view informed by affect theory would note that social anxiety is basically people's fears of having their shame activated in social situations (i.e., by disapproval).

16. Helen Block Lewis (1987c) has noted that sometimes therapy clients resist their therapists' influence because of a sense of shame. Lewis suggests the whole concept of therapeutic resistance is counterproductive and should be abandoned.

17. Sandra Murray and her colleagues conducted a series of studies on the power of being positively regarded among partners (Murray, Holmes, & Griffin, 2000; Murray, Holmes, Griffin, Bellavia, & Rose, 2001; Murray, Rose, Bellavia, Holmes, & Kusche, 2002). They found a relationship between feeling positively regarded and having better relationships, being a better partner, drawing closer to the partner when conflict arises, being less easily hurt, being less reactive to minor indications of disapproval, and being more resilient.

Chapter 14

1. The choice of whether to focus on early events or current life will be influenced by the therapist's theoretical orientation. The psychoanalytic therapist will probably seek to help the person understand the source of his shame; the cognitive-behavior therapist will focus more on current manifestations. In either case, the therapist must be able to see the person beyond the scripts, because the client will be absorbed in the scripts whenever shame affect is activated.

2. My emphasis on viewing the patient as a person with a problem rather than someone with something fundamentally wrong with himself counters his shame-derived view of himself. It also establishes a relationship between two functional adults. This is similar to what Gershen Kaufman (1989, 1992) has in mind when he emphasizes the establishment of the interpersonal bridge. It is that quality of relating to a fellow human being that ultimately transcends the shame.

3. This inner voice is literally expressed in words and sentences, often referred to as negative self-talk or automatic thoughts. The similarity to Freud's concept of the superego is hard to ignore. Perhaps in the case of individuals with severe shame scripts, a harsh superego takes on the manifestation of an inner voice. In any case, affect theory leads us to consider the role of shame in the development of that arena of functioning subsumed under the title of superego.

4. I am labeling the disconnection from self as a form of dissociation, but many theorists would reserve the term for more severe, symptomatic experiences.

5. The technique of inquiring about bodily sensations as way of interrupting dissociation and keeping a client anchored to the present moment is a trauma technique. It was pioneered by Pat Ogden at the Sensorimotor Psychotherapy Institute in Colorado and by Babette Rothschild, whose book, *The Body Remembers* (2000), is a modern classic on somatic therapy. Rothschild (2003) also has written a workbook that gives a careful description of the technique. I have found the technique to be particularly effective with people who are normally "in their bodies" until shame affect is activated and they then disconnect from themselves.

6. Mindfulness meditation is another activity that can help a person overcome the power of his or her shame. It is a form of meditation in which the person learns to focus on the

immediate moment, paying attention to the (external) data coming in from his senses rather than his (internal) thoughts. Mindfulness can help in two ways: it can diminish self-consciousness by helping the person shift his focus away from himself, and it can diminish the power of the scripts of Bad Self by helping the person become less absorbed in his thoughts. Thus, he is less influenced by self-consciousness and by the inner voice of shame. Mindfulness training is taught in classes similar to traditional yoga and meditation classes. The value of mindfulness meditation was established in this country by John Kabat-Zinn (1990, 1995), who demonstrated its value in helping cancer patients.

7. Unfortunately, I have also seen this angry focus on the other used within an intimate relationship. Needless to say, it eliminates all emotional safety. In abusive relationships, it is not uncommon that the controlling partner avoids his shame by maintaining a rigid, angry focus on the other partner. This is not simply the blaming reaction from Nathanson's compass of shame; it includes a dimension of control that is probably not restricted to moments of shame. Individuals who attempt to control their partners through the use of intimidation usually have serious character pathology.

8. I also noted in Chapter 7 that the four negative reactions can be viewed as fight/flight responses to fear. The third response to fear, freezing, is surrendering to the shame—experiencing it and accepting the shame-based view of self as reality. Young, Klosko, and Weishaar (2003) use the three response styles of fight, flight, and freeze in a similar fashion in their model of schema therapy. However, they do not confine these responses to fear but view them as more general maladaptive coping styles. From the point of view of affect theory, I view them as specifically motivated by fear. Hence, I assume a fear component to the fighting and fleeing of the responses in Nathanson's compass of shame.

9. Anger is best overcome by focusing on the irrational nature of the accompanying scripts, and these scripts achieve the status of beliefs when the individual is in the grip of the anger affect. This explains why cognitive approaches have been shown to be so effective in helping people overcome problems with anger (Ellis, 2001).

10. My reference to active empathy means being vocal and very involved. At such times, I find I am usually leaning forward in my chair, seeking eye contact, and sometimes will reach out and touch the person. David Read Johnson (2004) has a marvelous intervention for couples dealing with the shame associated with trauma. He has the partners face each other, look directly at each other, hold both hands and tell the shame story. He helps them to create such a powerful connection that the interpersonal bridge is maintained in the midst of experiencing and exploring the shame emotion.

11. Taking an objective look at oneself is not the same as accepting the shameful view (Bad Self). The view of self that is contained in a person's shame scripts is not an objective view, it is a view that is biased by shame affect (which works by amplifying whatever stimulated it). To reach a more objective view of the self, the person has to be able to examine his shame scripts independent of the affects that are normally assembled with them. When the intensity of his emotional state is relatively low, he can achieve a more objective view of himself.

12. David Schnarch (1991) emphasizes self-confrontation in his model of sex therapy. Although he doesn't conceptualize the process in terms of shame, the idea is similar. He emphasizes that self-confrontation in the presence of the partner can promote intimacy.

13. There is considerable evidence that a significant proportion of boys grow up with uncertainty about the quality of their masculinity. One of the societal solutions to that uncertainty are male fraternal organizations that typically shame the young man and require him to submit to various ordeals, and then reward him with pride and validation when he graduates from the hazing. Not all such organizations are restricted to men, but the structure of hazing and eventual acceptance is a long-standing male domain. I am referring to organizations such as the police/fire departments, military (with many levels of increasingly elite suborganizations within the military), law school, medical residencies, sports teams, and clubs/fraternities. By submitting to the shaming atmosphere of these organizations and tolerating the hazing, the aspirant earns the right to belong and replaces shame scripts with pride scripts.

14. David Schnarch's model (1991, 1998) would emphasize the need for the listening partner to stay differentiated in order to listen to the other partner's exploration without the listening partner getting triggered. He refers to this as the listening partner's need to "hold on to himself."

15. This quote is taken from the "big book," the basic text of Alcoholics Anonymous (Alcoholics Anonymous, 1976, p. 27). Isn't it interesting how clearly it describes the process of abandoning certain emotions and replacing them with new emotions?

16. From the way the meetings are conducted to the structure of the 12-Step program itself, the goal is to stop trying to fool people—especially oneself. The fourth step of the program is to make a "searching and fearless moral inventory" of oneself; and the fifth step is to admit to God, to oneself, and to another human being the exact nature of one's wrongs. As an ongoing practice, members are taught to promptly admit when they are wrong. The promptness helps prevent small problems from becoming large problems.

17. The 12-Step program of Alcoholics Anonymous, and the structure of their meetings, is ideally suited for overcoming shame. One of the premises of AA is that the alcoholic is always an alcoholic; he can stop drinking but he remains vulnerable to the threat of alcohol throughout his life. Another premise is that it is not the alcohol itself that is the problem, but the defects of character that lead to the misuse of alcohol. Thus, even AA members who have been sober for many years retain humility and gratitude. The result is that those members who are going through the painful process of self confrontation are accepted and not judged. It seems clear that shame is a significant part of alcohol addiction. Certainly, most alcoholics have shame about their alcoholic behavior; however, I think significant difficulties with shame precede the alcohol addiction with most alcoholics. In many of those cases, the excessive use of alcohol probably developed as a means of coping with the shame.

18. I fear that phrases like "being one's shame" may appear to the reader to be simply grandiloquent language, but I have found that many people with severe shame feel exactly this way.

19. These data come from a longitudinal study of sexual abuse survivors that began in 1987 when the survivors were still children and data were collected over a 7-year period (Bonannoet al., 2002). The children were identified by a local child protective services agency that had received reports of sexual abuse, hence, the opportunity to identify those who voluntarily disclosed and those whose disclosure was accidental (as a result of medical exams, third-person discovery, or perpetrator confession).

20. If his partner has a negative reaction but denies it, then he will not grow from the interaction. It is only when she can acknowledge her negative view, while effectively conveying that she also maintains the positive view, that he can take in a different attitude toward (and an emotion about) himself.

21. The process described here sounds very similar to the integration of good and bad objects that Melanie Klein and Joan Riviere (1964) emphasized in their discussion of the "depressive position." However, there are important differences, including: (a) focus on the other rather than the self and (b) the idea that the good object must be split off to protect it from the aggressive feelings directed at the bad object. Affect theory suggests that scripts for both kinds of emotions (Good Self, Bad Self) exist within the individual, and either one can be activated at any given moment. Resolution involves the gradual dismantling of negative views of self and development of positive views of self. On a surface level, these processes may look similar, but the affect theory view emphasizes the role of shame emotion rather than an aggressive drive. This distinction leads in a very different direction in treatment.

22. This phenomenon of experiencing a rupture of the bond with an important other, followed by a repair of that bond, has been identified as a central factor in the growth process in all interpersonal relationships. Psychiatrist Jerry Lewis (2000) has noted its significance in mother-infant attachment interactions, therapist-patient interactions, and in marital interactions. Heinz Kohut's (1984) model of self psychology is built on the idea that the patient's defective self is gradually changed by the analyst's empathic failures and subsequent reestablishment of an empathic connection. Kohut's model views the defect in the self as being its tendency toward fragmentation, weakness, or disharmony. I would say that this apparent defect is a manifestation of shame, and it is the disassembling of this shame emotion that leads to the stronger, or more cohesive, self.

Chapter 15

1. Pediatrician and psychoanalyst D. W. Winnicott (1963) described the role of the empathic mother in maintaining an environment that facilitates the child's development. He observed that the mother protects the child from disruptive influences (impingements)

so that the child is able to maintain a steady connection with his world and can thereby develop and learn to deal with his world. If too much disruption is allowed to intrude and excessive frustration occurs, the child's internal state of equilibrium breaks down—he then falls apart and is unable to learn anything from his experience.

2. Although men seem to be less attuned than women, this does not mean that men are less adept at tuning in to other people. Rather, most men have learned to tune into a different dimension of the other's emotional experience. For instance, most men are quite sensitive to any indication that a woman is angry or another man is feeling aggressive.

3. Some authors have noted that women pay a price for their attunement to others' pain because they have been found to be more exposed and more vulnerable to feeling distressed over events that occur to others (Turner & Avison, 1989).

4. A typical example is seen in an overview of 39 different research studies done on loneliness at UCLA. Males had the higher loneliness scores but were less likely to admit to feeling lonely than the females were. The authors did further research to assess people's attitudes toward lonely people and found that both men and women were more rejecting of a lonely man than were of a lonely woman. Men learn not to admit that they are lonely because it leads to negative consequences (Borys & Perlman, 1985). The Stone Center's relational model says the same thing about women, except that different aspects of their experience are considered unacceptable. Basically, females learn to suppress those aspects of their experience that are threatening to men and are not part of the traditional female role. Mary Pipher (1994) has described this process in detail, focusing on the period when exuberant young girls enter adolescence and suddenly feel pressured to shut down their natural capacities. She suggests girls tend to respond by conforming, withdrawing, being depressed, or getting angry.

5. We have long had theories about unconscious defense mechanisms that protect people from experiencing their own disturbing thoughts and feelings. However, it is difficult to produce meaningful research evidence of these processes; for example, to prove that a person is feeling one thing even though he reports another. But we get closer and closer to demonstrating such things. Research with undergraduates found evidence that they maintain their biases about gender stereotypes by not only discounting data that are inconsistent with their biases but by actually blocking their perceptions of events that require alternate explanations (Sanbonmatsu, Akimoto, & Gibson, 1994). This is an unconscious process involving perceptions of others, but it is possible that a similar process is involved when men fail to perceive their own feeling states. In effect, they may have a sort of stereotype of themselves—"these are the kinds of feelings I have"—and they block and discount those feeling experiences that do not conform to the stereotype.

6. A safe structure for checking in on feelings means the therapist must define the parameters of the task, such as a prohibition against commenting or offering advice on the other's feelings. These kinds of assigned tasks often do better if the couple practices them during the therapy session before instituting them at home. Of course, if a couple is too conflictual, assigning tasks at home sets them up for failure.

7. This comment reflects my view that the feeling of connection comes more from a partner's perception that the other partner is tuned in to him than from his attunement to the other partner's feelings and needs. The typical pattern is that the female partner is more attuned to the male partner. Thus, she more often feels disconnected, while he thinks everything is okay.

8. When a partner responds to the other partner's expression of attachment threat by intensifying his positive affect behaviors, then a systems theorist would say that the couple has an effective negative feedback mechanism for returning the relationship system to homeostasis. In this case, homeostasis coincides with the safe zone.

9. These techniques and others are summarized in Sherman and Fredman (1986, p. 149) and described in full on subsequent pages.

10. No, the most central component of positive attachment behaviors in not sex, though it is often the most pleasurable form of doing things together.

11. The quote refers to the young children whom Bowlby studied. They were separated from their mothers and the importance of the attachment suddenly showed itself.

12. The impact of negative support has been shown in diverse clinical populations from people traumatized in motor vehicle accidents (Holeva, Tarrier, & Wells, 2001) to patients with HIV (Nott, Vedhara, & Power, 1995).

13. In the past, many theorists viewed marital conflict as a clear indicator of a dysfunctional marriage. John Gottman's (1999) research has shown that "Both conflict-avoiding and volatile, passionate couples can have stable, happy marriages" (p. 14). His research has revealed that practically all couples have issues that never get resolved, but that does not prevent them from having satisfying marriages.

14. Chrys Harris (2004) discusses the value of sacrifice in a relationship and how it differs from compromise, in which neither partner may get what he or she wants.

15. Winnicott (1963) contended that the infant's development of his true self hinged on his maintaining a state of "going-on-being." The mother or maternal environment was viewed as responsible for fending off potential impingements to this state.

16. In a study of people in the process of divorcing, both men and women reported that the major reasons were unmet emotional needs/growing apart, lifestyle differences or boredom with the marriage, and high-conflict demeaning relationships; affairs per se were blamed only about a quarter of the time (Gigy & Kelly, 1992). A more recent study found that couples with infidelity issues had more marital instability, dishonesty, arguments about trust, narcissism, and time spent apart (Atkins, Yi, Baucom, & Christensen, 2005). John Gottman (1999) says that the most common myth about divorce is that it is caused by extramarital affairs.

Chapter 16

1. Harville Hendrix's Imago Relationship Therapy (1988, 1993) discusses the role of intimate relationships in healing wounds from childhood and how people seek partners with that in mind. Psychiatrist Jerry Lewis's book titled *Marriage as a Search for Healing* (1997) contends that people choose their partners with healing in mind (or else the marriage is unlikely to succeed).

2. Certainly esteem issues can be manifest in the transference, but attachment issues predominate. Esteem issues usually take the form of a perception of disapproval by the therapist; the transference being to a critical parent. However, attachment issues of feeling abandoned, unloved, needing to be special, and so forth would seem to be more common.

3. The idea that a partner could be fearful that someone might learn something that he couldn't handle hearing would seem to be the fear of a partner with a sordid past—fearful that the other partner might hear something he can't handle. However, sometimes it is the other partner who discourages talking about the past, but for that same reason—his fear that he may hear something that he can't deal with.

4. In tort law, this issue is referred to as the thin-skulled plaintiff, the individual whose pre-existing fragility is a major factor in his injury. Should the person whose minor act caused the injury be held liable if such an act would not injure most people? The law answers this question through the rule of proximate cause. If the injury would not have occurred without the act, regardless of how thin the injured person's skull may have been in the first place, then the person whose action caused the injury is responsible.

5. Gottman's (1999) research has led him to comment that stable, satisfied couples do not keep track in this way. They trust that each partner is doing his share.

6. Gordon and Baucom (1998) have studied the stages of forgiveness of a major betrayal in a relationship and categorized the process according to stages of trauma recovery: (a) impact, (b) search for meaning, and (c) recovery. Their research (Gordon & Baucom, 2003) has found significant differences between stages of the process; however, since they have not yet been able to acquire longitudinal data, we do not know whether people progress through the stages or whether different groups of people simply manifest different levels of forgiveness.

7. The primary measure of the health of an intimate relationship is how shame is handled. Robert Karen, whom I have quoted twice in this chapter, says much the same about forgiveness. But since I think it is some aspect of shame that makes forgiveness so difficult, I will stand by my assertion, and I hope the reader is beginning to understand how I have come to this view of the power of shame. Most readers would have thought I was crazy if I had made this assertion at the beginning of the book. Of course, some probably still think so.

8. Sullivan was not talking about intimate connections per se; he was expressing his view that interpersonal contact is a fundamental human need. He viewed the need for a love connection—in which the other is as significant, or nearly significant, as the self—as the measure of adulthood.

9. Russell Meares (2000) notes how intimacy can occur between strangers, such as the intimate conversations that occasionally occur between passengers seated next to each other on an airplane. He emphasizes a particular kind of conversation as being intimate (i.e., one in which the individual shares his inner thoughts and feelings without attempting to disguise them or organize them into more conventional form). This is quite similar to Vernon Kelly's (1996) definition of intimacy—the revealing of the inmost self. Such conversations can indeed occur between strangers—sometimes we feel safer with someone who does not know us and is not likely to see us again. This may also explain why people often are able to have more uninhibited sexual encounters with relative strangers than with their long-term partners.

10. There is an ever-increasing volume of studies supporting the observation that not talking about significant emotional events is a health risk. One of the best studies was conducted by James Pennebaker in his book *Opening Up: The Healing Power of Expressing Emotions* (1990/1997).

Chapter 17

1. This paragraph emphasizes: (a) the *bond* with the therapist, (b) agreement about the *goals* of the therapy, and (c) the relevance of the *tasks* designated to fulfill those goals. These are the core components of the therapeutic alliance, as identified by Edward Bordin (1979).

2. Mechanisms to stop conflict escalation range from counting to 10 to declaring timeouts in which either partner can declare an end to a discussion that feels like it is getting out of control. In the case of timeouts, it helps to have the partners agree that they will return to the topic at some future time when they are less aroused.

3. The communication task/tool that I have found most helpful with couples in conflict is the "couples dialogue" developed by Harville Hendrix (1988) for his imago therapy. The task is for one partner to listen while the other talks, but the response doesn't stop with paraphrasing what was said. The roles of speaker and listener do not change until the listening partner is able to see how the other partner's position makes sense from his point of view. The task ends with the listening partner finishing the sentence, "So I guess you must be feeling …"

4. One of the best structured tasks for increasing positive attachment behaviors is Richard Stewart's (1980) "caring days." In the task, the partners each develop a list of positive behaviors that they would like for the other to perform. Then they exchange lists and each partner takes a turn performing one of the requested behaviors.

5. I particularly prefer this check-in task because it goes to the heart of partners' feelings about themselves and touches on sources of both shame and pride. I learned the technique from Maggie Scarf's book, *Intimate Partners* (1988). However, I do not use tasks with all, or even most, couples. My criterion is that I do not use a task if the couple is likely to fail at it.

6. Gottman's (1999) research suggests that most partners do not resolve many of their long-standing individual issues, but this does not prevent them from having a stable, satisfying relationship.

7. Negative emotionality is now considered by some to be the primary personality risk factor for a symptomatic response to stress (Cox, MacPherson, Enns, & McWilliams, 2004; Miller, 2003; van Zelst, de Beurs, Beekman, Deeg, & van Dyke, 2003). Miller compared high negative emotionality and posttraumatic stress disorder, noting that both involved "tendencies to feel nervous, tense, sensitive, vulnerable, betrayed, mistreated, unlucky, etc." (2004, p. 2). This characterization of the manifestations of negative emotionality could easily be explained in terms of an abundance of scripts and the emotions in which those scripts are assembled.

8. The only seeming exception to the idea that she is responsible for his esteem threat is if she is not doing anything to threaten his esteem, but he wants her to pump up his esteem. This is not really a perception of threat, though some partners will occasionally describe it as though that were the case. It is actually a case of approval seeking, as with someone from a poorly differentiated family of origin.

9. The role of shame in depression is increasingly being noted (Fennell, 2004; Watkins & Teasdale, 2001, 2004).

References

Adler, A. (1923). *Understanding human nature*. New York: Garden City Publishing.

Adler, A. (1931/1958). *What life should mean to you*. New York: Capricorn Books.

Ainsworth, M., Blehar, M., Waters, E., & Wall, S. (1978). *Patterns of attachment: A psychological study of the strange situation*. Hillsdale, NJ: Erlbaum.

Alcoholics anonymous: The story of how many thousands of men and women have recovered from alcoholism (3rd ed.). (1976). New York: Alcoholics Anonymous World Services.

Allen, J. G., Stein, H., Fonagy, P., Fultz, J., & Target, M. (2005). Rethinking adult attachment: A study of expert consensus. *Bulletin of the Menninger Clinic, 69*, 59–81.

Atkins, D. C., Yi, J., Baucom, D. H., & Christensen, A. (2005). Infidelity in couples seeking marital therapy. *Journal of Family Psychology, 19*, 470–473.

Bartholomew, K. (1991). Attachment styles among young adults: A test of a four-category model. *Journal of Personality and Social Psychology, 61*(2), 226–244.

Bartholomew, K. (1997). Adult attachment processes: individual and couple perspectives. *British Journal of Medical Psychology, 70*(3), 249–63, discussion 281–290.

Bartholomew, K., & Horowitz, L. M. (1991). Attachment styles among young adults: A test of a four-category model. *Journal of Personality and Social Psychology, 61*, 226–244.

Basch, M. F. (1996). Affect and defense. In D. L. Nathanson (Ed.), *Affect, script, and psychotherapy* (pp. 257–270). New York: Norton.

Beck, A. (1999). *Prisoners of Hate: The cognitive basis of anger, hostility, and violence*. New York: HarperCollins.

Beidel, D. C., & Turner, S. M. (1998). *Shy children, phobic adults: Nature and treatment of social phobia*. Washington, DC: American Psychological Association.

Blake, W. (1794/1984). *Songs of experience*. New York: Dover.

Bodin, A. M. (1981). The interactional view: Family therapy approaches of the Mental Research Institute. In A. S. Gurman & D. P. Kniskern (Eds.), *Handbook of family therapy* (pp. 267–309). New York: Brunner/Mazel.

Bogells, S. M., & Mansell, W. (2004). Attention processes in the maintenance and treatment of social phobia: Hypervigilance, avoidance, and self-focused attention. *Clinical Psychology Review, 24*, 827–856.

Bonanno, G. A., Keltner, D., Noll, J. G., Putnam, F. W., Trickett, P. K., LeJeune, J., & Anderson, C. (2002). When the face reveals what words do not: Facial expressions of emotion, smiling, and the willingness to disclose childhood sexual abuse. *Journal of Personality and Social Psychology, 83*(1), 94–110.

Bordin, E. S. (1979). The generalizability of the psychoanalytic concept of the working alliance. *Psychotherapy: Theory, Research and Practice, 16*, 252–260.

Borys, S., & Perlman, D. (1985). Gender differences in loneliness. *Personality and Social Psychological Bulletin, 11*, 63–74.

Boszormenyi-Nagy, I., & Spark, G. (1973). *Invisible loyalties: Reciprocity in intergeneration family therapy*. New York: Harper and Row.

Bowen, M. (1978). *Family therapy in clinical practice*. New York: Aronson.

Bowlby, J. (1969). *Attachment and loss, Vol. I: Attachment*. New York: Basic Books.

Bowlby, J. (1973). *Attachment and loss, Vol. II: Separation: Anxiety and anger*. Harmondsworth, Middlesex, Eng.: Penguin Books.

Bradshaw, J. (1988). *Healing the shame that binds you*. Deerfield Beach, FL: Health Communications.

Branden, N. (1971). *The psychology of self-esteem*. New York: Bantam.

Branden, N. (1983). *Honoring the self: Self-esteem and personal transformation*. New York: Bantam.

Brennan, K., Clark, C., & Shaver, P. (1998). Self-report measurement of adult attachment. In J. A. Simpson & W. S. Rholes (Eds.), *Attachment theory and close relationships* (pp. 46–76). New York: Guilford.

Broucek, F. (1991). *Shame and the self*. New York: Guilford.

Buber, M. (1970). *I and thou*. New York: Scribner's.

Byrne, M., Carr, A., & Clark, M. (2004). The efficacy of couples-based interventions for panic disorder with agoraphobia. *Journal of Family Therapy, 26*, 105–125.

Carnelley, K. B., & Janoff-Bulman, R. (1992). Optimism about love relationships: General vs. specific lessons from one's personal experiences. *Journal of Social and Personal Relationships, 9*, 5–20.

Carrere, S., & Gottman, J. M. (1999). Predicting divorce among newlyweds from the first three minutes of a marital conflict discussion. *Family Process, 38*, 293–301.

Catherall, D. R. (2003). How fear differs from anxiety. *Traumatology, 9*(2), 76–92.

Chambless, D. L., & Hollon, S. D. (1998). Defining empirically supported therapies. *Journal of Consulting and Clinical Psychology, 66*, 7–18.

Cox, B. J., MacPherson, P. S. R., Enns, M. W., & McWilliams, L. A. (2004). Neuroticism and self-criticism associated with posttraumatic stress disorder in a nationally representative sample. *Behavior Research and Therapy, 42*, 105–114.

Damasio, A. (1999). *The feeling of what happens: Body and emotion in the making of consciousness.* New York: Harcourt.

Dreikers, R., & Soltz, V. (1964). *Children: The challenge.* New York: Hawthorn Books.

Dutton, D. G., van Ginkel, C., & Starzomski, A. (1995). The role of shame and guilt in the intergenerational transmission of abusiveness. *Violence and Victims, 10*(2), 121–131.

Ellis, A. (2001). *Overcoming destructive beliefs, feelings, and behaviors: New directions for rational emotive behavior therapy.* New York: Prometheus.

Ellis, A., & Tafrate, R. C. (1997). *How to control your anger before it controls you.* New York: Citadel.

Feeney, J. A. (1996). Attachment, caregiving, and marital satisfaction. *Personal Relationships, 3*, 401–416.

Fennell, M. J. V. (2004). Depression, low self-esteem, and mindfulness. *Behavior Research and Therapy, 42*, 1053–1067.

Fincham, F. D., Beach, S. R. H., & Davila, J. (2004). Forgiveness and conflict resolution in marriage. *Journal of Family Psychology, 18*, 72–81.

Fredrickson, B. L. (2001). The role of positive emotions in positive psychology: The broaden-and-build theory of positive emotions. *American Psychologist, 56*, 218–226.

Fredrickson, B. L., & Losada, M. (2005). Positive affect and the complex dynamics of human flourishing. *American Psychologist, 60*, 678–686.

Freud, S. (1923/1964). *The ego and the id.* Standard Ed., Vol. 19, Oxford, England: Macmillan.

Freud, S. (1926/1964). *Inhibition, symptoms and anxiety.* Standard Ed., Vol. 20, Oxford, England: Macmillan.

Gigy, L., & Kelly, J. B. (1992). Reasons for divorce: Perspectives of divorcing men and women. *Journal of Divorce and Remarriage, 18*, 169–187.

Gilliam, C. M., & Cottone, R. R. (2005). Couple or individual therapy for the treatment of depression?: An update of the empirical literature. *American Journal of Family Therapy, 33*, 265–272.

Ginott, H. G. (1965). *Between parent & child: New solutions to old problems.* New York: Avon.

Goldberg, C. (1991). *Understanding shame.* Northvale, NJ: Jason Aronson.

Goleman, D. (1998). *Working with emotional intelligence.* New York: Bantam.

Gordon, K. C., & Baucom, D. H. (1998). Understanding betrayals in marriage: A synthesized model of forgiveness. *Family Process, 37*, 425–450.

Gordon, K. C., & Baucom, D. H. (2003). Forgiveness and marriage: Preliminary support for a measure based on a model of recovery from a marital betrayal. *American Journal of Family Therapy, 31*, 179–199.

Gottman, J. M. (1994a). *What predicts divorce? The relationship between marital processes and marital outcomes.* Hillsdale, NJ: Erlbaum.

Gottman, J. M. (1994b). *Why marriages succeed or fail.* New York: Simon and Schuster.

Gottman, J. M. (1998). Psychology and the study of marital processes. *Annual Review of Psychology, 49*, 169–197.

Gottman, J. M. (1999). *The marriage clinic: A scientifically-based marital therapy.* New York: Norton.

Gottman, J. M., & Notarius, C. I. (2002). Marital research in the 20th century and a research agenda for the 21st century. *Family Process, 41*, 159–197.

Green, J., & Goldwyn, R. (2002). Annotation: Attachment disorganization and psychopathology: New findings in attachment research and their potential implications for developmental psychopathology in childhood. *Journal of Child Psychology and Psychiatry, 43*, 835–846.

Greenberg, L. S., & Johnson, S. M. (1988). *Emotionally focused therapy for couples.* New York: Guilford.

Greenberg, L. S., & Paivio, S. C. (1997/2003). *Working with emotions in psychotherapy.* New York: Guilford.

Griffin, D., & Bartholomew, K. (1994). Models of the self and other: Fundamental dimensions underlying adult attachment. *Journal of Personality and Social Psychology, 67,* 430–455.

Gunderson, J. G. (1996). The borderline patient's intolerance of aloneness: Insecure attachments and therapist availability. *American Journal of Psychiatry, 153,* 752–758.

Hanh, T. N. (1992). *Peace is every step: The path of mindfulness in everyday life.* New York: Bantam.

Harris, C. J. (2004). Family crisis intervention. In D. R. Catherall (Ed.), *Handbook of stress, trauma, and the family* (pp. 417–431). New York: Brunner-Routledge.

Hartling, L.M., Rosen, W.B., Walker, M., & Jordan, J.V. (2004). Shame and humiliation: From isolation to relational transformation. In J.V. Jordan, M. Walker, & L.M. Hartling (Eds.), The complexity of connection: Writings from the Stone Center's Jean Baker Miller Training Institute (pp. 103–128). New York: Guilford.

Hartmann, H. (1939/1958). *Ego psychology and the problem of adaptation.* New York: International Universities Press

Hazan, C., & Shaver, P. R. (1987). Romantic love conceptualized as an attachment process. *Journal of Personality and Social Psychology, 52,* 511–524.

Hendrix, H. (1988). *Getting the love you want: A guide for couples.* New York: Henry Holt.

Hendrix, H. (1993). *Keeping the love you find: A personal guide.* New York: Atria.

Heyman, R. E. (2001). Observation of couple conflicts: Clinical assessment applications, stubborn truths, and shaky foundations. *Psychological Assessment, 13,* 5–35.

Hill, E. M., Young, J. P., & Nord, J. L. (1994). Childhood adversity, attachment, security, and adult relationships: A preliminary study. *Ethology and Sociobiology, 15,* 323–338.

Holeva, V., Tarrier, N,, & Wells, A. (2001). Prevalence and predictors of acute stress disorder and PTSD following road traffic accidents: Thought control strategies and social support. *Behavior Therapy, 32,* 65–83.

Holinger, P. C., & Doner, K. (2003). *What babies say before they can talk: The nine signals infants use to express their feelings.* Wichita, KS: Fireside.

Holmes, J. (1996). *Attachment, intimacy, autonomy: Using attachment theory in adult psychotherapy.* Northvale, NJ: Jason Aronson.

Holmes, J. (2004). Disorganized attachment and borderline personality disorder: A clinical perspective. *Attachment and Human Development, 6,* 181–190.

Hwang, P. O. (2000). *Other-esteem: Meaningful life in a multicultural society.* Ann Arbor, MI: Sheridan Books.

Johnson, D. R. (2004). Critical interaction therapy with traumatized couples. In D. R. Catherall (Ed.), *Handbook of stress, trauma and the family* (pp. 513–532). New York: Brunner-Routledge.

Johnson, S. M. (1996/2005). *Creating connection: The practice of emotionally focused marital therapy.* New York: Brunner/Mazel.

Johnson, S. M. (2002). *Emotionally focused couple therapy with trauma survivors: Strengthening attachment bonds.* New York: Guilford.

Johnson, S. M. (2003). The revolution in couple therapy: A practitioner-scientist perspective. *Journal of Marital and Family Therapy, 29,* 365–384.

Johnson, S. M., & Lebow, J. (2000). The "coming of age" of couple therapy: A decade review. *Journal of Marital and Family Therapy, 26,* 23–38.

Johnson, S. M., Makinen, J. A., & Milliken, J. W. (2001). Attachment injuries in couple relationships: A new perspective on impasses in couples therapy. *Journal of Marital and Family Therapy, 27*(2), 145–155.

Jordan, J. V. (1989). *Relational development: Therapeutic implications of empathy and shame.* (Work in Progress, No. 39). Wellesley, MA: Stone Center Working Paper Series.

Jordan, J. V. (2000). The role of mutual empathy in relational/cultural therapy. *Journal of Clinical Psychology, 56,* 1005–1016.

Jordan, J. V., Kaplan, A. G., Miller, J. B., Stiver, I. P., & Surrey, J. L. (1991). *Women's growth in connection: Writings from the Stone Center.* New York: Guilford.

Jung, C. G. (1968). *Analytical psychology: Its theory and practice, the Tavistock lectures.* New York: Vintage.

Kabat-Zinn, J. (1990). *Full catastrophe living: Using the wisdom of your body and mind to face stress, pain, and illness.* New York: Dell.

Kabat-Zinn, J. (1995). *Wherever you go, there you are: Mindfulness meditation in everyday life.* New York: Hyperion.

Kalsched, D. (1996). *The inner world of trauma: Archetypal defenses of the personal spirit.* New York: Routledge.

Karen, R. (2001). *The forgiving self: The road from resentment to connection.* New York: Doubleday.

Kaufman, G. (1989). *The psychology of shame: Theory and treatment of shame-based syndromes.* New York: Springer.

Kaufman, G. (1992). *Shame: The power of caring* (3rd ed.). Rochester, VT: Schenkman.

Kelly, V. C. (1996). Affect and the redefinition of intimacy. In D. L. Nathanson (Ed.), *Knowing feeling: Affect, script and psychotherapy* (pp. 55–104). New York: Norton.

Kernberg, O. (1976). *Object relations theory and clinical psycho-analysis.* New York: Jason Aronson.

Kerr, M. E., & Bowen, M. (1988). *Family evaluation: An approach based on Bowen theory.* New York: Norton.

Kirkpatrick, L. A., & Davis, K. E. (1994). Attachment style, gender, and relationship stability: A longitudinal analysis. *Journal of Personality and Social Psychology, 66,* 502–512.

Kirkpatrick, L. A., & Hazan, C. (1994). Attachment styles and close relationships: A four-year prospective study. *Personal Relationships, 1,* 123–142.

Klein, M., & Riviere, J. (1964). *Love, hate, and reparation.* New York: Norton.

Kohut, H. (1971). *The analysis of the self.* New York: International Universities Press.

Kohut, H. (1984). *How does analysis cure?* Chicago: University of Chicago Press.

Kreuger, R. F., McGue, M., & Iacono, W. G. (2001). The higher-order structure of common DSM mental disorders: Internalization, externalization, and their connections to personality. *Personality and Individual Differences, 30,* 1245–1259.

Krugman, S. (1995). Male development and the transformation of shame. In R. F. Levant & W. S. Pollack (Eds.), *A new psychology of men* (pp. 91–126). New York: Basic Books.

Lansky, M. R. (1993). Family genesis of aggression. *Psychiatric Annals, 23,* 494–499.

Lebow, J. L. (2000). What does the research tell us about couple and family therapies? *Journal of Clinical Psychology, 56,* 1083–1094.

Lederer, W. (1964). Dragons, delinquents, and destiny: An essay on positive superego functions [Monograph 15]. *Psychological Issues, 4*(3). New York: International Universities Press.

Lerner, H. G. (1989). *The dance of intimacy: A woman's guide to courageous acts of change in key relationships.* New York: Harper and Row.

Lewis, H. B. (1971). *Shame and guilt in neurosis.* New York: International Universities Press.

Lewis, H. B. (1987a). Introduction: Shame—the "sleeper" in psychopathology. In H. B. Lewis (Ed.), *The role of shame in symptoms formation* (pp. 1–28). New York: Erlbaum.

Lewis, H. B. (1987b). The role of shame in depression over the life span. In H. B. Lewis (Ed.), *The role of shame in symptoms formation* (pp. 29–50). New York: Erlbaum.

Lewis, H. B. (1987c). Resistance: A misnomer for shame and guilt. In D. S. Milman & G. D. Goldman (Eds.), *Techniques of working with resistance* (pp. 209–226). New York: Jason Aronson.

Lewis, J. M. (1997). *Marriage as a search for healing: Theory, assessment and therapy.* New York: Brunner/Mazel.

Lewis, J. M. (1998). For better or worse: Interpersonal relationships and individual outcome. *American Journal of Psychiatry, 155,* 582–589.

Lewis, J. M. (2000). Repairing the bond in important relationships: A dynamic for personality maturation. *American Journal of Psychiatry, 157,* 1375–1378.

Losado, M. (1999). The complex dynamics of high performance teams. *Mathematical and Computer Modelling, 30*(9–10), 179–192.

Losada, M., & Heapy, E. (2004). The role of positivity and connectivity in the performance of business teams: A nonlinear dynamics model. *American Behavioral Scientist, 47,* 740–765.

Mahler, M., Pine, F., & Bergman, A. (1975). *The psychological birth of the human infant.* New York: Basic Books.

Markway, B. G., Carmin, C., Pollard, C. A., & Flynn, T. (1992). *Dying of embarrassment: Help for social anxiety and phobia.* Oakland, CA: New Harbinger.

Markway, B. G., & Markway, G. P. (2003). *Painfully shy: How to overcome social anxiety and reclaim your life.* New York: Thomas Dunne Books.

Maslow, A. H. (1987). *Motivation and personality* (3rd ed.). New York: Harper and Row.

Maugham, W. S. (1915/1986). *Of human bondage.* New York: Penguin Books.

McDonough, M. L., Carlson, C., & Cooper, C. R. (1994). Individuated marital relationships and the regulation of affect in families of early adolescents. *Journal of Adolescent Research, 9,* 67–87.

Meares, R. (2000). *Intimacy and alienation: Memory, trauma and personal being.* Philadelphia, PA: Taylor and Francis.

Mikulincer, M., Florian, V., Cowan, P. A., & Cowan, C. P. (2002). Attachment security in couple relationships: A systemic model and its implications for family dynamics. *Family Process, 41,* 405–434.

Miller, J. B., & Stiver, I. (1994). Movement in therapy: Honoring the "strategies of disconnection." (*Work in Progress* No. 65). Wellesley, MA: Stone Center Working Paper Series.

Miller, M. W. (2003). Personality and the etiology and expression of PTSD: A three-factor model perspective. *Clinical Psychology: Science and Practice, 10,* 373–393.

Miller, M. W. (2004). Personality and the development and expression of PTSD. *National Center for Post-Traumatic Stress Disorder PTSD Research Quarterly, 15*(3), 1–4.

Miller, S. B. (1996). *Shame in context.* Hinsdale, NJ: Analytic Press.

Muller, R. T., Lemieux, K. E., & Sicoli, L. A. (2001). Attachment and psychopathology among formerly maltreated adults. *Journal of Family Violence, 16,* 151–169.

Muller, R. T., Sicoli, L. A., & Lemieux, K. E. (2000). Relationships between attachment style and posttraumatic stress symptomatology among adults who report the experience of childhood abuse. *Journal of Traumatic Stress, 13,* 321–332.

Murray, S. L., Bellavia, G., Rose, P., & Griffin, D. W. (2003). Once hurt, twice hurtful: How perceived regard regulates daily marital interactions. *Journal of Personality and Social Psychology, 84,* 126–147.

Murray, S. L., & Holmes, J. G. (1998). A leap of faith? Positive illusions in romantic relationships. *Personality and Social Psychology Bulletin, 23,* 586–604.

Murray, S. L., Holmes, J. G., Dolderman, D., & Griffin, D. W. (2000). What the motivated mind sees: Comparing friends' perspectives to married partners' views of each other. *Journal of Experimental Social Psychology, 36,* 600–620.

Murray, S. L., Holmes, J. G., & Griffin, D. W. (2000). Self esteem and the quest for felt security: How perceived regard regulates attachment processes. *Journal of Personality and Social Psychology, 78,* 478–498.

Murray, S. L., Holmes, J. G., Griffin, D. W., Bellavia, G., & Rose, P. (2001). The mismeasure of love: How self-doubt contaminates relationship beliefs. *Personality and Social Psychology Bulletin, 27,* 423–436.

Murray, S. L., Rose, P., Bellavia, G., Holmes, J. G., & Kusche, A. G. (2002). When rejection stings: How self-esteem constrains relationship-enhancement processes. *Journal of Personality and Social Psychology, 83,* 556–573.

Nathanson, D. L. (1987). The shame/pride axis. In H. B. Lewis (Ed.), *The role of shame in symptom formation* (pp. 183–205). Hillsdale, NJ: Erlbaum.

Nathanson, D. L. (1992). *Shame and pride: Affect, sex, and the birth of the self.* New York: Norton.

Nathanson, D. L. (1993). About emotion. *Psychiatric Annals, 23,* 543–555.

Nathanson, D. L. (1996a). About emotion. In D. L. Nathanson (Ed.), *Knowing feeling: Affect, script and psychotherapy* (pp. 1–21). New York: Norton.

Nathanson, D. L. (1996b). Some closing thoughts on affect, scripts and psychotherapy. In D. L. Nathanson (Ed.), *Knowing feeling: Affect, script and psychotherapy* (pp. 379–407). New York: Norton.

Nott, K. H., Vedhara, K., & Power, M. J. (1995). The role of social support in HIV infection. *Psychological Medicine, 25,* 971–983.

Owens, K. A. (1995). Internalized shame, reclusive behavior, and intimacy in couples. *Dissertation Abstracts International, 53*(3A), 1143.

Peleg, O. (2005). The relation between differentiation and social anxiety: What can be learned from students and their parents? *American Journal of Family Therapy, 33,* 167–183.

Pennebaker, J. W. (1990/1997). *Opening up: The healing power of expressing emotions.* New York: Guilford.

Perls, F. S. (1973). *The gestalt approach and eye witness to therapy.* Palo Alto, CA: Science and Behavior Books.

Perls, F. S. (1992). *Gestalt therapy verbatim* (rev. ed.). Gouldsboro, ME: Gestalt Journal Press.

Pinckert, R. C. (1986). *Pinckert's practical grammar: A lively, unintimidating guide to usage, punctuation, and style.* Cincinatti, OH: Writers' Digest Books.

Pinsof, W. M. (1995). *Integrative problem-centered therapy: A synthesis of family, individual, and biological therapies.* New York: Basic Books.

Pipher, M. (1994). *Reviving Ophelia: Saving the selves of adolescent girls.* New York: Ballantine.

Pistole, M. C. (1994). Adult attachment styles: Some thoughts on closeness-distance struggles. *Family Process, 33,* 147–159.

Pistole, M. C., & Vocaturo, L. C. (1999). Attachment and commitment in college students' romantic relationships. *Journal of College Student Development, 40,* 710–720.

Prager, K. J. (1995). *The psychology of intimacy.* New York: Guilford.

Reber, K. (1996). Children at risk for reactive attachment disorder: Assessment, diagnosis and treatment. In *Progress: Family systems research and therapy,* Vol. 5 (pp. 83–98). Encino, CA: Phillips Graduate Institute.

Rothschild, B. (2000). *The body remembers: The psychophysiology of trauma and trauma treatment.* New York: Norton.

Rothschild, B. (2003). *The body remembers casebook: Unifying methods and models in the treatment of trauma and PTSD.* New York: Norton.

Sagan, C. (1997). *Billions and billions: Thoughts on life and death at the brink of the millennium.* New York: Random House.

Sanbonmatsu, D. M., Akimoto, S. A., & Gibson, B. D. (1994). Stereotype-based blocking in social explanation. *Personality and Social Psychology Bulletin, 20*(1), 71–81.

Sapolsky, R. M. (1997). The solace of patterns. In *The trouble with testosterone and other essays on the biology of the human predicament* (pp. 91–100). New York: Simon and Schuster.

Satir, V. (1967). *Conjoint family therapy: A guide to theory and technique* (rev. ed.). Palo Alto, CA: Science and Behavior Books.

Satir, V. (1988). *The new peoplemaking.* Palo Alto, CA: Science and Behavior Books.

Scarf, M. (1988). *Intimate partners: Patterns in love and marriage.* New York: Ballantine.

Scharff, D. E., & Scharff, J. S. (1991). *Object relations couple therapy.* New York: Jason Aronson.

Schnarch, D. (1991). *Constructing the sexual crucible: An integration of sexual and marital therapy.* New York: Norton

Schnarch, D. (1998). *Passionate marriage: Love, sex, and intimacy in emotionally committed relationships.* New York: Henry Holt.

Schwartz, R. C. (1997). *Internal family systems therapy.* New York: Guilford.

Schwarz, R. A. (2002). *Tools for transforming trauma.* New York: Brunner-Routledge.

Segal, Z. V., Williams, J. M. G., & Teasdale, J. D. (2002). *Mindfulness-based cognitive therapy for depression: A new approach to preventing relapse.* New York: Guilford.

Seldes, G. (1985). *The great thoughts.* New York: Ballantine.

Shadish, W. R., & Baldwin, S. A. (2003). Meta-analysis of MFT interventions. *Journal of Marital and Family Therapy, 29,* 547–570.

Sherman, R., & Fredman, N. (1986). *Handbook of structured techniques in marriage and family therapy.* New York: Brunner/Mazel.

Shi, L. (2003). The association between adult attachment styles and conflict resolution in romantic relationships. *American Journal of Family Therapy, 31,* 143–157.

Snyder, D. K., Castellani, A. M., & Whisman, M. A. (2006). Current status and future directions in couple therapy. *Annual Review of Psychology, 57,* 1.1–1.28

Snyder, D. K., & Whisman, M. A. (Eds.). (2003). *Treating difficult couples: Helping clients with coexisting mental and relationship disorders.* New York: Guilford.

Steel, R. (2000). *In love with night: The American romance with Robert Kennedy.* New York: Simon and Schuster.

Stein, H., Jacobs, N. J., Ferguson, K. S., Allen, J. G., & Fonagy, P. (1998). What do adult attachment scales measure? *Bulletin of the Menninger Clinic, 62,* 33–82.

Stern, D. (1985). *The interpersonal world of the infant.* New York: Basic Books.

Sternberg, R. J. (1987). *The triangle of love: Intimacy, passion, commitment.* New York: Basic Books.

Stewart, R. (1980). *Helping couples change: A social learning approach to marital therapy.* New York: Guilford.

Stiver, I. P. (1997). Chronic disconnections: Three family contexts. In B. S. Mark & J. A. Incorvaia (Eds.), *The handbook of infant, child, and adolescent psychotherapy,* Vol. 2: *New directions in integrative treatment* (pp. 439–459). New York: Jason Aronson.

Stone, H., & Stone, S. (1993). *Embracing your inner critic: Turning self-criticism into a creative asset.* New York: Harper San Francisco.

Sullivan, H. S. (1953/1997). *The interpersonal theory of psychiatry.* H. S. Perry & M. L. Gawel (Eds.). New York: Norton.

Teasdale, J. D., Moore, R. G., Hayhurst, H., Pope, M., Williams, S., & Segal, Z. V. (2002). Meta-cognitive awareness and prevention of relapse in depression: Empirical evidence. *Journal of Consulting and Clinical Psychology, 70,* 275–287.

Teasdale, J. D., Segal, Z. V., & Williams, J. M. G. (1995). How does cognitive therapy prevent relapse, and why should attentional control (mindfulness) training help? *Behavior Research and Therapy, 33,* 225–239.

Thomas, P. M. (2003). Protection, dissociation, and internal roles: Modeling and treating the effects of child abuse. *Review of General Psychology, 7,* 364–380.

Thomas, P. M. (2005). Dissociation and internal models of protection: Psychotherapy with child abuse survivors. *Psychotherapy: Theory, Research, Practice, Training, 42,* 20–36.

Tolle, E. (1999). *The power of now: A guide to spiritual enlightenment.* New York: New World Library.

Tomkins, S. S. (1962). *Affect/imagery/consciousness.* Vol. I: *The positive affects.* New York: Springer.

Tomkins, S. S. (1963). *Affect/imagery/consciousness.* Vol. II: *The negative affects.* New York: Springer.

Tomkins, S. S. (1979). Script theory: Differential magnification of affects. In H. E. Howe, Jr., & R. A. Dienstbier (Eds.), *Nebraska Symposium on Motivation – 1978* (Vol. 26, pp. 201-236). Lincoln: University of Nebraska Press.

Tomkins, S. S. (1991). *Affect/imagery/consciousness. Vol. III: The negative affects: Anger and fear.* New York: Springer.

Tomkins, S. S. (1992). *Affect/imagery/consciousness. Vol. IV: Cognition: Duplication and transformation of information.* New York: Springer.

Tucker, J. S., & Anders, S. L. (1999). Attachment style, interpersonal perceptions accuracy, and relationship satisfaction in dating couples. *Personality and Social Psychology Bulletin, 25,* 403–412.

Turner, R. J., & Avison, W. R. (1989). Gender and depression: Assessing exposure and vulnerability to life events in a chronically strained population. *Journal of Nervous and Mental Disease, 177,* 443–455.

Twain, M. (1957/1990). *The Mysterious Stranger.* In C. Neider (Ed.), *The Complete Short Stories of Mark Twain* (pp. 602–679), New York: Bantum.

Vanier, J. (1994). *From brokenness to community.* Mahwah, NJ: Paulist Press.

van Zelst, W. H., de Beurs, E., Beekman, A. T. F., Deeg, D. J. H., & van Dyke, R. (2003). Prevalence and risk factors of posttraumatic stress disorder in older adults. *Psychotherapy and Psychosomatics, 72,* 333–342.

Watkins, E., & Teasdale, J. D. (2001). Rumination and overgeneral memory in depression: Effects of self-focus and analytic thinking. *Journal of Abnormal Psychology, 110,* 353–357.

Watkins, E., & Teasdale, J. D. (2004). Adaptive and maladaptive self-focus in depression. *Journal of Affective Disorders, 82,* 1–8.

Watzlawick, P., Beavin, J. H., & Jackson, D. D. (1967). *The pragmatics of human communication.* New York: Norton.

Webster's New Universal Unabridged Dictionary. (1994). New York: Barnes and Noble.

Whitaker, D. J., Beach, S. R. H., Etherton, J., Wakefield, R., & Anderson, P. L. (1999). Attachment and expectations about future relationships: Moderations by accessibility. *Personal Relationships, 6,* 41–56.

Winnicott, D. W. (1963). *The maturational processes and the facilitating environment: Studies in the theory of emotional development.* New York: International Universities Press.

Wurmser, L. (1981). *The mask of shame.* Baltimore: Johns Hopkins University Press.

Young, J. E., Klosko, J. S., & Weishaar, M. E. (2003). *Schema therapy: A practitioner's guide.* New York: Guilford.

Index